D0050739

THE LEGEND

MARGINALIA

*Maddon's handwritten pregame notes
to himself, all in purple ink.*

TOP OF THE CARD

"C+B+L": "Courage plus belief equals life."

"H": In memory of his father, Joe, whose nickname was Howard.

"DNPTPTETP": "Do not permit the pressure to exceed the pleasure."

STRING OF CAPITAL LETTERS: Each one represents a deceased family member or friend.

"DSB": "Do simple better."

"DNBAFF": "Do not be a fucking fan."

"PROCESS!": Stick to the process; don't worry about results.

SPINE OF CARD

"B PRESENT, NOT PERFECT"

"Z IRREVERENT": Z honors the late Don Zimmer, who taught Maddon how to manage without being afraid to take chances.

LEFT-HAND SIDE

"POSITIVE/OPTIMISTIC": A reminder Maddon added to his cards in 2016 about keeping an upbeat attitude at all times.

PRINTED INFORMATION

BATTERS: Right-handed hitters in black, left-handed hitters in blue, switch-hitters in red.

"K" AND "GB": Percentage of plate appearances in which the hitter strikes out or hits a groundball. High strikeout rates are highlighted in red, medium rates are white, and low rates are shaded blue. For groundball rates, high rates are dark green and low rates are light green.

"MATRIX": The proprietary number Maddon assigns to each batter to capture how well the batter matches up against the starting pitcher. It follows a similar scale to batting average (.300 is very good, .200 very poor) but bakes every available hitting metric into one number, not just career hits divided by at-bats. The Matrix is color-coordinated. Moving from least favorable for the hitter to most favorable, the colors in the spectrum are blue, light blue, white, pink, and red.

"vLH" AND "vRH": Batting averages against relief pitchers, based on left-handed or right-handed hitters. Matchups favorable to pitchers are in red. Matchups favorable to hitters are in blue. Neutral matchups are in black.

IN-GAME NOTES

HEAVY BLUE MARKER

LINEUP CHANGES: Maddon puts a line through the names of position players who are removed and pitchers once they enter. Note that the name of Bauer had not been originally listed among Cleveland relievers.

FINE-POINT BLUE MARKER

NUMBERS IN CIRCLES: A circle is placed next to the name of the hitter who made the last out of an inning against the starting pitcher. The number denotes the total pitches by the starter at that point.

NUMBERS INSIDE A TRIANGLE: A triangle refers to the last out against a relief pitcher and his total pitches, with the name of the relief pitcher added.

"PIC" INSIDE A CIRCLE: Runners vulnerable to being picked off.

PENCIL WITH YELLOW HIGHLIGHTER

"B": Candidates to bunt.

RELIEF PITCHERS WITH ARROWS: Preferred usage through parts of Cleveland lineup.

Wednesday, November 02, 2016 — **8:08 PM**

CUBS

#	Player	POS	K	GB	Matrix
1	Fowler	CF	34%	42%	.260
2	~~Schwarber~~ (32)	DH	32%	37%	.307
3	Bryant	3B	36%	34%	.279
4	Rizzo	1B	24%	39%	.308
5	Zobrist	LF	17%	48%	.278
6	Russell	SS	33%	44%	.236
7	~~Contreras~~	C	29%	57%	.234
8	Heyward	RF	20%	48%	.287
9	Baez	2B	37%	46%	.232
P	Hendricks				

INDIANS

#	Player	POS	K	GB	Matrix
1	Santana	DH	20%	40%	.268
2	Kipnis	2B	19%	46%	.270
3	Lindor	SS	17%	54%	.244
4	Napoli	1B	30%	44%	.236
5	Ramirez	3B	10%	49%	.249
6	~~Chisenhall~~	RF	18%	41%	.258
7	Davis	CF	18%	53%	.219
8	Crisp	LF	13%	45%	.243
9	~~Perez~~	C	27%	59%	.197
P	~~Kluber~~				

CUBS — EXTRAS

	LEFT	SWITCH	RIGHT		
	LHP	RHP	LHP	RHP	LHP	RHP
~~Montero~~	.196	.233				
~~Coghlan~~	.114	.234				
Ross					.223	.191
Almora					.224	.274
Soler					.258	.258

INDIANS — EXTRAS

	LEFT	SWITCH	RIGHT
~~Naquin~~	.242	.293			
Martinez			.239	.233	
Gomes					.230	.194
Guyer					.297	.234

CUBS — RELIEVERS

LEFT	vLH	vRH	RIGHT	vLH	vRH
~~Chapman~~	.162	.173	Rondon	.257	.199
Wood	.188	.238	Strop	.165	.167
~~Montgomery~~	.233	.244	~~Edwards~~	.175	.118
~~Coster~~	.223	.225	Grimm	.231	.200
			Lackey	.261	.222

INDIANS — RELIEVERS

LEFT	vLH	vRH	RIGHT	vLH	vRH
~~Miller~~	.186	.144	Clevinger	.182	.287
Merritt	.250	.143	Salazar	.217	.239
			McAllister	.251	.266
			Manship	.241	.186
			Otero	.245	.274
			~~Shaw~~	.254	.230
			~~Allen~~	.202	.193

UMPIRES

HP	Sam Holbrook	1B	Chris Guccione
2B	John Hirshbeck	3B	Marvin Hudson
LF	Tony Randazzo	RF	Joe West

THE
CUBS
WAY

THE
CUBS
WAY

THE ZEN OF BUILDING

THE BEST TEAM IN BASEBALL

AND BREAKING THE CURSE

TOM VERDUCCI

CROWN
ARCHETYPE
NEW YORK

Published in the United States by Crown Archetype, an imprint of the Crown
Publishing Group, a division of Penguin Random House LLC, New York.
crownpublishing.com
crownarchetype.com

Crown Archetype and colophon is a registered trademark
of Penguin Random House LLC.

Credits for photograph insert appear on page 367.

Library of Congress Cataloging-in-Publication Data is available upon request.

ISBN 9780804190015
Ebook ISBN 9780804190022

PRINTED IN THE UNITED STATES OF AMERICA

Book design: Anna Thompson
Jacket photographs: (front) Kenny Chmielewski;
(back) Ezra Shaw/Staff/Getty Images Sport/Getty Images
Tip-in photograph: Courtesy of Joe Maddon

10 9 8 7 6 5 4 3 2 1

First Edition

For Kirsten, Adam, and Ben,
with love and pride

CONTENTS

CHAPTER 1

PRELUDE TO SEVEN

Three hours before the most important game for the Chicago Cubs in more than a century, the desk of Joe Maddon in the visiting manager's office at Progressive Field in Cleveland formed the cluttered tableau of a busy mind. Two opened, half-eaten, oversized bars of Ghirardelli dark chocolate. Eight-by-ten photos of deceased managers Earl Weaver, Chuck Tanner, and Dick Howser. All seven of his color-coded, two-sided, World Series lineup cards, complete with every piece of statistical information he needs in the dugout, not to mention a shorthand homage to deceased family and friends. An iPad Pro with stylus, which he used to design the lineup cards. And his smartphone, which buzzed with a text from one of his hometown buddies back in Hazleton, Pennsylvania.

Game 7 of the 2016 World Series between the Cubs and the Cleveland Indians, the two teams with the longest championship droughts in baseball, was drawing nigh.

Maddon faced two major questions heading into Game 7: How could his hitters possibly dent Cleveland starting pitcher Corey Kluber, the ace who had held the Cubs to one run over 12 innings in his two starts in the series? And what pitching plan could Maddon cook up to get the ball to his closer, Aroldis Chapman, whom he had taxed in the previous two games?

Maddon began this day with his usual daily meditation session. Then, as he does each game day, he mulled over what to do about his lineup over a cup of *caffè Americano*. He doodled ideas and batting orders on his iPad with his stylus, and when his lineup was ready he sent it, as always, to the recipients on his lineup chain: club president Theo Epstein, general manager Jed Hoyer, assistant general manager Randy Bush, assistant director of research and development Jeremy Greenhouse, first base coach Brandon Hyde, and director of media relations Peter Chase. The distribution of his lineup was done more as a courtesy, less for approval.

About Epstein, Maddon said, "He's never vetoed anything. He'll just write back sometimes, 'Have you thought about this?' The last two years they've given me a lot of freedom to do what I think is right. And it's been really enjoyable. We include each other in everything, but when it comes down to on the field, in the dugout, the clubhouse, he gives me all kinds of freedom."

Hyde then texted the lineup to the players, as he always did. If the lineup includes a significant change out of the ordinary—such as a position switch or a day off for one his regulars—Maddon will send a personal text to the player involved to open the door to a conversation.

Maddon is an inveterate lineup tinkerer. He started a different rightfielder in three of the first four World Series games (Chris Coghlan, Jorge Soler, and Jason Heyward). But Maddon did not ruminate long over his Game 7 lineup. He stuck with the same one that he used in Game 6, and why not? His team had thrashed the Indians, 9–3, while cranking out 13 hits. The key change he'd made for that game was to put designated hitter Kyle Schwarber in the number two spot, which moved third baseman Kris Bryant, first baseman Anthony Rizzo, and leftfielder Ben Zobrist down one slot each, to three-through-five. In Games 1 and 2 in Cleveland, with the designated hitter used in the American League park, Schwarber had hit fifth. It was the first time he had seen major league pitching in 201 days after rehabbing torn ligaments in his left knee. Amazingly, within a single series Schwarber had turned himself into a legitimate threat at the plate after missing virtually the entire season.

"Yeah, it changes the whole lineup," Maddon said in his office before Game 7. "I mean, everybody last night: K.B. didn't mind hitting third, Rizzo didn't mind hitting fourth, Zobrist, etc. They all like having [Schwarber] slotted in there. It sets up so different for the other side. It really does."

Still, the Cubs once again would have to contend with the swirling and spinning pitches of Kluber, who would make his second straight start on short rest. He'd flummoxed them in Game 1 primarily with a two-seam fastball that headed straight for the left-handed batters' front hip, only to swoop back over the plate just after they dodged out of what they thought was its intended path. Then Kluber had embarrassed them with a cruel game of bait-and-switch curveballs in Game 4. Most of Kluber's curves tracked the strike zone long enough to entice the Chicago hitters to swing, only to veer into the dirt or off the plate at the last second. You could almost hear his curveballs snicker as they pulled their trickery time and time again. In Game 4, the Cubs swung at 49 percent of Kluber's pitches that were not in the strike zone, the highest chase rate by any team against the right-hander all year.

Maddon knew if the Cubs took the same reckless approach against Kluber, they would likely ensure a 108th consecutive season for the franchise without a world championship. What concerned him most was that almost everywhere he looked on his color-coded lineup card, Maddon saw youth: Addison Russell, 22; Schwarber, 23; Javier Baez, 23; Bryant, 24; and Willson Contreras, 24. Only one other team in World Series history ever started so many players under age 25 in a Game 7, and that team, the "Impossible Dream" Boston Red Sox of 1967, played at home, and lost, 7–2, to the St. Louis Cardinals.

Now Maddon had to hope that a lineup packed with young hitters could show the discipline it had lacked against Kluber twice previously, this time on the road and with the World Series on the line.

"We're just trying to hit the ball up in the zone, and trying not to chase spin down," Maddon said. "Those are the two things we're trying to accomplish. The lefties must be on the [two-seam] comebacker, of course. But we've got to find out early where Kluber is at. This is his third game in nine days. So you don't know if all that is going to be present today. For me the biggest thing is for our youngsters to not chase.

"Zobrist does that. Addison, on a good day . . . after Addison's day yesterday I imagine he will not chase spin today. Contreras is in swing mode and Baez is in swing mode. We've been trying to get them not to do that. Yesterday, if you watched Baez's BP . . . he almost had two hits up the middle. At least he moved the ball. But we've got to get them out of swing mode and not chase spin. So, yes, we talked about it: we are not swinging at spin today.

"I just think with these kids, give them another year or two. They can hear it, but the training is still taking place."

A year or two? The game was just hours away.

As for his pitching plan, Maddon knew he would start with Kyle Hendricks, the low-key, low-velocity control artist, and end with Chapman, the hardest-throwing pitcher on the planet. But how could he bridge the gap between them?

Starter John Lackey was available, but, as Maddon said, the Cleveland lineup, with its heavy dose of left-handed hitters, "is a bad matchup for him."

Jake Arrieta, who threw 102 pitches only the night before?

"No," Maddon said. "I mean, he's like way out" if the game went extra innings. Arrieta was so far out of his thinking that Maddon didn't even list him on his lineup card among his available relievers.

The key piece to the planned bridge was another starting pitcher, Jon Lester, who had had two days of rest since throwing 90 pitches in his Game 5 win. But Maddon admitted he might need a second bridge just to get to Lester. The left-hander had been dogged for five years by a bad case of the yips throwing to bases. His inability to hold runners—Lester had not even tried a pickoff attempt since July—prompted Maddon to vow that he would not bring him into a game with runners on base, a situation he refers to as a "dirty inning."

"If Hendricks is not as sharp, he's coming out and Jonny Lester is coming in to that," Maddon said. "We need a bridge to Lester. Because I'm not going to bring Jonny into a dirty inning. So you have to bridge him with either [Mike] Montgomery or [Carl] Edwards to get to Jon—give him a chance to warm up.

"And being an American League game, it helps that somewhat. I don't have to worry about where the pitcher is in the lineup. That's such an advantage. The more you get a chance to manage in the National League, the more you see the differences more clearly. When you go out there to make a pitching change, there's nothing to think about but going out there and making a pitching change. So, yes, I'm watching Hendricks with high scrutiny tonight."

How many innings could he possibly get from Lester?

"I think a good two innings, and then [after that] it would be a matter of how many pitches he throws," Maddon said. "I have to talk to him about that. He was wanting to pitch yesterday, too."

Maddon was down to three true relievers he trusted: Chapman, Montgomery, and Edwards. Key relievers Hector Rondon and Pedro Strop, for instance, had not bounced back reliably enough from late-season injuries. There was no need, Maddon said, to talk to them about their reduced role—not under the coldhearted urgency of the World Series, anyway.

"I can't worry about that right now," he said. "It would be a disingenuous conversation on my part, just trying to ameliorate something. Ronnie has not been back to where he was. You saw Strop yesterday. Maybe the fastball command is not there. So maybe the intent is proper, but the execution isn't. All year he's been good. But to count on him to throw his fastball where he wants to, it's not always going to work out that way. Beyond that, C.J., Montgomery—all of these guys are in in short spurts—maybe one to three hitters. But I can't worry about that.

"Travis [Wood] is throwing the ball pretty good, but their lineup is so awkward it doesn't fit Strop and Rondon's strength—at all. That's part of it, too. It's just a difficult matchup. Whereas Montgomery with the curveball and changeup on righties is good, C.J. with the big old hook on lefties is good and the cutter is good. They play opposites well.

"They've been doing it all year, but this whole postseason has been a challenge, bullpen-wise, because of our skills versus their skills."

Just before game time, Epstein would visit Maddon in his office to review the game plan.

"Hendricks, Lester, and Chapman," Maddon told him. If all went well, he said, those were the only three pitchers he would use.

"How many innings do you want from Hendricks?" Epstein asked.

"Five," Maddon said. "I'll take five good innings."

Five? Epstein was surprised. It sounded like a curiously low number to him. Hendricks was the 2016 National League ERA champion and carried a run of 15 scoreless postseason innings into his Game 7 start. Epstein was hoping for more than five innings from him. Maddon wanted just five innings from Hendricks because he was counting on Lester and Chapman to take care of the other four. In Maddon's perfect world, Lester could get through three innings so that Chapman, who worked hard in Games 5 and 6, needed to pitch only one inning.

Maddon picked up his lineup card and studied it. Though it was small enough to fit into his back pocket when folded in half, the card was a veritable encyclopedia of information. Left-handed hitters and pitchers in blue ink, right-handed hitters and pitchers in black, and switch-hitters in red—just the way he always did it.

"Honest to God, if everything is the same color it screws me up," he said.

Next to every hitter on the front of the card was a number that looked like a batting average, but was Maddon's propriety number marked "Matrix." Under Epstein's leadership, the Cubs spent five years creating finely detailed strategies about how to score and prevent runs. Maddon's Matrix was the last dash of secret spice added to the recipe. As for every game, Maddon took a trove of information about a hitter—such as what types of pitches he likes, whether he hits well or not against velocity, how hot or cold he is at the moment—and distilled it into one number, the Matrix, that instantly told him how that hitter matched up against the starting pitcher.

"It's like a regular batting average," he said. "A .300 number is really good; .200 is bad. Those are color-coded also. So the high numbers are highlighted in red.

"I don't even know batting averages anymore. I don't even know how many hits you have against Chapman or whatever. I have no idea. I have no idea what you are against a pitcher. I just know my number, and my number has everything baked into it, man."

A hitter who is batting .100 in his career against a pitcher, for instance, might have a red .300 Matrix next to his name on Maddon's card.

"Correct. It happens all the time, and vice versa," Maddon said.

The color code worked like this, in ascending order of Matrix: the box with the number was highlighted blue for .239 and below, light blue for .240 to .260, white for .261 to .275; pink for .276 to .290; and red for anything above .290.

The highest Matrix on his card for Cleveland against Hendricks belonged to second baseman Jason Kipnis, who had a .270 in a white box to the right of his name. That meant that Kipnis represented the greatest threat in the Indians' lineup against Hendricks. But it also meant that nobody in the lineup posed either of the two highest levels of threat; there were no pink or red boxes on the Cleveland side of the card.

By contrast, though the Cubs had hardly dented Kluber in the series, the Chicago side of the card included five starters with pink or red Matrix boxes. Leading the way were Rizzo, with a red .308

Matrix, and Schwarber, with a red .307. Heyward followed with a pink .287, then Bryant, with a pink .279, and Zobrist, with a pink .278.

Maddon made an addendum to his Matrix system in 2016: on the back of his card he kept another set of Matrix numbers for hitters when they face the starting pitcher for the third time in a game, a reflection of how modern ball games often pivot on the decision point of when a manager goes to his specialized bullpen.

"Normally my Matrix increases by six one-hundredths," he said, "So, like it goes from .262 to .268, .270 to .276 the third time through. I incorporated that this year. I heard people talking about that so much I asked [the Cubs' analysts] if they could incorporate that into my card. The beauty of this system is if I have a thought, the information will be there for the next series, the next day, or when I want it."

Also on the card were strikeout and groundball percentages for hitters and pitchers. Like the Matrix numbers, these also were color-coded—the same light blue to red system for the strikeout percentages, but light green and green for the gradients of groundball percentages.

"Strikeout percentage is so good, groundball percentage is so good, whether to start a runner or not on a full count," Maddon said. "If the guy is high strikeout and fly ball, screw it. If you've got low-punch, heavy-groundball hitter, the guy's going. We'll take our shot. That's where those numbers are impactful.

"Even with the bullpen. You need a strikeout? I don't want the ball hit at all. You pretty much know, but this validates percentage point–wise the potential percentage you're going to strike out against this guy versus this other pitcher."

On a separate sheet of paper he folded inside his lineup card, Maddon kept information about the other manager's bullpen usage. He had tallies of appearances, pitches, and innings for each pitcher over the previous five days. That information provided him with clues about whom the other manager trusts or what pitchers may be unavailable because of recent workload.

"It's just stuff to know," he said. "When you're making decisions, it's nice to know. It makes you more confident making decisions, probably. Anything you want you can put on that card."

The card included a trove of personal marginalia handwritten by Maddon in purple ink. Toward the bottom of his card, down by the name of his starting pitcher, Hendricks, and running vertically up the left-hand side, he wrote "positive/optimistic." It was a personal reminder that Maddon added to his cards throughout the 2016 season.

"My mantra to myself was to stay positive and optimistic and to stay in the moment," he said. "That was my mantra to myself all year."

In the upper left-hand corner of the card, just to the left of the Cubs logo, Maddon wrote the letter "H." He has put an "H" on his card going all the way back to his first managing gig, with the 2006 Tampa Bay Devil Rays. The "H" is a remembrance of his father, Joseph Maddon. Why "H"?

"Howard," Maddon said. "That was his nickname. We called him that because every game we would watch on television Howard Cosell would say something, and two minutes later my dad would say the same thing Cosell said. Me and my brother said, 'Hey, Howard . . . ' And it stuck. Everybody called him Howard."

Running across the top center of the card was a long line of other letters, each of which represented the memory of a friend or family member Maddon has lost. Maddon recited the names in perfect order without looking at the card.

"I think about these people every day," Maddon said. "I look at the lineup card and I'm able to see Gig, Johnny, Didi, Freda, Peter, Peter, Michael, Michael, Frank, Murtz, Anthony, Mr. Arci, Joe, Milt, Booty, Irene, Irene . . . That's on the top of my card. I'm able to write that every day."

Running down the spine of the card, along the fold in a thin alley between the Cubs' side and the Indians' side, was another note he wrote to himself: "B Present. Not Perfect. Z. Irreverent." The first two key words recalled one of the six key principles he spelled out to his team on the first day of spring training: *Know we are not perfect, but can be present.* The "Z" stood for Don Zimmer, the late coach who influenced Maddon in Tampa Bay, and the "Irreverent" was an homage to the way Zimmer taught him how to run a game.

Maddon never ran a game by conventional means, never believed in reverence to the conformities of by-the-book baseball. Lord knows, as well as a nervous Cubs fan base who tried to think along with him, that Maddon would stay irreverent that night through the seventh game of the World Series.

In the upper right-hand corner of the card Maddon wrote, "DNBAFF," an acronym he wrote on all his lineup cards. It stood for "Do Not Be a Fucking Fan," a reminder that his job in the dugout was to take the emotions out of decisions and to stick to the word he wrote just below it: "Process!" In spring training of 2015, Maddon became good friends with Tom Moore, the 78-year-old assistant coach with the Arizona Cardinals. Moore grew up in Iowa, a Cubs fan. Later that 2015 season, Moore brought his son with him to Wrigley Field and, as guests of Maddon, stood by the batting cage for batting practice.

"He was like crying," Maddon said, "because he had the chance to take his kid to Wrigley Field. That was impressive. He's just a real man."

Moore told Maddon something at their lunch that stuck with him: "In football, you break the other team's will through the relentless execution of fundamentals."

Said Maddon, "I love that. I friggin' love that. 'The relentless execution of fundamentals.'"

Maddon believed the same principle applied to baseball. That's why he wrote "Process!" on the card. Stick to the process.

The splash of colors, numbers, symbols, and notes made for a Jackson Pollock of a lineup card: a kind of organized chaos that held in suspension both beauty and meaning.

Given the Cubs' history, Maddon could use all the help he could get in his pocket. Their 108-year wait for another title was the longest championship drought in sports. The last time they did win the World Series, in 1908, occurred in the lifetimes of Mark Twain, Florence Nightingale, Geronimo, Winslow Homer, and Joshua Chamberlain, and in a world when the Ottoman Empire still existed but the 19th Amendment, talking motion pictures, electric traffic lights, and world wars did not. The heritage of the Cubs had grown mythical, only in a Sisyphean kind of way.

This would be the third Game 7 in the history of the franchise. Each of the first two was played at Wrigley Field. Each one saw the Cubs yield nine runs. Each one ended in a painful defeat that ensured those series would stand as preeminent monuments to Cubs infamy, the kind of torment that convinced otherwise perfectly reasonable fans their team was cursed.

In 1945, the Cubs lost Game 7 of the World Series to the Detroit Tigers, 9–3, after falling behind by five runs before they even took a turn at bat. The loss gave perpetual life to an otherwise trivial, bizarre event in the fourth game of that series, when the club prevented local tavern owner Billy Sianis from bringing his pet goat, Murphy, to sit with him at Wrigley Field. An outraged Sianis declared the Cubs would never win again, a decree that came to be known as the Curse of the Billy Goat.

In 2003, the Cubs lost Game 7 of the National League Championship Series to the Florida Marlins, 9–6, after they took a 5–3 lead into the fifth inning. The loss perpetuated the ignominy of the sixth game of that series, when Cubs fan Steve Bartman deflected a foul fly ball that Chicago leftfielder Moises Alou thought he was primed to catch. The Cubs would have been four outs away from the World Series with a 3–0 lead if Alou had caught the ball. Instead, the incident triggered a cascade of events that produced eight runs among the next eight batters, condemning the Cubs to an epic 8–3 defeat.

Those were the sorts of legends and poltergeists that made this Game 7 the biggest, most anticipated game in baseball history. No game ever had more history riding on it. The Cubs and the Indians had waited 176 combined seasons to win another World Series, with the Cleveland drought dating to 1948. It was, by far, the most drought-stricken World Series there ever was, displacing the mere 90 years of combined waiting the Cincinnati Reds and Boston Red Sox brought to the 1975 World Series.

Since each team's last World Series title, the Cubs and Indians combined had played four games with a chance to win their next one—only to lose all four of them. The Cubs provided one of those failed World Series clinchers (Game 7 in 1945) while the Indians stumbled three times (Game 7 in 1997 and Games 5 and 6 in 2016). This time somebody had to win. And somebody had to remain cursed.

As Maddon sat at his desk, there was no way for anyone to truly imagine just how different the world would be the next morning with a Cubs victory. Cemeteries around Chicagoland would fill with people carrying to the graves of their loved ones white flags with a blue "W"—the symbol of a Cubs' win—mementos, newspapers, balloons, and assorted other pieces of evidence that the Cubs really did win the World Series.

At All Saints Cemetery in Des Plaines, 18 miles northwest of Wrigley, people would festoon the resting place of famed Cubs announcer Harry Caray with baseballs, beer bottles, and 15 bushels' worth of green apples, for it was Caray, in one of his 16 unfulfilled seasons broadcasting Cubs games, who said, "Sure as God made green apples, someday the Chicago Cubs are going to be in the World Series." Also interred at All Saints is Hall of Fame catcher Gabby Harnett, whose 19 seasons for the Cubs tie him with Ernie Banks for the second-longest tenure in franchise history without a World Series title. Only Phil Cavaretta, who spent 20 seasons with the Cubs, invested more time since 1908.

Flowers, rally towels, and notes also would cover the final resting place of Banks at Graceland Cemetery, just a half mile from Wrigley. And five miles from there, at Bohemian National Cemetery, people would flock to the columbarium built in 2009 to resemble the outfield wall at Wrigley. It is an ivy-colored redbrick wall with the same yellow "400" marker as in centerfield and a stained-glass image of the ballpark's iconic scoreboard. "Cubs Fans Forever, Beyond the Vines," it says, and from one of four ballpark seats facing the wall you can keep company with the ashes of those placed inside the wall's 288 niches.

At Wrigley Field, fans would turn the ballpark itself into a memorial. On the brick walls that face Waveland and Sheffield avenues, using chalk in many colors, they would draw their hallelujahs, including tributes and notes to loved ones, whether among the living or deceased, sometimes using ladders to find whatever empty space they could.

The returns from the television ratings would be staggering, the likes of which had never before been seen for a baseball game since satellite, streaming, and multiplatform services vastly expanded viewing options. Game 7 would draw an average audience of 40.035 million viewers, including 49.9 million at its peak, making it the most viewed baseball game in a quarter of a century, since Game 7 of the 2001 World Series. In the last 15 minutes leading to the last out, about 82 percent of the homes in the Chicago market with a television on would be watching the Cubs. More than 10.5 million tweets would be sent out about Game 7, the most ever for any baseball game.

Nowhere, though, would the scope of the catharsis be better understood than at the championship parade, held the day after the morning after. An estimated five million people, almost all of them in Cubs blue, would turn out for the team's victory parade. It would look as if a seven-mile river of fountain pen ink spilled across America's third-largest city. The crowd would be estimated to be the largest gathering of humanity ever in the Western hemisphere, and the largest in humankind's history for any nonreligious event, though to see the rewarded faith on the faces of the supplicants was to believe something very much ecclesiastical was going on here.

No championship ever bound more people than this one. No title was more defined by people pulling together than this one, right down to an impromptu team meeting during a rain delay that ignited the series-winning rally in Game 7. Theo Epstein, once known as the number-crunching wizard who broke the championship curse of the Boston Red Sox, built this team with an emphasis on people who would create the right ethos. The story of the Cubs' championship would not just be about 2016. It would be timeless. It would also be about the power of human connection—teammates to teammates, teammates to fans, generation to generation. The mass of humanity that would assemble at the parade to celebrate their Cubs gave awe-inspiring testimony to that power.

"We can win again next year, but it'll never be that again," Maddon would say. "It can't. Firsts are hard to beat."

In January 2015, soon after taking the Cubs job, Maddon made his first appearance at an annual pilgrimage called the Cubs Convention, a publicity event for fans.

"Joe, please take care of the goat," a fan beseeched Maddon.

Maddon didn't miss a beat: "Right between the eyes!"

Maddon laughed at the curse as much as his rejoinder. He was the new guy in town who gave no credence to generational talk about superstitions and unexplained oddities. One of his first orders of business was to scoff at this folklore. After all, as his lineup suggested, "DNBAFF." But sitting in his office before Game 7 of the World Series, Maddon literally surrounded himself with totems that suggested his own belief in the mystical.

The dark chocolate? He carried it with him everywhere he went because he believed it to be good for brain stimulation.

The pictures of Weaver, Tanner, and Howser? Maddon began the postseason with the eight-by-ten of Weaver out of supplication to the God of the Three-Run Homer, given Weaver's love of the long ball and his hatred for making outs on the bases. Maddon wanted to channel the Hall of Fame manager. He carried the photo with him from Chicago to San Francisco to Chicago to Los Angeles to Chicago to Cleveland and back to Chicago.

Then, before Game 5 of the World Series, with the Cubs trailing the Indians three games to one, Hyde, the first base coach, walked into Maddon's office and on his desk dropped pictures of Howser and Tanner. Howser's 1985 Royals were the most recent of only five teams to come back from a three-games-to-one deficit to win the World Series. Tanner's 1979 Pirates preceded the 1985 Royals, and remained the last team to finish off such a comeback on the road. After the Cubs won Game 5, Earl, Dick, and Chuck all accompanied Joe to Cleveland.

Finally, inside a backpack resting on the floor, was an old, faded, blue Anaheim Angels hat. The hat was nearly flat and showed dirt and grime from years of use. The hat belonged to his father. Joseph Anthony Maddon was a first-generation American of Italian ancestry who ran the family plumbing business in Hazleton that his father, Carmen, began in the 1930s. Beginning in 1975, Joe, his first-born son who wanted no part of pipes and faucets, spent 31 years with the Angels as a minor league player, instructor, and manager, and as a major league coach. As a minor league player, Maddon once was asked to fill out a standard questionnaire in which one question required prospects to list their heroes. Most prospects just named the major league player they had idolized growing up.

Maddon wrote: "My father, Joe. He's a plumber. He takes pride in it, so he's the best there is."

Maddon first reached the major leagues with the Angels as a coach in 1994. His dad grew partial to a periwinkle blue Angels hat in a style the club began wearing in 1997. The proud father would wear that hat all the time until the day he died, April 15, 2002. Later that same year, the Angels reached Game 7 of the World Series against the San Francisco Giants. Between innings, Joe—then the bench coach for Angels manager Mike Scioscia—would run from the dugout to his locker in the clubhouse to rub his father's hat for good luck.

In the ninth inning, with the Angels holding a 4–1 lead, Maddon brought the hat back with him to the dugout. He placed it on a shelf in front of him—facing the field so that his father could "see" his son's team win the World Series.

"I put the hat on that shelf so it was facing out," Maddon said, "and covered it with my papers because I didn't want to make it too obvious."

It was the only time Maddon was in uniform for Game 7 of a World Series—until this night, November 2, 2016. If the night turned out the way Maddon wanted—if his young hitters could resist chasing Kluber's assortment of devilish pitches, if he could build a bridge of pitchers between Hendricks and Chapman, and if the goat and Bartman really were nothing but meaningless fluke events—then his father's hat would be with him again to see the last out.

"I'm really not superstitious," Maddon said. "I'm—how can I say it?—I'm into *thoughts*. It's like you channel your thoughts in the right direction, and if you think it has a chance of happening, it has a better chance of happening. If you don't, it has less of a chance of happening."

It was approaching 8 p.m. First pitch, as was printed right there atop Maddon's lineup card, was scheduled for 8:08 p.m. It was time for Game 7. Maddon took his lineup card and rubbed it three times on the picture of Weaver on his desk, then he rubbed it three times on the picture of Howser, and then he rubbed it three times on the picture of Tanner. Only then was he ready to go. He folded the lineup card in half, stuffed it in the back pocket of his uniform pants, and headed to the dugout.

He left his father's hat in his office. He would be back for it later.

CHAPTER 2

READY FOR CHANGE

The secret meeting took place in New York, the better to keep reporters off the scent.

It happened in the apartment of Cubs owner Tom Ricketts the first weekend of October in 2011. The windows offered a spectacular view of Central Park. A playoff game between the Phillies and the Cardinals played on the television, though it was little more than background noise to the conversation between Ricketts and the man he wanted to rebuild his franchise, Theo Epstein.

Ricketts had met Epstein only once before, in passing at a baseball owners meeting. "My first concern," Ricketts said, "was what kind of person was he."

Ricketts knew all about Epstein's reputation. He expected a quant, someone who spoke with religious fervor about the power of numbers. He also expected someone with the air and attitude of a big shot, with an ego emboldened by winning two World Series titles as general manager of the Boston Red Sox, the first of which, at age 30, ended a supposed curse 86 years in the making.

"He was like Cher or Bono: people knew him by just one name—Theo," he said. "You wonder what kind of ego he had."

At dinner that night he immediately found Epstein to be different from the person he had expected. He found a humble, 37-year-old man who spoke with more passion about people than about numbers.

"I don't know what you think I am," Epstein told Ricketts, "but I'm not what people think I am. It's not about me. It has to be about the whole organization. To win you have to have a lot of people rowing in the same direction."

Ricketts would say later that he knew after just 10 minutes that he had found the right person to rebuild the Cubs.

"I was getting a good read on what kind of manager he would be, how he treats people," Ricketts said. "I've been in businesses where you hire really talented people, but they end up mistreating people beneath them. That is very uncomfortable.

"We spent a few hours, we had dinner, watched a little baseball, and it became clear who he was. He was the kind of person who treats people with respect. He was honest and candid about his successes and failures. A lot of people defend themselves so that every decision looks like a tough one. Theo doesn't get defensive. He gets very honest about it."

Likewise, Epstein discovered in Ricketts an owner who defied the expectations he brought to the meeting.

"I was really impressed with him personally, being humble and down-to-earth and easy to talk to, all the things you don't expect from a rich guy," Epstein said. "I was impressed by his desire to find someone to build a foundation and create a healthy, winning baseball operation, not look for a very quick fix for the 2012 Cubs. He seemed to know what he wanted, which was a modern, robust, thriving, healthy baseball operation, but he didn't know how to get there, and he had taken a lot of steps to do the search the right way to find the right person.

"We talked baseball and it was clear that he knew what he didn't know, but that he would also be very supportive and very patient and it seemed like he would be an easy person to get along with. He painted it very much like the blank canvas that it was. He wanted to develop a vision and a strategy."

The meeting went very well, but one key question remained, a question Ricketts kicked around in his head ever since he announced the firing of Cubs general manager Jim Hendry on August 19: Would Epstein actually leave Boston, his hometown, and with one year remaining on his contract?

The Cubs, in keeping with unwanted form, were a mess. The 2011 team lost 91 games while walking more batters and making more errors than any team in the league. A Cubs fan could shrug at the numbing familiarity of such ineptitude. Since 1945, when the Cubs last played in the World Series, losing seasons outnumbered winning seasons 45–19, with another two at flat even.

A century ago the Cubs were a dynasty. Led by the melodious double-play combination of Joe Tinker, Johnny Evers, and Frank Chance, the Cubs from 1906 through 1910 won four pennants and two World Series, while averaging 106 wins per year. Years of malaise and misadventure followed—so many years that the more optimistic of fans liked to crack, "Anybody can have a bad century."

Winning seasons happened for the Cubs like freak snowstorms: you never saw them coming, and they ended as quickly as they arrived. Those isolated times of success served only to set up epic, inglorious failure. The 1969 team suffered a 17–26 collapse, highlighted by a black cat scampering in front of their dugout September 9 in New York; it would be the last night the Cubs spent in first place that year. The 1984 team, needing one win to advance to the World Series, lost three straight games to the San Diego Padres in the National League Championship Series. The 2003 team reprised the collapse, losing three straight potential NLCS clinchers to the Florida Marlins, a downfall in which Bartman had an infamous hand.

Over the years, two ancient forces bound Cubs fans. One was Wrigley Field, the former site of a Lutheran seminary, where the Cubs have been playing baseball since 1916. With its bucolic beauty and a coziness as comforting as a grandmother's hug, Wrigley, especially on a warm day with a cold drink, was the perfect diversion from the other force: the unrequited yearning for a World Series championship.

Ricketts was the third owner to inherit those forces, following P. K. Wrigley, who ran the team from 1932 to his death in 1977, to the Tribune Company, which purchased the team from the Wrigley family in 1981. Ricketts also inherited Hendry, who upon his firing had been with the Cubs for 17 years, the last 10 seasons as general manager. His teams had won division titles in 2003, 2007, and 2008 under managers Dusty Baker and Lou Piniella, high-profile, old-school types who were the dominant personalities of the organization. But little about the organization was sustainable. After getting swept by the Dodgers in the 2008 Division Series, the Cubs in 2009 dropped from 97 wins to 83 wins. During that 2009 decline, Ricketts purchased the team.

Ricketts, the director of TD Ameritrade Holding Corporation, is the son of J. Joseph Ricketts, who established Ameritrade in 1971. The younger Ricketts became, like many fans, an ardent supporter of the Cubs in the magical playoff season of 1984, when he moved from Omaha to attend the University of Chicago. Ricketts would later live with his brother Pete on the corner of Sheffield and Addison, and he would meet his future wife, Cecilia, in the Wrigley Field bleachers. He deeply understood Cubs culture, and what a championship would mean to the fans.

The slide of 2009 begat the slide of 2010, when the Cubs dropped to 75 wins, which begat the slide of 2011, when they sank to 71 wins. On July 22 that season, Ricketts decided to fire Hendry. He informed Hendry of the decision, though he made no announcement at the time. Hendry agreed to keep the firing secret so he could stay on through the August 15 deadline to complete the process of trying to sign his selections from the June draft.

Hendry went out in a blaze of cash. On August 16 the Cubs announced they had signed 18 of their top 20 picks, many of whom were signed for bonus money that exceeded the recommendations of the commissioner's office, known as "slot" money. There were no penalties associated with "going over slot," other than incurring the wrath of commissioner Bud Selig. The slotting system was an unofficial strategy by baseball to try to curb spending on draft picks. But, by rule, teams could still flex their financial muscle to convince players to sign, especially the talented players who slid lower in the draft because of demands for an especially high bonus. Drafting players in later rounds and convincing them to sign with first- or second-round money was a popular tactic with higher-revenue teams, including Boston under Epstein. It was a tactic Hendry used on his way out from the Cubs in 2011.

Hendry's signings included first-round pick and high school infielder Javier Baez, who signed for $2.625 million, and Dillon Maples, a high school pitcher with first-round talent selected in the fourteenth round. (He slipped in the draft because teams considered him a difficult sign because of his scholarship offer to play football at North Carolina.) The Cubs signed Maples for $2.5 million, the largest bonus ever paid to a player drafted lower than the second round.

(Maples would turn out to be the more typical Cubs draft pick. Two days before reporting to a post-draft mini-camp, Maples felt a twinge in his forearm while using the TV remote control. He was diagnosed with a strained ligament in his forearm. The Cubs gave him a rehabilitation throwing program, but Maples did not strictly adhere to it. He developed "Steve Blass Disease," slang for the sudden, mysterious difficulty throwing strikes, which is named after the former Pittsburgh Pirates pitcher. In five years, none of them out of Class-A ball, Maples hit or walked 151 batters in 182 innings and threw 47 wild pitches.)

Three days after the signings, on August 19, 2011, Ricketts announced the firing of Hendry. Ricketts had no successor in mind yet, he said, but he did have specific ideas about what he was looking for in a top baseball executive.

"When I look at the candidates, I kind of see a couple of criteria," Ricketts told reporters. "I see, number one, they'll have to share a commitment to player development, which obviously is the key to consistent success. I think we can look for guys that have a little stronger analytical background than maybe some of the guys we have here. Someone who has worked with some of the new tools—that would be a plus.

"And then someone who's been in a winning culture and who can bring the lessons of that over and has a track record of success. The sabermetric stuff is important, but it's just a piece. We're not running the baseball organization by a computer model."

Ricketts's three major criteria—a commitment to player development, an analytical background, and a track record of success—made for an exact definition of Epstein. The media, though, did not immediately pick up on the possibility of Epstein leaving Boston for Chicago. Most of the initial speculation spit out the names of Oakland president Billy Beane, Yankees general manager Brian Cashman, Rays general manager Andrew Friedman, Padres general manager Josh Byrnes, and White Sox assistant general manager Rick Hahn.

Writing for Foxsports.com in mid-September, Jon Paul Morosi captured the popular media sentiment about the possibility of Epstein joining the Cubs:

"There is only one problem with this scenario: Epstein has a contract for 2012—in Boston.

"The Red Sox are on the verge of their seventh playoff berth in Epstein's nine seasons. The franchise is in the midst of its greatest era, in the baseball and business departments. For what possible reason would Red Sox owner John Henry—who, again, has control over Epstein's services for one more year—allow him to break the contract and leave?"

By then, Ricketts knew he wanted Epstein. That summer, Ricketts had asked 20 people he knew in baseball—owners, executives, and agents—to recommend the best person for the job. Nineteen of them told him Theo Epstein. What the media and Ricketts didn't know about Epstein was how much his moorings to Boston and the Red Sox had loosened over the years. They were about to reach the breaking point.

THEO EPSTEIN WAS born December 29, 1973, in New York City one minute after his fraternal twin brother, Paul, to proud parents Leslie and Ilene Epstein. Leslie told the *Yale Daily News* in 2002 that they decided on the name Theo because the baby was conceived in Holland, they wanted a Dutch name, it was popular at the time, and it had the added benefit of being the name of Vincent Van Gogh's younger brother. (Theo Van Gogh was a Dutch art dealer who died at 33, six months after Vincent died at 37.)

Writing coursed through the Epstein bloodlines. Epstein's father is a Rhodes scholar and an accomplished novelist who directed the creative writing program at Boston University. Epstein's grandfather and great-uncle, Phillip and Julius Epstein, won the 1944 Academy Award for screenwriting for the movie *Casablanca*, which also won for Best Picture. Phillip Epstein died in 1952. For years his Oscar rested in the den of Theo's parents. Theo's sister, Anya, would become a screenwriter.

Theo's life began on the Upper West Side of Manhattan. He lived there until 1978, when he was 4 years old, when Leslie and Ilene moved the family to Boston, not far from Fenway Park. They arrived just in time to see the Yankees' Bucky Dent break Boston's heart with a home run in a one-game tiebreaker. Leslie, Theo, and Paul would attend about a dozen Sox games every season at Fenway, with young Theo keeping score all nine innings. In 1984, as a fourth grader at Brookline Elementary, Epstein read for the first time Bill James's *Baseball Abstract*, which explained and analyzed baseball like nothing else before—from an advanced statistical perspective. Even at age 10, Epstein knew the book changed the way he looked at base-ball. The idea that one book could so deeply alter his vision of the game astounded him, and forever left him open to new ideas about a game hidebound by tradition.

Books would play an important role in shaping the future general manager. Leslie Epstein made sure that Russian novelists, Charles Dickens, William Faulkner, Ernest Hemingway, and the other great authors were as much of a part of Theo's childhood as the Red Sox. An Epstein house rule stipulated that every minute spent watching baseball on television had to be equaled by reading books.

"A doubleheader," Theo said, "was a lot of reading."

The reading material, nuanced and evocative, nurtured what would become one of his greatest traits as a general manager: em-pathy. The seeds were already there. "Maybe," he said, "it's part of being a twin. I'm a twin. My mom's a twin. My grandfather's a twin." He remembered what his parents would tell him about how he would drive himself crazy as a young child with thoughts of mortality. That someone he loved could die seemed so heavy and unfair to him.

Cubs manager Joe Maddon, after working with him for two years, did not hesitate to define what stood out most about Epstein.

"One word: empathy," Maddon said. "He's brilliant, he's saber-metrically inclined, he's old school, he understands old-school scouting techniques, he understands the game, but of all the guys I've met, he's more empathetic than all of them. He understands people. And he feels what they feel.

"When you have a conversation with him, it isn't sterile. There's feel. Feel is a part of his method. I don't know whether he does it intentionally or not. I just think that's who he is.

"What sets him apart from all the really good guys I've worked with is he's more empathetic than all of them. We get involved in [analytics], but we never get involved in that where other stuff doesn't matter. I might even be the cold one and he comes in with the warm and fuzzy to me, which normally never happens from the GM. That's my conclusion."

One day, when Epstein was about 10 years old, a man who ran a summer camp came to the house. He asked Theo to make a pick among three theoretical bunks with 15 kids: one with individualists who all did their own thing, one with team players who spent every moment together, and one with a mix of all types. It was a setup to steer a child toward being around kids of all kinds, except Theo quickly took the second option.

"It sounded fun for me," he said. "I always liked being with people I like and respect and seeing other people enjoy good times. I'm competitive, too, and that's why baseball's worked out for me: working shoulder to shoulder with people."

Epstein was 12 years old when Leslie took him and Paul to Game 3 of the 1986 World Series at Fenway Park between the Red Sox and the New York Mets. New York drubbed Boston, 7–1. But six days later the twins watched on television at home as the Red Sox held a 5–3 lead in the bottom of the 10th inning of Game 6 in New York. There were two outs and nobody on base. One more out and the Red Sox would be World Series champions for the first time since 1918. Theo and Paul climbed to the top of the living room couch, ready to leap off in celebration upon the final out. It never came. The Mets rallied on three singles, a wild pitch, and an error to win, 6–5. Theo and Paul climbed down and writhed in pain on the floor. Fully indoctrinated at age 13, Theo Epstein understood the visceral pleasure and pain of what it meant to be a Red Sox fan. Welcome to the club.

Epstein attended Brookline High School, where he played soccer and baseball, contributing as a part-time player and third base coach, before he went on to Yale, where he covered sports for the *Yale Daily News*. As a freshman at Yale in 1992, Epstein applied for an internship with the Baltimore Orioles, a team owned by a Yale graduate, Eli Jacobs, with a president who was a graduate of Yale Law School, Larry Lucchino, and a vice president of administrative personnel who was a Yale graduate, Calvin Hill. Epstein's application wound up on the desk of Hill, who walked it to the office of Dr. Charles Steinberg, one of Lucchino's top advisors. While Epstein's friends spent spring break that year in Cancun, Epstein visited Steinberg for an interview. The Orioles hired him, and liked him so much they brought him back for two more summers.

Epstein liked writing, but what he observed in the Orioles' press box of the life of sportswriters convinced him he wasn't cut out for the writing life. He saw the profession as a lonely, individualistic pursuit. He watched writers who sat by themselves and worked by themselves, then retired to the hotel bar. He wanted a more collaborative life, which he saw in professional baseball.

Lucchino left Baltimore to join the ownership group of the San Diego Padres in December 1994, 16 months after Jacobs sold the Orioles at auction to a group headed by Peter Angelos. Soon Steinberg joined him. And so, too, in 1995 after graduating from Yale but still without a driver's license at age 21, did Epstein. He began in the Padres' public relations department, mostly assigned to entertainment projects, such as displaying birthday wishes on the scoreboard. Steinberg drove him back and forth to work every day. Epstein worked his way up to a position as public relations assistant who wrote game notes for the media. His detailed work and diligence caught the eye of Padres general manager Kevin Towers, who in 1997 moved him to the baseball operations department.

In San Diego, Epstein's desk ostensibly made for the DMZ in the newly raging war between the few whip-smart number crunchers who were starting to fold quantitative analysis into the game and old-guard scouting and development men who were resisting the switch to analytics. His desk sat right between the team's analytics guru and the scouting director. They couldn't stand each other and rarely spoke to one another, but both of them enjoyed the company of Epstein.

Epstein obtained his driver's license at 23 and soon thereafter a law degree. When an Anaheim law firm offered Epstein a starting salary of $140,000 in 1998, Towers promoted him to director of baseball operations and boosted his salary from $30,000 to $80,000.

At a time when Triple Crown statistics (batting average, home runs, and runs batted in) still held sway among Major League Baseball decision makers, Epstein taught Towers about less familiar metrics that could give a more accurate assessment of a player's value, such as OPS (On-Base Plus Slugging, the sum of on-base and slugging percentages), strikeout-to-walk ratio, and ballpark factors.

In January 2002, Lucchino, with Steinberg in tow, left the Padres to join Henry and Tom Werner as the new owners of the Red Sox. Two months later Boston hired Epstein as an assistant to the interim general manager, Mike Port, whom ownership had installed as a placeholder after letting go of general manager Dan Duquette. Epstein was hired just two weeks after director of player development Ben Cherington hired Jed Hoyer, who, like Epstein, had just turned 28 years old, to work in the scouting department. Hoyer had played baseball at Wesleyan University, where Epstein's twin, Paul, matriculated and played soccer with one of Hoyer's roommates.

The first time Hoyer met Theo was when the Red Sox played an exhibition game in Houston just prior to Opening Day 2002. Already there was a sense that Epstein was on a fast track under the new Boston ownership.

"We hit it off right away," Hoyer said. "We were basically exactly the same age. Both of us were working all night, every night. It was pretty easy to connect. I remember everyone trying to curry favor with him. When he was brought onboard, his hiring was a big deal. He was a rising star in the game, and the Red Sox were able to bring the hometown kid back home. I tried to stay away at first. Like I said, I felt everyone was running up to him to curry favor. Then one night we were going to some event and it was just the two of us taking the subway. We hit it off on that ride. He started to find a lot of work for me.

"It was a pretty bare-bones operation then. People from the Duquette regime had been let go. It was a small shop. Theo, even as an assistant general manager, tried to build that up."

During that summer of 2002, Epstein heard that Billy Beane, the Oakland general manager, was cooperating with writer Michael Lewis on a book that would use the Athletics as an example of how the statistical revolution was changing baseball. The book would be titled *Moneyball: The Art of Winning an Unfair Game*. Epstein and Beane had become friends, based largely on their shared passion for leveraging advanced analytics. Epstein wasn't happy, however, when he heard about the book project. Said one Red Sox insider then, "I remember Theo being annoyed. He said, 'I can't believe Billy is letting him write this book. He's going to give everybody the same idea. He's handing out the blueprint.' After that, every owner in baseball read the book and said to his baseball people, 'Do this.' At the time at least 20 of the 30 teams still looked at stats crookedly."

The Red Sox were on the same cutting edge of analytics as Oakland, only they were more circumspect about it. Said Hoyer, "There were times in 2002 when I went to bed thinking Billy was my boss."

While Beane was cooperating with Lewis, Epstein went to Henry with an idea: "Why don't we hire Bill James?" Epstein had long admired James's work, so why not have the sabermetric guru produce exclusive work for the Red Sox? Henry loved the idea. After all, like Epstein, Henry had been reading James's *Baseball Abstract* since the mid-'80s, and he had built his fortune in the commodities trading business by relying on cold, hard data to drive his funds.

Henry convinced James to work for the Red Sox. The hiring was announced on November 5, 2002, but by then James already had produced his first project for the club.

"I have this vivid memory of being in the upstairs office," Hoyer said, "right after we hired Bill and getting his first piece of work. It came in a FedEx package and we just tore this thing open. We couldn't wait to read it. We both grew up reading the *Abstract*, and now we were sitting in a room with Bill's exclusive work."

The spiral-bound project ran 86 pages, much of it devoted to James's exclusive ratings of the upcoming free agent class as well as the historical benefit of having left-handed hitters populate the

Boston lineup, a counterintuitive thought because the nearness of Fenway Park's Green Monster in leftfield invites an emphasis on right-handed pull hitters.

Meanwhile, Lucchino drew up a document listing the top 10 qualifications of the ideal general manager. The second qualification he listed was "familiarity with, and willingness to use, modern quantitative approaches in evaluating players, in addition to traditional methods." Shortly after Henry, Werner, and Lucchino announced the hiring of James, they offered the general manager position to Beane with a five-year contract worth $12.5 million. Beane took the job, slept on it, and then changed his mind. On second thought, he did not want to leave California. He told the Red Sox owners they should hire Epstein.

The owners then turned to Toronto general manager J. P. Ricciardi, a Massachusetts native who had worked under Beane in Oakland before taking the job with the Blue Jays. Ricciardi declined to leave. He told the owners they should hire Epstein. Ricciardi's endorsement was another testament to how quickly Epstein made an impact around baseball, especially among forward-thinking organizations.

Finally, on November 25, 2002, the Red Sox made Epstein, one month shy of his 29th birthday, the youngest general manager in history.

What happened next was an immediate mushrooming of intellect and energy. Epstein and his group of top baseball operations advisors—many of them young and statistically savvy, including Jed Hoyer, Ben Cherington, Josh Byrnes, and later Jason McLeod—set about upgrading a Boston team that in 2002 missed the postseason with 93 wins and scored the second-most runs in the American League, trailing only the Yankees. They saw a roster that gave too many at-bats to players who were not very good at getting on base, such as Tony Clark, Rey Sanchez, José Offerman, Carlos Baerga, and Shea Hillenbrand.

"In September of 2002, Theo started talking to [James]," Hoyer said. "Theo started pushing your thinking in different directions. It became a completely different puzzle. What Theo does better than anyone is he wants as much scouting stuff and background stuff and makeup information as anyone. He believes in never having enough information and asking for more. It's probably his best quality. It's not about focusing on any one area, because if you do that you may miss the biggest piece of information. Listen, you're still going to miss. And you can be overly cautious to avoid missing, and he's not. He's as aggressive as it gets."

Epstein and his baseball operations people set about fishing in free agent waters in that 2002–2003 off-season. James's exclusive free agent ratings system was the equivalent of a fish-finder device. And as they fished, the Red Sox crew looked around them and happily noticed something: few teams were fishing in the same waters.

"It was amazing," Hoyer said. "There was just a lot of favorable talent out there. And we were hitting on guys like Bill Mueller, Kevin Millar, and David Ortiz. I remember we were all over Travis Hafner, and we weren't able to get a deal done . . . Carlos Guillén, Erubiel Durazo . . . there were a lot of guys who were freely available that were very talented. That was a group of players that was really undervalued. We were thinking, We can keep acquiring these guys as much as we can. That winter of '02–'03 led to much of the success to come in '03 and '07."

Epstein added infielders Mueller, Millar, and Ortiz, as well as second baseman Todd Walker, first baseman Jeremy Giambi, and pitchers Mike Timlin and Bronson Arroyo. Those seven players cost him only three nonprospects from his minor league system and $13 million in salary toward his 2003 payroll.

"We had a really frantic off-season," Hoyer said. "Looking back on those years there was so much energy and change. That first off-season may have been Theo's finest work. It was a really fun time. We were all around our early 30s and working nonstop. It felt like we never took a break, never had lives outside of work. We stayed at work."

THEY DID TAKE one fortuitous break one day in July 2003, while the team was on the road against Tampa Bay. Epstein was sitting at his Fenway Park desk when his secretary told him, "George Webb from Pearl Jam is on the phone."

Webb, the band's equipment manager, had heard that Epstein considered Pearl Jam his favorite band. Webb arranged for tickets to the concert in Mansfield, Massachusetts, for Epstein and his own "band," the whiz kids in his baseball operations office, including Hoyer, Peter Woodfork, and Amiel Sawdaye. They watched from the side of the stage. At one point Eddie Vedder threw Epstein a tambourine. After the show, Epstein told Webb that he and the band could take batting practice the next morning on the field at Fenway Park. So excited was Vedder, a Cubs fan who grew up in Evanston, Illinois, that he went to sleep with his glove near the nightstand. Alas, he did not get to sleep until after some all-night libations with the Buzzcocks, Pearl Jam's warm-up band. Vedder slept through the Fenway fun.

The next night Epstein and his Red Sox crew returned to Mansfield for the second show. Vedder played the first encore wearing a Red Sox cap. After the show, meeting him for the first time, Epstein could not resist needling Vedder about sleeping through the chance to hit at Fenway.

"Friends ever since," Epstein said.

Something else about Vedder, besides his thoughtful, piercing music, appealed to Epstein. He met Vedder at the same age Vedder had been in 1994, when his reaction to enormous fame—the release of a third platinum-selling album just months after he appeared on the cover of *Time*—was akin to treating a wildfire: you had to tamp down the beast, not stoke it. The band refused, for instance, to produce music videos. Building an image creates expectations of what a person should be, and those expectations, and the falseness of them, Vedder told *Melody Maker* that year, "just start tearing you apart."

Epstein shared the same ethos as Vedder. Upon being named Boston GM, Epstein had turned down offers to appear on *The Tonight Show with Jay Leno* and three morning network news shows.

"It felt wrong at that point," Epstein said. "I would have been on as a reward for being a young GM—a novelty, a gimmick. Even though it was appealing on the face of it, I felt it was wrong. I passed on all that.

"It really is the players' accomplishment. Not that I've been perfect in that regard, but once you thrust yourself out there in the public domain, it's really hard to retreat, to say no or reclaim that certain part of your life as private. It's hypocritical to say when things are going well, 'Interview me. Ask me how great I am. Ask me about family and personal life,' and, at some point later, when someone wants information and you want to draw the line, how do you draw the line?"

UNDER THEIR FIRST-YEAR general manager, the 2003 Red Sox pushed the Yankees all the way to the 11th inning of the seventh game of the American League Championship Series, only to see Aaron Boone, with his home run off Tim Wakefield, join Bucky Dent and Bill Buckner in the deep catalog of Red Sox villainy.

It has been said about the Beatles that their happiness was never so great as it was in the moments just before the boys from Liverpool first hit it big. If so, spring training of 2004 was the height of happiness for Epstein and his young bucks in the front office. Eight of them joined in renting a house in Cape Coral, Florida, about 20 minutes from Boston's training complex in Fort Myers. Under one roof were Epstein, then 30; Hoyer, 30; Cherington, 29; Woodfork, 27; Sawdaye, 26; Craig Shipley, 40; Galen Carr, 28; and Brian O'Halloran, 32. The house went by the unofficial name Phi Signa Playa. There were laptops everywhere, and pizza, beer, and poker to fill the few hours of downtime.

"We had such a great time," Hoyer said. "It was a huge house, and everyone would work different shifts. Some guys would leave super early and get back late. Other guys would leave late. We all carpooled in the mornings. We heard 'Seven Nation Army' by the White Stripes all spring in that car."

Sports Illustrated asked Epstein to cooperate for a story, with the guys posing around the house for a kind of team picture. He declined.

"We haven't accomplished anything yet," Epstein explained.

"That's the beauty of Theo right there," Hoyer said. "He would never allow something like that, even now. After we won the World Series [on Wednesday, November 2, 2016] we were right back to work doing something Saturday and Sunday right before the GM meetings. You don't see him touring different shows. That's the players' place. So it doesn't surprise me he said that back in '04. No one had camera phones back then, so it's lost to history."

In 2004, in his second season as general manager, Epstein won the World Series, unleashing a catharsis across New England the depths of which had been unknown in baseball history. It was in the wake of such emotional outpouring that the idea of someday running the Chicago Cubs first occurred to Epstein, even if it occurred to him in a fleeting manner.

"As far back as the aftermath of the '04 World Series I would talk about it with my friends a little bit," Epstein said. "'If I ever move on, the Cubs would be the one spot because it was so powerful to win in Boston.' The whole aspect of the job was seeing how much it resonated with people and families. You never let go of that. It adds meaning to the whole thing. I would joke around with friends—I remember telling Jed after '04—but it was also sort of a pipe dream, because I was focused on Boston."

Being a Beatle is hard work. Epstein discovered that quickly. The Red Sox won 95 games in 2005, but were swept in the Division Series by the Chicago White Sox. It was viewed as a disappointing year. A weary Epstein, rather than sign a renewal of his contract, resigned on Halloween, famously avoiding the media by slipping away from Fenway Park in a gorilla suit.

Epstein would return to the Red Sox a few months later, before the next season, and win the World Series again in 2007, and come within one win of another pennant in 2008. In six seasons from 2003 to 2008, Epstein's Red Sox won two World Series titles and twice came within one win of playing for more. The expectations of running at peak capacity never eased. In 2009, as they did in 2005, the Red Sox won 95 games but were swept in the Division Series, the kind of seasons that in Boston began to get relegated to the "failure" bin.

In 2010, Epstein, sensing that the years of pushing for 95 wins or more were starting to take their toll on the Boston player development system, made a subdued plea for some perspective. He mentioned that while the Red Sox were still trying to win, the team might be wise to consider 2010 a "bridge" season, in which the organization continued to build for the future, rather than pushing the chips all-in on a year-to-year basis. The sentiment did not go over well inside or outside the front office walls, not with the vast sums the Red Sox were paying their players and not with what the Red Sox were asking their fans to pay to watch them.

"But we were just—and this is a fight that goes back to when I first took the job and even when we won—we were just getting too big," Epstein said. "When we won, our fan base grew, our revenues grew, the expectations to keep creating revenues grew, our expectations of winning 95 games and getting deep into playoffs grew every year and it reached a point . . . One eye-opener is when we tried to have a little bit of a longer-term plan one year and I remember trying to be transparent with the fan base and saying, 'This is probably going to be a bridge year. We're going to try to compete but also get a little bit younger and some of our prospects will need one more year to mature and we're really looking forward to 2011.' It didn't go over too well internally or externally. The internal part was a little disappointing because I thought we were acting in our best interest—long-term interests and medium-term interests."

The environment around him had changed. And so, too, had Epstein.

"I sort of began to react to things emotionally that I shouldn't have," he said.

In that summer of 2010 Epstein attended the funeral of a Red Sox employee. The funeral pamphlet included a Red Sox logo. So did the casket. It shook him to see a man go to his grave so deeply associated with the team.

"I remember thinking, 'I really don't want this to be me,'" he said. "Because, when you're not unconditionally in love with a place anymore, I think you resent to a certain extent the degree to which you're identified with that place, or you self-identify with that place.

"So I just began to internally distance myself from it a little bit emotionally. I don't want to be buried in a Red Sox casket, and how long do I have to stay here until it's who I am? That's not really logical thinking. It's emotional thinking. Probably because of the pressure and the mistakes I made because I didn't do a good enough job taking care of my own environment.

"And it was the cumulative effect of taking the job at 28 and dealing with it for nine years, internalizing a lot of it, living season to season, game to game, and then seeing when you try to calm things and plan for the long term there's sort of a visceral, negative reaction. It doesn't leave you in a real stable [place] . . . It's hard to find a real stable safe haven to exist with that, unless you create it yourself, and I didn't do a good enough job of doing that."

The Red Sox won 89 games in 2010 and missed the playoffs for only the second time in eight seasons. Now the pressure really turned up to get Boston back into the postseason. Epstein's answer was to trade three prospects, including 21-year-old first baseman Anthony Rizzo, to San Diego to get veteran first baseman Adrian Gonzalez, with a seven-year, $154 million extension to Gonzalez tacked on after the deal was completed. Epstein also was close to trading for veteran outfielder Carlos Beltran from the Mets, who was entering the last year of his contract. The proposed deal would have come at a minimal cost: two fringe prospects, including pitcher Michael Bowden. But Epstein walked away from the deal when medical reports gave him concern about the stability of Beltran's knee.

Needing another bat, Epstein wrote a $142 million check to free agent outfielder Carl Crawford for the next seven years. Crawford became one of the worst big-ticket signings in Boston history.

"I thought the 2010–2011 off-season was me, for maybe the first time, taking the easy way out, giving in to the environment," Epstein said. "That was trading for Adrian Gonzalez and extending him and especially signing Crawford. In hindsight, Adrian is still a great player, he's in the last year of his contract [and] he's right on track. That worked out well. It was not received well in Boston. He had a great performance in Boston, but the clubhouse dynamic probably didn't work out great in Boston.

"The Crawford one was especially lazy. We almost avoided it. We were really close to trading for Beltran, and he ended up having an enormous year that year, getting traded for [Zack] Wheeler. Then we just got some bad stuff on his knee. The Mets would have been good with one or two end-of-the-roster guys.

"[Signing Crawford] was just unnecessary. We had just signed Adrian. I didn't do a good job of handling the environment and I took the easy way out. It was my fault. It's easy to sign guys to seven-year deals. It's hard to find guys that are more creative value solutions or plan ahead a couple of years.

"You don't admit it at the time what you're doing, but upon reflection that's not me, that's not what we built here. I didn't do it because I was leaving, but I knew once I did it, it reflected poorly on the fit going forward, regardless of results. And this was a stressful year. So we did that."

Crawford, hitting third in the lineup on Opening Day in Texas, went 0-for-4 in his Boston debut. He went 0-for-3 the next day, whereupon manager Terry Francona dropped him to seventh for the third game of the year. The Red Sox lost all three games to the Rangers, then lost all three games in Cleveland. So stressed was Epstein that he did something before the home opener that he rarely did: he addressed the team to try to shake it from its doldrums. The team continued to sputter, falling to 2–10. But the Red Sox soon marshaled all their talent to become the best team in baseball over the next four months. From that 2–10 start until September, Boston went 81–43, playing at the scorching pace of a 107-win team.

As the team played well, Epstein had a brief conversation with Henry and Werner about his future. The owners told Epstein they wanted him to stay for as long as he wanted. They told him he could write his own job description. Epstein told them about some "internal conflicts" he was experiencing, and that he wasn't sure if he wanted to stay in Boston forever. He recommended that Cherington succeed him someday.

"He's terrific," Epstein told the owners. "He's a lot more mature than I am in a lot of ways. He's definitely the next general manager here. Let's take this year to groom him so it could conceivably be a seamless transition if that's the way it goes."

It wasn't quite walking out in a gorilla suit, but Epstein did more than just hint about a succession plan to foretell his leaving.

"And they were onboard with it," he said.

Several factors began to push the kid from Brookline further away emotionally from the Red Sox. Epstein read a book by Hall of Fame football coach Bill Walsh that summer in which Walsh wrote that the voice of a coach or executive turns stale after about a decade with one organization.

"He talked about it as a sports executive, but it applied to almost any situation in a leadership role," Epstein said. "That it benefits not only the individual but also the institution to seek change every 10 years. And I've seen it, with managers or coaches in other sports, leaders.

"The same message or the same voice tends to get tuned out a little bit just by human nature. So it's impossible to have the same originality, same creativity, same freshness . . . it's impossible to look at things with an open lens. You start to close your lens based on your successes and failures a little bit. And so it got me thinking right there in the middle of that 2011 season."

Moreover, by August, Epstein had signed what he regarded as an especially deep class of draft picks, including pitchers Matt Barnes and Henry Owens, catcher Blake Swihart, and outfielders Mookie Betts and Jackie Bradley Jr. He was restocking the Boston cupboard. It fit his exit strategy. Epstein had begun to talk to his wife about the possibility of just taking a year off away from baseball. That's when the firing of Hendry was announced. Suddenly, the perfect landing spot opened.

"Everybody started asking me about the Cubs job," Epstein said, "and I said, 'I'm just focused on the Red Sox.' But it definitely got my attention because of all the factors—having it in the back of my mind for seven, eight years, the sort of internal struggle of identifying emotionally with the Red Sox, the Bill Walsh, ten-year thing. . . .

"This is before the collapse. We're the best team in baseball, we look really good, it's August of 2011, I'm thinking this would be really great if we can win a World Series and I can leave on top—a third World Series, they're set up for the future. That summer we drafted Betts, Swihart, Henry Owens, and Bradley and we had signed Xander Bogaerts, he was starting to come. They're set up for the future. This wave of prospects is going to be really good. Stable big league team, best team in baseball, if we can win the World Series it's the perfect opportunity to end it, nine years as a GM, ten years as a Red Sox, and move on to the next thing. And the Cubs would be awesome."

On Monday, September 5, the Red Sox held an 8-game lead over Tampa Bay for the wild card spot with 23 games to play, though they had just dropped back-to-back home series to the Yankees and the Rangers. A confident Epstein invited his top baseball operations advisors to Toronto, where the Red Sox would play a 4-game series against the Blue Jays, for pro scouting meetings. But the meetings had another purpose: a possible last chance for Epstein to simply hang out with his guys, as if it were the bookend to the 2004 Cape Coral spring. "I never do this," Epstein said about the off-site meetings jaunt. The more he thought about the Cubs' job, the more intriguing it became.

"So eight of us flew up there and we would have had a good time, but we played a horrific series," Epstein said. "It turned out to be the start of the collapse."

The Red Sox lost the first game of the series in a heartbreaker, 1–0 in extra innings. Jon Lester pitched superbly the next night in a 14–0 Boston laugher. The Red Sox seemed to be righting themselves as they took an 8–6 lead into the eighth inning in the third game of the series, with their best reliever, Daniel Bard, on the mound. A tall right-hander who threw sinkers that approached a hundred miles an hour, Bard had fashioned a 2.01 ERA in 134 appearances over the previous two years. He was as reliable as a manager could want with the game on the line. But that night in Toronto, something suddenly and strangely seemed to afflict Bard. Without warning, his sinker began to cut uncontrollably on him.

"All of a sudden it was, 'What the hell is going on?'" Epstein said.

Bard could not control his pitches. The eighth inning became a bonfire of mistakes: hit by pitch, groundball single, walk, two strikeouts to get to the edge of extinguishing the mess, but then two bases-loaded walks to tie the game, followed by a three-run double off Bard's replacement, Matt Albers. The Red Sox lost, 11–10. They made the last out of the game when a pinch runner, Mike Aviles, was thrown out trying to steal second.

Bard was never the same. Starting that night in Toronto, he went 0–4 with a 12.46 ERA down the stretch. He walked nine batters in 8⅔ innings. Never again was he effective. Bard mysteriously lost his ability to throw strikes and never got it back. He bounced from the Red Sox to minor league teams in the Cubs, Rangers, and Pirates organizations before his lack of control pushed him out of baseball. In 2016, at the age of 31, he tried a comeback with Palm Beach, the Class-A team of the St. Louis Cardinals. The comeback ended after he walked 13 batters in three innings.

Boston lost the final game of the Toronto series, 7–4. The Red Sox had now lost 6 of their previous 8 games and were fully caught in a downward spiral that would only get worse. The Red Sox had built such a big lead that they could have gone 8–19 in their final 27 games and still tied for a playoff spot. Instead, they went 7–20. They played their final 29 games without ever winning back-to-back games.

The more they lost, the more they broke apart from within. Pitcher Josh Beckett feuded with the front office. The *Boston Globe* would later report that Francona was distracted by personal issues and that starting pitchers Beckett, Lester, and John Lackey would drink beer, eat fried chicken, and play video games in the clubhouse during games when they were not pitching. Players feuded with one another. The egos that had created cracks in the clubhouse while they were winning caused deep fissures as they lost.

So toxic was the atmosphere that, as Boston's lead slipped away, one unidentified player began to shrug it off by saying, "Why we do we want to play in October anyway? We don't get paid for that." True enough—players get their annual salary based on the 26 weeks of the regular season—but the sentiment, even if expressed in a joking manner, revealed a deep problem with the character in the clubhouse. Epstein heard about it and wondered, "Who says *that*?" And he knew the answer: a losing player.

"It just got ugly," Epstein said. "It had been hidden by the winning. It was like a Shakespearean tragedy that year.

"It turns out we needed to go something like 8–19 to make the playoffs and we would have made the playoffs under the new [two wild cards] format [that began the next year]. Obviously, we didn't deserve to. It was like watching a monthlong car crash in slow motion.

"We just could not win. We ran out of pitching, we started making fundamental mistakes, defensive mistakes, and in Baltimore it was like a crushing blow."

The Red Sox still managed to get to within one out of tying for a wild card spot on the last night of the season in Baltimore. They led, 3–2, with two outs, nobody on base, and their closer, Jonathan Papelbon, on the mound. But the next three Orioles batters all hit safely: double, double, and single, the last hit a sinking line drive that fittingly wasn't caught by Crawford, Epstein's $142 million free agent albatross who that year hit a miserable .255 with a .289 on-base percentage. The Red Sox trudged off the field with a 4–3 loss, their season over. Boston finished with 90 wins. It wasn't good enough. For the first time under Epstein, the Red Sox missed the playoffs for a second consecutive year.

He never saw this coming. Before September Epstein had an exit strategy mapped out based on a successful season. Now what?

"So I had this thought in my head, 'Oh, we'll win the World Series, wrap it up with a neat little bow, and it's unassailable,'" Epstein said. "There can't be any critics with how I left. So now I was in a really rough spot, conflicted emotionally more than anything else about what to do. And so it took a lot of soul searching."

Two days after the loss in Baltimore, Ricketts called Henry and Werner to ask for permission to talk to Epstein. "It didn't surprise them at all when the Cubs called," Epstein said, remembering the conversation he had with the Red Sox owners at the beginning of the season about his internal conflicts.

"And John and Tom were great about it," Epstein said. "They basically said, 'Look, we'd like you to stay.'"

Said Ricketts, "John's a friend. It was very cordial. At that point I think he realized Theo wasn't going to sign an extension. It was a friendly conversation. He agreed to let me speak with Theo."

Epstein wrestled with his own thoughts in the immediate wake of the collapse.

"Now that we collapsed, is it important to stay?" he said. "There were some mixed feelings. There was the feeling that *Hey, there's kind of a mess here, we have to stay and clean it up* because everything was so public when you lose in that fashion, everything was dumped out there in the open, all the little things that go on behind the scenes became public.

"They also knew personally, for my happiness, the Cubs' opportunity was the right thing, because I had been open with them about how I was feeling and my long-term prospects. So they were great about it and I think a big part of them was they wanted to do the right thing for me, which I really appreciate. They said, 'Why don't you talk to Tom?' They gave permission."

The meeting with Ricketts in New York went even better than Epstein could have imagined. As if stuck in a relationship that had run its course over a decade, and with the worst aspects of the otherwise invigorating Boston fanaticism fresh in his mind—the hypercoverage, the daily strain of your happiness defined by whether you won or lost, the exhaustive autopsies of every defeat, and, in this case, a historic collapse—Epstein was ready for change. But Ricketts came bearing not just the opportunity for change. He also brought the opportunity to go back to the Cape Coral house, a chance to rediscover the energy and passion that only comes with a project at its start. And there was no project in sports as meaningful as this one: the chance to build the first championship Cubs team since 1908.

Epstein could easily imagine its meaning because of the 2004 championship in Boston, when he felt the powerful catharsis. Cubs fans had been waiting even longer, a burden that transferred to the 1,728 players and 52 managers who wore a Cubs uniform between 1908 and 2016. As the Cubs were making their fluky playoff run in 1984, for instance, former third baseman Ron Santo, who played the most games for the franchise without getting to the postseason except for teammates Ernie Banks and Billy Williams, made a confession. "I've got everything I want in life," he said then. "I'm a happy man. But I've got this guilt. I don't think I could have done more than I did, but it was a failure. I felt guilty for the fans. For Chicago. If they win the pennant this year—and they're going to win this—believe me, it's going to take all that guilt off me."

The Cubs did not win the pennant in 1984. Santo was 70 years old when he passed away on December 2, 2010. The guilt of being an unrequited Cub remained to his very last breath.

Ricketts wasn't interested in one fluky season. He and Epstein shared a vision: to rebuild the Cubs from the ground up to create a sustainable champion. Such a plan allowed for a few years without the day-to-day pressure of winning, a respite from the cauldron in Boston that was wearing on Epstein. Ricketts talked about the construction of a champion in physical terms, too. He loved Wrigley Field, but he hated that it presented his players with substandard working conditions. Players, for instance, had no batting cage to prepare for at-bats during games. They had to construct a net in the clubhouse in order to hit off a batting tee, but only after they hung a board and netting to protect a nearby television. A first-class organization, he told Epstein, deserved first-class facilities. The more Epstein heard, the more he remembered Cape Coral.

"Back in that cocoon. That's what it represented," Epstein said. "It wasn't a conscious thing, but it represented all the redeeming aspects of the Boston experience that were now a lot tougher to attain in Boston: the building, the excitement of a new challenge, working shoulder to shoulder with people . . . I still love my baseball operations family in Boston, but once it was clear I could reunite with Jed [Hoyer] and Jason [McLeod], that was a big part of it.

"Frankly, I have to admit—I never thought about it this way—but deep down knowing it would be a build but the pressure of the standings for the first year or two wouldn't matter at all . . . That appealed to me, having just gone through the torture of yet another loss, another loss, another loss in September of that year. It represented a respite from that. Because that wears on you. I probably aged five years that month of September.

"And the chance to re-create the thrill of '04, the region-wide joy and relief and catharsis that championship represented. That's why you go to Chicago, to try to bring that to people again, watching an organization and a fan base experience something like that in such an intimate, personal way that connects fans and families and generations. It was by far the most meaningful part of the whole decade in Boston. You're lucky to ever think about playing a small part in that at least once, but you never think you could re-create it or duplicate it, even just the chance of it is super appealing."

Epstein soon agreed to Ricketts's offer, though it was not immediately announced. Epstein wanted Hoyer, who was then general manager of the San Diego Padres, and McLeod, Hoyer's assistant there, to reunite with him in Chicago. Hoyer was an ascendant star in his own right. He interviewed for general manager positions in Pittsburgh after the 2007 season and in Washington and San Diego after the 2009 season. Hired by the Padres, Hoyer inherited a 75-win team and immediately improved it by 15 wins. The Padres slipped back to 71 wins in 2011.

Hoyer was in Arizona with his wife, who was eight months' pregnant, looking at spring training rentals for 2012 when his phone rang. It was Epstein. He wanted Hoyer, and he wanted McLeod. It was the chance to go back to Cape Coral.

"I thought, *What an incredible opportunity for Theo. They're going to be great,*" Hoyer said. "We had this whole conversation. I had a good job. I was happy. A big part of me started to think about building something there in San Diego, the challenge of building something without a big payroll.

"But as we started talking through it, it was clear this was a once-in-a-lifetime opportunity. The door wouldn't swing open again. Once it was clear Jason might go, it became incredibly appealing. It was a great city with a great fan base and a great story. This was the one place we could replicate '04.

"One thing I thought about was our relationship. We knew the size of the task. We knew the responsibility on both of us. Neither one of us is great at being super specific at those responsibilities, but I knew he would give me a ton of autonomy and that's what happened. This is ultimately a situation where Theo is the final decision maker. But I felt as though I was able to have an impact. I never would have left for anyone else. It was more about our relationship."

Epstein broke the news to Henry, Werner, and Lucchino: he was gone. His departure happened over years and involved the slow incubation of personal and emotional conflicts, but much of the press boiled it down to a simple narrative: after learning at the foot of Lucchino, the student had to leave to get out from the heavy hand of his mentor. Epstein never bought that facile presentation.

"I blame myself for this more than anything." Epstein said, "I hate it when people blame their environment, because, especially in a leadership position, you're responsible for how you react to your environment and how you change your environment, and being a positive force to change it for the better if you think something is toxic.

"I wouldn't blame anyone else for it or any one person. I know everyone said, 'Well, it was you and Larry . . . it was a power struggle.' It really wasn't. Our dynamic never really changed. He never got super involved in baseball operations, but he was my boss and always had the right to question me on things and I never really resented that.

"It wasn't any one person. It was just the weight of the nine or ten years in Boston."

On October 25, 2011, twenty-seven days after the season-ending debacle in Baltimore, and exactly one month from what would have been his ninth anniversary as general manager of the Red Sox, Epstein made his departure official. Ricketts introduced Epstein as the Cubs' president of baseball operations. Epstein agreed to a five-year contract worth $18.5 million. Hoyer, as executive vice president/general manager, and McLeod, as senior vice president/scouting and player development, both agreed to leave the San Diego Padres to join him.

"I firmly believe," Epstein said at his news conference, "that we can preserve the things that make the Cubs so special and over time build a consistent winner, a team that will be playing baseball in October consistently and a team that will ultimately win the World Series."

If anything, though, Epstein underestimated the difficulty of the job.

CHAPTER 3

THE FIRST PIECE

Theo Epstein knew where to begin with the rebuilding of the Cubs: pour gobs of money into the draft. No one expected the Cubs to contend in 2012, so Epstein concentrated on becoming what he called "a scouting and player development machine"—the same metaphor he had used when he took over in Boston. The first step toward that goal was, as he put it, to take "a huge chunk of the major league payroll, put it into the draft and try to have three drafts in one year."

He had worked the system well in Boston. With no hard caps on spending on amateur players, clubs were free to spend as they wished to sign players they drafted. All it took to pull off such a strategy were money and thick skin. The money was needed to convince hard-to-sign players to sign by paying them more than Major League Baseball's recommended bonus commensurate with that pick—the practice known as "going over slot." The thick skin was needed to withstand an angry phone call from commissioner Bud Selig for doing so.

In Boston, Epstein used the hammer of over-slot money to sign Ryan Kalish ($600,000, ninth round, 2006), Will Middlebrooks ($925,000, fifth round, 2007), Anthony Rizzo ($325,000, sixth round, 2007), Mookie Betts ($750,000, fifth round, 2011), and Jackie

Bradley Jr. ($1.1 million, supplemental first round, 2011). Such players typically slid lower in the draft than their level of talent because of the "signability" issue.

The strategy didn't always yield future big league contributors. Epstein also went over slot for players such as Pete Hissey ($1 million, fourth round, 2008), David Renfroe ($1.4 million, third round, 2009), Madison Younginer ($975,000, seventh round, 2009), and Brandon Jacobs ($750,000, tenth round, 2009), none of whom have played a day in the big leagues with the Red Sox.

The point of over-slot money, however, was not to hit on every signing, but for a club to buy more chances—more lottery tickets to try to win the jackpot. When a talent like Rizzo, for instance, slides in the draft because of his stated goal to attend Florida Atlantic University, over-slot money allows a team like the Red Sox to take him in the sixth round and change his mind by paying him third-round money.

Just as Epstein planned to bring the same buying power to Chicago, Major League Baseball took away the hammer. Epstein was on the job just 28 days as president of baseball operations for the Cubs when MLB and the Players Association announced a new collective bargaining agreement, one that significantly curtailed spending in the draft. Each pick would have an assigned value—the so-called slot money—but this time there were teeth in the rules to enforce it, not just Selig's temper. Each club would have a cap on its spending: the sum of the slot money associated with the picks it held. Any club that exceeded that cap by 5 percent was subject to a 75 percent tax on the overage. Exceeding the cap by more than 5 percent called for the forfeiture of a first-round pick the following year, an onerous penalty that no rational team would dare incur.

In his office at Wrigley Field, Epstein used magnets with names on them to track prospective Chicago rosters for the next five years. It was an exercise in hope, built on the idea that prospects developed at a steady rate and to the level that could best be expected. Alas, there was only so much hope available in the Chicago system.

Epstein looked at the board and knew something very important was missing: he had no impact players. Impact players take the guesswork out of roster building. They are so talented that they provide All-Star-caliber performance that is reliable. They hit at the top or in the middle of a batting order or pitch at the front of the rotation.

To build a championship team, Epstein knew he needed a minimum of four impact players on that board before entering 2016, the fifth and final year of his contract. He also knew that most drafted players, even the ones drafted in the first round, typically need three to five years of development before they can have an impact in the big leagues. The new draft rules killed his plan for "three drafts in one," which might have put two or three such impact players in the system right away.

"The collective bargaining agreement happened like right after we got there," Epstein said. "That was sobering. There were a lot of sobering moments the first year or so, like how are we going to get enough impact talent? We looked up at the future year rosters on the board, like 2014, 2015, 2016, and said, 'How are we going to get enough impact talent? There's not enough drafts. There's not enough talent.'"

The change in draft rules affected the Cubs immediately. In 2011, Hendry's last draft, the Cubs spent a franchise-record $12 million on draft picks. In 2012, Epstein's first year, the Cubs were allotted a pool of $7.9 million to spend. Epstein essentially saw the team's draft budget slashed by 33 percent as soon as he walked in the door.

(The Cubs spent $8,273,800 on their picks in 2012, incurring a tax of $280,350. In 2016, with no picks in the first or second rounds as penalties associated with signing free agents John Lackey and Jason Heyward, the Cubs had a draft pool of just $2,245,100, the smallest of all 30 teams. Epstein had spent more on three over-slot, nonimpact players in 2009 than he did in his entire 2016 draft. Building teams quickly through the draft became much more difficult.)

"There was some . . . maybe not panic, but we didn't quite know how we were going to have enough transactions and opportunities to acquire the impact talent we needed in time," Epstein said. "And we knew we couldn't do an eight-year rebuild, like the Royals essentially did: eight years to the World Series, nine years to win it. Brilliant job by them dealing with a lot of obstacles we wouldn't face, but we knew we probably didn't have eight years. We had five-year contracts and that seemed like an awfully long time in a big market. We knew we had to hit at an awfully high rate and we were desperate to find opportunities to transact."

Despite his concern, Epstein knew just where to start: a .141 hitter with the San Diego Padres who had just lost his job there not just once, but twice.

In the spring of 2007 major league scouts packed the games of Stoneman-Douglas High School in Parkland, Florida, to see a catcher named Danny Eliorraga-Matra. One of those scouts was Laz Gutierrez of the Red Sox. Gutierrez, then 31 years old, was a former minor league pitcher from Miami. This was his second year working as a scout for Boston. (He is now the team's mental skills coordinator.) The more Gutierrez watched Stoneman-Douglas play, the more he liked the team's first baseman more than he liked the catcher. The first baseman's name was Anthony Rizzo.

The more background work Gutierrez did on Rizzo, the more he kept selling him to the front office. He kept using the word "special" to describe the kid's character. McLeod, Boston's scouting director, pivoted the team's attention from Eliorraga-Matra to Rizzo. The world of scouting is filled with subterfuge. Half the trick is finding great players. The other half is making sure the other teams don't draft them before you do. For instance, in that same spring of 2007 the San Francisco Giants sent their best pitching expert, Dick Tidrow, to follow up on an area scout's report on a North Carolina high school pitcher named Madison Bumgarner. Teams had mixed reports on Bumgarner because he threw with an unconventional, crossfire delivery.

Tidrow traveled from San Francisco to North Carolina to see one of Bumgarner's starts. Suddenly, after just three innings, Tidrow bolted from his seat in the scouts' section of the stands behind the plate and walked out. A week later an area scout from a rival team told the Giants' area scout, "I knew it! I knew he wouldn't like his arm action! He left after three innings."

Here's what the scout didn't know: as soon as Tidrow reached his car that day he told his area scout, "I love him." He didn't need to see any more. He left early to hide his team's interest in Bumgarner. The Giants took Bumgarner with the tenth overall pick that year.

McLeod had a similar plan in mind to disguise the Red Sox's interest in Rizzo. When scouts watch hitters, they typically stand on the "open" side of the hitter to see as much of his swing as possible: the third-base side for a left-handed hitter, and the first-base side for a right-handed hitter. McLeod told Gutierrez and his other scouts not to stand on the third-base side when Rizzo was hitting. He didn't want to tip off other clubs about their interest.

Anthony Rizzo is the son of John, a bartender and security firm manager, and Laurie, who worked in New York City when the couple lived in Lyndhurst, New Jersey—that is, until a winter's vacation in Florida convinced them to move there in 1986. The next year their first son, Johnny, was born. Anthony came along two years later. His parents, as they still do, called him "Ant" or "Antnee," while his friends called him "Little Rizz" in deference to his older brother, a football star. Laurie said she knew that Ant would be a major league ballplayer from a very early age.

"When he hit a home run in T-ball," she said, "that's when I knew. I'm serious. I don't want to sound like that cocky mom, but he was always better than all the other kids—in any sport. Plus, he's determined. No matter what he did, he kept going and going until he turned out to be the best at it. He's competitive with everything."

Laurie also saw something at a young age in her son that Gutierrez would see in 2007: people gravitated toward this born leader.

"He was always the leader," Laurie said. "He always organized our vacations and, even when he was young, when it came to planning a party or homecoming or anything like that, he'd be the one in charge. Always. He had a lot of friends. Johnny was big and Johnny was a football player with a lot of friends. Everybody would come over to our house, and Anthony would be part of the group and just fit in."

Said Anthony, "I think I get it from my parents and then my brother. My brother set the path for me in high school. He's two years older. Everyone knew me as Little Rizzo. Whenever we would go to football summer practices, my brother was *the guy*. I was his little brother. So when I was playing baseball, it was one of those things. I don't know, I try to get along with everyone and hope my work and what I do on the field and outside the field guys could see and gravitate toward."

"Laz did a great job," McLeod said of the background work the Boston scout filed on Rizzo. "He fell in love with the person, not just the player."

The difficulty for Epstein and McLeod was deciding when they should draft Rizzo. They were confident that he would not be drafted in the early rounds.

"He didn't put up monster numbers," McLeod said. "He was a thicker-framed kid. You just saw the body structure—a big-boned kid—and you could see he either was going to get really heavy or he would be able to be a big, strong kid. He didn't show lightning bat speed, not like [Eric] Hosmer. We loved his approach at the plate. He stayed in the middle of the field and we liked the kind of professional way he took batting practice. He wasn't trying to show you 70 power [on an 80 scale] on every pitch."

The first day of the draft, five rounds went by and nobody took Rizzo. The Red Sox scouts and executives reconvened. They held the 20th pick of the sixth round, the first round of the second day of the draft. During the break between the first and second day they heard rumors that the Detroit Tigers, picking 27th in the sixth round, had interest in Rizzo. They knew the Tigers were one of the teams willing to robustly spend over-slot money to convince a player to sign. The Red Sox decided they could no longer afford to wait. They took Rizzo in the sixth round. Two hundred and three players were drafted ahead of Rizzo. Boston gave him third-round money to sign. They sent him to rookie ball in time to play six games there and then to Instructional League in the Dominican Republic.

"Laz was right," McLeod said about Rizzo's leadership skills. "It became quite apparent in his first season. We heard from coaches about the leadership qualities this kid had and how he took to everybody on the team. Latin players, American players . . . it didn't matter. They all gravitated toward him. And once you got to meet his parents, you could see why.

"That fall in the Instructional League in the Dominican Republic was an eye-opening experience for him, to see where those kids came from and how little they had. I'll never forget Anthony talking to his parents and saying, 'Is there anything we can do for these guys? How can we help?' Immediately a lot of us took notice. Here was a 17-year-old kid looking to do whatever he could to help these people he'd never met before."

The following season, 2008, Boston assigned Rizzo to Class-A Greenville. He was the third-youngest player on the team, and yet he was one of the team's best hitters. He hit .373 in 21 games. But something wasn't right. He gained 15 pounds in a matter of days. His legs and feet were swollen. Rizzo didn't want to say anything; he was 18 years old and hitting well. But team officials finally noticed the swelling and sent him to Massachusetts General Hospital in Boston for tests. They speculated that he might be suffering from a kidney infection.

It was far worse. Laurie was at his bedside and John was on the telephone when doctors broke the news to him: he had cancer. It was Hodgkin's lymphoma. The doctors found two tumors, one on each side of his pelvis.

"Am I going to die?" Anthony asked them through tears.

Doctors told him the good news: they'd caught the cancer early and the success rate for treating it was 97 percent.

"Can I play baseball?" he asked.

No, they told him, he would need a six-month regimen of chemotherapy, and then they would reassess his condition.

"I didn't know what anything was," Rizzo said. "I didn't know what chemotherapy was. I thought chemotherapy was cancer. I had no idea. So they explained it and explained what they had to do and I was like, 'Okay, let's go.' It was obviously tough. I'm an emotional person. There were tears. But there was never a doubt. I truly believed after my first treatment I was all better. You still had to go through the process. It was six months."

Said Laurie, "It was shocking, devastating. But we had a lot of support at the hospital. And once he got a hold of himself, it was, 'Let's do this. I want to get this out of my body.'"

Rizzo underwent treatment in Boston. On May 16, Epstein invited Rizzo to visit Fenway Park. Epstein was rattled by the news of Rizzo's illness, but when Rizzo arrived at the ballpark the general manager was blown away by how easily this 18-year-old kid with cancer was calming everyone else around him. Epstein arranged for Rizzo to meet Red Sox pitcher Jon Lester, who had fought and won his own battle with lymphoma just a year earlier.

"Don't worry about it," Lester told Rizzo. "There are little things that are going to happen . . ."

And just then Rizzo fainted right in front of him, falling to the ground. When Rizzo came to, he and Lester spoke for nearly an hour. Three days later, in his next start, Lester threw a no-hitter.

"Going through the sickness, not being able to play any sport was the hardest part," Rizzo said. "You do something 18 years and then not to be able to do anything but watch the different highlight shows, it's like, that was the hardest part for me.

"Afterward, it validates everything my parents ever preached to me: live up every moment that you can because you never know.

That's what we do. I feel like when I do things I do them to the best I possibly can. I don't shortchange anything."

After six of months of treatment, Rizzo received word that he was in remission. The tumors were gone. Rizzo returned to baseball, and went back to crushing the ball. He climbed from Greenville to Salem, in High-A ball, in 2009, then from Salem to Portland, in Double-A, in 2010. He hit 20 home runs in Double-A ball at age 20, which put him on the fast track to the big leagues. But Rizzo was one level behind another left-handed-hitting first baseman in the Boston system, Lars Anderson, who in 2009 was rated as the 17th best prospect in baseball, according to *Baseball America*. Rizzo had not yet begun to show up on such "hot stocks" lists.

Meanwhile, the 2010 season had gone badly for Boston. The Red Sox won 89 games, the second fewest in Epstein's decade with the club, and missed the playoffs. That winter, as Epstein admitted, is when he abandoned his core principles of development and "took the easy way out." It was the winter he traded for Adrian Gonzalez and signed Carl Crawford, two players who cost $296 million. There was an additional cost: one of the players Epstein traded to get Gonzalez was Rizzo.

Epstein made the deal with Hoyer, his friend who had left to become general manager of the Padres, taking McLeod with him as his scouting director.

"Hands down the Red Sox were the most aggressive team," said Hoyer, who received lesser interest in Gonzalez from the Cubs, the White Sox, and the Mariners. "They were calling me often. It was clear from early on that Adrian was the linchpin of their off-season plan.

"Theo was very judicious. He doesn't like to trade prospects, and they knew they could sign Gonzalez to a long-term deal. The fact that Jason and I knew their prospects probably made it more difficult for them. You always hope a team asks about prospects you don't like.

"So that knowledge made it more difficult, but it made it more transparent, too. There was no BS. Adrian was a guy Theo always had a crush on. Going back to when Adrian played for the Rangers, he wanted to acquire him then. Theo had watched him play as a high school player in San Diego. Theo, to his credit, never got off him."

The personal cost was high for Epstein. He had drafted Rizzo in part because of Gutierrez's reports extolling his character, and he had seen that for himself in the way Rizzo beat cancer. He placed a call to Rizzo after the trade was completed.

"Someday," Epstein told him, "I'll get you back."

Hoyer and McLeod knew exactly what they were getting.

"When you have your player who's going to be looked upon as a leader," McLeod said, "and he's also your best run producer, that's the one who can take you where you want to be in the postseason. Not all guys are that way. Some great players want to be left alone. Some are snarky.

"It's something that's so cherished to have on a team, especially a team pushing into the postseason. Anthony has high expectations of his teammates and himself, and he makes everyone feel comfortable. He's somebody they can go to and talk to, or just go to and have a laugh. He is someone that's just wired that way from the time he was 17. He genuinely likes people, has a great heart, and certainly cares about his teammates."

Hoyer's phone immediately started to blow up over the trade—from people in the Red Sox organization.

"It was amazing how many texts I got from coaches and coordinators," Hoyer said. "They all said they think this guy is a great player and a great person and they were sad to see him go. His makeup stood out right away. He became such a favorite among coaches in the minor league system. In a short amount of time he was a favorite of the player development staff. He was a beloved person."

The Padres started Rizzo in 2011 at Triple-A Tucson, where he continued to rake. Rizzo hit .365 with a 1.159 OPS there.

On June 9, entering a home series against Washington, San Diego was in last place in the National League West with a 28–35 record. Hoyer decided it was time to promote Rizzo for his major league debut.

"I look back with regret at bringing him up when I did," Hoyer said. "But we were getting zero production out of first base, we were struggling following a 90-win season, he had a 1.050 OPS and [was] tearing up the Pacific Coast League, and he was a guy we had gotten as a marquee name in a big trade. It was hard not to bring him up.

"He started pretty well that first week or so, but then he started struggling, and he did not have the survival skills at that point to handle it. It sort of snowballed on him."

Rizzo hit .143 in 98 at-bats. On July 21, Hoyer demoted him to the minor leagues and handed his first-base job to a journeyman named Kyle Blanks. The Padres brought back Rizzo in September when rosters expanded, but he fared no better. He finished the year at .141 in 128 at-bats.

"When I was up there [in San Diego] I was missing pitches I had never missed in my life," Rizzo said. "And I said to myself, *Why am I missing this pitch? I don't understand it. It's a fastball right down the middle at 90 miles an hour and I can't hit it.*

"It was more, *What is going on?* And then it got to the point where I got sent down, I was hitting well again in Triple-A, and got called back up in September. Then I was at that point where my brain just needed a rest. I was overthinking: *Try this, try that.*

"I remember I had to go to winter ball that year, which I did not want to do at all. I just knew I needed a break. But at the same time I was going to do everything I could to be on the team next year. I ended up playing two weeks. I ended up rolling my ankle and went home."

It was after that season, in October, that Hoyer and McLeod left the Padres to reunite with Epstein in Chicago. Another former young buck from the Red Sox player development office, Josh Byrnes, was hired to replace Hoyer in San Diego. One of Byrnes's first moves was to trade for a first baseman, Yonder Alonso from Cincinnati, on December 17.

"I get a call after that from our GM saying I was still a big part of the organization," Rizzo said, "and I was going to be there and a part of their future.

"A week later I get traded."

Said Hoyer, "The Cubs are really fortunate. If when he came up he played really well, there's no chance the Padres would have traded him. There's no way when Jason and I came out to Chicago that the idea of acquiring Anthony Rizzo was even possible. He was their first baseman of the future and there was no one to compete with him.

"Once they traded for Yonder Alonso, Josh Byrnes said he didn't want a quarterback controversy. Anthony had lost his main sponsors. And I knew how much Theo wanted him."

"The trade," Epstein said, "was not a slam dunk."

Epstein's inner circle debated the merits of giving up Andrew Cashner, a 24-year-old, big-bodied pitcher who threw 97 miles per hour—the makings of a future ace—for Rizzo. The game was pivoting toward a pitcher-dominated era. Young, cost-controlled, power arms like Cashner were highly valued currency, especially for teams rebuilding. Hoyer and McLeod had seen how badly Rizzo looked against major league pitching. His swing was too long. He couldn't catch up to average velocity.

"Hey, this is a 21-year-old who struggled his first couple of months seeing big league pitching," Epstein argued. "Great. That's exactly when you can get him."

Hoyer and McLeod agreed with Epstein in general about the principle of buying low, but cautioned him that they had seen every one of those big league at-bats; Epstein hadn't.

Eventually, the three of them came to a consensus: now was the time to buy low on Rizzo, with the faith in his character that he would do whatever it took to make adjustments with his swing. On

January 6, 2012, the Cubs traded Cashner to San Diego for Rizzo. The clubs also exchanged lesser prospects in the deal.

"When I got traded I was ecstatic," Rizzo said. "I'm from Florida. I'm not the biggest West Coast fan, so Chicago is closer to home. I had the opportunity out of high school to go to Arizona State to play baseball, and I decided to stay closer to home at Florida Atlantic. I like being able to stay closer to home.

"Obviously, when I got here we weren't very good. I had no idea about the fan base. My first time I came to Chicago it was snowing and it was cold. Then I get called back up in June and it's like a whole different ballgame. Everyone's out in the city having a good tine, taking advantage of the nice weather, the games are rocking—we weren't good and they're still rocking—and just how the fans embraced me and all the stories you hear, I feel like Chicago is home now."

Epstein had been on the job with the Cubs for less than three months when he made the Rizzo trade. It was his third trade in that period. The first didn't work out so well: he traded DJ LeMahieu, a future All-Star, Gold Glove winner, and batting champion, with Tyler Colvin to Colorado for two former hot prospects who fizzled, Casey Weathers and Ian Stewart. He also traded reliever Sean Marshall for versatile pitcher Travis Wood, who was part of the 2016 championship team.

But the Rizzo trade was a watershed moment for Epstein. Rizzo was one of the four impact players Epstein needed to build a championship team. One down, three to go.

Just as importantly—though so subtly the rest of baseball didn't pick up on what he was up to—Epstein signaled his intentions about how he was going to rebuild the Cubs. The clues were right there in the Cashner-for-Rizzo trade. This was going to be a very different blueprint than the one Epstein used to win championships with the Red Sox. It had to be.

CHAPTER 4

GAME 1

The Cubs' lineup for Game 1 of the World Series sat on the desk in front of Joe Maddon with a name that had not been in there in 201 days: Kyle Schwarber. He was listed as the first Cubs designated hitter in World Series history, batting fifth. The World Series opened in Cleveland for the first time among the 112 ever played, and did so because the American League had won the All-Star Game back in July, a game in which the winning pitcher was Corey Kluber, the Cleveland Indians' Game 1 starter, and a game that Cubs pitchers Jake Arrieta and Jon Lester had skipped in order to take the rest.

If the downside to the NL losing the All-Star Game meant the Cubs would not have the home-field advantage in the World Series, the upside was that the designated hitter rule allowed Maddon to start the World Series with the use of Schwarber's bat, a turn of events that shocked the manager himself.

"I really didn't expect this—at all," Maddon said at his desk. "I'm not being disingenuous. I had no idea until a couple of days ago when they said, 'Schwarber was cleared by the doctor in Texas to do this.' I said, 'Okay, what are we going to do?' 'Well, we're going to have him take some BP and we'll send him to Arizona.' He goes to

Arizona and the guys watching him go, 'He looks normal.' And I saw the video of him swinging and running. Very normal.

"So he could run into something tonight very easily, there's no doubt."

What kind of hitter was this? How could the manager actually expect somebody to hit a home run in the World Series after missing six months with a blown-out knee? That Maddon could think it was possible—"very easily"—said much about both Schwarber's freakish hitting skills and how much the club had come to love and believe in this 23-year-old who looked and hit like a linebacker.

Schwarber had not seen major league pitching since April 7, when, playing leftfield against the Arizona Diamondbacks in Phoenix, he collided with centerfielder Dexter Fowler while both were trying to catch a ball hit between the two of them.

"I was watching on my couch in Chicago and it was awful," Theo Epstein said. "I almost got physically sick. It was bad. We all felt that way. We were talking ourselves into, 'Maybe it's just a bone bruise or something.' But we kind of knew."

Doctors would have to wait until the next day, when the swelling subsided, to perform an MRI. The news was not good: Schwarber had torn ligaments in his left knee. On April 19, Dr. Daniel Cooper performed surgery to reconstruct Schwarber's anterior cruciate ligament and to repair his lateral collateral ligament. The Cubs said he was expected to be ready for 2017 spring training. Privately, they hoped in a best-case scenario he would be cleared in time to play the second half of winter ball.

"Once you hear he's out for the season, it's just sickening," Epstein said. "It's denial for him and the team, because he's such an integral part of the lineup. He creates fear with his left-handed bat."

Epstein had grown personally attached to Schwarber, ever since September of 2013 when, after watching about 80 videos of Schwarber as a sophomore catcher at Indiana University, he fired off an e-mail to his scouting director and others who were preparing for the 2014 draft: "Take your scouts off the road. We have our pick.

We're taking Schwarber with our first pick." Schwarber had just hit .366 with a school-record 18 homers, the third most in the country.

Recalled Epstein, "I said, 'I don't care who pitches for us, we're going to let him play leftfield for a decade and put up Big Papi numbers. We can get anybody to pitch.'

"Nobody talks about how left-handed hitters tend to have that longer swing. No one has a shorter, more powerful left-handed swing than Schwarber—with a lot going on in his swing. He's a rhythm hitter and there's a lot going on with his prepitch movement, but he's always on time. He has a natural instinct to be on time. Not like one of these skill guys who just happen to be on time. He recognizes movement, he understands pitching."

The Cubs held the fourth overall pick in the draft. Epstein wanted Schwarber, even having just watched him hit on video. Then he actually met him, and he was convinced even more that Schwarber was the best player available to the Cubs in the draft.

In February 2014 Epstein and the Cubs' front office personnel had just moved into their new spring training quarters in Mesa, Arizona. Epstein noticed that Indiana was scheduled to play games that month in Arizona as part of the Pac-12 versus Big Ten tournament, so he extended an invitation to the Hoosiers to take batting practice at the Cubs' new complex. His motivation was more than altruistic. Epstein wanted an up-close look at Schwarber and teammate Sam Travis, a first baseman who would be picked in the second round by Boston.

Schwarber had been a second-team, all-Ohio middle linebacker at Middletown High School who drew the interest of Big Ten schools to play football. No major league baseball team bothered drafting him out of high school, so he enrolled at Indiana. He was a three-year hitting star as a catcher at Indiana, following up his big sophomore season with a .358 average in his junior year. Scouts wondered, however, if at 6 foot and 240 pounds he had the defensive skills and athleticism to succeed in the majors. MLBPipeline.com rated him as the 16th best player available in the 2014 draft. *Baseball America* rated him 17th, and in a mock draft in May had him going 24th.

Epstein and Jason McLeod met with Schwarber in Epstein's office after the hitting session in Mesa. The conversation lasted an hour.

At one point Epstein told him, "Hey, some guys even out here in our own organization don't think you can catch."

Schwarber paused and looked him square in the eye, the anger evident.

"Well, I look forward to proving those fucking people wrong," he said.

Said Epstein, "He dropped an F bomb! It was great! He came away as an incredibly likable baseball rat with a football mentality whose teammates are going to love him and the ultimate, grounded, Midwestern kid who wants to do the right thing and have fun doing it. He wants to go to battle with his teammates and win at all costs, but in a really relatable, likable, fun way. He's so magnetic and such a baseball rat it's ridiculous.

"Once we met and shared our vision for the organization and he got to tell us what he's all about, there was a mutual feeling that this was meant to be. And we needed to make this happen."

Said Schwarber, "It just kind of clicked. It was like we had the same beliefs in baseball terms. It's all about winning. So that's the only thing that matters at the end of the day—making sure that we get a win."

The three teams that drafted ahead of the Cubs all picked pitchers: the Astros took high school pitcher Brady Aiken, the Marlins took high school pitcher Tyler Kolek, and the White Sox picked college pitcher Carlos Rodon. There was some doubt about what the Cubs would do next, even within their own draft room and despite Epstein's enormous regard for Schwarber. A healthy discussion followed about whether Schwarber was worth the fourth overall pick. Some in the room felt Chicago needed a pitcher, the position everybody else in baseball seemed to want. That year teams drafted 13 pitchers with the first 19 picks. College pitchers such as Aaron Nola, Jeff Hoffman, and Brandon Finnegan remained on the board.

"By the time we got to the draft room, typically guys like [Schwarber] who are bat-first or bat-only, they don't go that high in the draft," Epstein said. "So he was more a consensus late-first-round guy. But we had a lot of conviction. Scouts loved the bat. We all loved the bat. Our statistical model loved the bat. And makeup was huge. Stan Zielinski, the area scout, did a great job getting to know Kyle inside and out. Jason and I felt like we knew him.

"And there were a lot of good arms available so the debate in the draft room really crystallized. It was like, 'We can choose a pitcher who is going to move quickly and can help us win every fifth day, but pitchers have a really hard time leading. They can lead the starting rotation after they get established a little bit, but it's hard for them to lead the team. We draft Kyle Schwarber, he's on the field every day, he's going to rake, and he's going to be right in the middle of everything that is going to happen in this organization.'"

Epstein continued stumping on behalf of Schwarber.

"He is what we want to be: how he prioritizes winning, how he cares about his teammates, how hard he plays, how much he loves the game, how much he wants to win," he said.

The room started to turn. Epstein put Zielinski, the scout, on the phone. Zielinksi also gave a heartfelt speech in support of Schwarber.

"There was a lot of passion about him," Epstein said. "And we went from kind of split to consensus."

The Cubs took Schwarber with the fourth overall pick and quickly signed him for less than the assigned value of that slot. Most people considered the pick a reach, especially for a National League team, which would not have the option of using Schwarber as a full-time designated hitter.

Wrote *Baseball America*, "His bonus of $3.125 million, which was $1,496,200 under the slot allocated for the fourth overall pick, was also seen as both a compromise and a negative reflection of his overall ability."

Upon signing him, Epstein invited Schwarber to Wrigley Field, where they sat together in Epstein's box during a game.

"He became part of our heartbeat," Epstein said. "You can't put a dollar figure on that. That's so hard to find. When he showed up here, after he signed, he was up in the box watching the game and he kept saying, 'I can't wait. Just trust me, I'm going to do everything I possibly can to help this organization win a World Series. I'm going to do everything in my power to help this team win. I won't let you down.'"

Schwarber zoomed through three levels of Class-A ball that summer, hitting .344 in 72 games. Only five months after drafting Schwarber, Epstein was dropping his name to help sell the Cubs in an attempt to lure free agent veteran pitcher Jon Lester to sign with the team.

Schwarber reached the big leagues one year after being drafted. In just 69 games in 2015 he smashed 16 home runs. No Cubs player ever had hit so many homers in so few games in his first season. What happened in 2015 was shocking in terms of impact hitting from the Chicago rookies. Until then, only two first-year players in franchise history ever hit as many as 13 home runs: Mandy Brooks, with 14 in 1925, and Vince Barton, with 13 in 1931. The Cubs had three such rookies in 2015 alone: Schwarber; Kris Bryant, who hit 26; and Addison Russell, who hit 13. Schwarber added 5 home runs in nine postseason games.

The knee injury may have kept Schwarber out of action in 2016, but not out of mind. The renovated clubhouse facilities at Wrigley Field allowed Schwarber to attend to much of his rehabilitation work in Chicago, whereas in past years he would have been assigned to the spring training complex in Mesa. By staying in Chicago, Schwarber immersed himself in the team's daily preparations for home games. He sat in on and contributed to the pregame meetings between the catchers, the starting pitcher, and coach Mike Borzello, as if he were starting behind the plate. He sat with Epstein as an advisor in the Cubs' draft room during the June draft.

"Well, if you know me as a person, that's the kind of guy I am," Schwarber said before Game 1 of the World Series. "I'm a baseball rat. I want to be involved in it as much as I can. A lot of things go to this team and this organization for allowing me to be around. They were a big rock in my rehab. I could have easily just gone to Arizona, gone through the motions in rehab, but these guys really made me kick it up a notch. I'm here, sitting here today mostly because of those guys."

The process was grueling. Teammate Pedro Strop would tell him, "You're going to be back this year," but Schwarber was far from certain himself, especially in the first few weeks after the surgery.

"At first I didn't think I was ever going to have a normal knee again," he said. "I had to do six weeks of just keeping it straight, no walking on it, no anything. And then trying to get range of motion back after that—that was probably the toughest part for me mentally. You're going to the field every day and trying to get your knee to bend and it just won't. It's painful. You're getting strapped down to a table, they're pushing back on it.

"But then after that, we got that range of motion back, it went to the strengthening portion of rehab, where you want to try to get all your strength back in your knee and then in your quads, hammies, things like that. Then after that, there goes the running. Running was like trying to learn as a kid again. You're limping all over the place. You can't figure out why you're limping. Then, after that, it goes to swinging the stick. That went about as good as possible."

Even while injured, Schwarber was one of the most coveted players in baseball. As Epstein scoured the trade market in July for bullpen help, teams kept asking for Schwarber. When Epstein called the Royals about Wade Davis, Kansas City asked for Schwarber. The conversation ended there. When Epstein called the Yankees about Andrew Miller, New York asked for Schwarber. Epstein told the Yankees he was an untouchable franchise player. (The Cubs shifted the focus to trading for Aroldis Chapman in a deal in which they surrendered top infield prospect Gleyber Torres.)

The big day on Schwarber's calendar was October 17. That's the day he was scheduled to visit Cooper for his six-month checkup. The Cubs were in Los Angeles, where they were tied with the Dodgers in the National League Championship Series at one game each.

"I'm going to see the doctor," Schwarber told catcher David Ross as he left for his flight to Dallas, "and he's going to tell me I'm good to go. I'll see you at the World Series."

The World Series was eight days away.

Schwarber did pass his checkup. The doctor was surprised at the stability of his knee. He gave Schwarber the okay to resume hitting. Schwarber flew back to Los Angeles and took batting practice that night at Dodger Stadium before NLCS Game 3. He hit again in Los Angeles the next day, then flew the day after that, Thursday, October 20, for the Cubs' training facility in Mesa.

The World Series was just five days away.

Over the next four days, Schwarber underwent the speed version of spring training. He played in two Arizona Fall League games (he went 1-for-6) and faced live pitching in two simulated games at the Mesa facility. His hands opened up blisters on the very first day from so much hitting. Schwarber hit or tracked 1,300 pitches in four days, many out of a pitching machine that fired major-league-quality breaking pitches, some from two Class-A pitchers the Cubs brought in to pitch to him in the simulated games, and some from coaches assigned to assist the AFL team, which is a co-op team involving several organizations.

One of the AFL coaches throwing batting practice to Schwarber, unwittingly helping in this crash course to get Schwarber ready to face the Cleveland Indians in the World Series, was Larry Day, a coach from Lynchburg, a Class-A minor league affiliate of the . . . Cleveland Indians.

The Cubs won the National League pennant on Saturday, October 22. Schwarber, in between at-bats of his first game action in the Arizona Fall League, watched the game on an iPad in the dugout of the Mesa Solar Sox, getting strange looks whenever he would scream when the Cubs scored a run. In the training room after the game the Solar Sox doused Schwarber with champagne, a celebration from afar of the Cubs' first pennant in 71 years.

On Monday, October 24, the day before Game 1 of the World Series, Schwarber played in an Arizona Fall League game in front of only about one hundred people. He drilled a double, slid into second base, and scored a run. He also lined out to second base on a ball hit with an exit velocity of 110 mph. Epstein took in this information on his phone, including a live feed of the game, and smiled. He knew Schwarber was ready. The Cubs had a private plane waiting for him in Mesa to take him to Cleveland that night. Schwarber told the driver meeting him at the Cleveland airport to take him directly to the ballpark, rather than the hotel.

"I wanted to just get a little sneak peek what it would be like for today," he said before the World Series opener. "You know, just tried to soak it in as much as I can."

He then checked into his hotel, where, despite his long day, he "didn't really sleep. I had a lot of thoughts running through my mind. I told myself I wanted to go to sleep at a good hour. That didn't happen, but as expected."

Maddon had offered encouragement to Schwarber throughout the rehab, assuring him that he expected him back as good as new—but for the 2017 season.

"There are maybe five people, if that, who could have done what he did," the manager said.

In ways Epstein never could have imagined, Schwarber rewarded the faith Epstein had put in him just two years earlier, when critics accused the Cubs of overreaching to draft Schwarber so high.

"His bat and his intangibles are why we drafted him," Epstein said. "He's a complete impact hitter with the bat, but more than that he's the perfect player to have as a franchise player because he can be one of your best players who everybody else wants to follow because of his character. He's a special player and a special person."

Maddon immediately put Schwarber in the lineup without reservations.

"I think from watching him, first of all everything looks right," he said. "He's running well. I don't know what he's going to show you tonight, but he can run normal without injuring himself. The biggest thing would be timing issues—breaking ball, etc. But that's something that's always been a part of his game. If you get him in swing mode, you can get him to chase. He did that last year. But if he's not in swing mode and he stays off that stuff, heads up! His swing looks normal. If you get a chance to watch BP, you're going to see the ball go really far."

Even with rust, Schwarber was the least of Maddon's concerns as the World Series opened. The manager had to make a decision about what to do with Jason Heyward, who had managed only two hits in 28 at-bats in the postseason while getting beat by fastballs with regularity. Heyward, a left-handed hitter, was his everyday right-fielder throughout the season, and in the postseason had started every game except three games started by tough left-handers, Madison Bumgarner, Rich Hill, and Clayton Kershaw.

To bench Heyward against a right-hander, Kluber, and to do it in the first game of the World Series, would take a bit of courage on Maddon's part, especially because Heyward already had confronted Maddon about being left out of a lineup. After the Cubs needed 13 innings to beat San Francisco in Game 3 of the NLDS, 6–5, the game in which Maddon did not start Heyward against Bumgarner, Heyward poked his head into Maddon's small office at AT&T Park.

"Can we talk?" Heyward asked.

Heyward is one of the most physically intimidating players in the big leagues. He is 6-foot-4 and a ripped 240 pounds. Coincidentally or not, Heyward walked into Maddon's office with no shirt on. He practically filled the room. He clearly was upset and hurt, but his words were measured. Heyward told Maddon he didn't take kindly to the benching, that he felt he could help the team in many ways, no matter who was pitching for the other team.

"That wasn't a difficult meeting," Maddon said. "I love that he would do that, but it was not a difficult conversation. He just wanted to tell me what he thought. It wasn't a disrespectful, 'I'm angry with you' kind of thing. He wanted me to understand where he was coming from—that he is a proud man. 'I'm here to contribute. If I'm on the field consistently I will show you what I am,' which I knew.

"I pretty much listened, which I normally do. I can tell when a guy is hot, and there's not a whole lot I'm going to do as far as having an exchange with him. Listen, it happens. It happened enough during the season so that they talk, I listen, and then we're fine the next day, or even right after the meeting is over. But they have to come see me."

When Maddon did not start Heyward against Hill in Game 3 of the NLCS, he did not tell Heyward in advance of his decision. Maddon explained that Heyward didn't attend the voluntary workout on the previous day—when he planned on telling him—nor did he have a chance to speak with him before the lineup was texted to players for Game 3.

A similar scenario occurred before World Series Game 1. Around midday, Maddon texted his lineup to the front office chain, and coach Brandon Hyde retexted it to the players. Heyward wasn't in it—this time against a right-hander, the biggest sign yet of the manager's lack of confidence in Heyward. Maddon sent an individual text to Heyward regarding his exclusion from the lineup.

"He didn't return the text," Maddon recalled later. "So, okay, he's pissed. There's nothing I can do about it at that point. Sometimes the guy is going to be upset and not want to talk about it. There's not a whole lot I can do about that. I expect that. It's part of the landscape. It happens to everybody. I don't take it in a bad way. It's part of the job. Because you're not going to keep everybody happy, I promise you. If he's upset, then somebody else is happy that they're playing."

In Heyward's place Maddon chose to start Chris Coghlan, a .188 hitter who had started only 18 games in rightfield all year.

"Obviously J-ward has been struggling," Maddon explained. "Just

give C.C. a chance. Kluber's pretty good. Americar
you have to take advantage of that extra hitter if yc
ing with J-ward. Definitely go to his defense in the ..
game.

"[Coghlan] was swinging the bat really well, and still is. You just watch him working. It could have been one of the right-handers, [Willson] Contreras. I just wanted to get another lefty on him. C.C. was swinging the bat well."

Maddon's biggest concern, however, had to do with the matchup of his starting pitcher, Jon Lester, against the Indians, one of the best baserunning teams in baseball. Lester's phobia about throwing to bases could be exploited by a team that stole the fourth most bases in baseball, the most in the American League.

Maddon had learned long ago the best way to deal with Lester's yips was to leave him out of the game-planning about how to defend the running game. Maddon already had talked the previous day with David Ross, Lester's catcher, about calling more "disguised" pitchouts. A pitchout is a ball intentionally thrown far away from the batter when a stolen base attempt is anticipated so that the catcher can rise from his crouch early, essentially gaining a head start toward throwing out the runner. But Maddon knew that Lester's throwing yips also sabotaged his ability to throw an accurate traditional pitchout. So Lester threw only "disguised" pitchouts, which are simply fastballs thrown off the corners of the plate, and usually up. Maddon could call for such a pitch from the bench or Ross could call for it on his own.

Lester, Maddon added, might actually throw to first base on a pickoff attempt for the first time since July. The manager was encouraged by a throw Lester made in Game 5 of the NLCS, when Lester fielded a bunt by Joc Pederson of the Dodgers and threw him out, albeit on an ugly, bounced throw to first baseman Anthony Rizzo, who advised Lester to keep his throws along the ground, where at least he had a chance to catch them. Anything well over his head would leave Rizzo with no chance.

"My point is since he did that the other day you may see something to first base today," Maddon said. "We've practiced everything. Everything. We've practiced everything. My point is he may have gained some kind of weird confidence from that moment. The minute he threw that ball to first base, I thought his game was elevated on the mound. I thought everything got better.

"I've talked to Rossy. I've communicated with him to have him communicate with Jon. I don't want to talk to Jon, so David does a great job. Me and David talked here yesterday. We went over some things."

So this is how Maddon would begin the World Series for the Cubs, their first World Series game in 71 years: with a rightfielder making only his 19th start at that position all year, his $184 million left-handed-hitting rightfielder benched against a right-handed pitcher, not talking to a pitcher who has a mental block throwing to bases facing a team that led the American League in stolen bases, and a designated hitter who was seeing major league pitching for the first time in 201 days. What could possibly go wrong?

It took only four batters to confirm Maddon's fears about Lester facing the running game of the Indians. Cleveland's first baserunner, shortstop Francisco Lindor, swiped second base on the second pitch after reaching on a single. It cost Chicago a run. Lindor scored what was the first of two first-inning runs for Cleveland.

With the way Kluber pitched, the game effectively was over right there. Kluber's nickname is "Klubot," as much for his stoicism as for the machinelike consistency of his pitching. But after throwing his last warm-up in the bullpen before the game, Kluber actually let loose a rare smile. It was the rough equivalent of a Haley's comet sighting, a Thomas Pynchon book tour, or a Cleveland professional sports championship. The expression came in recognition of the stuff Kluber had that night.

"When you can make the ball move like that," Indians pitching coach Mickey Callaway said, "you should smile. Yes, I saw it. I could tell right away. You could definitely tell the movement he had today from the bullpen."

The Cubs had no chance against Kluber. None. He was that good. They lost, 6–0. In six innings Kluber threw 30 sinkers, which is a misnomer because his two-seam fastball runs more than it sinks. Twenty-four of those 30 sinkers were strikes, an outstanding percentage for anyone, but especially for someone with so much movement and mid-90s velocity. Kluber obtained 24 called strikes on just 88 pitches. Most of the called strikes occurred on pitches Cubs hitters were certain would stay far out of the zone, only to come darting back over the plate. Kluber had pitched in 143 major league games, postseason included. Never before did he obtain so many called strikes in so few innings.

Three men iced down after this game: Lester, the losing pitcher; Kluber; and Larry Vanover, the home plate umpire who practically strained a right rotator cuff calling strikes.

Kluber's insane movement at peak velocity produced one of the greatest pitching lines in World Series history: no runs, no walks, and nine strikeouts. Only one other pitcher in World Series history had struck out so many batters with no walks and no runs: Roger Clemens, in Game 2 of the 2000 World Series for the Yankees against the Mets.

Facing Kluber and relievers Andrew Miller and Cody Allen, the Cubs struck out 15 times. Only one team in World Series history had ever been shut out with so many strikeouts: the 1968 Detroit Tigers, who ran into a buzz saw named Bob Gibson. The Cardinals ace struck out 17 that day in Game 1.

The box score told a story of Cleveland domination. The Cubs had waited 71 years for *this*? Maddon left the park that night, however, in good spirits. For one reason, the loss was easy to dismiss because the Indians pitched incredibly well.

"I mean, I'm not disappointed by any means except for the fact that we did not win," he said. "I thought we came out ready to play.

They pitched well . . . I know we had 15 punch-outs. I get it. But the quality of the at-bats was not that bad."

There was one more reason for Maddon to be optimistic about the shutout defeat: Schwarber looked like Roy Hobbs. In four plate appearances Schwarber saw 18 pitches, drew a walk, and banged a double off the wall in rightfield, very nearly coming close to hitting a home run while seeing big league pitching for the first time in 201 days. It was an astounding display of natural hitting ability. Maddon knew right away that Schwarber would be a force in the World Series.

CHAPTER 5

THE PLAN

A few weeks before spring training of 2012, in the ballroom of a budget hotel in Mesa, Arizona, Theo Epstein stood before nearly every person connected with the baseball operations of the Chicago Cubs and told them how the Cubs were going to win the World Series. His long speech would be the first and easily the most important one he would give as president of baseball operations. It kicked off four days of organizational meetings. It was his vision of the future.

Many of those in the ballroom—managers, coaches, instructors, scouts, trainers, analysts, etc.—figured Epstein, Jed Hoyer, and Jason McLeod would simply try to re-create what they had done in Boston. Others worried that their jobs weren't safe under the new regime; many of those people would turn out to be right.

Epstein, who had just pulled off the trade for Anthony Rizzo, spelled out the hallmarks he wanted from a championship Cubs team. He wanted an offense that grinded out at-bats, got on base at a high rate, drove balls with authority rather than simply making contact, and boasted a relentless batting order, not one reliant simply on its few big hitters in the middle. He told them, however, that the Cubs would not sacrifice defense for the sake of fulfilling his offensive wish list.

"We're going to have both," he told them, "and we're going to have it at every position."

He told them he wanted a pitching staff populated by pitchers who threw a heavy percentage of strikes but also featured swing-and-miss stuff. He wanted those pitchers also to have high groundball rates, so they could induce weak contact into the teeth of a premier defense.

He wanted a baseball operations department that would be the best in baseball—"a scouting and player development machine," to use his signature phrase.

"We're going to have the resourcefulness of a small market team," he told them, "and the resources of a big market team."

And then Epstein told them about one of the strongest pillars of his entire building plan: he wanted players with strong character.

"We are not going to compromise character for talent," he told them. "We're the Cubs. We're going to have both. Talent and character."

The idea of so strongly emphasizing character may have struck some in the room as odd, especially coming from a Bill James disciple who built two World Series championship teams in Boston as an early adopter of analytic principles. Numbers had been his pre-eminent guiding principle. There was that first off-season in Boston, when Epstein and Hoyer could do their fishing in uncrowded waters for undervalued players, like David Ortiz and Bill Mueller, with a high rate of getting on base, while old-school general managers continued to emphasize batting average and runs batted in.

The next year, in the 2004 draft, Epstein found Dustin Pedroia, an undersized shortstop from Arizona State, with the help of data. That same year Epstein sent a flock of interns to NCAA headquarters in Indianapolis to collect 30 years' worth of archived college baseball statistics. The interns photocopied the information and brought it back to Boston, where the baseball operations team developed an algorithm to predict major league success from the college statistics. One of the hitters the algorithm liked was Pedroia, an on-base machine who rarely struck out. Many clubs undervalued Pedroia because he was only 5-foot-9 and was not a plus runner.

After 64 players were picked, including 15 college hitters, the Red Sox could not believe their good luck that Pedroia was still available to them. He turned out to be even better than the algorithm forecast. After Boston converted Pedroia to second base, he became Rookie of the Year in 2007 and Most Valuable Player in 2008. A four-time All-Star, Pedroia has more hits and home runs than any Boston second baseman, with the exception of Hall of Famer Bobby Doerr. Eleven of the 15 college hitters drafted ahead of Pedroia played less than 200 games in the majors, including 5 who never played a day in the big leagues.

By 2012, overlooked value buys like Ortiz and Pedroia were getting harder and harder for Epstein and Hoyer to find. The use of advanced analytics was becoming commonplace. Old-guard general managers were being phased out by an entire generation of Epstein 2.0s—young bucks armed with degrees from elite universities and a hunger for data.

"The landscape was flat now," Hoyer said. "There were so many smart people working for teams. Thinking back to that energy in the room in Boston when we could go after the Millars and Muellers and Guilléns and Hafners, it was so different now. It was really great that all us were here in Chicago, but we knew we couldn't fall back on the way we used to do it. We had to keep evolving. We realized this was going to be really different."

Epstein devoted the first day of the 2012 Mesa meeting to hitting philosophy. He devoted the second day to pitching philosophy, and the third to defense and baserunning. The entire last day was devoted to character. The Cubs, Epstein insisted, would acquire only players with outstanding makeup. Even Epstein realized himself how far he had evolved since he put so much faith in numbers when he began as general manager of the Red Sox. Now character did not just matter. It was essential to Epstein's blueprint to win the World Series.

"I used to scoff at it, when I first took the job in Boston," he said. "I just felt like, you know how we're going to win? By getting guys who get on base more than the other team, and by getting pitchers who miss bats and get groundballs. Talent wins, but . . . It's like every year I did the job I just developed a greater appreciation for how much the human element matters and how much more you can achieve as a team when you have players who care about winning, care about each other, develop those relationships, have those conversations . . . it creates an environment where the sum is greater than the parts."

How did character become so important to Epstein?

"It was a lot of things," he said. "It was living through the Nomar [Garciaparra] trade and how we played in the aftermath of that."

Epstein made the bold move at the 2004 trade deadline of trading Nomar Garciaparra, a fan favorite because he had been a Rookie of the Year and two-time batting champion, mostly because Epstein's proprietary defensive metrics showed Garciaparra to be among the worst shortstops in the league. But Epstein also made the move because he was concerned that Garciaparra's brooding over his contract situation and intense media coverage created a negative clubhouse dynamic. The Red Sox went 42–18 without him. The lesson for Epstein was that the character of players in the clubhouse mattered, especially in a major market where negative issues get amplified.

"Probably on the other end of things," Epstein said, continuing, "was coming off the 2011 experience and how things fell apart in the clubhouse there despite our best intentions. And then also it was coming to a place that was kind of vanilla for a long time. What was the personality of those Cubs teams? They had been to the playoffs in '07, '08, but what was the personality? Who were the leaders?"

Epstein wanted leaders who were everyday players to define the personality of his team. That's why the quick acquisition of Rizzo was so telling about how Epstein wanted to rebuild the Cubs. Rizzo was his prototype. He was the first of the four impact players Epstein knew he needed in his lineup to win a World Series. But Epstein also knew that getting a building block like Rizzo in a trade was like hitting a walkoff homer: a rarity he could not count on. The key to building a winning culture did not exist in trades.

"It starts in the draft room," Epstein said. "That's the one time all year when you decide proactively, affirmatively, what type of person, what [kind of] human being, you want to bring into your organization. When you trade for players, you can only trade for those players who are available. It's a small subsection of players. When you're signing free agents, you can only sign those free agents who are available—a very small percentage of players who are available.

"In the draft, when it's time for your pick, the entire universe of eligible players is out there for you. You choose one of them. Whether you sort of admit it or not, you're saying, 'This is what I want my organization to be. This is what I want my organization to be about. This is a Cub.' Every time you pick, especially in the first round, that's what you're saying."

At the time Epstein left Boston for Chicago, baseball was falling into a deep, offensive recession. A rise in fastball velocity and a surge in the inventory of pitchers who could throw in the mid- and upper-90s—coupled with advances in defensive strategies, including the widespread adoption of shifts—turned baseball into a game that emphasized run prevention. The game was sinking into its lowest offensive trough in a generation. In 2011, the Major League Baseball earned run average fell below 4.00 for the first time in 19 years (3.94), strikeouts set an all-time high for the fifth straight year (now at 11 consecutive years and counting), the strikeout-to-walk rate hit an all-time high, home runs per game declined to its lowest level since 1993, runs per team per game sank to its lowest rate since 1992, and batting average dropped to its lowest mark since 1989.

The 2011 draft mirrored this rise of pitching. Clubs drafted pitchers with 18 of the first 28 picks, including the top four selections (Gerrit Cole, Danny Hultzen, Trevor Bauer, and Dylan Bundy).

Throughout its history, whether in times when pitchers dominated or times when hitters dominated, baseball lived by mantras such as "You can never have too much pitching" and "Good pitching stops good hitting." Drafting pitchers seemed, at least in a traditional way of thinking, the proven, safe route.

In Chicago, however, Epstein decided to zig while everyone else zagged. Pitching, he decided, was something he would worry about later. Most important to him was establishing what it meant to be a Cub, and the ones who most determine the culture of a team are the ones who play every day, not the ones who pitch every fifth or sixth day. Epstein believed that starting pitchers, at best, become leaders of the rotation once they get established, but not leaders of an entire team.

"There's lots of reasons why we went toward position players instead of pitchers in the first round, but that was a big one," Epstein said. "We are going to define our identity. We're going to define it through our best players. We're going to define it through our young nucleus. So we want character, too.

"We want players who are invested in their teammates, we want players who are going to understand what it means to play in a World Series for the Cubs and their fans. We want players we trust can respond to adversity. We want players other players like being around. We want guys who care about winning, and prioritize it, and are happy when the team wins and they are 0-for-4 and are pissed even if we lose and they are 3-for-4."

There was another reason that Epstein emphasized drafting position players with character for the foundation of his team. Despite the traditional emphasis on pitching, hitters are more reliable than pitchers, especially because the increase in pitching velocity has dovetailed with and even caused a rise in arm injuries, particularly blown elbow ligaments that require Tommy John surgery.

"We really focused so much on acquiring bats and position players because we knew that was the safer path for us to take," Hoyer said. "People thought, *You guys are taking the wrong path because you win through pitching.* But that's not the way we saw it.

"Safety. That was a big part of it. We knew we had one chance to do this. We only had so long to draft at the top of the draft. So we took the safest route. We bought bonds instead of stocks.

"The Mets were really close to winning the World Series [in 2015]. They went the opposite way. There are plenty of examples of teams that drafted well. The Giants drafted [pitchers] Matt Cain, Tim Lincecum, and Madison Bumgarner. How often does that happen? The way we happened to do it was safer. We emphasized building up our core players. It became such a buzzword that people mocked us. But we felt sustained success came from position players. They were the rock on which you build the rest around."

While baseball fell deeper into a pitching-dominated era, and while teams continued to chase pitchers at the top of the draft, even as elbows were blowing out at an alarming rate, the Cubs under Epstein chose a path no other club saw. In the first five years since Epstein joined the Cubs (2012–2016), teams used 47 percent of the top 30 picks in the draft on pitchers (71 of 150 picks). But only one team did not select a single pitcher with one of those 150 top 30 picks: the Cubs.

Chicago's avoidance of pitchers proved prudent. Of those 71 pitchers other teams selected among the top 30 picks over the five drafts, just as many pitchers have had either Tommy John surgery or thoracic outlet syndrome surgery (14) as reached the major leagues.

Even if you narrow the sample to pitchers taken with one of the first 10 picks—the ones who should be the safest selections—the returns on investment remain poor. Of the 25 pitchers picked in the top 10 over the previous five drafts, only 2 have a winning record in the majors: Carlos Rodon of the White Sox and Aaron Nola of the Phillies, neither of whom is a front-of-the-rotation pitcher.

For Epstein, deciding to build the team around high-character position players was an easy, if novel, choice. Having the infrastructure to find those players loomed as one of Epstein's biggest challenges.

Since the draft began in 1965, few if any teams have drafted worse than the Chicago Cubs. A 2014 study by ESPN ranked the Cubs dead last in average wins above replacement from first-round picks. The Cubs' top picks were particularly abysmal from 1999 to 2010. In those 12 drafts, Chicago took 16 players in the first round. Half of them never played a day in the big leagues, and only 2 of them played more than two seasons with the Cubs: Mark Prior and Tyler Colvin.

When Epstein arrived, the Cubs were still relying on the old-school wisdom of scouts, but they were a decade behind the rest of the industry when it came to the number of scouts and front office employees, and the sophistication of their databases. Their software program, at least when it was used, was an outdated one that other teams had used in the mid-'90s. Many scouts still filed handwritten reports on paper. The internet was not being fully utilized. Twice a day—midmorning and midafternoon—the Cubs' information manager, Chuck Wasserstrom, would print out multiple copies of baseball news and notes from the internet, staple them into packets, and drop them on the desk of front office executives, even though such information was available to anybody who knew how to use a web browser.

"That's how behind we were," one employee said. "We were killing a lot of trees in the digital age."

Epstein was stunned at how small an investment the Cubs were putting into scouting and player development, both in terms of money and processes. He was coming from Boston, where the Red Sox were among the most advanced clubs in that department. The draft rules had changed on him, he faced the daunting task of changing a losing culture, and he inherited no homegrown impact players. But of one thing Epstein could be sure.

"We knew how to do this: build a scouting and player development department," he said.

There would be no more short, handwritten reports on players.

No more photocopied printouts of internet news. Epstein immediately would have to replicate the deep, diligent system he used in Boston, especially now that he was placing an even greater emphasis on finding players with character.

"Okay, we know our principles," he said. "We built our scouting department around the idea that the currency in the draft is information. That's *it*. The currency in the draft is not, 'I'm a little bit better of a scout than you.'

"We're going to have great scouts. We're probably going to have some that are not so great mixed in. You don't know it. It takes years. But the currency of the draft is information. So yes, scouting *information*. We're going to have more scouts and better scouts and make sure they see the right players and see them more often than the other teams.

"Give us makeup information. It's not going to be 'Check a box on a scouting report: excellent, good, fair, poor.' That's what it was. 'Good kid.' I saw it a hundred times. 'Good makeup. Good kid.' Tells you nothing. Explain.

"Everyone's life is really complicated and involved and there are myriad influences and background factors and transformative experiences and challenges and times when they responded the right way to adversity and times they responded the wrong way. And you have to dig and figure out what makes this person tick and how he's going to respond in pro ball."

Epstein gave his scouts very specific marching orders. On every prospect he wanted the area scout to give three examples of how that player responded to adversity on the field, and three examples of how that player responded to adversity off the field. They were to dig into the player's makeup by talking to just about anybody who knew him: parents, guidance counselors, teammates, girlfriends, siblings. He wanted as many questions answered as possible: What's the family situation like? How does he treat people when no one's looking? What do his friends say about him? What do his enemies say about him? How does he treat people he doesn't necessarily have to treat well? What motivates him? Is he externally motivated where he wants money or followers?

"You really want people who are motivated by the competition," Epstein said, "especially by winning. You try to find the guys that want to thrive in that environment."

Cubs scouting reports would never look the same again. Epstein wanted reports that went on for pages, like the Russian novels his father had him read as a boy. The scouts who didn't take to the long-form scouting reports didn't last. Epstein ran them off.

Epstein had to have this information. It wasn't hard, measurable data. But it was information nonetheless, and if Epstein was going to build a team around high-character, high-impact, position players, he wanted as much of it as possible.

"MEDICAL INFORMATION IS important, too." Epstein said. "So if you can dig deep in all those buckets, if you can find some new way of looking at players no one else has, you can really separate yourself. That's where the neuroscouting stuff was huge for us."

Neuroscouting? In 2007 Drs. Wesley Clapp and Brian Miller founded NeuroScouting LLC in Cambridge, Massachusetts. Their self-defined mission involved "paving new roads in converting the latest neuroscience research into actionable technologies for elite performers in 'read and react' sports." Think of what they do as providing the services of an athletic trainer, not for the body but for the brain.

Epstein heard about the company while he was with the Red Sox and, around 2009–2010, entered into an exclusive agreement with NeuroScouting, establishing Boston as the only major league club that could use its services. Ever on the hunt for information, Epstein was curious if neuroscouting could provide predictive information about draft-eligible hitters. A hitter has four-tenths of a second—the equivalent of the blink of an eye—to see, decode, decide, and, if he chooses, swing at an average big league pitch. What if neuroscouting could provide data on how well and how quickly players processed all that information?

NeuroScouting developed three games as an evaluative tool. One example is a game in which the player sees pitches coming at him as if he is in the batter's box. The graphics are very simple, because if they appeared too lifelike—too much like a sophisticated video game—the players with vast gaming experience would score better than the ones who do not have such familiarity. The "baseball" coming at the hitter is a green circle, and it is moving with the speed and spin of real major league pitches. The game uses actual pitch data from the motion-capture technologies of PITCHf/x and TrackMan, MLB-licensed technology services. The hitter must hit the space bar when he judges the ball to be in the hitting zone.

The game then takes a twist. The ball may or may not turn red on the way to the plate. If it does turn red, the hitter is to avoid hitting the space bar—the equivalent of "taking" the pitch.

Sometimes the ball turns red right out of the "pitcher's" hand. That's an easy take for a hitter. Sometimes it turns red two-thirds of the way to the plate. That's a much harder take, the equivalent of a slider that looks like a fastball, only to break late and out of the strike zone. Researchers have discovered that the human brain can no longer complete the swing-or-don't-swing decision once the ball gets to within 10 feet of home plate. In technical terms, it's the measurement of a neural pathway called inhibitory control. So the game can push the hitter right up to the human limit of inhibitory control.

The Red Sox began their use of NeuroScouting's technology by trying it on their major league hitters. The collection of that data gave them basis points for some of the elite hitters in the world when it came to "read and react" and inhibitory control. Beginning in 2010, the Red Sox used that data as context when measuring the neural skills of draft-eligible players.

One day in the spring of 2011, Red Sox personnel visited John Overton High School in Brentwood, Tennessee, and waited for one of the students to stop by on his lunch period. Mookie Betts, who had gained acclaim as an all-state bowler but was lesser known around the heavily scouted elite travel baseball landscape, sat down at a table with the NeuroScouting games on a laptop. The Red Sox evaluated Betts as someone who figured to go in the tenth round of the draft that year. When the results reached Epstein, he was astounded.

"Mookie was up there with David Ortiz and Dustin Pedroia," Epstein said. "That got our attention. We moved him up from the tenth round to the fifth round. We got him in the fifth round."

A total of 171 players were drafted before Boston took Betts. He has developed into one of the best players in baseball—the Most Valuable Player runner-up in 2016—who is known for how fast his hands work as a hitter.

In Boston, Epstein was happy with the use of neuroscouting as an evaluative tool. Then the idea occurred to him and the Neuro-Scouting team that it might also work as another application: as a training device. If the laptop games served as a means to collect data on the neural pathways of potential draft picks, what if they could train players already in the system—a kind of batting practice for the brain?

Epstein noticed that the players were getting better at the games the more they played them. So he required all minor leaguers to play the games for about 15 minutes before they took the field for batting practice. They were instructed to do this a minimum of three or four times per week.

"We could track how much they trained on it and how they were developing," Epstein said. "We started to see a soft correlation to performance on the field: improvement in neuroscouting led to improvement on the field, which is cool."

When Epstein joined the Cubs he took neuroscouting with him, though the team's contract became exclusive to the National League, not all of the major leagues. (The American League's Tampa Bay Rays began using neuroscouting with their minor leaguers in 2013.)

In the flattening landscape of information available to major league teams, Epstein managed to find and hold an edge over his competitors.

In the spring of 2012, armed with neuroscouting reports and the Russian novel–length scouting reports from his newly challenged scouts, Epstein still needed one more piece of information before deciding how to use his first draft pick as the architect of the Cubs: he had to speak with the top candidates himself.

The Cubs held the sixth overall pick in the draft. The draft class was weak when it came to elite college hitters—the type most likely to be impact players. The only college hitter who would be selected among the top 14 picks was Florida catcher Mike Zunino, who had been a bust for Seattle. The Cubs set their sights on two high school players: Carlos Correa, a shortstop at Puerto Rico Baseball Academy, and Albert Almora Jr., an outfielder at Mater Academy Charter School in Hialeah, Florida. As it turned out, Houston, picking first overall, would take Correa.

"To Houston's credit, they played their cards close to the vest," Hoyer said. "We spent the year talking about Correa or Almora, and then—bang!—they took Correa. We didn't know which direction they were going to go."

Picking sixth, Epstein remembered his meeting with Almora. Epstein and McLeod flew to Miami in May 2012 and drove to Almora's house in Hialeah. They sat in the family living room. Out back was a batting cage. When Almora was a small child, his father gave him a choice for the backyard: he could have a pool or he could have a batting cage. The child chose the batting cage. Once the cage was installed and through high school, Almora hit in that cage every day, usually with his father throwing to him.

"Every. Single. Day," Almora said. "I didn't miss a day."

As a senior at Mater Academy, Almora hit .603 and struck out only three times in 87 plate appearances. He also maintained a 4.1 grade point average. He had made a commitment to play at the University of Miami.

The year before Epstein and McLeod paid their visit, Almora lost both of his maternal grandparents. His grandmother died six months earlier, just as he was leaving to catch a flight to Colombia to play for the 18U USA team in the Pan American Championships. His parents decided not to tell him about her passing until he returned, leaving him to his task of being the team leader and trying to win a gold medal. His team did win the gold medal and Almora was named Most Valuable Player of the tournament and later USA Baseball Player of the Year. When he arrived home and heard the news about his grandmother, Almora buried his gold medal next to her, saying he won it for her, so he wanted her to have it.

Epstein and McLeod already were working with glowing scouting reports from area scouts Laz Llanos and John Koronko, who became a scout after his 13-year pitching career—which included 31 big league games—had ended the previous year. But Epstein and McLeod wanted personal confirmation of what made Almora tick. Most importantly, what they wanted to know was what motivated him. Was he motivated by external factors, or was he motivated by winning? They were blown away by his responses.

"I'm telling you," he told the Cubs executives, "all I want is a chance to go out there and help the Cubs win the World Series. I'll do anything. I'll make a catch. I'll run the bases. I'll get a hit."

He began to break down emotionally.

"Just trust me," he said. "I win. I'm a winner. I know how to contribute to winning. I want to be a part of it. Trust me. I won't let you down."

"He got emotional," Epstein said. "His grandparents had just died and he had just won another gold medal for Team USA and he was crying at times during the meeting."

They were sold. The Cubs took Almora with the sixth pick of the draft. They signed him to a $3.9 million bonus. Epstein was thrilled with the pick, but he knew that as an 18-year-old high school pick Almora needed four or five years of development. Almora was a potential impact player, but his development curve was too long for Epstein to count him as one of the four impact players he knew he needed by 2016. Epstein still needed three impact players to add to Rizzo.

He would get one of them in the draft the next year.

The Cubs "earned" the second pick of the 2013 draft by losing 101 games in 2012, Epstein's first year in Chicago. It was the third-most losses in franchise history, trailing only the 103 losses from 1962 and 1966. Epstein had arrived in Chicago to such fanfare that at the start of the season the *Chicago Sun-Times* published a photo illustration of Epstein walking on water—Lake Michigan, to be exact. By the end of the season the newspaper had reprised the image to show Epstein with all but his head under the same waters. The headline read "S.O.S." with a subhead that warned, "Forget walking on water. Cubs boss Theo Epstein might sink if he doesn't focus on the present."

The 2013 draft was, of course, loaded with pitchers, and other teams continued to gobble them up. Twenty of the 39 picks in the first round, including supplemental picks, would be pitchers.

Finding big-bodied pitchers who threw in the mid-90s, even in high school, was becoming easier and easier. Because of advances in youth coaching and training, the development of velocity began earlier and reached higher heights. The supply of hard throwers kept growing, but baseball teams kept drafting them as if the supply were shrinking—except the Cubs.

Two big-bodied throwers, in particular, stood out in the 2013 draft class: Mark Appel from Stanford University and Jon Gray from the University of Oklahoma. The Astros again owned the first pick in the draft, the Cubs owned the second, and the Rockies owned the third. The Cubs had Appel, Gray, and a third baseman from the University of San Diego, Kris Bryant, rated as the three best talents in the draft. Epstein, Hoyer, and McLeod met with all three players. They met Bryant in late May in the lobby of a hotel in Stockton,

California, where San Diego was competing in the West Coast Conference baseball tournament, a tournament San Diego would win as Bryant hit his 31st home run, far and away the most in the nation.

Wanting to build his team around high-character position players, Epstein was leaning away from the pitchers and toward Bryant all along. But that day in Stockton solidified his decision.

"It was like, 'How can you not love everything about the guy?'" Epstein said. "He's a machine. We all came out of that meeting like, 'If we have daughters, that's the guy we'd like her to marry.' He can handle any situation, he knows exactly what to say, he's a genuinely good person, he cares about baseball, he's awesome, but always looking to get better. I don't think there's a situation that could throw him off his game, on the field or off the field.

"He's the safest stock, the best bet, that there is. He was just so polished. We came away thinking, *That's a face of a franchise right there. And we want it to be ours.*"

Houston, however, controlled Bryant's fate. The Cubs would not get their franchise player if the Astros took Bryant with the first pick. And Chicago did not see another impact position player in the draft like Bryant. So for weeks leading up to the draft, the Cubs created a smokescreen. Their executives and scouts downplayed their interest in Bryant. They played along with the big narrative in baseball that everybody wants pitching and that Appel and Gray were The Next Big Things to come along to a big league mound. The Rockies, picking third, were so convinced by this chatter that the Astros would take Appel and the Cubs would grab Gray that they began to focus heavily on Bryant.

"[Rockies GM] Dan O'Dowd just assumed we were taking Gray," Hoyer said. "He said, 'We thought Bryant was ours' and they were over the moon about it."

The Astros bought into the established narrative about prioritizing pitching. They took Appel with the first pick. Appel also was attractive to them because he grew up in West Houston and because, as a college senior, he did not have much leverage in negotiating his signing bonus. Houston saved $1.45 million by signing him under slot money for $6.35 million, money they could use to sign other players.

"This is the most significant investment the Astros have made in their history in an amateur player and we hope we're investing a lot in him in the future," Astros general manager Jeff Luhnow said when he announced the signing. "We believe it's going to be a long-term relationship. This is the beginning step. It's not the end. It's very exciting."

Appel never threw a pitch for the Astros. They traded him to Philadelphia in a deal to acquire a relief pitcher, Ken Giles, after Appel struggled for three seasons in their minor league system.

The Cubs, thankful, signed Bryant to a $6.7 million bonus. Gray fell to the Rockies.

"That was a turning point for us," Hoyer said. "Everybody was really excited. There was one position player that was in the top three and we got him. We knew we had a really good player. But we didn't think he'd be this good this fast. We didn't have any idea about how quickly he would make adjustments. It was incredible. We kept pushing him, waiting for him to struggle, and he just didn't struggle."

Bryant, in annual succession, was College Player of the Year, Arizona Fall League Most Valuable Player, Minor League Player of the Year, National League Rookie of the Year, and, in 2016, National League Most Valuable Player.

"What's most impressive," Hoyer said, "is that, as good as he is, I think he's going to figure out what he didn't like about his game and go fix it. He's someone that truly wants to be great."

Two years on the job, Epstein had acquired two of the four young, high-impact, high-character position players to build a championship-ready team for 2016: Rizzo and Bryant. The next year, in the June draft, he would add a third: Schwarber. And less than a month after that, Epstein found his fourth young, high-impact, high-character player in a place known to be difficult to acquire such gems: he went back to the trade market.

In May 2014, in preparation for the July 31 trade deadline, Epstein and Hoyer split up the teams they talked to about possible deals. Epstein's biggest chip to trade was Jeff Samardzija, a pitcher who had rejected the team's offer of a contract extension worth nearly $80 million. One of the teams assigned to Hoyer was Toronto. The Blue Jays had expressed strong interest in Samardzija as far back as spring training. Hoyer talked to them about young pitchers Daniel Norris, Aaron Sanchez, and Marcus Stroman.

One of the teams assigned to Epstein was Oakland. The Athletics were in the thick of the American League West race and needed a starting pitcher. Beane let Epstein know he was interested in Samardzija.

"I'm not sure you guys have enough," Epstein said to Beane, "unless you want to talk about Addison Russell."

"We would consider that," Beane said.

The hair on Epstein's arms nearly stood on end. Russell was only 20 years old and rated by *Baseball America* as the 14th best prospect in baseball. As a high school shortstop in Florida, Russell played on the same 18U USA Team as Almora. The Cubs had acquired loads of information on Russell and were especially impressed with his makeup, but they regarded Almora as the safer pick because of his longer track record of success. They had data on Almora going back to when he was 15 years old.

Also, in his junior season Russell fell out of shape and ballooned to 225 pounds. He grew so big that scouts wondered if he would have to move off shortstop, a doubt that decreased his value. Russell did drop his weight to 190 by his senior year, but by then his stock had slipped slightly. Russell fell to Oakland with the 11th overall pick.

"To defend our scouts," Hoyer said, "we were drafting sixth. And once you have a hiccup on a guy, you don't have much time to overcome it. We liked him a lot, but he was written off as not quite good enough for six."

Russell hit .369 in his first year in pro ball, 2012. That fall Epstein and Hoyer watched Russell play Instructional League games against Chicago's prospects.

"He destroyed us," Hoyer said. "Watching this guy hit doubles in the gaps, we hadn't seen the same player in high school. He was just so impressive. We went back and dug into all the reports again. Reading the reports, he was super young back then, had the ability to play multiple positions, and every scout who went to go watch him mentioned how attentive he was in the field. He was locked in on every single pitch."

In reviewing their original reports on Russell, the Cubs had no questions about his character. Russell was the oldest of four siblings raised in Pensacola, Florida, by his mother, Milany, and his stepfather, Wayne Russell, who has been part of his life since he was a toddler. With both parents often working, Addison took on many responsibilities in the raising of his two younger sisters and his younger brother. He always played against older competition, yet seemed to be one of the more mature, quietly confident players.

(So humble and reserved is Russell, in fact, that in time Maddon would encourage him to be more outgoing. Once Maddon began managing him, in 2015, he found Russell to be too quiet for a middle infielder. To get Russell more engaged with the coaching staff and teammates, Maddon gave him a reading assignment: Stephen King's *11/22/63*, the historical novel about the Kennedy assassination. Maddon asked Russell to report back to him every 50 to 100 pages to discuss it. It was Maddon's way of not only connecting with a 21-year-old who had played only 14 games above Double-A, but also helping develop the communication skills of someone he regarded as a future leader. The book gave them plenty of opportunities to chat—it runs 849 pages.)

Once Beane mentioned that Russell could be had, Hoyer said, "Then we went into overdrive scouting Russell. He had been out with a hamstring injury. We scouted his rehab in Arizona. We followed him every step of the way."

After the draft in June—when Epstein obtained Schwarber—Beane and Epstein spoke again. Beane told Epstein he would not trade Russell for Samardzija straight up.

"Is there a way I can get Samardzija from you without Russell?" Beane asked.

"No," Epstein replied.

"Well, you don't have much time, because we'll go somewhere else to get a pitcher."

Beane was deep into discussions with Tampa Bay about trading for David Price.

Then, on July 1, while the Cubs were playing in Boston, Toronto general manager Alex Anthopolous called Hoyer there.

"We're out," Anthopolous said.

"What?" Hoyer replied. He couldn't believe it. The Blue Jays had been in on Samardzija since spring training. Talks had proceeded without hitches.

"It's an ownership decision," Anthopolous said. "We're out. Totally out."

Hoyer quickly called Epstein.

"Toronto's out," he told him. "If you can get Oakland done you've got to do it. Toronto was our next best bet and now that's gone."

Epstein accelerated talks with Beane. On July 3 he sweetened the deal by adding another starting pitcher, Jason Hammel. The appeal for Beane was that he could make a playoff run with the addition of two veteran starters, Samardzija and Hammel—and by the end of the month his go-for-broke wheeling and dealing would also net him Jon Lester in a trade from Boston.

The next day Epstein attended a Fourth of July party with his wife, his son, and his mother. Beane called. Epstein left the party, sneaking behind some bushes for privacy. There he completed the deal: Samardzija and Hammel for Russell, pitcher Dan Straily, and outfield prospect Billy McKinney. The trade was announced the next day.

"We were ecstatic," Epstein said. "We were ecstatic because we never felt like we'd be able to get one singular talent like Russell in the deal. You usually have to take a package and get lesser guys you're hoping on, but we were really convicted on Russell. It was hard to get elite prospects like that in any deals at that time. So we were ecstatic about that."

Done. Mission accomplished, at least as far as the mission of acquiring pillars to the building plan was concerned. In two and a half seasons, Epstein had obtained the four high-impact, high-character everyday players he regarded as essential to fielding a championship team by 2016: Rizzo in a 2012 trade, Bryant in the 2013 draft, Schwarber in the 2014 draft, and now Russell in a 2014 trade.

The 2014 season marked Epstein's third season running the Cubs, and this would be his third fifth-place team. While Chicago might have offered him a respite from the daily obsession with the standings in Boston, Epstein knew he was testing the patience of Cubs fans. The Cubs still drew between 2.6 million and 2.8 million people in those three years, ranking in the top half of the league despite losing teams on the field.

"Of course, the whole thrust of the organization, which we were transparent about, was to be single-minded about acquiring young talent at all costs," Epstein said, "and I said it at my opening press conference. I said, 'Look, we're going to do everything we can to build for the future and acquire young talent. That's number one. We also have a big league team and every season is sacred, but where those two ideas conflict we're going to side with the future, and with the long term and acquiring talent.'

"So we put our fans through a lot and we put our big league players through a lot. It was, 'Oh, good, we're excited about Andrew Cashner.' Bang! He's traded for Rizzo.

" 'Oh, Sean Marshall, he's one of the few reliable guys we have in our pen.' Bang! He's traded for Travis Wood, who was a bit of a buy low. He had come up and pitched great but had kind of a mediocre year after that.

"It was, 'Cool, Ryan Dempster, he's popular and funny, and having a great year.' Bang! He's gone for a Low-A ball pitcher who throws 87.

" 'Oh, cool, we signed this Scott Feldman guy. He's having a great year.' That was actually a great sign. Bang! He's gone for a guy with a six-and-a-half [ERA] who's in Triple-A with the Orioles and a reliever with a seven.

" 'Oh, at least we have Matt Garza. He's having a great year.' Bang! He's gone for two youngsters and two players to be named later.

" 'Oh, at least we have good old Jeff Samardzija. Maybe they'll sign him and he'll be on the mound when they finally make the playoffs.' Bang! He's gone. And Hammel, too? The third straight year we've traded 40 percent of our rotation leading up to the deadline? Three straight years of 40 percent of the rotation, gone."

But, deep down, Epstein knew the Russell trade was a watershed moment. The minute it was completed, he knew the Cubs were entering an entirely new phase. The heavy lifting was over. Like a home builder, he had slogged through building the foundation and the structure. It was time to start the finishing pieces.

"If we were right about what was emerging," Epstein said, "that would be the last time that we'd have to trade significant pieces off our big league team for minor league players. And we still hope to make trades like that from time to time. But it was sort of the last piece of the rebuild, the last time we would make a trade that devastated our big league clubhouse and sort of flummoxed or confused a certain cross section of our fan base. It really added to our future.

"All of a sudden you look [and] it's not just one future impact talent you're counting on, it's not just two or three, we had a whole wave, we had a whole generation of players who were within a year or two of each other age-wise and broke within a year of each other and we started to get really, really excited about the future."

Said Hoyer, "I remember that summer being so much fun. We felt like we were in on a secret—a secret about how good we were going to be. Every night in the box we could look up on the internet to see how Schwarber and Bryant and Russell and Baez and Soler, before he came up, and Almora were doing. We had so much young talent playing in the minors. It was like, 'Man, oh, man, this is starting to come together.'

"Post-Russell trade at the end of 2014 was exciting. Then we started to get some love nationally and won some big series against contenders. That's when people could start to see what was happening."

Five days after the Cubs acquired Russell, Epstein witnessed another watershed moment. The team was playing the Reds in Cincinnati. Reds closer Aroldis Chapman, pitching the top of the ninth, buzzed fastballs by the heads of Chicago left-handed hitters Nate Schierholtz and John Baker. Rizzo yelled at Chapman from the Chicago dugout.

After the half inning, as Rizzo walked to his position at first base, he heard somebody in the Cincinnati dugout yell at him. Rizzo threw down his hat and glove and headed toward the dugout, challenging the entire Reds team. The Cubs won the game, 6–4, in 12 innings, though it wasn't especially the win that struck Epstein as important. It was confirmation about the character and leadership abilities of one of the pillars of his team.

"Those are two important, transformative events: the Russell trade and Rizzo challenging the other team," Epstein said. "We didn't start playing better right away, but like three or four weeks after that I think Baez and Soler had come up and at the time we were excited about [Arismendy] Alcantara. We started playing great. We flashed a lot of exciting talent those last two months.

"We played pretty well, and one team we played pretty well against was Tampa. That got Joe Maddon's attention a little bit while he was in here at Wrigley. Meanwhile, Lester was traded to Oakland and for the first time could picture himself out of Boston and also started to think about what was important to him from an organization and city and he didn't have a great experience out there necessarily. So us playing better in 2014, our young guys breaking in, created a lot of momentum to really try to have an off-season that would help us turn a corner and compete in 2015."

The pieces were coming together. Epstein made a bet on the importance of the makeup of the players he acquired, not to replace the edge in analytics he once wielded in Boston, but to enhance it. He made this bet just as baseball teams more and more resembled technology companies. The baseball operations offices swelled with brilliant people with math and science degrees. The spin rates of pitches and the launch angles of balls hit off bats were being studied with the rigor of major science research projects. Players were donning "wearable" technology to collect data on how hard their bodies were working. Teams were fiercely guarding all kinds of proprietary statistics to find hidden value in players. Catchers were being schooled on how to subtly cradle pitches with their fingers to influence umpires into calling balls as strikes. Baseball teams were obsessed, at unprecedented intellectual and scientific levels, with finding "the next inefficiency," and Epstein's belief in neuroscouting stood as just one of the many such endeavors.

The brilliance of what the Cubs did was to put their faith not just in numbers, but also in the type of people they acquired. The four pillars of the rebuild—Rizzo, Bryant, Schwarber, and Russell—as well as the regime's first number one draft pick, Almora, all were acquired because the Cubs valued their character, not just their skill.

"It's not luck," Hoyer said. "It's definitely something you focus on. Having the experience we had in Boston, we knew if we were going to overcome the challenges in a big market—what we needed to overcome in terms of the history and dealing with the media every day—that was definitely a focus."

Epstein and Hoyer had come a long way from when they couldn't wait to tear into a Bill James analytics project for Boston in 2002. This time there was no propriety formula, no algorithm, for acquiring self-motivated, high-character players and creating an environment to allow them to flourish. They never stopped searching to find edges, but they made a fundamental decision early after coming to Chicago that the one edge they could exploit was found in a very old-school resource: people.

Said Epstein, "Interestingly, during the push for the next competitive advantage and how flat everything's gotten now and how smart everyone is, and how everyone is using basically the same technology, I feel like I've pushed our organization back to the human being. And thankfully so.

"If we can't find the next technological breakthrough, well maybe we can be better than anyone else with how we treat our players and how we connect with players and the relationships we develop and how we put them in positions to succeed. Maybe our environment will be the best in the game, maybe our vibe will be the best in the game, maybe our players will be the loosest and maybe they'll have the most fun and maybe they'll care the most. It's impossible to quantify.

"The Cardinals were, like, teasing us about it. [But] when people do things they weren't even sure they were capable of, I think it comes back to connection. Connection with teammates. Connection with organization. Feeling like they belong in the environment. I think it's a human need—the need to feel connected. We don't live in isolation. Most people don't like working in isolation—some do, but they typically don't end up playing Major League Baseball."

CHAPTER 6

THAT'S CUB

The four-day summit in the Mesa hotel ballroom before the 2012 spring training produced the road map to the first Cubs championship since 1908. It was Epstein's opportunity to take everything he learned from Boston and treat it like wet clay. He, Hoyer, and McLeod wanted the input of every scout, coach, manager, and instructor in the Chicago organization.

"We said, 'We're going to meet and we're going to get it all out there on the table: what we believe about baseball, all of our collective wisdom about baseball, and we're going to come up with the Cubs Way,'" Epstein said. "How we want to play the game, how we're going to teach the game, what kind of human beings we want in the clubhouse, and what we're going to stand for as an organization.

"Obviously, we took some core principles from the Red Sox, the Red Sox way, obviously controlling the strike zone. . . . We weren't going to come out of that meeting saying, 'Yep, we're going to be a free-swinging team.' Everything was going to revolve around controlling the strike zone. But we were open-minded about a lot of things."

It was important to Epstein that he involved everybody in the room. Yes, he opened the summit with a long speech about what was important to him about winning baseball, and his overall vision to turn the Chicago Cubs into an elite franchise with sustained success. But he knew just about everybody in the room had been hired by somebody else, and he wanted to establish the kind of environment in which he and most humans worked best: a collaborative one.

"There were a lot of people there who thought maybe they would get fired right away," Epstein said, "or 'These guys are going to come in from Boston and try to re-create what they did there' or 'They have their own ideas.' But I think it created some buy-in, some sort of collective investment in the vision.

"So I laid out this big vision for everybody and then I said, 'Now it's up to us. That's the vision. We can all agree on that. Now it's up to all of us to collectively figure out the strategy. How are we going to get there? What's the journey going to look like?' And that's when we met and talked about the Cubs Way. I think it created a lot of buy-in."

The room became a baseball think tank in which no detail was too small to be debated. The people in the room discussed the proper pregame warm-up routine for pitchers, how the uniform should be worn, innings limits for pitchers, curfews, nutrition, cutoffs and relays, clubhouse protocol, strength training programs, pitching and hitting mechanics, mental skills, the proper way to take batting practice, rules about facial hair, bunt defenses, rundowns, the proper way to slide, and much more. The discussions became as precise as determining the proper foot a runner should use when running through first base and for rounding any base.

When the meeting was over, Epstein collected all the wisdom and the best of everything he had learned about baseball and put down on paper exactly what he wanted the Cubs to be. This was the 259-page, spiral-bound road map known as *The Cubs Way*, the 2012 player development manual. Shortstop Starlin Castro was featured on the cover.

The first chapter of the manual was titled, "Departmental Principles." It began, "The Chicago Cubs are committed to building and maintaining the best Scouting & Player Development system in Major League Baseball." It went on to list the six core principles on which the organization would be built:

1. We will treat the development of every player as if we were making a personal investment in him.
2. We will stay objective in evaluating the player's strengths and weaknesses in order to devise the most precise and thorough Individual Player Development Plan.
3. We will continually challenge ourselves to better communicate our method of teaching.
4. We will put the organization's goals ahead of our personal ambitions always.
5. We will embrace the cultures and backgrounds of all of our players, foreign and domestic, as we recognize the growth we can achieve as an organization from this experience.
6. At all times we will keep this in mind: Our mission is to help the Chicago Cubs win a World Championship!

Emphasis on personal character and conduct rang out loudly in the manual. The book included a Minor League Code of Conduct that held development staffers to the same code as the players, reasoning, "If we ask our players to act a certain way, it is critical that we do the same." The code included 10 promises by which a Cubs minor leaguer must abide. Among them was the recognition that "I am viewed as a 'role model' and as such, assume the responsibility to demonstrate a professional demeanor in word and deed, on and off the field."

Another one of the 10 standards of conduct required every player to "make a commitment to team spirit by maintaining a positive attitude, treating my coaching staff and fellow teammates with dignity and respect while appreciating individual differences."

Forming the bulk of the manual were the highly detailed expectations for playing baseball the Cubs way, with chapters on pitching, hitting, bunting, team fundamentals, infield play, outfield play, catching, baserunning, base stealing, strength and conditioning, the mental skills program, and the rehabilitation program. Those expectations included details as fine as the exact sequence and number of pitches in the proper pregame warm-up (exactly 38 pitches) and the answers to the discussions on how to touch first base while running through it ("<u>always</u> hit the front edge of the bag with the **left foot**") and how to touch all bases while rounding them ("<u>always</u> hit the front corner of the bag with the **right foot**").

(The first page of the manual noted, however, that "rather than a 'how to' reference guide," it should be considered "a living, breathing document that will change over time as we continually challenge the status quo." Indeed, later editions of *The Cubs Way* removed the preferences to touching bases with a certain foot. The instructions were modified to allow a runner to touch a base with either foot; what was more important was that a runner not break stride while doing so.)

A key component to *The Cubs Way* was what Epstein called Individual Player Development Plans. The germ of the idea began in 2006 when Epstein hired former major league infielder Gary DiSarcina in Boston as a baseball operations consultant. Sitting around the office one day, Epstein suggested, just for fun, that they look up the old carbon copy scouting reports on the young DiSarcina that were buried in the Boston files. The scouting reports included a notation that DiSarcina was slow at turning double plays.

"Why didn't anybody tell me I needed to work on my turns?" DiSarcina erupted. "I would have gotten to the big leagues so much quicker!"

The reaction impacted Epstein. It caused the second big *a-ha!* moment in his career when it came to dealing with players. The first such moment occurred in San Diego back in 1996, when Epstein, then 22, was working only his second full-time year in professional baseball. Epstein was chatting with Padres infielder Craig Shipley near the batting cage when Shipley told him, "Theo, don't you understand every single player in Major League Baseball at one point or another has been flat-out lied to by somebody in the front office?" Recalled Epstein, "That defines how players look at the business of baseball. It was really powerful. I've always remembered that, and because of that I feel like I've bent over backwards to be honest with players."

The DiSarcina moment jolted him in the same way as the Shipley moment. It was another epiphany. For years baseball teams rarely shared evaluations about players with the players themselves. Scouts and evaluators filed reports, and the information remained closely held internally, buried in file cabinets or kept to one's opinion about the player. It occurred to Epstein that the first time a team truly tells a player he's not good enough is when it's too late—when it releases him. It sounded absurd to him that a team wouldn't tell a player about his strengths and weaknesses. Around the same time, he discovered that Mark Shapiro, then the Cleveland Indians' general manager, had regularly shared evaluations with players since he worked in that organization as its player development director. Epstein decided in Boston to start using Individual Player Development Plans.

"To their credit I think Cleveland was the first to start it. Mark Shapiro [did it] when he was farm director there," he said. "We stole it in Boston and stole it again in Chicago. It does really create a great connection with the player and helps him develop himself. And we just try to make it fun."

Minor league players meet with the vice president of player personnel three times a year: spring training, midseason, and after the season. Major league players meet with Epstein, Maddon, Hoyer, and either the pitching, hitting, or catching coach in spring training. The review covers the player's physical, fundamental, and mental strengths and weaknesses. The information is logged on a review sheet that the player must sign. The player keeps one copy and the team keeps another.

Epstein wanted a culture in which the players could trust the front office. And the way to help build that trust was to develop an open and honest personal connection.

"The player plans were a huge part of that," he said. "'Here's what we see. Here's what you need to work on to become a big leaguer. Here's a plan to work on it.' Then a player gets to give their feedback and give their input. They get to argue, 'No, that's actually not a weakness. I do that fine. Here are things I want to work on.'

"And you see this transition. Their first year they're just listening. They sign the page. But by the time they reach Double-A, the guys who are starting to reach their ceilings, they're starting to take responsibility and accountability for their own development.

"The kids who really start to take responsibility start to run the meeting. 'Okay, here's what I need to work on. Here's where I'm at.' That's the key to player development—when you stop developing them and they start to develop themselves. They start to trust you that you're in it for their best interests because you're being transparent. You're not hiding the ball. It's really different from the way it used to be."

Epstein knew that having a 259-page manual was important, but even more important would be how those ideals were carried out. The organization's managers, coaches, instructors, and coordinators were responsible for turning those words into a workplace environment that promoted growth. It took Epstein a year to sort through the skills of the people in his system. Many of those at the 2012 preseason summit meeting who feared change under the new administration were let go after the season.

In April 2012, Epstein hired Vanderbilt pitching coach Derek Johnson as organizational pitching coordinator. After that season, Epstein hired Tim Cossins out of the Marlins organization to be the Cubs' minor league field coordinator. Brandon Hyde, who held that job, was promoted to director of player development. Both Cossins and Hyde recommended to Hoyer that he hire Anthony Iapoce, who played 11 minor league seasons with the Marlins and Brewers and had spent the previous three seasons as the roving hitting coach in the Blue Jays organization. Epstein and Hoyer hired Iapoce as special assistant to the general manager/hitting coordinator.

"I give most of the credit to changing the culture in the minor leagues to the coordinators," Epstein said. "Mostly Cossins and Iapoce. Those guys made it really fun to be around, and created a great vibe. Now, all of a sudden, you're a minor leaguer in the Cubs system, you are looking around, and it's like, 'Wow, Bryant is pretty good, Baez is really good, Schwarber is really good. . . . We're going to win, and this is fun.'

"In 2012 we were more about just getting our team in place. We really had it in place in 2013."

The 2013 Cubs, with 96 losses, were only slightly less terrible than the 2012 Cubs, who lost 101. Under manager Dale Sveum, the 2013 Cubs used 56 players, of whom not a single homegrown player would remain three years later. The pitching staff walked the most batters in the league for a fourth straight year, and ranked in the bottom four in ERA for the fourth of five straight seasons. The team batting average was .238. Only one Cubs team ever hit worse over a full season: in 1892, back when Benjamin Harrison was president.

Underneath the flotsam on the surface, however, the Cubs were changing the very definition of what it meant to be a Cub. The best place to see such change was completely off the major league radar.

"The morale was incredible in the minor leagues, down below," Epstein said. "It was not great in the big leagues, understandably, because we were losing. But you'd go to Instructional League, you'd go to the back fields of spring training, and it was so much fun to see the talent emerge."

Morale was so high at that 2013 Instructional League camp in October in Mesa that an image-changing mantra emerged. Whenever somebody executed a winning-type fundamental play—advancing a baserunner, executing a relay, taking an extra base, or anything straight out of *The Cubs Way*—a coach or coordinator might shout, "That's Cub!" Soon players picked up on shouting the honor themselves.

"Meanwhile," Epstein said, "the narrative that surrounds the big league team is that 'That's Cub' is still a reference to lovable losers. So there was a real dichotomy between the secret we all knew we had—this mass base of talent and morale and character that was developing in the minor leagues—versus the understandable ongoing struggle that we had in the big leagues just to be respectable."

"That's Cub" started organically and grew into an official source of pride. By 2016, Epstein had folded it into the latest version of *The Cubs Way*—the one with Kyle Schwarber on the cover—carving out a space for it in the player development manual under the Mental Skills Program.

"Ultimately what it means is that something was done that is right on point with what we are working to accomplish in this organization," the manual stated. It even turned "That's CUB" into an acronym: C stands for the courage "to do the right thing," even if it is scary or uncomfortable; U is for the urgency "to do the right thing right now"; and B is for the belief "that we can do it."

Every time "Cubs" was mentioned in that section of the manual, it was put in boldface, including this summary of the organization attitude:

> The **Cubs** attitude is positive, powerful, action-oriented, and resilient. It is an attitude that says, "I am" and "I do." It is an attitude that says, "No matter what happens, I will continue to grow, and I will always find a way."

In sight and sound, that 2013 Instructional League camp was the most obvious evidence yet to Epstein that the organization had turned a corner—even if the rest of the world didn't know it yet. For the first time in more than half a century, Cubs players, albeit in the minor leagues, were developing with an attitude that they were winners—that they were *supposed* to be good.

―――――――

CHAPTER 7

GAME 2

H ow many 24 and unders do we have in there?"

Joe Maddon looked at his lineup card before Game 2 of the World Series and began counting. He answered his own question.

"Six."

No one had ever said that before. Until this night, managers had filled out exactly 1,300 World Series lineup cards and never once before had started six position players who had not yet reached their 25th birthday. The previous record was five such starters, used by manager Dick Williams of the 1967 Boston Red Sox. Here were the Cubs in danger of falling behind two games to none in the World Series, playing on the road and reeling from a 15-strikeout shutout loss the previous night, and Maddon was counting on an unprecedented youthful lineup to bail him out. The kiddie corps consisted of shortstop Addison Russell, 22, designated hitter Kyle Schwarber, 23, second baseman Javier Baez, 23, catcher Willson Contreras, 24, rightfielder Jorge Soler, 24, and third baseman Kris Bryant, 24—none of whom had been in the big leagues as recently as two and a half years before.

Maddon wasn't worried. In fact, he recalled Game 4 of the

National League Championship Series against the Los Angeles Dodgers, when his young team was playing on the road coming off *two* shutouts, and by the time it reached the fourth inning it had not scored a run in 21 consecutive innings. But after a leadoff bunt single by Ben Zobrist in the fourth inning, youngsters Baez, Contreras, and Russell all smashed hits en route to producing four runs. A two-run homer by Russell was the biggest blow in the revival inning. It was the turning point of the series. Chicago never lost again to Los Angeles.

"Look what just happened against the Dodgers," Maddon said. "Not hitting, down two games to one, in Los Angeles, crazy crowd, tremendous tradition they have of winning in the postseason, and we came through it and bounced back. Addison starts hitting homers. I mean, to me that was a real growth point for us.

"Moving forward, I just see all of this as a positive. Hopefully, we win it but even if you did not win it, just like last year, the way it influenced this year, based on getting eliminated by the Mets, it didn't bother us. I don't see it. I just see this as one big positive moving forward. With good health, these guys are going to get better.

"There are others on the way. I'm good with all this stuff. I don't see the negative. Like last night, that's all great starting pitching. That's not unlike what Kershaw did to us. It happens every postseason to somebody."

Maddon also felt confident because of how Schwarber looked at the plate in Game 1. Schwarber had ripped a double against Cleveland ace Corey Kluber and drew a walk against über reliever Andrew Miller, the two toughest pitchers on the Cleveland staff, in his first major league action since tearing up his knee in April.

"I loved the walk against Miller," Maddon said. "I thought that was outstanding. The double I thought was a homer when it left the bat. If the wind isn't blowing in that's a homer right there. Did you talk to him? It's like he's in Indiana right now and they're playing friggin' Notre Dame or Indiana State. That's where he's at right now. He's just really good. He's fine."

Against Cleveland's Game 2 starter Trevor Bauer, Maddon did not play rightfielder Jason Heyward again, nor did he start left-handed-hitting catcher Miguel Montero. Bauer, he said, was "a reverse split guy," someone with better numbers against left-handed batters than against right-handed batters, primarily because of his wicked curveball. So Maddon started Jorge Soler in rightfield—"Soler is definitely capable of going crazy the next couple of days," Maddon said—and Contreras behind the plate.

The key for the game would be a running theme for the Cubs throughout the World Series: Would a lineup stacked with a record number of young players have the discipline to lay off teaser breaking balls? Batters hit just .126 during the regular season off Bauer's curveball, which ranked among the six best curveballs in baseball. (Kluber's curveball also ranked among the best hooks in baseball.)

"Spin strikes we're actually pretty good with," Maddon said. "Bryant hits the breaking ball strike well. Schwarber [does] if he's hot. Baez will kill a breaking ball strike. Contreras will hit a breaking ball strike. Soler will hit a breaking ball strike. It's there, but it has to be a strike. If we're chasing, we're screwed. But if we're spitting on the ball and make him throw it over the plate, we'll hit it.

"Zobrist is all about velocity. Even at this age he hits velocity. Rizzo, middle down. K.B. will crush a breaking ball strike. One-handed, too. It just goes.

"The biggest thing with Bauer is make him throw the ball over the plate. He's going to want to make you chase. He likes the cutter on lefties, elevated fastball, and he wants you to chase that breaking ball in the dirt. I think if we're patient and score first—you see teams are 12–0 in the postseason when they score first—I've seen it before. When this guy gets on a roll, he gets going good, but if you can put just a little doubt in his head he starts making mistakes."

On paper, the Cubs looked to have the decided advantage in the pitching matchup. Maddon was giving the ball to Jake Arrieta, the 2015 Cy Young Award winner, who was well rested. This was his third postseason start, and he had made them with 12, 7, and 7 days

of rest, respectively. Arrieta inevitably slipped back from the amazing heights of his Cy Young season, in which he won 22 games and
posted a 1.77 ERA. But the slippage was noticeable: 18 wins and a
3.10 ERA.

The biggest difference in the 2015 and 2016 versions of Arrieta
was that he had lost the command of his sharp breaking ball, the
one that resembles a cutter when it is thrown hard and with a tight
break, and a slider when it is thrown with slightly less velocity and a
bigger break. For most of the year, Arrieta fought his mechanics on
the pitch. In trying too hard for movement and velocity, he reached
too far behind him on his arm swing, causing his torso to overro-
tate, which caused timing problems in his delivery. Timing problems
cause command problems because they prevent the pitcher from
repeating his delivery. Late in the season, Maddon noticed something in Arrieta's prepitch routine that caused the overrotation, and
suggested a change.

"When he was off for a bit, I got involved," Maddon said. "There
[were] some dramatic differences in him in his prepitch, compared
to the year before. A lot of times when guys get like that, it's usually
more of what he's thinking than what is physically wrong. I think
he was physically off in his setup. It got a little bit better in the lat-
ter part of the season—balls and strikes, being able to repeat his
delivery well . . . If you remember before then he was missing by a
lot. When he set up, he was laying back so much he was overrotating.
When he got to the position he's supposed to, he was better."

The game plan seemed obvious to Maddon. To even the series,
he needed the good version of Arrieta to show up, and he needed his
hitters to put doubt in the head of Bauer, forcing him into mistakes.

He got exactly what he wanted.

ARRIETA WAS BRILLIANT. He no-hit the Indians through $5\frac{1}{3}$ innings, and gave up two hits and one run before departing one out
later. He struck out six, the most in a World Series win for a Cubs

starter since Orval Overall in 1908. Arrieta walked off the mound with a 5–1 lead—it would remain the final score—as Chicago's young hitters pounded a rattled Bauer early and often.

The record six 24-and-unders in the Cubs' lineup reached base 10 times against seven Cleveland pitchers, including 5 times by walks. They were cool under pressure. Most dramatically, Schwarber kept raking as if he had never missed those six months with the knee injury. He twice drove in runs with singles and walked another time. In two nights in the World Series, fresh off only six at-bats in front of just dozens of people in the Arizona Fall League, Schwarber reached base 5 times in nine trips to the plate. He saw 40 pitches in those nine plate appearances. He left his teammates in awe.

"People have no idea how hard it is to do what he just did," Cubs first baseman Anthony Rizzo said. "Only someone who is a freak of nature could do this. He's a natural-born hitter. This is the stuff of legends as the World Series goes on."

Said teammate Kris Bryant, "To do this, especially with the stuff that staff has? No way. I couldn't do it."

Said Hoyer, "I asked Rizzo, 'How long would it take you to get ready?' He said, 'Thirty at-bats.' And Anthony Rizzo is a great hitter. But that's in spring training after you've been hitting since January. What he just did is crazy.

"How could anybody have expected this? We couldn't. But because of who he is, he gets the benefit of the doubt. He's just a freakishly good hitter and a genuinely great guy."

The World Series never had seen anything like this. The closest historical comparison to someone playing this well after missing so much time occurred in 1945, the last time the Cubs played in the World Series. Detroit pitcher Virgil Trucks missed virtually the entire season while on military service for World War II. Three days after he was discharged, he pitched the pennant-winning game for the Tigers. Shortly thereafter, he beat the Cubs with a complete game in Game 2 of the World Series. Schwarber's story is even more amazing, given the severity of his injury and the demands and speed of the modern game.

"To use 'shocked' and 'Kyle Schwarber' in the same sentence is probably a bad combo," said Cubs catcher David Ross. "The legend of Kyle Schwarber—the guy is a legend already."

The least nonplussed of the Cubs was Schwarber himself.

"I'm just trying to put in team at-bats right now," Schwarber said. "I want to help this team get to the ultimate goal. That's why I did all of this—it was for these guys in the clubhouse and for our organization. It wasn't for me. So, like I said, I just want to put in good team at-bats every time I go to the plate and take that result."

The Cubs had regained their equipoise. They had just won their first World Series game since 1945, and they had done so with the youngest starting lineup in Fall Classic history. With a core of young position players, it was happening just as Epstein had planned. None of it would have been possible, however, unless he found pitchers like Arrieta.

CHAPTER 8

THE BEAST

One day in February 2016, inside a workout room at the Cubs' spring training headquarters, pitcher Jake Arrieta stood with teammates Matt Szczur, Anthony Rizzo, and Kyle Schwarber in front of a wood contraption called a Pilates reformer, a sledlike device developed by German-born Joseph Pilates in the first half of the 20th century to stretch and strengthen the muscles in the body, particularly in the core. Arrieta had the reformer custom-built and delivered to the Arizona facility. A fierce devotee of the training method, Arrieta wanted not so much to spread the gospel of Pilates as he wanted his teammates to know he was there for them.

"I want you guys to feel comfortable coming to me if there's anything you need," Arrieta told them. "If you have anything with your hips, stiffness in your back, anything, that's the time when I want you guys to feel comfortable coming to me. Just ask me, 'What are the one or two movements on this reformer that can help me prepare that day?'"

The offer to help his teammates illustrated just how far Arrieta had come in his career. The classic underachiever had become a leader.

"One of my biggest motivating factors obviously is to make myself as good as I possibly can be in all areas of my life, but also to benefit my teammates," Arrieta said. "This is something I talked about at the [Texas Christian University] alumni banquet. I talked about how, when my career first started, I was trying to be the best I could be for myself, and I think that's how a lot of guys are initially. You want to be the best player you can possibly be on an individual level. I talked about how that's drastically changed for me, based on relationships that I've developed, how I've grown and matured mentally and physically, not only as a player but as a person—getting to know teammates' families and getting to know their kids. I want them to know I will help them anytime."

The construction of a championship team is granular. The final picture is a Seurat painting. As with many tiny dots of color, there are millions of reasons and thousands of cascading events that help explain how in five years the Cubs morphed from a 101-loss team into a world championship team. It would be difficult, if not impossible, to find a handful of those reasons and events that were more significant than the acquisition and transformation of Jacob Joseph Arrieta, better known as Jake to the baseball public, and, because of his competitiveness and hirsuteness, Beast to his family and friends.

Theo Epstein, sitting on a cache of hitting prospects with designs to draft even more, knew his plan to rebuild the Cubs was nothing but a sleek sports car without wheels unless he came up with elite starting pitching. He had none of it in 2012, his first season with Chicago. He tried 12 starting pitchers that season, relying mostly on Jeff Samardzija, Travis Wood, Paul Maholm, Chris Volstad, Ryan Dempster, and Matt Garza. Then he found Arrieta.

The story of how his team turned the worst starting pitcher in the history of the Baltimore Orioles into a Cy Young Award winner for the Cubs is emblematic of all of the Cubs' best practices rolled into one: the shrewd evaluation of talent; the emphasis on the growth of the whole person, not just the player; and the culture of teamwork, both in the front office and at the playing level. The story begins with Epstein casting a wide net of opinion that stretched far beyond metrics.

After the 2012 season, as he does each year, Epstein took a Change of Scenery survey. He asked his 40 or so scouts and baseball operations people to submit a list of names of major and minor league players they believed would flourish with a change of scenery and why. Clashes with a manager, problems at home, an injury kept quiet, a positional logjam—anything could be holding back a player that didn't show up in traditional metrics. As the lists came in that year, one name kept turning up more than others: Jake Arrieta. The Cubs' intelligence was clear on Arrieta: he was healthy, he had an excellent work ethic, he had an elite power arm, but he was stymied in Baltimore, where he had spent six years in the organization, much of it going back and forth between the Orioles and the minors while listening to enough different pitching coaches to fill a choir. Arrieta's time with the Orioles would only worsen in 2013, which gave the Cubs the opening they needed.

JAKE ARRIETA WAS blessed with a great arm, the kind of blessing that becomes a curse when the pitcher does not deliver well enough and quickly enough, according to expectations.

"I heard from day one, even in college, 'You have the best stuff on the team. Your stuff is incredible,'" Arrieta said. "I almost got tired of hearing it."

Arrieta grew up in Plano, Texas. His father, Lou, had been an outstanding ballplayer himself, with a full ride waiting for him at the Air Force Academy. That's when he met his future wife, Lynda. Jake came along quickly when Lou was 18 and Lynda was 19. That was the end of Lou's college plans.

"My dad put it all aside and went to Dallas to drive an 18-wheeler for several years," Arrieta said.

Lou eventually took a job with his father's construction company in Dallas before becoming a senior estimator with another company. Every day when Lou came home from work, Jake would be waiting for him. Lou would grab a bucket of baseballs, they would walk across the street to a Little League field, and Lou would throw batting practice to his son until it was too dark to see his pitches.

One day Jake, a right-handed hitter, tried to pull every pitch over the leftfield fence. He constantly "stepped in the bucket," opening his front side in an exaggerated manner to try to pull the pitch. Lou told him to stop. Jake kept trying to pull home runs. So Lou threw his next pitch right at his son, and then another, and another.

"He started drilling me," Arrieta said, "and after the third or fourth time I had a few choice words for him and flipped him the bird. And he chased me around the field for like 30 minutes. I tried to tire him out until he couldn't run anymore.

"Now, being a father going to work every day and coming home tired, I know how difficult it can be to have the energy and do that two to three hours a night. I don't know how he did it. I don't. But every day I thank him for it. He coached me in every sport until I was 14. He was dedicated and allowed me to have every opportunity to play this game."

The boy noticed traits in his father that he would adopt as part of his own identity: a fierce work ethic and imposing physicality.

"I learned how to be resilient and how to be relentless in how I work from him," Arrieta said. "I can remember as a kid—I was probably 12 years old—and I always did chores with my dad, especially in the yard, mowing the lawn, raking leaves, trimming trees and bushes. We really bonded over that. One of the things I really enjoyed was taking everything out of our garage, cleaning it out, and putting everything back in nice and neat and perfect the way I saw it. As I cleaned the garage out, I would Rollerblade in the garage in circles with dumbbells in my hands for at least an hour.

"I didn't develop physically until I think my sophomore year in high school. That was something that kind of bothered me. Looking back, it was just a matter of time that I hit my growth spurt and filled out. But my interest in fitness and nutrition started when I was about 10 to 12 years old, and I slowly got into it."

As a junior at Plano East High School in 2003, Arrieta didn't pitch all that much. He was stuck behind three senior pitchers who threw in the 90s for a team that reached the regional finals. Plano East, hurt by graduations, fell the next year to 11–19. Arrieta did pitch as a senior—he also played third base—but wound up with more home runs (three) than wins (two). Arrieta was not named to the first team all-district team, nor was he named to the second team. He was listed as an honorable mention.

The Cincinnati Reds took a flier on Arrieta that year with a selection in the 31st round of the draft. He had no interest in signing.

"I wasn't ready," he said. "Both parents wanted me to go to school. The draft kind of changed my outlook a bit. In a sense I thought, maybe if I got to a JUCO for a year I'll keep developing and growing and be ready after that."

Arrieta attended Weatherford Junior College, and though he didn't have a big year statistically, his velocity climbed to the mid-90s and he earned a spot in the Texas Collegiate Summer League. One day that summer, Texas Christian University coach Jim Schlossnagle planned to scout a relief pitcher on Arrieta's team. TCU assistant coach Todd Whitting told the coach, "You don't have to get there until the fifth or sixth inning."

"If I'm going," Schlossnagle said, "I'm going to watch the whole game."

Arrieta happened to be the starting pitcher that game. Schlossnagle had never seen him pitch before. By the second inning Schlossnagle turned to Whitting and said, "Forget the reliever. Who is this Arrieta guy?"

"I'm not sure," Whitting said.

Schlossnagle immediately wanted Arrieta on his team. Even before the game was over, he approached Arrieta and spoke through a chain-link fence between the two of them.

"Listen," Schlossnagle told Arrieta, "my best pitcher just left and about 130 innings went with him. I need you to come on campus and be our Friday night starter."

Arrieta quickly agreed to attend TCU.

"I tell everybody, to this day, that's the best opportunity I've been given my entire career," he said. "For somebody like that to have the faith in me after seeing me pitch just once—I never looked back from that moment. I took that not only as an opportunity but as a wake-up call. It was an opportunity to take my career to the next level at a really prestigious private school. I didn't grow up with a lot of money. I wouldn't have been able to go to TCU. I probably would have gone to Oklahoma State or a small school, but from the first day I stepped on campus I wanted to be the best I could be academically and on the field."

Arrieta went 23–7 in his two seasons at TCU. Baltimore took him in the fifth round of the 2007 draft. Arrieta signed too late to pitch that season, but in 2008, his first pro season, he tore up the Class-A Carolina League (2.87 ERA in 20 starts) and earned an invitation to Orioles spring training camp in 2009, along with fellow pitching prospects Chris Tillman and Brian Matusz.

"I've been watching pitchers for a long time," Orioles manager Dave Trembley said then, "and I would say those three guys are as good as I have seen at any one time coming up through somebody's system."

Trembley was fired by the time Arrieta made his major league debut in 2010 under Juan Samuel, the interim manager between Trembley and Buck Showalter. Thus began four turbulent seasons for Arrieta in which he shuttled between Baltimore and the minor leagues, worked with four different pitching coaches in the majors and minors (Rick Kranitz, Mark Connor, Rick Adair, and Rick Petersen) and constantly tweaked his mechanics to try to please whatever coach he worked with at the time.

The relationship with Adair, who took over for Connor midway through the 2011 season as Orioles pitching coach, never clicked. At the time Adair took over, Arrieta pitched with his natural cross-fire style—stepping toward the right-hand batter's box and throwing across his body—from the first base side of the rubber and with his hands at his belt to start his delivery. A month later he was pitching from the middle of the rubber and swinging his hands over his head. A few months after that, the Orioles banned pitchers in their organization from using the cutter, one of Arrieta's best pitches, out of fear it sapped fastball velocity.

By the next April, Arrieta still pitched from the middle of the rubber, but his hands were back at his belt. By May he was back on the first base side of the rubber. By September he had trimmed his windup to a modified stretch position. By the next year he was back to the middle of the rubber with a huge change: Adair took away his cross-fire step in favor of having him stride directly to the plate. The Orioles wanted Arrieta to be a conventional four-seam fastball/overhand curveball pitcher. Over the two calendar years, trying to be that pitcher under Adair, Arrieta went 6–16 with a 6.30 ERA.

"There were so many things in Baltimore not many people know about," Arrieta said. "I had struggles with my pitching coach. A lot of guys did. We got to a point—three or four guys, Tillman, Matusz, [Zach] Britton—that guys were just really uncomfortable in their own skin at the time, trying to be the guys they weren't. You can attest how difficult it is to try to reinvent your mechanics against the best competition in the world.

"I feel like I was playing a tug-of-war, a constant, continuous tug-of-war, trying to make the adjustments I was being told to and knowing in the back of my mind I can do things differently and be better than what I was showcasing on the field. It was such a tremendous struggle for me because, as a second- and third-year player, you want to be coachable. I knew I got [to the majors] for a reason and I was confused about why I was changing that now. You feel at that moment everybody has your best interest in mind, but you come to find out that's not necessarily the case."

So lost was Arrieta that on one night, June 3, 2012, in St. Petersburg, he found himself back in the clubhouse after getting knocked out in the fifth inning by Tampa Bay and he could not recall how it happened. All he could remember was how he was consumed by thoughts about his mechanics on the mound. *Am I balanced? Is my front side where it needs to be? Is my landing spot good?* The actual game was a blur. He had to look at the video the next day to know how he gave up four runs.

"And I was looking at somebody who wasn't myself," he said.

The low point was yet to come. That happened in June 2013. Arrieta was 27 years old and banished to Triple-A Norfolk. His ERA in seven starts for the Orioles that year was 7.32, and for his Orioles career it was 5.46, the worst for any pitcher with 60 starts since the franchise moved to Baltimore from St. Louis in 1954.

When the Orioles demoted Arrieta to the minors that year, Showalter said, "I can't sit here and tell you that anything going on there physically is going to be a big difference. Most of us are looking at how we're failing him."

So down was Arrieta while in Norfolk that he told his wife he was about ready to quit baseball.

"I'm thinking about not playing any more after this season," he told her. "I'm close to my business degree from TCU. I'm really good with people. I can easily go into business."

Said Arrieta, "But then the next hour I'd go, 'How crazy an idea is that that I would stop playing this game that I love so quickly?' But those really are some of the thoughts lots of players go through when they get adversity on a consistent basis. It was difficult to fail on such a frequent basis. It became hard.

"They wanted me to throw in a direct line to the plate. So if 80 percent of left-handed pitchers throw across their body, what's the difference for a right-hander? There is none. People don't have answers for that. I developed the way I threw. I look at pictures when I'm 10 years old, pitching off a mound, and I threw across my body slightly."

As the Cubs' good fortune would have it, the Orioles established themselves as a contender in 2013 and Baltimore general manager

Dan Duquette needed a veteran starting pitcher to chase down Boston in the American League East. By late June, Duquette opened trade discussions with Chicago general manager Jed Hoyer about Cubs right-hander Scott Feldman. Epstein and Hoyer had signed Feldman straight out of the bargain bin of free agents just seven months earlier: it took only a one-year, $6 million contract to get a 29-year-old pitcher who was 6–11 with a 5.09 ERA the previous season. Now the Orioles were knocking loudly on the Cubs' door ready to give up talent to get him. Feldman was simply a placeholder for Chicago. He wasn't part of the rebuild, not at his age and not when he was eligible to leave as a free agent after that season.

Hoyer remembered the Change of Scenery survey. He asked Duquette right away for Arrieta in return for Feldman. Duquette, knowing how Arrieta never flourished in the Baltimore system, quickly agreed. Hoyer was taken aback a bit by how quickly the deal seemed to be coming together. Most trade talks are much more rigorous tugs-of-war to try to even out the value going back and forth. Sensing more room to negotiate, Hoyer decided to make a play for another hidden power arm, reliever Pedro Strop, a right-hander with a 97-mph sinker who, like Arrieta, was underachieving with an ERA north of seven.

Duquette balked. He told Hoyer he would need another player from him to make such a deal work. Talks hit a snag. Hoyer grew nervous. He desperately wanted Arrieta and at one point virtually had him in hand, but by pushing for Strop he risked overplaying his hand and losing Arrieta. Duquette might easily move on to another club to find the veteran starter he wanted. To get the deal back on track, Hoyer offered up Steve Clevenger, a 27-year-old backup catcher who had hit .199 for the Cubs over parts of three seasons. The sweetener to adding Clevenger was that the catcher grew up in Baltimore.

On July 3, 2013, the clubs agreed to the deal. Epstein and Hoyer had just traded three months of control of a journeyman pitcher

(Feldman) and a 27-year-old backup catcher (Clevenger) for nine years of combined service for two young pitchers with mid-90s velocity. Duquette called Arrieta in Norfolk that night to give him the news.

"We appreciate everything you've done in an Orioles uniform," Duquette told him. "We just think it's appropriate to move on."

"Thank you," Arrieta responded. "I enjoyed my time in Baltimore."

"I really did," Arrieta said in hindsight. "I learned so much. I was a young, dumb kid coming to the big leagues and had to be whipped into shape from time to time. It got me to this point. I'm better for it. I'm stronger for it."

Soon he heard from the Cubs. The first to call was Chris Bosio, the Cubs' pitching coach and a former right-handed pitcher who lasted 11 years in the majors with a cross-fire delivery.

"Look, man, I've been through a lot," Arrieta told him. "All I want to do is come over there and be myself and be a winner. That's the guy I was my whole life, and now I want to put it on display for a new organization."

"Jake," Bosio said, "we know what kind of stuff you have. We want you to come over here and be yourself."

The Cubs assigned Arrieta to Triple-A Iowa. Bosio monitored his starts by reading scouting reports and watching video.

"He was having a really hard time with pitch efficiency," Bosio said. "His stuff was nasty, and he wasn't getting hit, but he was throwing like 110 pitches in five innings. And I was getting the feedback from [manager] Marty Pevey and Mike Mason, who was the pitching coach. I said 'Listen, just try to get him more aggressive right now. There's nothing I can do over the phone.' But I know what I saw on the videotape and it was so exciting.

"As soon as we saw his stuff, I was like, 'Theo, please God, get him here! Get him here!' Then I think he had four or five starts there and Theo texted me and said, 'We're going to bring Arrieta up.' I was like, 'Yes!' I couldn't wait. I knew where we were going to go with him. For selfish reasons I wanted to work with him, because I knew he could help the club. The first thing I found out was he didn't have any warm-up routine."

Pitchers are classified in two categories: right-handed and left-handed. But all of them could be split into two camps that are less obvious to the casual fan: their dominant side of the plate. Some pitchers naturally control the baseball to their arm side of the plate and others control it naturally to the glove side of the plate. For instance, former pitcher Tim Hudson, a right-hander, worked the baseball naturally to his arm side with sinkers and splits. He had to learn how to work it to his glove side with sliders. Cubs left-handed pitcher Jon Lester and San Francisco left-handed pitcher Madison Bumgarner have a natural ability to feed the ball to spots on their glove side—that is, on the inside corner to right-handed hitters. Both do so with fastballs and cutters. But each of them reached a higher level of success when they learned how to command the baseball to their arm side—fastballs and breaking balls.

A champion chess player commands the middle of the board. Pitching is the opposite of chess. It's about keeping the baseball out of the middle. The areas to get weak contact with the bat or none at all are on the edges of the plate. A baseball is slightly less than three inches in diameter. When you think about how a pitcher can find his greatest success, imagine two "lanes" that are about only six inches wide: the width of two baseballs—one baseball just inside the vertical edge of the strike zone and one just outside it—on each side of the plate.

When Bosio watched Arrieta throw, he knew he had a glove side–dominant pitcher. Arrieta owned only one of the two six-inch lanes. With the twisting action of his torso, which sometimes caused his head to follow in the same direction, Arrieta easily "pulled" pitches to the glove side of the plate. He was throwing 93 mph with cutting action down and away to right-handers.

"His stuff was absolutely filthy," Bosio said.

But there was a problem. Arrieta's heavy rotational action caused him inconsistency. His stuff may have been filthy, but he lacked control over it.

So Bosio had an idea. At the start of every warm-up Bosio would have Arrieta emphasize throwing the ball to his arm side of the plate. The trick would be to calm the rotational torque of his body without losing it altogether and especially to quiet his head, making sure it stayed in line with the plate rather than tilting toward the glove side.

"As soon as he started doing it, we started to see more consistency," Bosio said, "and once he found that consistency the confidence started growing."

The Orioles wanted Arrieta to throw conventionally with a neutral stride. That is, if you imagine the outline of the pitching mound as a giant clock, with 12 o'clock directly in front of the pitcher, they wanted Arrieta to step with his left foot toward the 12. Arrieta, however, found it more natural to stride toward 1 o'clock. Once his front foot landed, his torso twisted over his front leg, creating that cross-fire action. Bosio didn't want to take away Arrieta's natural cross-fire delivery and he didn't want to take away his cutter. He only wanted to refine his approach.

"I threw across my body," Bosio said. "I didn't see anything wrong with it. He's a one o'clock, front side, toe-down guy. So when I saw it, I was like, 'Fine. I don't see anything wrong with it.' I was that kind of guy. I was basically a two-pitch guy: fastball and slider. Once we started flipping his thoughts to more arm side, everything started to quiet down."

Once Bosio had success emphasizing the arm-side work, he then introduced a visual reminder to Arrieta's warm-up routine. After Arrieta made four or five pitches, Bosio would draw a rectangle in the dirt of the mound around the footprints from his left spike. He also would draw a circle around the marks left by the ball of his right foot. When Arrieta first starting throwing for Bosio, the rectangle and the circle were fairly large, to accommodate the variations in where his feet landed.

"At end of 2013," Arrieta said, "they started to tighten up pretty good. Then in 2014 you basically had a rectangle that was exactly around my foot and a tiny little circle where my toe hit. I landed square in a really good spot. I wasn't falling to first base or falling toward third base. I tell people, 'If you're falling off to the first base side, where is the ball going to go?' You fall this way the ball is probably going to run or tail.

"That's why Pilates is so important to me: body control. Because I can get into positions and I can even do it with my eyes closed and land square almost every time."

In nine starts for the Cubs in 2013, Arrieta was 4–2, pitched to a 3.66 ERA, and held opposing hitters to a .185 batting average. Never did he have a nine-start stretch quite like that in Baltimore.

"It was honestly like starting from scratch," he said. "I knew I was going to get to Chicago and not be judged based on what I did in the past. I was going to get a fresh start.

"I was able to come here and not hold anything back or feel like I was judged. People had lost so much faith in me in Baltimore, and rightfully so. I didn't pitch well. I had a really short leash, and that's what happens. I knew that was not the guy that I was. And I was ready to change that. I was letting it out as hard as I possibly could in a controlled way—across my body. I felt strong. I felt explosive. I didn't feel limited. I started to throw my cutter in hitter-friendly counts and get outs. I pitched differently with my fastball. I was just being comfortable with who I was. I pitched two years not being comfortable with anything I was doing. I was trying to be somebody else."

Arrieta began to fully flower in 2014. He made a career-high 25 starts and went 10–5 with a 2.53 ERA. It was an impressive season, but nothing like the historic one he crafted the following year. In 2015 Arrieta posted a 1.77 ERA while holding hitters to a .185 batting average. Since the mound was lowered after Bob Gibson's 1.12 ERA in 1968, only Arrieta and Pedro Martinez of the 2000 Red Sox have dominated hitters with an ERA and batting average that low. His second half was astonishing: a record-low 0.75 ERA in 15 starts.

After mid-July more men ran for president of the United States than scored an earned run off Arrieta (nine).

Flourishing in the Cubs' culture of individualism for the betterment of the team, Arrieta unlocked the very best from his gifted right arm. With Chicago he learned how to combine extreme velocity and extreme spin with exceptional control.

"That's when I was 'Okay, I trust how much my ball moves,'" he said. "I know generally how much it's going to move, and I can account for that. I can throw it at you this far off the plate and end up black or outer third. And that's where I kind of went to the next level. I knew what all my pitches were doing and I knew how to account for that.

"Even in 2014 I didn't have the ability to do that. I would go fastball away and have the catcher sit in that exact spot, and how many times does the ball wind up exactly where you want it? Especially sinking fastball or the slider. So that was something I really put a lot of time and effort in—set up middle of the plate, and let's just be down. Down with everything: cutter, slider, fastball, it doesn't matter."

Arrieta threw a career-high 229 innings in the 2015 regular season. He threw a five-hit shutout in the wild card game at Pittsburgh. He threw $5\frac{2}{3}$ innings to beat St. Louis in Game 3 of the NLDS, but he knew even in the days leading up to that game he wasn't right. Actually, he felt it in the final innings against Pittsburgh. His pitches didn't have the same explosiveness. His arm didn't have the same snap.

The Mets swept the Cubs in the NLCS. Arrieta lost Game 2. He allowed four runs in five innings in one of his worst games of the season. He finished the year with $248\frac{2}{3}$ innings.

"I felt like I didn't have the explosive life at the very end," he said. "I felt strong throughout, and I was able to spin the ball, but it was a feeling I didn't have all year."

When Arrieta showed up for spring training in 2016, Maddon told him he would not work him as hard as he had in 2015. The manager told him, "You might not like me for it, but if we have a lead I'm not going to let you finish the game or even go past the seventh inning." The message was clear: this year the Cubs would be budgeting bullets to last through a seven-month season. They planned for a deep run in October, and Maddon wanted Arrieta to have strength in reserve for that month this time around.

True to his word, Maddon pushed Arrieta beyond the seventh inning only five times in 2016—half as many times as he had in 2015. Thanks to Chicago sprinting to a big early lead in the standings—they owned a 10-game lead after just 56 games—Maddon enjoyed the luxury of giving him extra rest between starts 19 times, two more times than the previous year. He cut Arrieta's innings by 31⅔ and his pitches by 314.

Alas, Arrieta's 2015 season had been so sublime—the true height of his powers—that even with Maddon easing his burden he was fated to fall short of such excellence. By any other measure, Arrieta pitched well in 2016. His regular-season numbers (18–8, 3.10 ERA, 190 strikeouts) bore resemblance to the numbers that won the Cy Young Award for Brandon Webb just 10 years earlier (16–8, 3.10, 178).

The worst starting pitcher in Baltimore Orioles history also continued to place himself among the best starting pitchers in Chicago Cubs history. There have been 279 pitchers in the live ball era (since 1920) who have started as few as five games for the Cubs. Arrieta has the lowest ERA among them all (2.52). His .720 winning percentage is the best in franchise history for all those pitchers who started more than 60 times for the Cubs.

Something was missing, however, in 2016: the same laserlike command of his cutter. The pitch is one of the great wonders in baseball, one that defies easy classification. Arrieta can change the velocity on the pitch from as slow as 84 miles per hour, when it has a bigger break and more resembles a slider, to 93 miles per hour, when it resembles a fastball with a bad attitude, darting away from a hitter's barrel in the last five feet before the plate.

Though the pitch appears violent in its speed and spin, Arrieta does not torque his wrist when he throws it. He takes an off-center grip on the baseball—looking from behind on release, his pointer and middle fingers are slightly on the eastern hemisphere on the baseball—and throws it like a fastball with one major thought upon release: to get his middle finger on the front side of the baseball, which emphasizes extension and a loose wrist. If he wants to slow down the pitch to create a bigger angle of break, he simply offsets his fingers slightly more. Everything else about how he throws it remains exactly the same.

In 2015 Arrieta threw 969 cutter/sliders that held hitters to a .188 batting average. In 2016, after seeing so many of them, hitters adjusted to that pitch. Realizing that the Arrieta cutter was both hard to hit and often destined to wind up outside the strike zone with its late movement, they more often passed on swinging at it. And the more they took the pitch for a ball (35 percent of the time in 2016, up from 30 percent in 2015), the less Arrieta threw it. He threw only 556 cutter/sliders in the regular season, and the batting average against it rose to .221.

Force, in overabundance, is the enemy of artistry. When the level of effort begins to redline, whether flooring a four-cylinder engine, swinging for the fences, or reaching back for extra velocity, the results tend to worsen. As Arrieta's cutter elicited fewer swings and fewer strikes, he tried even harder to get the results he had obtained in 2015. And the more force he applied, the worse the pitch became.

The increased effort prompted two mechanical problems. It caused Arrieta to swing his arm farther behind him, which began to bring back the overrotational problem he endured in Baltimore. It also caused his body to jump more quickly toward the hitter, causing his arm to lag behind him, which resulted in a duller, flatter cutter. Maddon had talked to him late in the year about adjusting his prepitch setup to get himself into better position.

By the time the World Series began, however, Arrieta believed he had rediscovered some of the magic in his signature pitch.

"I'm so close," he said on the eve of the World Series. "I know what I have to do. If I just stay on my back leg a little longer—just get a little deeper into my back leg over the rubber—I'll be on time. That's the whole key. Then I can get to here"—he displayed that extended release point, with his middle finger just coming over the front of the baseball—"on time."

Timing, as historians, comedians, and pitching coaches like to say, is everything. Once he stopped forcing it, Arrieta rediscovered the magic. He would throw 41 cutter/sliders in his two World Series starts. The Indians would get only one hit off the pitch. The Beast would be unbeatable.

CHAPTER 9

THE RECRUIT

Money and hope. The pockets of Theo Epstein overflowed with both resources as he sat across a conference table from free agent pitcher Jon Lester and his wife, Farrah, on November 18, 2014, in the "recruiting room" at the team's offices on North Clark Street in Chicago. The wood-paneled room was decorated with memorabilia and historical Cubs photographs. What Epstein could not offer Lester was on-field success in his time as president of the Cubs. In three years running the team, Epstein fielded teams that lost 289 games and finished a combined 84 games out of first place. Without success, and with a rebuilding plan that now banked entirely on somehow getting two front-of-the-rotation pitchers, Epstein had to dig deep into his reservoirs of money and hope. The meeting would last all day.

"You," Epstein told Lester, "are a key piece to everything we are doing here. You can be for us what Curt Schilling was for us in Boston in 2004."

The Cubs' recruitment of Lester officially began two weeks earlier with the first day of free agency. An overnight package arrived at the suburban Atlanta home of the Lesters and their two sons, Hudson, then 4, and Walker, then 14 months old. Inside was a boatload of Cubs swag, including Cubs hats and shirts in camouflage style, and bottles of fine wine. The contents indicated how well Epstein and general manager Jed Hoyer already knew Lester, and his tastes for hunting and wine, from their eight years together with the Red Sox.

The key item in the box, however, was a 15-minute DVD. Lester popped it into his DVD player and pushed "play." Epstein had commissioned the DVD to explain why the Cubs were close to winning and why Chicago was a great place to live and play. Former Cubs pitchers Kerry Wood and Ryan Dempster, both of whom had become advisors to Epstein, were among those who gave a players' perspective on the unique opportunities of playing for the Cubs. The recruitment video was slickly produced, never more so than in its concluding segment.

Epstein had hired special-effects masters from Hollywood and producers from the gaming industry to make a lifelike movie of the Cubs hosting and winning the World Series. He didn't want Lester to just imagine what it would be like to win the World Series in a Cubs uniform, he also wanted him to *see* what it would look like.

The movie showed the World Series logo on the iconic hand-operated scoreboard in centerfield at century-old Wrigley Field. It cut to a shot of the ballpark's famous art deco marquee that faced the corner of Addison and Clark. Across the electronic message board part of the marquee scrolled this message: "Cubs vs. Yankees. Game 7. Lester vs. Pineda."

Then, with an appropriately epic orchestral soundtrack playing over it, and from a vantage point at the top of the third-base grandstand, the movie showed Lester on the mound getting the last out of the World Series, the Cubs rushing to dogpile in the middle of the field, and "live" news reports from the mass jubilation on Waveland Avenue.

When Lester saw Epstein in person at the November 18 meeting, he complimented him on the production of the DVD, telling him, "That was a bad-ass video."

Epstein's next mission was to hyper-target his sales pitch to Jon and Farrah. They got up from the conference table and walked into an adjoining room. In the middle of the room on a large table, and occupying most of the room's space, was a huge architectural model of a fully renovated Wrigley Field. Epstein explained what the Cubs were calling "The 1060 Project," which borrowed from the ballpark's Addison Street address and would include $575 million worth of renovations over four off-seasons, the first of which was about to begin. The Cubs' home clubhouse and training facilities were among the worst and most cramped in all of baseball, and would not be remediated until after the 2015 season. But Epstein even managed to use the outdated quarters as a selling point.

"It's good that you'll have the old facilities for a year," Epstein said. "You'll get to appreciate the history, but in another year you will truly appreciate how far we've come."

Then a Cubs community relations staff member picked up the presentation, emphasizing how the Cubs would get behind the Lesters' Never Quit Foundation, which is dedicated to fighting pediatric cancer, how the Cubs fly the fewest miles in baseball over the course of a regular season, and how a home schedule heavily tilted toward day games would allow the Lesters to have breakfast with their kids and tuck them in at night on 63 game days. The Lesters heard about the designs of a new family room at Wrigley Field, about dedicated security personnel in the family section of the ballpark, and how a doctor, a nurse, and security personnel would be on round-the-clock call to families whenever the team was on the road. Team owner Tom Ricketts stopped by and engaged in a long discussion with Lester about hunting.

For their part, Epstein and Hoyer sold Lester on the young talent in the Chicago system. They specifically mentioned first baseman Anthony Rizzo; infielders Starlin Castro, Kris Bryant, Javier Baez, and Addison Russell; and catcher Kyle Schwarber.

The obvious omissions from such a list, however, were the names of talented young pitchers. But Epstein and Hoyer did tell Lester he was just the first of two planned big-time additions to the rotation. Once the Cubs signed him, they told Lester, they would still have enough money to trade for another ace-level pitcher—they had their eye on Noah Syndergaard in the New York Mets' system—or acquire one from what looked like a blockbuster class of free agents the next winter, including David Price, Jordan Zimmermann, Johnny Cueto, and Jeff Samardzija.

That's when Epstein laid out the time line. The meeting with Lester took place 20 days after the surprising Kansas City Royals lost Game 7 of the World Series to the San Francisco Giants. The Royals punched their postseason ticket as an 89-win wild card team (they famously rallied against Lester and the Oakland Athletics to win that wild card game) after a 14-win improvement in 2013.

"We think we're getting somewhere," Epstein told Lester. "If you come here, in 2015 we have a legitimate chance to be the 2014 Royals. We should contend for the second wild card, and if things break just right, we could do some special things. We could also go in the other direction. We could crumble under the weight of relying on so many young players. But I don't see that with this group."

He told Lester the window was just beginning to open for the Cubs—that the team could contend for multiple championships over the next decade.

"We could present it in forceful, compelling terms because we believed it," Epstein recalled. "We really believed in the talent and the character of this group. We could tell him that the Bryants, the Russells, the Schwarbers—these guys had the kind of makeup that was off the charts. We told him that we totally trusted in the ceiling and the character of these players and that this was the nucleus of a championship club."

Lester would later say, "You never know when prospects work out and I know sometimes the free agents you want to go after sign extensions. So those plans don't always work. But I believed in the core and the plans they have for more additions.

"I don't really want to say it was a sales job, because I really believe what they believe, that this could be the next dynasty over the next six, seven, eight, nine years. That interested me. Having that comfort with Theo and Jed was important. I think I'm pretty good at knowing when it's somebody you can believe or when you can see through the BS. I felt like there was no BS. This wasn't a used car salesman sitting there trying to sell you something."

Epstein ran Lester through statistical projection models and scouting reports on the young players in his system.

Said Lester, "It didn't take much for him to convince me about these young guys. He sat there and gave me highlight after highlight and number after number on these guys and what they projected them to do and what position they wanted them to play. I think the biggest thing that sold me, especially on not only these young guys, but the whole organization, was just how arrogant he was about it, and I mean that in a good way. He was very confident in what he had done to this point or to that point to get this team to the next step, and I thought that was the most impressive part. Just how confident he was in these guys because these guys were not going to be failures.

"They weren't going to be a bust when the scouting report gets out and going to get exposed and all that stuff. Now, getting to play with these guys, you really understand what he saw."

Lester would later tell Epstein, "That day of the presentations was a home run. That's when we started envisioning ourselves as Cubs."

The meeting was all about hope. Nobody said anything about money. That would happen the next day.

The Cubs had money to spend on Lester because they had missed out on signing Japanese free agent pitcher Masahiro Tanaka 10 months earlier. Tanaka hit free agency after a 24–0 season for the Rakuten Golden Eagles. Interested teams would have to pay a $20 million posting fee to his former club and win a bidding war to gain Tanaka's services. In January 2014, Tanaka's agent, Casey Close, rented the Beverly Hills home of one of his colleagues, a basketball agent, to host two "recruiting days" for Tanaka. Representatives from

10 teams, waiting in black SUVs on the street for their one-hour turn over the two days, literally lined up in America's leading neighborhood of $10 million homes to convince a 25-year-old pitcher, fresh off a flight from Japan and eating sushi on a couch inside one of the mansions, to take nine digits worth of their money.

Those 10 teams were not scared off by the obvious risks: that Tanaka had never thrown a pitch in the major leagues, that since he was a teenager his arm had endured a massive workload these same decision makers believe would wreck their own pitchers, and that the transition from playing baseball in Japan to playing in the United States was fraught with competitive and cultural differences that threatened the entire investment. The Yankees, Rangers, Astros, White Sox, Dodgers, Cubs, and Diamondbacks were among the teams that lined up.

"It was like *The Dating Game*," said Kevin Towers, the Arizona general manager at the time. "First of all, it was a beautiful home. We were all waiting. You see all these cars parked up the street. And he's sitting there on the couch and then it's like, 'Now it's bachelor number one!' You come down and try to sell yourself, your entire organization, in 15 minutes. You have a chance to make that first impression."

The Yankees sent eight people to Beverly Hills. They brought a video presentation that included a recruiting pitch from former Yankees outfielder Hideki Matsui and a tour of Yankee Stadium done in the style of MTV's *Cribs*. Twelve days later, Tanaka took the Yankees' money: $155 million over seven years. With the $20 million posting fee folded in, their $175 million investment represented the second largest bet ever made on a pitcher at the time, trailing only the $180 million extension Detroit handed Justin Verlander. Rather than spend the money they had bid for Tanaka that winter, Epstein and Hoyer put it back in their pockets.

"Missing on Tanaka allowed us to do Lester," Epstein said. "When we missed on Tanaka, rather than spend the money in the 2014 budget we set it aside. We rat-holed it and didn't spend the $25 million [average annual value]. We said, 'That will be a big part in pursuing a free agent.' That became the signing bonus for Jon."

The key question for Epstein was this: If Tanaka at age 25 was worth $155 million over seven years, how much money and how many years would he pay for Lester, who would pitch in 2015 at age 31?

The clues began in spring training of 2014, when the Boston Red Sox opened negotiations on an extension for Lester at four years and $70 million. The industry generally regarded that opening salvo as a lowball offer, particularly because Philadelphia had given left-handed ace Cliff Lee five years and $120 million four years earlier. If Boston regarded the offer simply as a start to lengthy back-and-forth negotiations, it was a miscalculation, because Lester, famously stubborn in how he pitches and approaches the game, told them he would not negotiate once the regular season began. Boston simply didn't have the time to make up the chasm between its opening offer and Lester's market value.

It didn't help matters, either, when Red Sox principal owner John Henry expressed general agreement with a report that long-term contracts for pitchers in their 30s were bad investments. Boston wound up trading Lester to Oakland midway through the season, with designs on making a run at him after the season, though by then they had lost the advantage of incumbency and would have to line up with all others interested in his services.

The day after Epstein and Hoyer made their presentation to Lester, they put together a formal offer: $130 million over six years. How could they justify paying Lester through age 36 when the landscape was filled with bad investments on older pitchers?

"Contracts of this size for pitchers are a risk regardless of age, especially for starting pitchers in their 30s," Epstein acknowledged at the time. "There's no way around that. But I don't believe that means you never do them. You go in with eyes wide open. [One] of our primary goals was to build an organization that was so healthy that you don't need to go into free agency very often, and healthy enough so you can afford to fail in free agency. You can't sign a free agent if you can't recover if you get little or no production.

"The only reason we can sign a contract like this is because of the potential impact position players we have in the organization. A good deal of our strategy is accumulating impact position players, and when the time is right to go out and get the impact pitching guys to go along with them.

"For three years we've slowly been building up a stable of position players and we knew sometime over the next 15 months we were going to add an impact pitcher or two from outside the organization, one through free agency and probably one through trade.

"It's such a risky thing, but sooner or later you have to put your trust in someone. And when you're a last-place team pursuing and attracting free agents, the free agents have to put their trust in you. We felt a lot better knowing the player. We've known Jon Lester since he was 18 years old. We studied his mechanics inside out.

"We believe nobody has perfect mechanics, but, according to the model we hold up when we send pitchers to biomechanical labs, his mechanics rate higher than anybody we've seen. Does that fully mitigate the risks? No, but it helps. And it helps knowing he's been on a state-of-the-art shoulder [conditioning] program since he was 18, it helps knowing the family and the workload and what makes him tick. All that stuff helps. They are small factors in mitigating the risk. He has a tremendous pitcher's body with ideal mechanics, he wasn't abused as an amateur as a pitcher because of growing up in cold weather, and he has a very strong and undamaged shoulder."

Epstein also knew that in Boston in 2009 he had ordered four MRIs of Lester's shoulder before giving him a five-year extension. Those MRIs came back impressively clean. The two of them had a long shared history. Epstein and Lester had joined the Boston organization just three months apart a dozen years earlier.

In January 2002, Henry, Tom Werner, and Larry Lucchino agreed to join forces to purchase the Red Sox. One month later Henry divested himself of the Florida Marlins by selling them to Montreal

Expos owner Jeffrey Loria, who in turn sold the Expos to the 29 other owners. Loria replaced many of the Marlins scouts and executives with the people who had worked for him in Montreal, leaving many of the former Marlins people to scatter to the wind. In March, many of them reunited with Henry in Boston, including evaluators David Chadd, Ray Crone, and David Finley, all of whom had been keeping an eye on a pitcher from Bellarmine Prep in Tacoma, Jon Lester. Epstein arrived in Boston from San Diego that same month as an assistant general manager. One of his duties was to assist with the draft.

Lester, who was throwing between 89 and 93 mph when his senior season began, looked like a first-round pick. By midseason, however, his velocity began to drop. When the Major League Scouting Bureau paid a visit to watch him pitch, Lester topped out at 88 mph. When that video circulated, Lester's stock sank. But Chadd, Crone, Finley, and Gary Rajsich, the Boston area scout, all had seen Lester on his best days, and they knew that a high school pitcher who also played another position (outfield) and who also played other sports (basketball and soccer) might typically hit a dead-arm period during the season. They were unbowed by the Scouting Bureau report.

That June, the first draft for Epstein with Boston, the Red Sox did not have a pick until number 57, in the second round. Much to their good fortune, Lester slipped to them. They signed him for $1 million.

Four years later, on June 10, 2006, Lester made his major league debut. He was spectacular right from the start. Lester, then just 22 years old, went 5–0 with a 2.38 ERA in his first eight starts. But then he hit a rough patch. His back began to ache. On August 18, while Lester was driving to Fenway Park for a start against the Yankees, a car rear-ended his vehicle. He gave up seven runs that night before getting knocked out in the fourth inning. His back grew worse. He lasted just five innings in his next start, giving up three runs against the Angels in Anaheim, after which he flew to Seattle to see his doctor about his back.

After that exam, Henry arranged for a private jet to take Lester back to Boston for more exams. It wasn't simply about his back any longer. On Thursday, August 31, the Red Sox announced that Lester had been admitted to Massachusetts General Hospital with enlarged lymph nodes. The next day the club announced that he was diagnosed with a rare form of non-Hodgkin's lymphoma, a blood cancer, and would immediately begin treatment. They'd found it early. In late November 2006 he was declared cancer free.

Lester spent the first half of the 2007 season in the minor leagues, regaining his strength and his form. He earned a second-half promotion, and was the winning pitcher in the clinching game of the 2007 World Series—just 13 months after his cancer diagnosis.

After that, and up to his free agency, Lester proved to be one of the best and most reliable pitchers in baseball. From 2008 through 2014, Lester averaged 15 wins and $207\frac{1}{3}$ innings, ranking fourth and sixth among all pitchers over those years in those respective categories. He kept up his velocity with his clean mechanics. In those years Lester's fastball maintained an average velocity in the narrow range of 93.1 to 94.7 mph.

Meanwhile, while trying to sign Lester, Epstein and Hoyer were running concurrent negotiations with a soon-to-be-38-year-old backup catcher who hit .184 in 2014 while starting only 47 games, 18 of them with Lester on the mound for Boston. David Ross, despite his modest statistics, was a free agent in demand because of his reputation as an excellent receiver with impressive leadership skills. For anyone interested in signing Lester, Ross had the added benefit of having established himself as the left-hander's personal catcher.

What became one of the most renowned pitcher-catcher relationships in baseball began in earnest on September 3, 2013, in Boston. The first-place Red Sox began play that night with a $5\frac{1}{2}$-game lead in the AL East, though they had been shut out the previous night by Detroit, the AL Central leaders. Lester had thrown much of that season to catcher Jarrod Saltalamacchia. Ross had missed much of the season with complications from concussions, which sometimes left him in such dark moods that he would find himself snapping at other people while driving with his wife and kids in the car. Manager John Farrell that night put Ross behind the plate for what was only his fourth start in 13 games since coming back. The fun started when Ross and Lester began going over the scouting report on Detroit.

"We all have different days," Lester said. "We all have good days, we all have bad days. You're in a good mood, you're in a bad mood, whatever. He was in one of those David Ross bad moods and we went over the report and it was like, 'This guy, he's got it. He's got it under control.' I can just sit back and just see what he wants and I'll throw it, you know what I mean? So it just so happened we had a good start."

Lester and Ross combined for seven innings with one run allowed. Boston won, 2–1. Still, Farrell continued to mix Saltalamacchia and Ross behind the plate for Lester's starts. It wasn't until the American League Championship Series that year that Farrell fully committed to Ross as Lester's personal catcher. The results were stunning. Starting with the September 3 game against Detroit and until his trade to Oakland, Lester went 15–5 with a 1.99 ERA in the 25 games Ross caught him.

Speaking about Ross's thoroughness and intensity, Lester said, "Going into the [2013] postseason, I just felt like that wore off on a lot of our pitchers. That intensity, and where he wanted the ball, and he expects so much out of you that you want to almost do more sometimes to kind of get that approval-from-your-dad type thing. And it just evolved from there."

Epstein put in an early call to Ross when the free agent period began after the 2014 season. He told Ross he was trying to sign Lester.

"We definitely have interest in you, Lester or no Lester," Epstein told Ross. "We're going for it. If we get Jon, we're definitely going for it. If we don't get Jon, we'll wait one more year to go for it. We'll be 80 percent in this year and with one more off-season we'll be all-in."

The Red Sox wanted to keep Ross. The Padres made a strong push for him. Meanwhile, Epstein arranged for Ross to get his personalized version of the Cubs' recruitment video. In that one, the public address announcer at Wrigley Field announced his name for his turn at bat in the World Series.

"I got chills watching it," Ross said. "Theo laid out the plan to me. When Theo started talking to me, I started thinking, *What if I was on the team that won the Holy Grail of championships?* If you win that, you're set for life. You sign autographs the rest of your life, like guys like [Kevin] Millar and [David] Ortiz with the '04 Red Sox.

"If you could be a part of all that, why wouldn't you try? If you really want to compete at the highest level, that's the biggest stage. That's what was calling me. I'm a guy that lays out the pros and the cons, but when it came to which way my heart was going, it kept pulling me to Chicago."

Ross would have to wait. Lester was the Cubs' priority. Epstein and Hoyer moved quickly with their November 19 offer to Lester, and soon thereafter bumped it from $130 million to $150 million, "hoping for an impulse buy," as Epstein put it. Even so, the pitcher's representatives, Sam and Seth Levinson, formulated their own game plan. They wanted to slow-track negotiations so that Lester remained in play until the winter meetings in early December, when an auction atmosphere can take root while teams gather under one roof for the equivalent of baseball's annual convention.

Other teams began to jump in. On December 1, Lester's doorbell rang. He opened the door and heard the man standing there say, "Hi, I'm Buster Posey, and I want to be your catcher for the next six years." Posey, the San Francisco Giants catcher, had driven three hours from his Georgia home. He was accompanied by Giants president Larry Baer, general manager Brian Sabean, and assistant general manager Bobby Evans. The Giants had just won their third World Series title in five seasons.

Four days later, there was another ring of the doorbell. It was John Henry paying Lester a visit from Boston.

The winter meetings began three days after that, on December 8. The Levinsons told all teams to bring their best offers. The Red Sox came in at $135 million over six years. The Giants were close to $150 million over six years, and showed some appetite for a seventh year. The Cubs were at $150 million over six years with a seventh-year option. The mutual option would vest if Lester threw 200 innings in the sixth year or 400 innings over the fifth and sixth years combined. The Levinson brothers locked in on negotiations with the Cubs late into the night. They grinded on Epstein for more money. By four in the morning, they had extracted another $5 million, in addition to perks such as a full no-trade clause, a suite on the road rather than a standard hotel room, and 25 hours of private jet travel each year of the contract.

They called it a night with the framework of a $155 million deal in place. The Cubs had separated themselves from the pack with money, after having started the process already in a unique spot. The Red Sox and Giants had won five of the previous eight world championships, with Lester earning rings with the 2007 and 2013 Red Sox. In a way, he was in a similar spot to the one Epstein had been in three years earlier: whatever good happened again in Boston, or whatever he added in San Francisco, would be only the repetition of success. And whatever failure might occur in those places would fade the glory of what had been accomplished. Chicago offered not just a new challenge, but also the biggest of championship blank slates. Lester was a 20-year-old kid in Class-A ball in 2004 when Boston won the World Series for the first time in 86 years. He never forgot the impact of that championship.

"Those guys are legends in Boston," Lester said. "I always use the comparison that Dave Roberts stole one base, and this guy hasn't paid for a meal or drink since."

The next night, December 9, Lester made his decision. The Levinsons were in a hotel room with Epstein, Hoyer, and Maddon when they put Lester on the phone with Epstein.

"I want to come play for you," he said.

Privately, the Cubs believed all along that Lester was looking for a reason not to return to Boston. The Cubs provided that reason. Epstein sold him on the path to a World Series title. History was calling. Lester heard it.

"The lure of bringing the World Series to [Chicago] and this team really interested me and my family," Lester said. "You go back to the '04 Red Sox and think about the free agents they brought in and the players they traded for. Those guys are legends for the rest of their lives. You bring that here and that's an exciting time to be a part of. I'm really interested in being part of that, of breaking that curse. I know what breaking a curse can do for a city and an organization. Hopefully, I can be a part of that."

Fourteen days later, Ross agreed to a deal with the Cubs for $5 million over two years.

"Jon was kind of the last straw," Ross said. "That's when things were picking up. The Cubs weren't sure what they would do with [catcher] Welington Castillo, whether they would trade him or not. But signing Jon put it over the edge for me. What better way to go? I love the city. I knew they were going to be good. I knew Jake Arrieta had great stuff—he almost no-hit us in Boston in 2013. Now we've got Jon, so we've got two number ones. I thought, yeah, maybe this is going to be a pretty good team."

What signing Lester meant to Epstein and Hoyer was that they were all-in on the 2015 season, rather than using the year as another ramp-up season toward 2016. He was the ace pitcher they needed to front a rotation. He would join Jake Arrieta and Kyle Hendricks, both of whom showed promise in 2014, and Jason Hammel, who rejoined the Cubs as a free agent three days before Lester signed. All four starting pitchers were acquired in the first three seasons Epstein and Hoyer were in Chicago. Later that off-season the Cubs added switch-hitting centerfielder and ebullient clubhouse presence Dexter Fowler, whom they acquired in a shrewd trade with Houston for pitcher Dan Straily and infielder Luis Valbuena.

Epstein and Hoyer had targeted two top free agents as priorities that off-season, both of whom they identified as playoff-hardened leaders who could help show a young team how to win: catcher Russell Martin and Lester. They gave Martin the same recruiting pitch they gave Lester—the stocked farm system; the statistical projections for the young players; the cool, expensive architectural model of the renovated Wrigley Field; the CGI images of a World Series at Wrigley Field—but it didn't work. Martin signed quickly—before Thanksgiving—to take a bigger offer from the Toronto Blue Jays, the national team of his home country. Epstein and Hoyer pivoted toward Miguel Montero, acquiring the catcher in a trade with the Arizona Diamondbacks.

"We knew to acquire someone like Jon, an elite free agent with choices, would mean somebody taking a risk on us," Hoyer said. "I feel like, when Lester signed, it really upgraded our team in so many ways. It took us to another level. I can't tell you how big that was. We tried to get Russell Martin as well, but we couldn't get it done. He didn't take the risk, which is understandable. Jon was the one who took a chance on a team that won 73 games."

Lester took the leap of faith that Martin did not take. By choosing to sign with Chicago, Lester turned down two franchises that had combined to win four of the previous five World Series titles in order to play for one that had finished in last place two years in a row. Money and hope won him over.

CHAPTER 10

BROAD STREET JOEY

J oe Maddon opted out of his contract as manager of the Tampa Bay Rays on October 23, 2014, with one year remaining on the deal at about $2 million. One of the first calls his agent, Alan Nero, made after the decision was to Cubs president Theo Epstein.

"Joe Maddon is a free agent," Nero told him.

Epstein, who claimed the phone call was the first he heard about Maddon hitting the open market, couldn't believe his good fortune. He instantly knew he wanted Maddon to manage the Cubs, even if his own manager, Rick Renteria, was under contract for another year after leading Chicago to a seven-win improvement in 2014. As soon as Epstein hung up the phone, he called owner Tom Ricketts.

"We have to pursue this," Epstein said. "It's a great opportunity."

Said Epstein, "I knew right away that he was our guy, that it was a once-in-a-generation opportunity for the perfect guy at the perfect time for this place that we had all invested so much in, and we had struggled as far as finding that finishing piece. How do you create the same environment—the same morale and environment that we were so proud of in the minor leagues and front office and scouting department—how do we re-create it in the big league clubhouse where we're losing and where no one wants to hear about young guys? That was the missing piece.

"We could not create the environment. Look at Rizzo and [Starlin] Castro and their ups and downs, the pressures they had to deal with, the criticism they had to deal with, and, understandably, in a losing environment. But we could not create the environment at the big league level that was conducive to young players developing, and young players making adjustments and thriving and relaxing and letting their talent take over. We ran the risk of really retarding our growth because we were so single-minded about developing our young nucleus, but what happens when they get up here?"

Epstein and Jed Hoyer had considered Maddon for a managing job once before. It was the Boston job after the 2003 season, a job that became available after the Grady Little Game—the seventh game of the American League Championship Series, when Little, the Red Sox manager, allowed a tiring Pedro Martinez to blow a three-run lead with Boston only five outs from winning the pennant. It cost Little his job.

At that point, Maddon had been a major league coach with the Angels for 10 years. Epstein and Hoyer asked him to meet them at the Biltmore Hotel in Phoenix. Maddon bought a new suit at Men's Wearhouse just for the occasion. This was his third interview for a managing job. The first two interviews both occurred with the Angels, and both seemed to be done out of respect for his years in the organization: once by general manager Bill Bavasi before the job went to Terry Collins, and once by general manager Bill Stoneman before the job went to Mike Scioscia.

"It was more of an old-school conversation," Maddon said about the Angels' interviews, "as opposed to . . . This was totally different."

Epstein and Hoyer spent all day with Maddon, first at the Biltmore, and then at Roy's in Scottsdale for dinner. The interview was probing at times in the manner of an essay test.

Epstein and Hoyer, for example, gave him a long list of a manager's responsibilities, including empowering the coaching staff, working with the media, handling the bullpen, creating lineups, dealing with a petulant superstar, and running spring training. They asked Maddon to place them in order of importance, and to explain why.

"By the end of the day I felt like I knew them pretty well," Maddon said. "And I think they knew me at that time pretty well, too. It stuck that these are guys I could work with and for."

Maddon didn't get the job. Epstein and Hoyer ultimately decided they did not want to take a chance on hiring a rookie manager in Boston. Prioritizing experience, they hired former Philadelphia Phillies manager Terry Francona. The Red Sox won the World Series the next year.

This time around, in 2014, Maddon had nine years of experience managing the Rays. Epstein told Nero that he and Hoyer wanted to meet with Maddon as soon as possible. Nero told him that Maddon and his wife, Jaye, were driving their 43-foot Winnebago recreational vehicle from their home in Tampa to their place in Long Beach, California. (Maddon calls his RV "Cousin Eddie," after Chevy Chase's RV-driving cousin in the *Vacation* movies. Others call it the Maddon Cruiser. He also owns a '56 Belair named Bella, a '67 Ford Galaxie named Aunt Hen, a '72 Chevelle named Babalou with a 1908 Cubs emblem in the carpet of the trunk, a '76 Dodge van he calls "my shaggin' wagon," and his most recent purchase, to mark the '16 world championship, a 707-horsepower, purple '16 Dodge Challenger Hellcat. As his Jaye likes to say, Maddon has "a sweet tooth" for cars.)

Nero wasn't sure exactly where Maddon was at the moment. He put Epstein in touch with him by phone. Maddon happened to be at an RV park on a tiny gulf beach in Navarre, Florida, near Pensacola. Epstein told Maddon he would be happy to meet him anywhere on the road, as long as it was as soon as possible. He didn't want to allow time for other clubs to get involved. Maddon pulled out a map.

"San Antonio," Maddon said. "We can meet up in San Antonio."

"Great."

But then Maddon remembered something: the RV park in San Antonio, not too far from a garbage dump, wasn't the most scenic spot.

"Let's just stay here," he said. "Our beach in Pensacola."

"We'll be there tomorrow afternoon," Epstein said.

Maddon was 60 years old. He was a baseball lifer. He had been in pro ball for 39 years, the first 20 in the minors in this labor of love. His agents and his wife, he said, "have been really disappointed in me in the past because I really don't push on the money side of things." And now the top baseball executives of the Chicago Cubs were hopping on a plane to meet him at an RV park near Pensacola, Florida.

"When was the last time a 60-year-old dude became a free agent in the Major League Baseball world?" he said.

He had waited his whole life for this kind of leverage.

JOSEPH JOHN MADDON was born February 8, 1954, to Joseph Anthony and Albina "Beanie" Maddon of 9 East 11th Street in Hazleton, Pennsylvania, a town of about 32,000 then and built literally on coal and figuratively on a misspelling. It was supposed to be "Hazelton," but a town clerk misspelled it during its incorporation on January 5, 1857, and the error stuck.

Hazleton was as blue as blue collar gets. In the early 19th century, railroad developers from Philadelphia sent a young engineer from New York named Ariovistus Pardee to survey the land of Northeast Pennsylvania to determine the feasibility of extending railroad service there. The area was discovered to be sitting on a massive anthracite coal field. Pardee bought acreage himself and formed a coal company. The coal industry in Northeast Pennsylvania in the mid-19th century boomed, supplying much of the coal that powered the enormous blast furnaces of Bethlehem Steel Corporation. The coal jobs attracted immigrants from Germany, Ireland, Italy, Russia, Poland, and Lithuania.

Among the second wave of European immigrants to settle in Hazleton was Carmen Maddonini, a red-haired Italian from Abruzzo, in the mountains east of Rome. To fit in with the Irish coal miners who lived on his block, Carmen Anglicized his name to "Maddon," and, after working in the mines himself, in the 1930s opened a plumbing shop called "C. Maddon and Sons Plumbing." Carmen had nine children. Three of his five sons, including Joseph Anthony Maddon, who followed his father in the business, lived in the family apartments above the plumbing shop.

Joseph's firstborn son, Joe—or Joey as everybody called him—loved his father but hated the plumbing business. He sometimes would accompany his father on jobs just to enjoy his company, with no regard for learning the trade. What Joey did learn from his dad was that working hard and having fun were not mutually exclusive, and that a truly rich man did both.

Joe the Plumber was the kind of diligent, humble man typical of the Greatest Generation. He served as a foot soldier in Germany in World War II but never talked about it. With a Phillies Cheroot cigar typically clenched in his teeth, Joe worked long hours—many of the pipes in Hazleton today were installed or serviced by C. Maddon and Sons—but made sure to always allow time with his son at the end of the workday. In baseball season they would play catch, or Joe would throw Joey batting practice. In football season Joe would hang an old tire from a tree in the backyard for Joey to practice his passes. And in basketball season they would retreat to the filthy plumbing shop in the basement and play basketball using rolled-up socks for the basketball and an old coffee can for the hoop. Joe and Joey would go at it amid the grime and dust until Beanie would call from the top of the stairs, "Time for dinner!"

It was an idyllic life in its simplicity. Hazleton was a place where doors remained unlocked and so did neighbors' hearts. Joey Maddon enjoyed the greatest gift a child can know: he was loved. Beanie worked as a bookkeeper and waitress around the corner on Garibaldi Court at the Third Base Luncheonette—so named because it is the "next best place to home." Joe took Joey to Yankee Stadium for his first major league game in 1962, when Joey was eight years old, to see the Mick and the Yankees play the White Sox. On the way out through centerfield—fans could file out through the field in those days—Joey saw on a merchandise stand a blue Cardinals cap with a red "STL" on the front panel. Little Joey was smitten. Joe bought him the hat, and a Cardinals fan was born. That same year, Joey awoke on Christmas morning to find under the tree a red Flexible Flyer sled with a chrome bumper, still his best Christmas present ever.

The boy proved to be a skilled athlete. Up Ninth Street, past the cemeteries, Maddon would hit home runs off the water tower in left-field at the Little League field. In high school he excelled at football, as a quarterback, and baseball, as a pitcher and shortstop. Friends called him "Broad Street Joey," the Hazleton version of Broadway Joe Namath, his favorite player, or "Termite" because he was small and feisty, or "Monsignor," because of his clean language.

"I never cussed," he said. "My dad would go nuts now."

Joey never had slept outside of his own bed in Hazleton until as a senior at Hazleton High School he went on football recruiting trips to Gettysburg and Brown. He felt uncomfortable on both trips. Eventually, he decided to play football for coach Neil Putnam at Lafayette, about 55 miles from home. Joseph and Beanie drove him there in the fall of 1972, dropped him off at Room 123 with a footlocker to hold his belongings, and said good-bye. Three days later Joey walked to a pay phone at the end of the hallway and called Beanie.

"I'm out of here," he told her. "I can't do this. I want to come home and be a plumber just like dad."

Beanie knew her son had no interest in plumbing.

"No, you're not," she told him. "You are not coming home, so just put that thought out of your head. Everything is going to be fine."

Just two weeks later, after starting well with the freshman football team, Joey decided he never wanted to go home.

"Lafayette was the best thing that ever happened to me," Maddon said. "The people that I met, learned some social skills finally—I was really shy. I was painfully shy. So going down there, meeting the people that I did, living under that environment, the educational component, the liberal arts education—all that stuff. I didn't realize at the time how important it was going to be to me."

During freshman football practices, Joe could hear the *crack-crack-crack* of batting practice on the baseball diamond being played two fields over. Baseball in the fall? The idea was foreign to him. He had never heard of such a thing. But one thing he knew when he heard those sounds: he wanted that. Now that he knew it was possible, he wanted baseball all year round.

Maddon missed spring football that school year with a badly sprained ankle, though he was still in line to be the varsity starting quarterback come fall. As he packed up his Volvo for the drive to Lafayette to start fall football practice, he felt an ache in his heart. He wanted baseball. He went through football conditioning drills and wanted to throw up. He ran the required six-minute mile and wanted to throw up. That's when he told the coaches he was done with football. He wanted to play baseball.

"My dad didn't talk to me for six months," he said. "But I had to do it."

The coach of the Lafayette baseball team was a man named Norm Gigon, who had signed with the Philadelphia Phillies in 1958 out of Colby College, where he'd earned a degree in history and government. Gigon toiled eight years in the Phillies minor league system. During three of those off-seasons, Gigon earned a master's degree in history from the University of Rhode Island. He wrote his master's thesis on British imperialism in East Africa. Veteran Philadelphia manager Gene Mauch once summed up Gigon's place in the Phillies organization succinctly: "He doesn't even look like a ballplayer."

Convinced the Phillies were not giving him a chance to reach the majors, and wanting nothing of being a career minor leaguer, Gigon was on the verge of quitting. He gave away all his equipment, except his glove. That's when former major leaguer Pete Reiser, an executive with the Cubs, told him he needed a change of scenery. He

After nine years as general manager of the Boston Red Sox, where he broke one curse, Theo Epstein arrived in Chicago on October 25, 2011, as President of Baseball Operations for the Cubs with one mission: Break another curse.

Theo Epstein signed Manager Joe Maddon as a free agent after the 2014 season. Said Epstein, "As soon as I found out he was available I knew we had to have him."

After owner Tom Ricketts launched a $575 million renovation of Wrigley Field, the 2016 Cubs won 57 home games, a record in the franchise's 100 seasons at the Friendly Confines.

Joe Maddon and Jake Arrieta show off their duds during the Cubs' 2016 "minimalist zany suit trip"—one of Maddon's favorite team-bonding exercises is the themed trip.

Drafted second overall in 2013, Kris Bryant quickly defined Theo Epstein's idea of an impact player: 2015 Rookie of the Year and 2016 Most Valuable Player.

Obtained in a trade with Baltimore, where his 5.46 ERA relegated him to the minors, Jake Arrieta became a dominant force and the 2015 Cy Young Award winner with the Cubs.

Following Anthony Rizzo, Kris Bryant, and Kyle Schwarber, shortstop Addison Russell became the fourth key impact player Epstein acquired. Russell arrived via a July 2014 trade with Oakland.

The "buddy battery" of Jon Lester and David Ross, signed before the 2015 season, worked together in 68 of Lester's 72 games over two seasons, including three World Series games.

For the first time in 71 years, the iconic Wrigley Field marquee announced a World Series game.

Kyle Schwarber became an instant legend when he hit .412 in the World Series after not seeing Major League pitching for 200 days because of a serious knee injury.

The first significant piece acquired by Epstein, Anthony Rizzo became a linchpin of the lineup and the clubhouse.

A moment 108 years in the making: Kris Bryant and Anthony Rizzo share a mid-air hug after combining for the out that ended the longest championship drought in sports.

Actor and Cubs superfan Bill Murray, who was born and raised in the Chicago suburbs, salutes Theo Epstein with a champagne shower.

Manager Joe Maddon and General Manager Jed Hoyer enjoy the spoils of victory: the Commissioner's Trophy, given to the World Series champion.

A crowd estimated to be five million people—the largest gathering of humanity in the
Western hemisphere in history—turned out to salute the world champion Cubs at their
parade. Whether they waited through many of the 108 years or only a few,
the fans expressed pure joy.

promised him Chicago would give him an opportunity. In June 1966 Chicago gave him that opportunity. The Cubs traded for Gigon.

A year later Gigon went to major league spring training camp with the Cubs. When third baseman Ron Santo suffered a spike wound that would keep him out 10 days, manager Leo Durocher gave Gigon playing time at third. Gigon, taking advantage of the opportunity, swung a hot bat and made the team. In his first major league start, at the age of 28, he hit a home run at Wrigley Field off Juan Pizarro. He cooled off, though, and hit .171 that season in 34 games at second base, third base, and rightfield. After the season, he quit to take the job at Lafayette.

Gigon knew what it took to be a professional baseball player. In Maddon Gigon saw a tough, smart kid from Hazleton with a good bat, but one who was not fast and a bit undersized. He called Maddon into his office one day and gave it to him straight: "The only chance you have at playing pro ball is as a backup catcher," Gigon said. And with that, Maddon became a catcher, a position that literally and figuratively gave him a view of the whole field.

Like Maddon, Nick Kamzic was born in Pennsylvania with a love for baseball. He moved to Chicago after his father died, and he signed out of high school there to play minor league baseball in the Detroit Tigers organization. His career was interrupted when he was drafted into the army in 1942. He spent four years in Europe, during which time he was shot in France and hit by shrapnel in Germany. When he returned to the states, Kamzic played briefly in the minor league systems of the Cardinals and the Reds before he quit in 1947 to become a scout. Kamzic drove 100,000 miles a year, from Texas to Canada, as a scout for Cincinnati, Milwaukee, and the Angels, where oral history has it that he was the first hire by Angels owner Gene Autry.

To supplement his meager income from scouting, Kamzic sold car wax and shoes, helped build bridges, and worked in factories. Kamzic became a legend in scouting circles. He helped the Angels sign future big leaguers, such as Jim Fregosi, Doug DeCinces, Jim

Abbott, Frank Tanana, and Andy Messersmith. In the summer of 1975 a junior catcher from Lafayette caught his eye. The Angels, on Kamzic's advice, and with the backing of cross-checking scout Loyd Christopher, signed Maddon.

Maddon spent the next three years in Class-A ball with the Angels, hitting a respectable .269, but mostly as a backup without much playing time. Then one day, after he hit .261 in just 42 games for Salinas in the California League, a letter on Angels stationery arrived at his tiny apartment in Salinas—"a closet," Maddon called his pad. The letter was from Mike Port, the Angels' farm director (and later the Boston Red Sox general manager who would be replaced by Theo Epstein). It was a notice of his release.

Maddon wasn't ready to go home. He was 24 years old, did not have a college degree and, most importantly, was convinced that he could still play. He worked out that winter at Horton Junior College in Salinas and called around for a job. After failing to find one in affiliated baseball, he tried out for the Bakersfield Outlaws, an independent team in the Class-A California League. One day Loyd Christopher came walking on the field toward Maddon with a bag filled with small, plastic Wiffle balls.

A former outfielder, Christopher had played 16 years of professional baseball, but only 16 games in the majors, split among three teams, the Red Sox, the White Sox, and the Cubs. His Cubs career was but a sip of coffee: he spent six weeks with the 1945 Cubs but his entire playing time consisted of just two innings in one game as a defensive replacement. A knee injury forced his retirement from baseball in 1952 (though he tried a brief comeback in 1955). He took a job selling Chevrolets in Richmond. But in 1957 Christopher began what would be a 35-year run as a scout, bouncing among six teams, right up to his death in 1991.

Most scouts sit in the same section of seats behind the plate. Christopher was the rare scout who sat by himself at games. He didn't want to be distracted. He preferred being alone with his thoughts. When he saw Maddon trying out for the 1979 Bakersfield Outlaws, he figured he could help him. Flipping small Wiffle balls to Maddon from 20 feet away—a common drill now, but almost unheard of back then—Christopher retooled Maddon's swing.

"That spring I hit the ball as well as I ever hit the ball," Maddon said. "I made this independent team in Bakersfield, but it didn't quite work out. That's the kind of guy Loyd was. He'd come out and work with his guys with a bag of Wiffle balls. He was well ahead of his time. He had his own thoughts. If you get a guy who is not active with his top hand when he was swinging, have him take the batting glove off the bottom hand and just keep it on top to get their top hand active. That was Loyd."

Maddon left the Outlaws before the season started, looking for a more stable place to play.

"I wanted to still play," Maddon said. "Of course people thought I couldn't play anymore. I still thought that I could."

He called Joe Gagliardi, the president of the Cal League, which was running a co-op team called the Santa Clara Padres. The Mariners, A's, Angels, Padres, and Cardinals supplied players to the Santa Clara team. The team wore green, red, gold, and white uniforms designed to honor the many Italian, Mexican, and Portuguese families in the area. Maddon asked Gagliardi for a job with the Santa Clara Padres.

"We don't really need you," Gagliardi said. "We don't need another catcher."

Maddon begged him for a spot.

"Tell you what," Gagliardi said. "Two hundred bucks a month. That's it. Take it or leave it."

Maddon took it.

"I wanted to play so badly I took the two-hunski," he said. "Listen, I just wanted to put on a uniform and I thought I could still do it."

The Santa Clara Padres were supposed to play their home games at Washington Park, which was built in 1935 and featured a wooden grandstand with seating for only 1,000 people. But issues with the field forced the team to play most of its games at San Jose Municipal

Stadium, which they shared with another team in the same league, the San Jose Missions.

The Santa Clara Padres were terrible. They finished in last place with a record of 47–93 and finished last in the league in attendance. Maddon was the fourth-string catcher. He played only 20 games: 11 behind the plate, 5 in the outfield, 2 at third base, and 2 more as a pinch hitter. He hit .250 with no home runs. Most of his starts behind the plate happened because the Padres had a knuckleball pitcher named Tracy Harris, and the three other catchers wanted no part of catching his knuckleball. Maddon had five passed balls in his 11 games.

One day during that 1979 season his scout friend Loyd Christopher came up to Maddon with some advice.

"When are you going to stop playing and start coaching and managing?" Christopher asked him.

Maddon was only 25 years old, still too young to give up on his dreams of the big leagues.

"I was like, 'You've got to be kidding me!'" Maddon said. "I was upset. I was very upset.

"Obviously, he was right."

Maddon began to take stock of his career as a baseball player at that moment. He was living in that closet of an apartment in Salinas and commuting 120 miles round-trip to be the fourth-string catcher on a terrible co-op team in Class-A for the salary of $200 a month, nearly all of which he put toward gas money for his Volkswagen.

Late in the season, the Santa Clara Padres were playing the Fresno Giants. It was late in the game when Maddon, dressed in the colors of the Italian flag, with an interlocking "SC" on his helmet, took a turn at bat. It was his 579th plate appearance in his 170th career minor league game.

"And I hit a double down the leftfield line," Maddon said. "It was my last pro at-bat. And I moved on from there."

He tossed aside his dreams and took Christopher's advice. In 1980 he quit playing and returned to the Angels as a scout, beginning what would be his 25-year run in the organization as a scout, coach, manager, instructor, and personnel director. Maddon earned his first managerial gig the following year, 1981, with the Idaho Falls Angels, a rookie league team. He was 27 years old. The team was miserable. The Idaho Falls Angels went 27–43. The team ERA was 6.37. But Maddon was on his way.

One day in spring training of 1984, Maddon, then-manager of the Peoria Chiefs, an Angels Class-A team, was throwing batting practice in cage number one at Gene Autry Park in Mesa, Arizona, when an unmistakable man with perfectly coiffed white hair and his warm-up jacket collar standing up on the back of his neck walked up to the netting.

"C'mere."

It was Gene Mauch, the legendary manager and, at the time, the Angels' director of player personnel.

Maddon stopped throwing and walked over to him.

"What's up, Gene?"

"You've created a great atmosphere here."

"Thank you."

And just like that, Mauch walked away. Maddon resumed throwing. Coming from an icon like Mauch, the words made an impact on him.

"I remember going home that night, going, 'What is he talking about?'" Maddon said. "[Angels pitching coach] Marcel Lachemann, right around the same time, told me how positive I was. I had never thought about it. Never knew that about myself. He made me think about being positive, and Gene made think about creating atmosphere, in a good way.

"So my next thought was, *What are they talking about?* I had to understand first what Gene was talking about, because my concern was, *What if I can't do this again next year? What am I doing? How do I do this again?* I thought it started with communication. I really did."

Mauch affirmed Maddon's natural inclination to create a positive working environment by creating trust with his players, which he believed began with honest, open communication. Maddon, though, still was learning how to manage. Two years later, managing the 1986 Double-A Midland Angels, another bad team, he flipped out after another languid loss. He ran to a newspaper stand and bought all kinds of newspapers. He grabbed a pair of scissors and cut out the classified ads, then taped them all over the clubhouse, including on the back of the bathroom stalls so that the players could read the HELP WANTED notices when they used the toilet. He threatened them.

"If you're not going to play baseball hard and you're not going to play baseball well, these are your alternatives!" he told his players.

Said Maddon, "I thought this was a great idea because I was so upset over what I perceived to be a lack of caring and a lack of effort, and I did not have a good team and I resorted to my lowest level ever."

The lesson Maddon learned from his Midland gimmick stayed with him: there was no room for negativity in a clubhouse. He told himself he would never forget that lesson if he ever had the chance to run a big league team.

Maddon had been managing in the minors for six years—all without a winning team. Bill Bavasi, the general manager, reassigned him to serve the minors as a roving instructor.

"He got me into roving because I was probably getting too intense," Maddon said. "And the best thing that ever happened was I became a rover because I got to see everybody—go to town for five or six days, you saw both teams' styles; your team, the other team—and you learn what you like and you really learn what you didn't like. I loved that. Roving is the best minor league job.

"I was hitting coach, catching coach, field coordinator, baserunning coach, eventually I did outfield, and I always consulted with the pitching coaches because I love pitching. I pretty much was involved in everything. At that time you had to wear several hats. There wasn't a specific guy for each one."

The education of a future big league manager continued in

Europe. Maddon signed on as an advisor for a company that sold pitching machines, a role that included staging clinics across the country and, after the 1993 season, in Europe. Maddon gave one-hour presentations on nine different topics between a Friday afternoon and Sunday morning. Before he left on the trip, Maddon wrote an outline on nine different facets of baseball—he still has the papers today. The preparation and the teaching emboldened him.

"You will remember 75 percent of what you write down," Maddon said. "And you will remember 90 percent of what you teach. So I wrote it down and then I taught it. And of course I was always open to amending, but the clinical work really helped me learn my stuff, to the point when I get on the field to teach, I feel a hundred percent comfortable with what I'm saying and how I'm saying it. I still do.

"I like to empower the coaches and not overpower their message, but if I don't like it I've got to jump in there once in a while, and I will. I'm very confident in that."

Maddon finally earned a big league job in 1994. Lachemann, then the pitching coach for the Marlins, was hired as manager of the Angels in May. From his days as the Angels' pitching coach, Lachemann remembered the minor league manager with the positive outlook. He hired Maddon as his bullpen coach. Maddon ran the Angels' next spring training, using a laptop to organize and print out the daily schedule. The old-school baseball men around the Angels would see him bent over his laptop, tap-tap-tapping away, and mock him.

"There's no place in baseball for computers," they'd cackle.

"If you criticize me for using a computer," Maddon would retort, "don't turn on your air conditioner in the car on the way home."

Maddon began using his computer to log hitting spray charts to customize the Angels' defense. During games, another Angels coach, Bobby Knoop, would chart by hand where balls were hit and on what pitches they were hit. After the game he would sit with a tall beer and classical music and input the information into a laptop. Maddon would then take the data and convert it into charts that he printed out: two for every hitter on the opposing team, one against left-handed pitchers and one against right-handed pitchers, with notations on where the defense should be positioned. He would copy the charts, staple them together, and place them on players' chairs in the clubhouse. It required four hours of work before the first game of every series. Some of that work had to be done after a late flight into the next city.

"I was killing myself," he said.

One day, before a series against Seattle in September 1998, Maddon printed out the chart on Ken Griffey Jr. and was stunned to discover that Griffey had not hit any balls on the ground to the left side of the infield. He approached Angels manager Terry Collins and said, "The numbers show that Ken Griffey Jr. almost never hits a ground ball to the left side of the infield. What do you think if we shift the shortstop over and play three infielders on the right side?"

"Let's do it," Collins said.

The modern shift was born on September 20, 1998. Griffey came to bat in the first inning against Angels right-hander Omar Olivares with runners on first and second and no outs. He looked up and saw just one infielder on the left side. Griffey took one pitch for a ball. Then he decided to exploit the defense by dropping a bunt—except when he tried to do so on the next pitch, he popped out. The Angels won the game, 3–1. Maddon would later tell Griffey, "If you want to bunt every time up, that's fine with us."

Said Maddon, "That stuff I did in the mid-'90s, it was labor-intensive. You had no idea. There was one year we had like 25 two-game series. When we were on the road I had like a big anvil box, with my printer in it and my laptop. I'd get in at two o'clock in the morning and I'd do all this before I went to bed so I could have it ready in time the next day. I don't know how many times I did that.

"You talk about learning your craft. All this stuff we can talk about now, it's about all the stuff I did to prepare myself for these moments, the labor-intensive work, the 10,000 hours. My God, it had to be way more than 10,000 hours."

After missing out on the Boston job in 2003, Maddon interviewed with Tampa Bay after the 2005 season. He arrived at the interview with general manager Andrew Friedman in Houston (where the World Series was being played), armed with a thick binder of his own reports on players in the Tampa Bay system. He got the job, his first big league managing gig, as pilot of the 2006 Devil Rays, who would be playing the ninth season in franchise history. In his first spring training, Maddon, in a harbinger of the boon he would be for the silkscreening business in Chicago, handed out to his players T-shirts that read, TELL ME WHAT YOU THINK, NOT WHAT YOU'VE HEARD. They lost 101 games in Maddon's first year, but two years later won the American League pennant, beating the Red Sox of Epstein and Hoyer in a thrilling seven-game American League Championship Series.

Epstein saw plenty of Maddon over the years as intradivision rivals. Under Maddon, the small-market Rays played baseball in the manner of an annoying little brother. They never went away easily. They played a loose, unconventional style of baseball, but never compromised on fundamentals, especially on defense. Before Maddon, Tampa Bay had never won more than 70 games in its eight seasons. With him over the next nine years, it averaged 84 wins and made four postseason appearances, including a 2008 run to the World Series. Twice Maddon was named American League Manager of the Year (2008 and 2011).

"Joe's different," Epstein said. "He's special. When I had a chance to interview him, I kind of knew how he thought about the game. I knew how his mind worked. But I got to see him across the field for the better part of a decade. Every time we played the Rays it felt like they dictated the game to us. We were constantly on the defensive. Some of that was personnel-related. A lot of it was how he was able to put his imprint on the game.

"You could tell there was a lot of thought involved, that he had thought through the game situations, such as the defensive positioning, and he had thought in advance in a really creative way. There was a lot of innovation with respect to strategy. I think there was a fearlessness associated with his style. He wasn't afraid to look silly. If he thought something worked, he was never afraid to try it in the most important part of the game.

"The safety squeeze had been around forever, but he realized that the first-and-third bunt was too hard to defend. As far as the shifting, he realized it worked in principle, but he also realized it worked psychologically against the hitter, so he took it to extremes. He relished the opportunity to be different, not just to be different but because it begs thoughts and questions and analysis. It makes life a little more interesting and fun."

Epstein saw Maddon's vibe reflected on his young players in Tampa Bay. Epstein thought they played with a coolness and creativity on the field. He attributed such ease to the environment Maddon created. Maddon gave them room to be their genuine selves.

"'Vibe' is a good word when talking about him," Epstein said. "He creates a certain vibe. He needs a certain vibe. He needs feedback to operate. He needs a more open, relaxed vibe. I think he's really intuitive. He can read situations, people, and environments, and engage with people, connect with them."

Sitting on a cache of young players ready to win, Epstein couldn't believe his good fortune when Nero called him about Maddon. Great managers in their prime simply don't become available. The pool of available managers typically requires taking a risk on a rookie manager or hiring somebody coming off a bad breakup. Maddon became a free agent by such an overlooked provision in his contract that he wasn't even aware of it.

The cascade of events that made Maddon available to the Cubs began with a hanging curveball from Clayton Kershaw, a rare event in itself. Kershaw, the Los Angeles Dodgers ace, held a 2–0 lead in the seventh inning of the fourth game of the 2014 National League Division Series against the St. Louis Cardinals when he hung the curveball to Matt Adams with two runners on. Kershaw had thrown

409 curveballs to left-handed hitters in his career without ever giving up a home run—until this one.

Because Adams hit the curveball for a home run, the Dodgers lost. And because they lost, the Dodgers were eliminated. And because they were eliminated, they reassigned general manager Ned Colletti and replaced him by poaching Friedman from the Rays, where he had been working without a contract. (Dodgers president Stan Kasten disputed that the Dodgers sought change simply because they were bounced in the first round, but would they have cleaned house if they reached the World Series?) And because Friedman left, Maddon was free to opt out of his contract—a provision Maddon knew nothing about until Nero phoned him with the news, and Nero recalled it only because Rays president Matthew Silverman had called Nero and asked, "So what will you do about the opt-out?"

"If nobody had told me I would never have known about it," Maddon said. "Of course, I think my agent would eventually have said something to me, but I had no idea."

Maddon's first instinct was to work out an extension with the Rays. He gave it two weeks. The top managers in the game were making near $5 million a year. The Rays made an offer. Maddon countered. One source familiar with the talks said Maddon asked for about $14 million over four years. The Rays declined, the source said. When it became obvious that no agreement was in sight, Maddon exercised his opt-out.

(The Rays filed a complaint of tampering against the Cubs, claiming the club contacted him before the opt-out was official. Major League Baseball investigated the complaint and found no evidence of tampering.)

At 60 years old, as a dues-paid-in-full-and-then-some, tried-and-true baseball lifer, Maddon at last had reached his time. It was time after all these years—all the bus rides through the Midwest, California, Pioneer, Northwest, and Texas Leagues; all the clinics; all the hours spent crunching numbers on crude software; all the sweat equity invested over nearly a decade in turning Tampa Bay from a joke into an honest rival to the deep-pocketed Red Sox and Yankees—to find out what he was worth.

"People just see what you do now, and it's beautiful and that's the way it should be," Maddon said. "And I'm not one to pat myself on the back. But when you do take the time to really reflect on it and exactly figure out where it began and how it got here, it's okay. There was a time when I was not making a whole lot of money and there were many times when it was paycheck to paycheck and it was kind of difficult. So I guess, I've always been a late bloomer. I've never wanted something before it was my time. So maybe it was just my time."

Epstein thought the timing was just about perfect. He saw Maddon as a critical piece of his rebuild.

"We've tried to create an organization that cultivates the whole player, the whole person," he said. "We take a holistic approach to player development. We try to be a humanistic organization. But sometimes it's so hard in baseball not to be impacted by convention and routine, by uniformity and falling in line with the same thing every day when you play 162 games in 183 days. It's hard to change that.

"That's when the leader in uniform becomes the most important person in the whole organization, by his very nature, by leading the life he wants to lead. He turns it on its head. The idea of change becomes instant and inevitable instead of difficult."

Epstein knew that, inevitably, the essence of the Cubs would belong to the four pillars: Rizzo, Bryant, Schwarber, and Russell. But until they fully matured, with the wisdom and experience to be true leaders, Epstein needed a willful manager to establish the environment to allow them such personal growth. Epstein's belief in the importance of the manager represented a quantum leap from how Beane, his rival from the early years of quantitative analysis, cast his manager as little more than a middle manager, who occupied the narrow space of implementing the will from above.

The timing, Epstein understood, wasn't entirely perfect. Epstein already had a manager under contract, Renteria, a man he liked and admired. Shortly after talking to Maddon over the phone for the first time, Epstein and Hoyer called Renteria. They were up front with him. They told him they were going to meet with Maddon. They promised him a resolution within a week.

"As soon as I found out [Maddon] was available, I knew we had to have him. I also just dreaded the situation we were in for Ricky," Epstein said. "The only way we could handle this with any sense of integrity was to tell Ricky what we were doing. We told Ricky that, and we told him [Maddon] would be the only person we would replace him with, and no matter what happened it would be over as quickly as possible."

The next morning Epstein woke up, threw on a pair of his oldest jeans, pulled a Chicago Bears trucker hat low on his head for cover, so as not to be recognized, and headed to the airport to meet Hoyer for their clandestine trip to Pensacola. Upon arriving in Florida, they rented a car and punched in the RV park on Google maps. Just as they were about to drive into the park at 3 p.m., they realized they had forgotten to bring a gift for Joe and his wife, Jaye. They pulled into a Publix supermarket across the street and, knowing Maddon's love of fine wines, headed for the wine section. They started on the extreme left of the aisle, where the bottles were marked at $2.99. They started walking down the aisle . . . $3.99, $4.99 . . . by the time they made it to the end of the aisle, they grabbed the most expensive bottle in the house: $9.99. The clerk wrapped it in a plain brown bag.

Epstein had never before been to an RV park. Given the clandestine nature of the meeting, the location was perfect: Navarre Beach touts itself as "Florida's Best Kept Secret." Joe and Jaye were parked in space number one. There was a little pool in the complex. There was just a sliver of beach—a few feet of sand between the RV and the gulf. Theo, Jed, Joe, and Jaye grabbed four lawn chairs and some 16-ounce bottles of Miller Lite out of the RV's fridge and sat down in the sand and talked. They talked for three or four hours, left to eat dinner at a Mexican restaurant, where they talked some more, and finished up back at the RV park, where they talked some more. In all, they talked for six hours.

"It was purely, purely philosophical," Maddon said. "You get to a certain point career-wise, you want to be able to go to work where you want to go to work. And with people you want to work with."

The Maddons had deep roots in the Tampa Bay area. They lived in Tampa. Jaye had opened a boxing and fitness studio there. Joe considered his nine years in the Tampa Bay area his "baseball Camelot."

That night Epstein called his wife, Marie Whitney.

"How'd it go?" she asked.

"'I think he wants to be a member of the Cubs,'" Epstein said, "'but he's really connected to Tampa—both the organization and the city. I think he really wants it, but he's not emotionally there yet as far as leaving.' I recognized it. I had a lot of similar feelings when I left the Red Sox."

Maddon would later say that Epstein was right; he wasn't emotionally ready to leave Tampa. "No, not at all," he said. He also had other things to worry about: he had to get up the next morning to make it during daylight to Beaumont, Texas, the next stop on his RV trip.

Another day passed and Joe and Jaye were driving somewhere between Junction, Texas, and Las Cruces, New Mexico, when Nero called. The Cubs had made a formal offer: five years, $25 million. Somehow Maddon kept Cousin Eddie on the road. The annual value would put Maddon on par with his former boss, Mike Scioscia of the Angels, as the highest-paid managers in the game at the time.

"I was like, 'Whoa!'" Maddon said. "It staggered me. I'll be honest. So you are driving along, driving along, trying to process all this stuff, and of course when someone makes you an offer you can't refuse, you don't refuse."

He took the job. The trip from Tampa to Long Beach became not only a life-changing one, but also a reflective one.

"If you are blown away by good fortune," Maddon said, "and you have the chance to retrospectively look at your life in an RV, maybe it was okay."

Epstein was thrilled to get his missing piece, but he knew there was an ugly side to this. Renteria was out. The Cubs would offer him another position in the organization, but Renteria declined.

"I stayed here [in Chicago] to finish up Joe, and Jed went out to see Ricky," Epstein said. "It was horrible. I wrote the press release articulating the dilemma, which was basically—I didn't surgarcoat it—we had to decide whether we were going to be fair to Ricky or fair to our organization, and that was the choice. And there was only one answer."

On November 3, 2014, the Cubs introduced Joe Maddon as their new manager, the 52nd person to take a crack at winning the franchise's first championship since 1908. They held the news conference in a sports bar across from Wrigley Field, the Cubby Bear. The joint was packed. Maddon, taking over this fifth-place team five times running, said he would be talking about making the playoffs from the start of spring training. He used words such as "synergy" and "philosophically," vowed "I play well in the sandbox," and quoted a line he wrote on the top of his lineup cards in Tampa Bay: "Don't ever permit the pressure to exceed the pleasure." Just when the news conference appeared wrapped up—Epstein, Hoyer, and Maddon rose from their chairs to leave—it suddenly wasn't. Maddon remembered something, wheeled, and grabbed a microphone.

"One more thing," he told the assembled media crowd. "Where's the bartender? Barkeep? Anywhere? I've got the drinks right now. What do I got?"

Epstein laughed and raised one finger.

"Theo said I've got one round. Actually, I hadn't thought about that, so . . . One round's on me! Please."

He put the microphone down, then remembered something else. He grabbed the mic again.

"That's a shot *and* a beer. That's the Hazleton way. Shot and a beer."

Broad Street Joey was the toast of Chicago. Buying the media a round of drinks was pure genius. The news conference was a hit. He immediately changed the "lovable losers" narrative. It was one of his gifts. With the sleight of hand and witty wordplay of a magician, Maddon could comfortably create narratives for the media to run with, which took some of the spotlight off his young players.

Maddon wore many hats: Renaissance man, polyglot, car enthusiast, polymath, bicyclist, oenophile, Springsteen fan, restaurateur, community activist, humorist, bibliophile, and dugout contrarian. But what Chicagoans saw most in Maddon was the Hazleton in him: a working-class dude with whom you wanted to have a drink. He was genuine, and already he was one of their own.

IT WAS STRANGE how the 2014 Major League Baseball schedule worked out. It had brought the Rays to Wrigley Field that August for the first time in 11 years, and only the second time in their history. Incredibly, it also had brought Maddon to Wrigley Field for the first time in his life. It was the same place where Babe Ruth hit his "called shot" in the 1932 World Series, and the same place where Norm Gigon, Maddon's coach at Lafayette, the biggest influence on his baseball life, hit his only major league home run, in 1967.

The first game of the series was played on a late Friday afternoon in spectacular weather—77 degrees and sunny. By the late innings, as the sun slipped lower in the sky, golden sunbeams poured through the ballpark's open gap between the third-base field-level seats and the second deck, a phantasm of natural light no longer possible in the fully enclosed modern stadiums. The wonder of it caused Maddon, perched like a great-horned owl at the rail of the first-base dugout, to occasionally divert his gaze from the field.

My goodness, he thought, *it's cinematic, all this golden light. It's like the opening scene from* Gladiator.

He considered the place a baseball cathedral. Less than three months later, Epstein would call him with what Maddon joked at his news conference was "a once-in-a-hundred-and-seven-years opportunity."

The Angels had never won a World Series until 2002, when Maddon was there in the dugout as bench coach. The Rays had never been to a World Series until 2008, when Maddon was there in the dugout as manager. Chicago was different. Chicago was the Old Testament of droughts. Maddon knew it and felt it, even before he managed his first game for the Cubs.

"The biggest difference so far to me are the fans," he said a few weeks before his first spring training with the Cubs. "Regardless of the fact that the Cubs have not won in a long time, meaning the World Series, the fan base is incredibly loyal to the group.

"The refrain I keep hearing is there is constant dialogue about their parents or their grandparents and how they tie into the moment today. This is truly a fan base that has been derived from history and previous generations. Everybody today wants to have the Cubs win because of their dad or grandpa or grandma.

"We need to get this straightened out, so all of a sudden they can go out to the gravestone and have a shot and beer with somebody."

CHAPTER 11

GAME 3

When the World Series returned to Wrigley Field for the first time in 71 years, the big box of a scoreboard in centerfield still was run by hand; vines of ivy, some of it turning umber and crimson in the midautumn evening, still clung to the brick outfield walls; and the subterranean concrete dugouts still threatened the heads of anybody who made the mistake of leaping in excitement.

But Wrigley winked at you. It gave you the impression that, within its brick walls, baseball and time had stood still since 1945. But that picture was an illusion.

First proof was the powering on of the great big arc lights on the roof, installed in 1988, as well as the two state-of-the-art videoboards, one in the rightfield bleachers and its colossal big brother lording over the leftfield bleachers, demanding your attention.

Second, when the World Series returned to Wrigley Field in 1945, following a "drought" of 7 years, it marked the fifth one played there in 17 years.

In 2016 such familiarity had long since faded. The return of the World Series to Wrigley Field was a first-in-a-lifetime event for almost all living fans. All day, hours and hours before the game, people filled the Wrigleyville neighborhood streets, simply milling about, smiling, chatting with strangers, and, whether they held game tickets or not, generally behaving as if the World Series was not merely something to be watched, but to be breathed in through great gulps, coursed through the lungs, and exhaled.

Wrigley was about to get her first-ever World Series close-up on television. Back in 1945, there were only about 5,000 television sets in the country. One poll that year found that a majority of Americans had never even heard of television. The first televised World Series game was still two years away.

Out of sight and out of camera range, underneath Wrigley, was one of the starkest differences between 1945 and 2016 at the ballpark: the home team clubhouse, new for 2016. The old clubhouse had the shape of a shoebox—a shoebox for narrow-width shoes. To get to the manager's office, you walked to the end of the shoebox, and took a quick left up a very short flight of stairs. At the top of the stairs was a door on the right, which opened to an office the size of a janitorial supply closet. The desk filled half the room.

By contrast, Joe Maddon's office in the new digs was the equivalent of a studio apartment, replete with a huge desk, two chairs, a sectional sofa, coffee table, bathroom, wine refrigerator, bookshelf, and wood cabinets. On his desk, facing out, was a Hollywood publicity shot of *The Munsters*, from the 1960s television comedy show, that was signed by Butch Patrick, who played Eddie Munster, as well as bobblehead dolls of four of Maddon's buddies; a small piece of driftwood engraved with one of his many slogans, "Try not to suck"; and various assorted such tchotchkes. Stacks of hardcover books filled a table behind him.

Maddon looked over his lineup card. Without the use of the designated hitter while playing under National League rules, there was no Kyle Schwarber on it. The previous day, during a workout at Wrigley Field, doctors refused to grant him clearance to play defense on his surgically repaired left knee. He wasn't even close, they said, to being able to withstand the reactionary starts and stops required of playing the outfield. They said he probably needed at least four weeks for such clearance. Maddon wasn't surprised—not after watching Schwarber simply stand in leftfield and read balls hit off the bat in batting practice during the workout.

"The doctors said, 'Don't do it,' which really galvanized my thought process," he said. "I was standing by the batting cage just watching him react in leftfield. No chance. Just watching his first movement, I said, 'He can't do that.' Because he might knock in one or two, but there's a good chance he lets in more than that.

"It's not about standing. It's about the movement to either side. At least running the bases I know I'm going here and I can control all that. If a ball is hit down the line, he has to break and go and I know he's going to dive. He's going to do what he does. I don't think his first movement, as the ball is hit off the bat, it's just not there. I saw it. For me, standing behind the cage—and he wasn't really even trying—I said, 'This is not going to work.' There's too much outfield for this guy to cover under those circumstances."

Listed at catcher on Maddon's card, batting fifth, was 24-year-old rookie catcher Willson Contreras, who had signed with the Cubs out of Venezuela as a 17-year-old third baseman. Contreras and second baseman Javier Baez were the only two players remaining on the 40-man roster who were there when Epstein arrived after the 2011 season. Right around the same time that Epstein signed, Contreras, while playing on the Cubs' Instructional League team, saw a set of catcher's equipment on the floor of the clubhouse. Not in the lineup that day, and with oodles of energy to spare, Contreras simply decided to put on the equipment, walk to the bullpen, and begin warming up pitchers.

"I wanted something to do," Contreras said. "I thought it would be fun."

The Cubs' director of player development, Oneri Fleita, who had been instrumental in signing Contreras, happened to walk by the bullpen. He did a double take.

"Will, what's up?" Fleita said. "Do you really want to catch?"

"I've never caught before," Contreras said.

"Want to try?"

"Sure."

Five years later Contreras was catching Kyle Hendricks in the first World Series game at Wrigley Field in seven decades—with an arm unlike anything Maddon had ever seen before. "I've never had a weapon like that on one of my teams," Maddon said. It was Contreras's second straight start. Game 2, a 5–1 Cubs win, was excruciating in its surfeit of dead time. It took four hours, four minutes, much of it seemingly wasted away by frequent visits to the mound by Contreras to speak with reliever Mike Montgomery, sometimes within the same at-bat.

"Honestly, he was right with Montgomery," said Maddon, who applauded his young catcher for sticking to the game plan when Montgomery wanted to improvise. "[Montgomery can] take that cutter and stick it you-know-where against righties. And we told him that and Willson's going out there to tell him, 'No! Curveball, changeup.' He did everything right. That was on the pitcher, not on him. He was doing what he's supposed to do. I was very proud of him. So everybody's on his ass, [but] he goes out there and he does what he's supposed to do.

"I like when he works with Chapman, too. They laugh. Him and Baez and Contreras, they laugh. When Chappy's missing the plate, I like when Javy comes in and makes him laugh."

On the wall next to Maddon, figuratively looking over his right shoulder, hung the very large color photo of a man in a baseball uniform. The man was sitting, level with the field, on the ledge of a concrete dugout that is obviously not in a major league park. It is the biggest photograph in Maddon's office. The man in the photo is a middle-aged man with dark, somber eyes—sad even. His eyebrows angle up and the edges of his mouth turn down. With his elbows resting on his thighs, dangling from his hands are a pair of eyeglasses like the kind Vince Lombardi would wear, with black rims atop the lenses. He is wearing a dark windbreaker with no shirt underneath, a dark cap with an Old English "B," and . . . are those? . . . yes, he is wearing black wingtip shoes instead of spikes. There is no identification of who this man is. He is a paradox. He looks at once familiar—an Everyman kind of coach—and also broodingly mysterious. Who is this man who occupies such a prominent place in Maddon's office, if not his life?

"Bauldie Moschetti of the Boulder Collegians," Maddon said with pride.

Bauldie A. Moschetti was born in Brookside, Colorado, on March 12, 1909—six months after the Cubs' most recent World Series title until 2016—to Rocco Alfonso Moschetti and Gentina Mary Merlina Moschetti. The family moved to Boulder so Rocco could work at the Black Diamond Mine, and, as it turned out, his son, too. Bauldie started working in a coal mine when he was nine years old, attending to a hoist powered by mules. If strangers happened to wander by, young Bauldie would run and hide because he was too young to work there legally.

The mines gave the Moschettis an income, but they took Bauldie's father. Rocco died in an accident in 1925. To support the family, the teenage Bauldie bought a small coal trucking company. He started with one truck. Soon he was the boss of 20 people. As the trucking business grew, he invested in real estate and a liquor store, Baseline Liquors, and became a multimillionaire. His real loves were his wife, Sybil, and baseball.

In 1964, at the age of 55, Bauldie started the Boulder Collegians Baseball Club, an elite, semipro, summer team he populated by recruiting the best college players from around the country, particularly from the West and the Plains. Bauldie's Boulder Collegians quickly became a national powerhouse. In only their third year, they won the National Baseball Congress World Series, then repeated as champions the next year.

In 1975, after his junior season at Lafayette, Maddon was playing summer ball for the Scranton Red Sox of the Atlantic Coast Baseball League, a college league with teams mostly in Pennsylvania and New

Jersey. In his second summer with the team, he was hitting .358, second in the league, and was selected to the all-star team. Two top college players who were drafted that June and later played in the major leagues, Paul Hartzell of Lehigh and Rick Cerone of Seton Hall, knew Maddon from competing against him in the ACBL and recommended him to Bauldie. Moschetti called Maddon, who had been treated so well by the Scranton team that he was unsure about heading West.

"How many catchers do you have there?" Maddon asked Moschetti.

"Oh, a couple."

"How many exactly?"

"Three."

Great, Maddon thought, I'd be leaving to be a fourth catcher.

"Okay, I'll come play for you," Maddon told him.

The way Maddon figured it, if he wasn't any better than the three catchers in Boulder, he didn't have any business even thinking about playing pro ball, and the sooner he found out the better. He also knew that more scouts spent their time watching players in the West than the East.

He noticed that one of his Lafayette teammates the previous year, infielder Art Fischetti, didn't get drafted until the 28th round. Maddon thought Fischetti should have been drafted higher, but blamed his low stock on never having played outside the East.

Maddon quickly became the Boulders' starting catcher. After a 6-for-34 start, Maddon hit better than .350 over the next dozen games. A Boulder writer wrote a column extolling Maddon as a cinch to play pro ball.

During the day Maddon shared groundskeeping duties at Scotty Carpenter Field with Stan Jakubowski, a pitcher from Miami, and Rod Boxberger, a pitcher from USC who later would father a son, Brad, who pitched for Maddon with the 2014 Rays. But Maddon spent much of his time after night games hanging out with Bauldie in the back office of Baseline Liquors.

"He was Italian and he loved me because I was Italian, too," Maddon said. "He had this real giggle . . ."

Bauldie would put on his glasses, the ones Maddon swore made him look exactly like the great Lombardi. The two of them would order pizza and swig drinks pulled from the cooler—Maddon would grab himself a beer and Bauldie would shout to him, "Get me a Squirt!"

"God, he loved Squirt," Maddon said.

They would stay up until three in the morning, just the two of them, talking about baseball, about life, about anything.

The Boulder Collegians won the National Baseball Congress (NBC) World Series again that summer. After the last game in Wichita, players filed in and out of Bauldie's motel room. He was sitting there in his boxer shorts, peeling off bills from a stack of hundreds.

"I promised you a thousand bucks . . . two thousand bucks for you . . ."

Bauldie was making good on the money he'd promised these top players from top programs to come to Boulder for the summer.

Maddon, the kid from Lafayette, walked in.

"Hey, Bauldie? Where's my money?"

Moschetti just laughed. There would be no money for Maddon. Bauldie was paying him in other ways: with his time and love.

"I didn't get any money," Maddon said. "Because he treated me like family. Swear to God. I was like a kid to him, so I didn't get anything. He was the absolute best. That's Bauldie."

Maddon identifies Norm Gigon, his coach at Lafayette, as the biggest influence on his baseball development, the man who turned a freshman quarterback into a minor league catcher. But Bauldie Moschetti holds a special place in Maddon's heart.

"I wouldn't be here without him," Maddon said. "He took a chance on me."

Because Bauldie invited the kid from Lafayette to play with the big-time Boulder Collegians, Angels scout Nick Kamzic watched Maddon play that summer and recommended him to cross-checking scout Loyd Christopher, which is how Maddon came to join the Angels organization and professional baseball, instead of the plumbing business. It might not have happened if he had remained in Scranton that summer.

Maddon and Moschetti stayed close friends. Moschetti had terrible allergies that acted up every fall in Colorado, so the two of them would switch homes for a month. Moschetti would move into Maddon's place in Laguna Beach and Maddon would live in Bauldie's house in Boulder. Maddon painted the place while he was there and tooled around Boulder in a 1969 Volvo that would not go into reverse. Bauldie, the tough son of a gun, told Maddon he wouldn't help him cover the cost of a new transmission.

In 1980, after Christopher encouraged Maddon to quit playing and become a coach or a manager, Moschetti offered him a player/coach gig with the Collegians. The team included future major league stars Joe Carter, Spike Owen, Al Newman, Mark Langston, and Tony Gwynn. Maddon once pinch-hit for Carter at the NBC World Series in Wichita. He found the coaching responsibilities to be a great training ground for his next career. The manager Maddon is today first emerged that summer.

It was not until May 17, 1994, that Maddon made it to the big leagues. That was the day Marcel Lachemann hired the guy with the positive outlook to join his Angels coaching staff. The last paragraph of the United Press International story announcing the change included this notation:

"The Angels also announced the addition of Joe Maddon to the coaching staff. Maddon had been the Angels' director of player development."

Maddon's first day in the big leagues came 19 minor league years after Bauldie took a chance on him, the break that made his pro career possible. Six days after Maddon made it to the majors, Bauldie Moschetti died. He was 85 years old.

Bauldie was buried in Canon City, Colorado, with a photographic portrait on his tombstone. In the picture, different from the one on

Maddon's office wall, Bauldie is wearing a blue windbreaker with no shirt underneath, a Boulder Collegians cap, and a dark, mysterious look with arched eyebrows.

Thirteen years later, in June 2007, Maddon's Rays were playing an interleague series in Denver against the Rockies. Accompanying Maddon on the trip was Jaye Sousoures, his girlfriend. After a game one night, around 10 o'clock, Maddon told Jaye, "C'mon. Let's take a road trip to Boulder."

They drove the 30 minutes to Boulder. First Joe took Jaye to the Dark Horse Bar and Grill, which opened in 1975, the year Joe first came to Boulder. They enjoyed burgers, fries, and beer at one of his favorite spots, all the while with Joe keeping his cool. After all, Maddon had an engagement ring in his pocket. His plan was to drive after dinner to Scotty Carpenter Field, the old home of the Boulder Collegians, and propose to Jaye there. It was dark and late, and Joe no longer was as familiar with Boulder as he once had been. He couldn't find the field. After wandering around a bit, he adjusted his plan. He knew where to go: Baseline Liquors.

It was 1:30 in the morning when Joe dropped to a knee in the parking lot of a liquor store in Boulder, Colorado, and asked Jaye if she would marry him. She said yes. It was perfect.

In 2014 Maddon was poking around online when he came across a slide of Bauldie Moschetti, the one with him seated field-level on the ledge of a dugout. He had to have it. He arranged for two poster-sized photographs of the shot, each of them framed and each without any identification. He hung one of them at Ava, his restaurant in Tampa.

He knew just what to do with the other one when he moved into the beautiful new manager's office at Wrigley Field.

Tom Ricketts knew he needed to do something about the home clubhouse facilities at Wrigley Field as soon as he saw them for the first time. It was right before he closed on the purchase of the team.

"It was terrible," he said. "I was stunned. It was like a junior high school clubhouse. So that was always a priority for me. We wanted to get a better clubhouse. I give a lot of credit to guys like Anthony Rizzo and Travis Wood, who were around back then, because we would tell them, 'Hang in there. We're getting a new clubhouse.' You can't tell people you're a first-class organization and have third-rate facilities. We definitely wanted to get the facilities taken care of as soon as we could."

In January 2013 the Cubs announced a $575 million renovation of Wrigley Field that would include not only the new clubhouse, but also the new scoreboards, renovation of the bleachers, luxury suites, upgraded wiring and plumbing, and renovations to the press box and visiting clubhouse facilities. The project would occur over four phases of off-season construction. After structural work was done after the 2014 season, Ricketts prioritized the home clubhouse facilities to be completed in time for Opening Day 2016. The new digs covered 30,000 square feet, making it the second-biggest such facility in the majors, behind only the Yankees' facilities at Yankee Stadium.

The entire shoebox that was the old clubhouse essentially became a batting cage, with most of the other space built behind it under street level of what had been a parking lot. Epstein was involved heavily in the project, making sure, as Hoyer half-joked, that the *feng shui* was just right for a baseball team. To avoid pockets of perceived value-enhanced spaces—which happens with corner lockers in rectangular rooms—Epstein ordered the main dressing area to be a rounded room to promote democracy. The diameter of the room was no accident, either: 60 feet, six inches, same as the distance between the mound and home plate. In the middle of the room, beneath a giant Cubs insignia and mood lighting are leather couches, enough giant television monitors to shame a sports bar, and a granite-topped counter.

Beyond the dressing area are a maze of rooms: a weight-training room; a video room; a therapy room that includes a cryotherapy machine, a float pod, and portable hyperbaric chambers; a lounge with recliners, Pop-a-shot, Ping-Pong, foosball, Golden Tee golf, air hockey, and guitars with amps; and a kitchen and dining area staffed by a chef and a nutritionist.

Between the batting cage and the dressing area is a designated "party room," where the Cubs immediately celebrate wins as soon as they come off the field. The lights dim, electronic dance music starts to play, strobe lights and smoke machines fire up, and videos with the star of the game begin to play. The players dance, sing, chant, and splash bottles of water on each other.

For years Maddon believed players wasted too much time in the clubhouse, sitting for hours watching movies and killing time under fluorescent lighting. It's one reason that in Tampa Bay he instituted "American Legion Week," in which he ordered his players to show up just an hour or so before game time, just as they did when they played American Legion baseball. He took the same concept to Chicago. But even Maddon had to admit that the environment in the new facilities was so comfortable that he started to rethink his position about clubhouse time.

"One of the things Tom Ricketts focused on," Hoyer said, "was that if we were supposed to be a first-class organization then we would have to make sure we took care of everything for the player. If they feel that we take care of every little detail for them, then all they need to do is go play. The more we can do for them has value as far as showing we care about them and their families as people.

"That hadn't happened here before. When it was run by a company like the Tribune Company it was an entertainment product. The Tribune never was able to invest the money in doing stuff like that. In some ways we went overboard, making sure that they knew, 'That isn't true about the Cubs anymore. You are going to be treated great and have the best of everything.'"

Coincidentally or not, in the first year with the new clubhouse facilities, the Cubs won 57 home games, the most in franchise history at Wrigley Field.

Wrigley Field actually is two ballparks, and for as long as it has been around players will know as soon as they arrive which one is in store on that day: they check which way the flags atop the roof and scoreboard are blowing. Most often, the wind blows in from Lake Michigan, turning the park into a haven for pitchers. Then there are some days, such as May 17, 1979, when the flags are starched stiff toward the lake and Wrigley becomes a bandbox. The Cubs scored 22 runs that day—and lost, 23–22, to Philadelphia. For Game 3, the signs were bad for starting pitchers Kyle Hendricks of Chicago and Josh Tomlin of Cleveland: the flags were blowing straight out, buffeted by 15-mile-per-hour winds that gusted up to 25 miles per hour. Maddon wasn't worried about how Hendricks would handle the elements and the excitement of the first World Series game at Wrigley Field since 1945.

"I haven't even thought about that, because if he pitches badly, it's not because he was nervous," Maddon said. "He would have pitched badly just because he pitched badly. I think he is ready for it. He is bright. And when you really open up a conversation and stay in there a long time he's really good. He's exactly as you saw him. He's just a nice fellow. He's a nice human being who happens to be a good pitcher."

WITH THE WIND howling straight out to centerfield, the Cubs and Indians played the most opposite kind of game the conditions encouraged: Cleveland won, 1–0. Maddon gave Hendricks a quick hook—two on and one out in the fifth inning of a scoreless game—but it mattered little because of how Cleveland pitchers Tomlin, Andrew Miller, Bryan Shaw, and Cody Allen stifled the Chicago bats. The Cubs managed just five hits.

"Unbelievable," Maddon said. "I'm looking at the flags, and we can't hit a ball on the fat part of the bat. It was un-friggin-believable. It was the most unlikely of everything. And Kyle was fine and then all of a sudden he wasn't fine. I don't know what happened. When he gets up to 85 [pitches] in the fifth inning—ugh, I don't like that at all."

The Indians manufactured the only run in the seventh inning. Catcher Roberto Perez singled off Carl Edwards Jr. Pinch-runner Michael Martinez moved to second on a sacrifice bunt and to third on a wild pitch. With the count 3-and-1 on Rajai Davis, the Cubs called for a disguised pitchout: a fastball thrown intentionally out of the strike zone to allow the strong-armed Contreras to try to pick off Martinez at third. Maddon didn't care about walking Davis, as the intentional ball would cause. He didn't want Edwards to give in to the hitter while behind on the count and risk a hit that put a big inning in play.

Edwards threw the pitch slightly low and outside, causing Contreras to start from a somewhat compromised position. His throw was strong, but a little farther inside the baseline than he preferred. Third baseman Kris Bryant reached for the ball, caught it, reached for Martinez, and tagged him a fraction too late for the out. Everything about the play was slightly off by the narrowest of margins—enough to lose the chance for the out.

"K.B.'s not a good tagger," Maddon said. "Watch the replay. He goes and gets the ball and then he tags. Let it travel and just drop it.

"I thought we could do it. I'm always watching the runner at third. And Willson's so good at it. Again, just let the ball travel just a click."

The next batter was pinch-hitter Coco Crisp, a .231 hitter for Oakland and Cleveland in 2016. Crisp is a notorious fastball hitter, especially early in counts. On first-pitch, four-seam fastballs during the season, he hit .290. On all other first pitches, he hit .206. Contreras, wanting to make use of his strong arm, signaled to first baseman Anthony Rizzo that he was looking to pick off Davis from first base after the first pitch to Crisp. To expedite such plays, catchers call fastballs, not off-speed pitches, on possible pickoffs. The preferred spot for such a pitch with a left-handed hitter at the plate is on the inside corner. So Contreras asked Edwards to throw a first-pitch fastball to Crisp—the pitch that turned Crisp into a .677 slugger in the regular season. Crisp lined his favorite pitch into rightfield for a single, sending Martinez home with the only run of the game.

"We were going to pick when Coco got the hit," Maddon said. "Wanted curveball there, but wanted to be aware of picking, so I think they went with fastball there as opposed to curveball because of the pick."

The Cubs had waited 71 years to get back to the World Series for this: they became the first team in Fall Classic history to strike out a combined 23 times in two shutouts—and it took them only three games to do it. It was the second time the Cubs lost a 1–0 World Series game. The first time occurred 98 years earlier against Boston. The winning pitcher that day was Babe Ruth.

CHAPTER 12

THE ZEN OF JOE

The first assignment Theo Epstein gave Joe Maddon after hiring him as manager of the Cubs was to go see Javier Baez in Puerto Rico at the end of January 2015. Baez was their top prospect, a 22-year-old infielder with the kind of wicked bat speed that reminded scouts of former major league slugger Gary Sheffield.

One morning during the previous spring training in Mesa, Arizona, Epstein said to me, "Come with me. You have to see this," and we headed to a back field, where Baez was taking batting practice. It was like watching the golfer John Daly blast tee shots on the driving range. Baez sent one ball after another high and far beyond the outfield fence, but it was the brutal violence in his swing that was more arresting than the ball flight. Swing after swing, Baez created tremendous torque with a looping motion with his hands just to get himself ready to swing—the barrel of his bat wrapped behind his head and pointed at the pitcher, as if making a personal threat he would make good on. When the bat did come around to meet the baseball, Baez swung as if his life depended on it. One manager in the Pacific Coast League, where Baez played with Triple-A Iowa most of that summer, said the highlight of his season was watching Baez take batting practice. Opponents stopped what they were doing to watch when he took BP.

Baez made his major league debut late in the 2014 season, and did so with unprecedented impact. He hit a home run in his first major league game. He hit two home runs in his third game, becoming the first player in Cubs history to post a multihomer game so quickly. But Baez's grip-it-and-rip-it approach came with a downside: he piled up strikeouts and rarely walked. He also was prone to emotional outbursts on the field that gave away his youth.

Epstein asked Maddon to watch Baez play for Santurce in the winter league playoffs. He had two reasons for dispatching his new manager to visit his top prospect. One, he wanted Maddon to establish a personal connection with Baez. And two, knowing that Baez figured to be a part of the Cubs' 2015 plans, he wanted Maddon to evaluate Baez's skills before spring training. Epstein and Jed Hoyer already had extensively reviewed players on the roster with Maddon, who was growing excited about the young talent available to him.

"It's really fascinating, and I kind of relate," Maddon said shortly before flying to Puerto Rico. "I started out as a scout through those different states. I definitely have the scouting gene in me. [Former Angels scouting director] Larry Himes was the guy who nurtured that within me. Larry was outstanding, so I feel like I'm a good scout. Looking at these players right here, I'm not being a genius: these are really interesting players.

"The big thing is, can we make them accountable? And how professional are they going to be about the day? I don't know that yet. What is their makeup like? I'm hearing good things, but you can have the greatest skill set in the world, but if you are not an accountable Major League Baseball player you are probably not going to get better. It's probably going to somehow hurt the fabric of the team and eventually that's not going to work.

"So, yes, on paper, physically, this is a really, really talented and interesting group—no question. But beyond that I've got to get in the dugout and clubhouse and find out what makes these guys tick."

The visit to Baez was the first step in that process. Was Baez an accountable player, or was he someone who might hurt the fabric of the team?

"The big thing," Maddon said about the trip, "was to get to know him because he was going to be a part of the future soon, to develop a relationship with him. The swing and miss, the long swing . . . but I had heard about the defense and how wonderful that was . . . but primarily it was just to get to know him and observe.

"In Puerto Rico, he was playing for Santurce at Hiram Bithorn Stadium, a stadium named after a pitcher who played for the Cubs in the mid-'40s. So all these crazy connections started jumping out at me. His defense and his instincts on the bases stood out."

Baez went 0-for-9 with six strikeouts in the first two winter league championship games. Maddon could see he was trying too hard to try to impress him.

"Hit a couple of singles," Maddon told Baez, "and above all, I want to see you smile."

Baez had three hits in his next eight at-bats before Maddon returned home. Maddon's first impression was that Baez needed a lot of work on his swing mechanics and his plate discipline. But Maddon took that impression and simply stashed it away in a file cabinet in the back of his brain. The emphasis on that kind of work would have to wait. His first concern with Baez was establishing a connection with him, as it is with any new player.

Maddon's entire managerial philosophy begins with those interpersonal relationships. His golden rule of managing can be summed this way: before you can manage and lead, first you must establish trust, and before you can establish trust, first you need to establish a personal relationship with your players.

This emphasis on connecting with people is what so attracted Epstein to Maddon. It was at the heart of what Epstein emphasized in those first three years of the rebuild. Epstein wanted an organization with a holistic approach to development. Epstein looked for an edge over the rest of baseball in the character of his players. Finding a manager who not only believed in that edge but also could nurture it to its greatest potential was the missing piece.

"A lot of challenges we face here are analogous, but not directly, to the same ones he faced in Tampa Bay," Epstein said just before he sent Maddon to Puerto Rico. "He used creativity and originality and personality to overcome some obstacles they faced: payroll, stadium, fan apathy. Here we have the curse and day games and an intense media market and a young team. A manager can help overcome that, but he has to be creative to do that.

"I do think Joe is a driver within an organization. He helps define the culture and sets the tone. His personality is inescapable. I think he's an asset who touches all aspects of the organization. He helps create a humanistic organization. His personality and his intellect and his heart are almost too big not to make a difference in whatever organization he's in. He creates possibility. He's one of a certain subset today that creates opportunities for an organization just by his mere presence."

Given their like-minded approach to holistic player development, the marriage between Epstein and Maddon created a blissful honeymoon as the Cubs prepared for the 2015 season. Epstein's wife, Marie, could see it on her husband's face. Only one week after Epstein hired Maddon, she told him, "Look at you. I can't remember the last time you were like this."

"What?"

"You've been *smiling*. You're always in a good mood."

Epstein pleaded guilty as charged.

"He's so engaging you find yourself sitting up a little more, leaning forward in your chair a little more, your mind is going a little faster and you want to make him laugh and smile," Epstein said. "You want to rise to his level of energy, intellect, and accomplishment. I think he has that effect on players. They want to match his energy and offer him ideas. You see that even in his young players, guys like [Evan] Longoria and [Chris] Archer. There's a lot of creativity you see in them. He allows individualism that promotes personal growth. It's about the environment he creates."

This new age approach seemed novel for someone who grew up in a Pennsylvania coal-mining town he considered "a subdivision of Europe" because of the influence of so many immigrants with old-school values, not to mention someone who grew up in a baseball age of taciturn and autocratic managers, such as his beloved and brilliant Gene Mauch. But the strong male figures in Maddon's life were men of great depth and empathy, beginning with his father. As a kid in Hazleton, Maddon once broke a window playing baseball. His uncle fumed. Joe felt terrible. His father came by to see what was going on, took stock of what happened, and said, "Nice arm, Joey." Maddon loved his father so completely he believed he could do no wrong. Pipes would burst in the middle of a cold night in Hazleton, and his father would respond not with complaint but with patience and positivity. Joey saw it. He believed his father never had a bad day in his life.

There was Norm Gigon, his Lafayette baseball coach, a worldly man with his degree in history and government from Colby College and his master's degree in history from Rhode Island. There was Bauldie Moschetti, the self-made millionaire who was smart enough to treat him like a son on the Boulder Collegians, rather than pay him. There was Loyd Christopher, the scout who cared enough about him to tell him the truth. They were givers, not takers. Maddon learned from them. He learned that the value of connecting with people exceeded whatever could be gained from ordering them around.

Under these men, and buoyed by his liberal arts curriculum at Lafayette, where he discovered James Michener and became a voracious reader of books, Maddon brought his own philosophy to baseball. He was open to new ideas. What really grated on him was the traditional inertia in baseball, created by the thinking of "because that's the way we've always done it." He liked to say that he read a lot of books, but "I never read the proverbial one," a reference to playing and managing baseball "by the book," the phrase that refers to using traditional, risk-averse strategies that date back to John McGraw.

The books he did read, by writers such as James Michener, Leon Uris, and Pat Conroy, not only entertained him, but informed him. Within every book Maddon looked for lessons he could apply to baseball. He scoured them for methods and ways of thinking that changed a group in a positive way.

Like billboards on a highway, Maddon's outlook on life and baseball were never hard to miss. On his very first day as a big league manager, at the 2006 spring training camp of the Tampa Bay Devil Rays, Maddon asked the clubhouse manager, Chris Westmoreland, to order and hang signs in several languages that said, ATTITUDE IS A DECISION.

Over the years his favorite canons of baseball wisdom typically found their way onto T-shirts for the players. He started the practice in the late 1980s with the Angels with a shirt that said, EVERY DAY COUNTS. Among the many such classics since then from the Maddon oeuvre, with translations, were GET LOUD (strive only for hard, or "loud," contact, rather than fixating on results); 9=8 (all nine players playing hard for nine innings each day equals one of eight teams in the playoffs—the slogan of his 2008 pennant winners); ALL ABOARD MADDON'S BUS. THERE'S A DIFFERENT BUS DRIVER EVERY NIGHT (everybody on the team contributes); and BE PRESENT on the front and FUH-GEDDA-BOUDIT on the back. (One day Maddon saw a player struggling to shake adversity and yelled, "Forget it!" A lightbulb went off in his head: *that's exactly what "being in the moment" is about*.)

Beneath the humor and the silkscreening T-shirt madness is an actual baseball philosopher who believes deeply in people and questioning conventional wisdom. He has an established track record, not only as a winner but also as a manager with a unique aesthetic.

Bits of that aesthetic may sound like slogans, but the expanse of it requires a longer form. Here are the 13 core principles of managing, according to Joe Maddon:

1. MAKE A PERSONAL CONNECTION FIRST; EVERYTHING ELSE FOLLOWS.

The greatest responsibility of the manager is to create a positive environment that promotes growth and success. "That's the most important thing," he said, "and that's what everybody overlooks."

The key to creating that environment is to first make a connection with your players on a personal level.

"You want to impart information and knowledge and methods and how-tos," Maddon said. "And that's a lot of people's first thought going into a new moment. For me, my first thought is to get to know you. Then we trust each other. And then we can exchange ideas. *Then* we can talk about methods and ideologies and whatever you want to call it. We can go there then. But if you try to go there before all this other stuff has been established, a lot of this fertile seasoning lands in bad spots, in infertile areas, and all of a sudden it's going to go away."

How does Maddon create that connection?

"You do that by conversation, you do that by talking," Maddon said. " 'How is your family? What's going on? What are you thinking? Where are you from?' All kinds of personal questions. Just get in there a little bit and try to find some common ground. 'What makes you light up a little bit? What interests you?' And as we keep moving along, from that there are going to be these moments and baseball. I've got to be brutally honest with the guys. I think over a period of time they know you are being straight up with them, because baseball players want straight up. They don't want any kind of sugarcoating.

"When a player finally understands that, if I tell you the truth you may be upset with me for a week to 10 days maybe. But if I lie to you, you are going to hate me forever.

"What eventually occurs after that is that we have arrived at this point of trust. Now I can be constructively critical, and you are not going to push back. You are not going to think I'm picking on you. And it works both ways. If you are really upset with me I want you to tell me also. And you are going to know that I'm going to accept the constructive criticism also."

2. THERE IS ONLY ONE TEAM RULE.

"Respect 90." It's the message Maddon had painted on the grass of practice fields in his first spring training with the Cubs. The "90" refers to the number of feet between bases.

Shortly after being hired by the Cubs, Maddon recalled a plane trip he took back in the mid-'90s. He was flying from Arizona to Midland, Texas, upset about being passed over for a big league coaching job to serve again as a minor league instructor, and not too happy about being stuck in a middle seat, and not too thrilled that a woman next to him wanted to chat. It was one of those days. But something the woman said rang like a bell within him: "Whatever you put out there will come back to you."

It changed his outlook and stuck with him. In deciding on a theme for his first spring camp with the Cubs, he remembered that conversation and chose "Respect 90" because it captured the sentiment that if you give respect you get respect in return.

If a player respects those 90 feet between bases enough to run hard all the time, good things flow from such an attitude.

"I ask the players to respect 90 and I ask the pitchers to work on their defense," Maddon said. "I really like to see the pitchers spending time on getting better, whether it's holding runners, whether it's fielding bunts, backing up bases, stuff that's really important in the moment. If we do that, and if a position player respects 90 feet, I think he'll play baseball as good as he possibly can."

3. FREEDOM IS EMPOWERING.

Maddon has no other rules besides "Respect 90" because he believes rules inhibit people from reaching their potential.

"I believe in freedom," he said. "I don't believe in overmanaging. I don't believe in micromanaging. I believe in players being players, players being themselves, playing without restrictions. I never want to coach instincts out of you. I want your instincts to soar.

"The more you restrict freedom the more you restrict creativity. To restrict creativity—which a lot of people do unknowingly, they don't even realize they are, they don't even realize the importance of creativity, they don't understand the role freedom plays in all this—to restrict that you really are losing out on a tremendous opportunity to find out how good someone actually is. When you attempt to create a contrived version of somebody before permitting that person to show you what they are, you're automatically setting restrictions. Automatically. You don't know that you are. But you are.

"I've used that line over the course of a season. If I ever coach instinct out of a player, shame on me, man. Shame on me. That may be the mortal sin of coaching, to limit or inhibit somebody's intrinsic abilities out of them. That would be awful. And that comes primarily from anger, when you get angry with somebody, when you don't attempt to understand why they're doing that and where they're coming from, or you want to enact your mores on them because you think your way of doing something is the only way to do something, that's the only way that's right. That's dangerous thinking. It's inhibiting. It's restrictive. It doesn't work with baseball teams, it doesn't work with countries, it doesn't work in society. It just doesn't work.

"So I'm super aware of that. I think growing up when I did in the '60s and '70s contributes to that mind-set. At that time my peers were anti-establishment. They did not want to be told what to do all the time. We saw the flaws. We didn't want to be like them.

"I still have those old-school Hazleton values. I question methods. Just because something has been done one way for a long period of time doesn't mean it's the right way. I don't question traditions. I question methods. Traditions are solid, whether my Catholic church, within my family, what your grandpop wanted you to do within the family structure—that's fine. But why can't you play the infield in in the first inning? That run counts, too. Things like that—why? 'Well, because Wes Westrum told me that 20 years ago.' Well, I don't agree with that."

4. NEVER HOLD A TEAM MEETING IN YOUR HOME CLUBHOUSE.

"It poisons the room," Maddon said.

Team meetings are a reaction to negative events, such as too many losses, a lack of effort, or a lack of discipline. Calling out such negativity in what you have strived to create as a positive, physical place is harmful to the environment. The negativity lingers.

"To show up at home every day and have it be this negative room and a lot of yelling and screaming and throwing of things and name-calling?" Maddon said. "Not good."

Maddon said he blew up on one of his teams once as a big league manager. It happened in 2008 after a sloppy win by his Tampa Bay Rays in Kansas City. As he walked back to the clubhouse, a steamed Maddon said to bench coach Dave Martinez, "Get 'em in here. Right now."

"We made all kinds of mistakes," Maddon said. "We weren't running hard, mental errors . . . we were doing well so we thought we were hot stuff. I went off."

He hates team meetings in general. "Most of them, I'd say 97 percent of them, are not necessary," he said. "I think a lot of it's for show. A lot of times when a manager gets upset like that and has to have a meeting, it's for his own feelings, and also to produce the effect to say, 'I had a meeting and I got suitably angry because the guys aren't winning.' Any time you blow up on your guys publically I think it's to protect yourself. I refuse to do that.

"I've been on teams when the team meeting happens and I'll be sitting on the floor as a coach, thinking, *This sucks.* The players are just giggling inside. They're going to make fun of it when you're done. They'll use it against you. There may be a couple of real rah-rah kids that it's going to affect a little bit, but there's no lasting impact of that. None. And the more meetings you have to have, it means you're pretty bad.

"I prefer meetings by players, among each other. I prefer that. I like when players talk to one another more than when coaches [address them]. I like my coaches' meetings when they talk preseries. It's empowerment, too. But I think if there's an issue, when it comes to players talking amongst each other I think it's more impactful."

Maddon prefers to hold just three team meetings each year: one at the start of spring training, one just before the All-Star break, and one before the start of the postseason. All of them are planned meetings to project a positive message.

"I read once a really good line, 'Praise publically, criticize privately,'" he said. "I love that. That's exactly how you should do it, I think. So I attempt to live by that."

5. DO NOT HAVE A FINE SYSTEM.

Maddon seemed to have a fine system when he began managing in Tampa Bay, but he chose to consider it as an educational and team-building exercise. Maddon would write the names of certain bottles of wine on slips of paper, fold the slips, and place them in a jar that he kept in his office. If a player violated a principle of the game Maddon thought deserved a fine—such as a lack of hustle or missing a sign—he called the player into his office after the game and asked him to pick a piece of paper from the jar. The player would have to buy the bottle listed, and bring it to the clubhouse.

"Poor Joey Gathright," Maddon said about an outfielder on his 2006 team. "He always picked the most expensive bottles.

"I was trying to make a point and make it fun. Because the wine was going right into the [clubhouse] kitchen. So after the game I was trying to teach them wine, about a good glass of wine. The group was way too young in the beginning.

"I had a victory chalice there. A big wine glass with 'Victory' on it and I called it the victory chalice. After we won a series, I would take some of the really good stuff—the whole bottle went in there—I put it in the kitchen. 'Drink out of the victory chalice!' They'd put it in their glass, sip out of the chalice. That was so cool."

With the Cubs, Maddon no longer uses the wine-in-a-jar system, nor any formal fine system. Martinez, his bench coach, will sometimes fine a player if he misses a sign or doesn't run out a ball in play he thought was a home run. Often money does not change hands.

"It's like they don't even have to say it," Maddon said. "They'll just bring me a bottle of wine. They know they screwed up."

6. WEAR WHATEVER YOU THINK MAKES YOU LOOK HOT.

Dress code? Fuh-gedda-boudit.

Maddon is famous for arranging themed trips a few times each season on getaway days. He began the tradition in Tampa Bay, where he asked the entire team to dress in costumes to match a theme he picked, such as *Miami Vice* (all white), Johnny Cash (all black), and varsity lettermen (cardigan sweaters with a "TB" monogram).

"There were a lot of times guys wouldn't even dress up," Maddon said. "They thought it was silly, unprofessional. I never worried about that. That's fine. You don't have to do it, then don't worry about it. But I can promise you the guys that didn't do it really weren't the team guys we were looking for. I promise you that.

"It's a method where you are building camaraderie, the team-building situation. If we can impact one guy every day, whether it's by the 'thought of the day' or the 'joke of the day,' that's always good. All these little things that you do every day definitely serve the bond bringing people together."

Maddon brought the themed trip tradition to Chicago. In 2015 he pulled off the pajama trip, the shorts trip, and the Blackhawks jersey trip. In 2016 he cooked up the "minimalist zany suit" trip, the basketball warm-up suit trip, and the football jersey trip, on which the first-year Cubs players had to wear female cheerleader's outfits. Maddon arranges the trips not just as a team-bonding exercise, but also for the sheer fun of it—not to mention to give a poke in the eye to old-school rules that players adhere to a formal dress code.

On an everyday basis Maddon has no rules at all about how players should dress. He really does tell them in spring training that they should wear "whatever you think makes you look hot."

"I've had guys come up to me in the past and say, 'Do you see how he's dressed on the road?'" Maddon said. "I'll say, 'So? So? Listen, you saw it. To me I would have never noticed that because to me it doesn't matter. Doesn't matter. So if you want to inhibit him and his development mentally and how he is as a person and on this field, then go ahead and bust his balls about the way he's dressing. But it doesn't matter. You're attempting to enforce your mores on him based on how you were taught. Doesn't make it right. It's just that's what you heard from some old dude that wore polyester. It doesn't mean it's right. So go. Go do what you've got to do, but just understand I don't care.'"

7. EMPOWER YOUR COACHES.

"Empowering the coaching staff is huge," Maddon said, "because I had been in a situation where the coaching staff was not empowered. I never felt *not* empowered myself. I think that's something you feel if you lack self-confidence, the fact that you've not been empowered by somebody. But if you have self-confidence, nobody can ever take that power away from you.

"But I've been around guys I know who felt a lack of power because the manager would not give them specific things to do or they felt they were not being listened to. And that never bothered me. Never. Because I was always very confident in what I did and my opinions. But I listened. And getting in that position I never wanted to be that guy who made my coaching staff feel like they couldn't say what was on their mind.

"My thought was, any time anybody shows up to work they need to feel as though they can make an impact. And if they feel like they can make an impact and they feel a part of this thing, then when things don't go well, they can't jump ship and can't do the infamous backstabbing. They can't do that because they've been part of the planning.

"Now if you exclude them from the planning, and you have these moments when things don't go so well, that's when guys jump ship. So this was all obvious to me coming up. All this stuff I've been doing since '81, and I have strong opinions about how to do it and how not to do it based on people I thought did it well and more importantly people I thought didn't do it well."

8. BUT DON'T ALLOW YOUR COACHES—OR VETERANS—TO BE HARSH ON YOUNG PLAYERS.

"I saw it when I first got to the big leagues," Maddon said. "I thought some young players' abilities were being negatively impacted by veteran players, managers, and coaches. They were kind of subduing the personalities of these young guys, whether by making fun of the way they dressed, being hyper-angry at mistakes, intolerant of mistakes. Definitely young players had a big target on their back. The more veteran players had a small target on their back.

"The way the rookie mistake was treated always bothered me. I saw guys who had been playing for seven years making the same mistake, but when it's a rookie mistake, people think it requires a heavier hand than the guy who's been doing it for seven years. It bothered me. If you want these young guys to play as well as they can quickly, then you've got to change your approach with how you deal with them. You have to permit them to be themselves, and, of course, like everybody else, if they mess up they have to be told about

it. But you don't have to get hyper-angry at them or send them back
[to the minors], or explain it to them in a way that absolutely frac-
tures their self-confidence. And I have seen it."

Maddon had a small problem in 2016 with one of his veterans
on the Cubs. The veteran was riding one of the young players about
making mistakes. Maddon thought the veteran was overly severe. He
called the veteran into his office.

"I get where you're coming from with that," Maddon told the veteran, whom he declined to name, "but don't you think you're being
a little bit harsh, a little bit over the top in your explanation and how
you went about it?"

The veteran quickly agreed to tone it down.

"By the end of the season these guys had the best relationship in
the world," Maddon said. "But you just can't give the veterans a free
wheel regarding how they interact with these guys and instruction.

"I don't like when guys get in other guys' heads. A veteran may
see this guy coming at his position, and he may want to start creating doubt in this young guy's head. I've seen it. This group? No.
Absolutely not. But I've seen it. Just because a guy is a veteran doesn't
mean he's going to have good influence. Just because the back of his
baseball card reads well doesn't mean he's a leader. Just means he's
been playing seven or eight years. You can have leaders that absolutely take it the wrong way. You can have coaching staffs that take
it the wrong way.

"That's why, as a manager, you've got to coach the coaches on
top of that and not permit them to carry a message that's not your
message."

9. QUESTION DATA WITH FEEL.

You never will find Maddon managing a game from the bench. He
needs to be standing near the rail of the dugout. He needs to be as
physically close to the game as possible because he needs to "feel"
and sense the vibe of the game.

"I've trained myself to do this. The part I'm trying to convince all the sabermetricians about is trends," he said. "You have to pay attention to trends. Don't tell me trends don't matter. Don't tell me that. You go sit in the dugout. Because everybody wants the large sample size. I get it. I get large sample size. I'm not dumb. I get it. But here's August 15 to August 30 and this .220 dude is *en fuego*. So you mean to tell me like I have to treat him like these numbers? No way.

"The dudes that are solely based on numbers, they can't see through trends because they don't believe in them. They believe it's going to correct itself, and I agree with that, but for right now . . . Matty Joyce was a great example: great in the first half, horrible in the second half. He gets to like September and he's hitting like .350 against this guy today. But I know Matty has no confidence. He's popping up to the third baseman on 2-0 counts. He's just not right. But I'm supposed to play him based on this friggin' number? No. Ain't gonna do it. He's my classic example. He's the large-sample-size dude. He's going to appeal to every sabermetrician, and I love Matt.

"All this different stuff that's available is good and I believe in it, but you've heard me say it a lot in the postseason: I've got to feel it. I've got to feel what's going on right now. And that's why I don't sit in the dugout. I've got to get up where I can feel everything because when you get isolated in this little cubicle you don't feel around you. I don't like it. I don't think I'm making as good of a decision. I've got to feel it."

10. PREGAME WORK IS EXCESSIVE.

Players hit far more before games today than they did 20 or 30 years ago. There is early hitting on the field, hitting in the cage, regular hitting on the field, and more hitting in the cage.

"It doesn't make sense," Maddon said. "You've got a cage inside. Guys need to get loose. Why do they have to hit on the field? Come on. The biggest thing for me would be groundballs. You need that. Take a couple of groundballs. Throw over to first if you need to do that. But if you don't have to be outside you can work on something inside. And if you stay off your feet longer, I think it benefits you. It's nothing you ever did when you were kids playing. You didn't go out there and practice five hours before you played the game—ever. I don't know where that became ritual. I think maybe the '80s. I think in the '80s it became popular to get that extra work in. Work, work, work. I think it can be very counterproductive.

"Everybody talks about infield practice. Infield practice the way it was done before was ridiculous. Because you had to warm up your arm so many different times in a day that they never even considered guys getting sore arms just taking infield too often. You want to take infield? The right time to do it is at home before batting practice. Get your arm loose one time, go out there, and take your ground-balls. What they used to do is you come out, play catch, hit, take your groundballs, come in, sit around for a bit, go back out and play catch again, take infield, throw again, then come back in and get changed and go back out. That is insane. It really is. It makes no sense other than that somebody said it's supposed to be that way. So I think the more rest you can give guys the better you are."

11. KEEP SIGNS SIMPLE AND TO A MINIMUM.

Cubs players rarely look for a sign on 3-and-0. That's because Maddon rarely gives one.

"Because I don't like to give them signs," he said. "I like them to rely on their baseball instincts. I don't want to insult. If it's 3-0, you're leading off, we're down by a couple of runs, why would you want to swing at that pitch? So you want me to do this [he gives hand signals] to tell you to do the right thing?

"But I tell them if it's 3-0, two outs, even runner at first base, I want you to go. I say, 'Doubles or better.' You're looking for doubles or better, especially with two outs. That's what you're looking for. I do let them go under those circumstances."

When he does give signs, Maddon keeps them simple—American Legion simple. The only twist is that if he's thinking about a play somewhere in an at-bat—say, a safety squeeze bunt—he might give the sign before the first pitch but place it "on hold," which puts the players on alert. When and if he decides to use the play, he gives another to put it "on."

12. A LINEUP CARD IS ALL A MANAGER NEEDS IN THE DUGOUT.

Major League Baseball in 2015 approved the use of tablets in the dugout. The tablets do not have connectivity, but they are loaded with scouting information and data. Maddon has no use for a tablet in the dugout.

"It's too slow," he said. "That's my point. Paper is faster than a tablet could ever be. Paper's much quicker. You have it in advance. You know what you want to do. I mean, I love it for my research and my work, but in the moment, paper's quicker.

"You use it to get ready to do that, but when you're out there, there's no piece of paper that I could possibly ask for that I don't have. I have two sheets with everything I need to know for the game, so why do I need more, technologically speaking?"

13. FORGET "THE BOOK." MAKING THE FIRST OR THIRD OUT AT THIRD BASE IS OKAY.

One of the oldest tenets of the game is that a runner should never make the first or third out at third base. It's about the risk-reward ratio. The thinking behind the theory goes like this: trying to get to third with no outs is overly risky because you still have three more outs with which to play—you're likely to score from second with no outs, so the reward is small—and taking a risk to get there with two outs makes little sense because you cannot score from there on an out. The problem Maddon sees with this long-held belief is that it encourages a passive mind-set on the bases. The entire premise is based on playing it safe before the ball is even hit.

"I don't mind making the first or third out at third base," he said.

"I don't give a rip—as opposed to using that line, which you've heard a hundred thousand times. I like to get to third base with less than two outs as often as possible. That's what we say.

"If everything is set up right and you're making your reads and this guy makes a great play, so what? I'd rather us be aggressive at third, even making the first out there. But to make the first out at *home* would really bum me out. I don't like that at all. It really fries your oysters."

Maddon's slightly offbeat take on the game might rub traditionalists the wrong way. To them it may smack of gimmickry, and from his constant perch at the rail of the dugout, call attention to him. Baseball is a game with great regard for its elders and its lineage. It is a generational game, traditionally taught to sons by their fathers, who learned from their fathers. Its mythology relies on the idea of "timelessness," the idea that the game came down from on high in perfect form, like commandments in stone, and revisions or rebukes of it can be seen as blasphemous.

Innovation is not easily accepted in baseball. Traditionalists can be so hidebound by "The Book" that freethinkers like Maddon may be criticized for "trying to reinvent the game." He gives them plenty of material. Maddon deployed a four-outfielder alignment against Boston designated hitter David Ortiz as far back as 2006. He once intentionally walked Detroit Tigers slugger Miguel Cabrera with runners at first and second—putting the tying and winning runs in scoring position—to pitch to Brennan Boesch. (It worked.) He once intentionally walked Josh Hamilton with the bases loaded. (He won the game.) In Game 5 of the 2008 American League Championship Series, holding a 7–0 lead, he refused to play "no-doubles" defense in the outfield—"The Book" version of a prevent defense. (He lost, 8–7). He once used an outfielder, Sam Fuld, to kill time warming up on the game mound so his relief pitcher would gain more time to get ready. (It was against the rules, for which he later apologized to the umpires.)

Maddon has managed postseason games wearing a cap with

sewn-in felt earflaps (the "Elmer Fudd" look) and a wool ski cap. He likes to squeeze-bunt with two strikes, to have his second baseman hold the runner on first base with the opposing pitcher bunting so the first baseman can charge, to play a five-man infield, and to disguise his pitchouts by throwing fastballs just off the outside corner.

"If guys are really upset with me for some of the things that I do, I prefer they come and ask why I do them, and I would tell them," Maddon said. "There is always a reason behind it. I never worry about stuff like that. I never have.

"Reinventing the game? If you look back into the days in the mid-'80s on the back fields of Gene Autry Park we were doing crazy stuff back there, trying different things then. It's not about reinvention. It's about trying to stay ahead of things, especially when you are managing the Rays. You have the limited payroll. You are playing the Yankees and the Red Sox. You are playing all these big-market teams often, anyway. How do you beat them?

"If you try to go with the conventional, you are going to get your brains beat out. They have greater ability to win with more tried-and-true than you do. You've got to figure out different angles or ways to get through all that.

"I never really worried about people saying things like that. I hope that doesn't sound conceited in any way. I mean, there is self-confidence there, or it's the fact that I know what I'm doing and why I'm doing it. It's not that I'm trying to impress anybody."

CHAPTER 13

GAME 4

T hree games into the World Series, two of which ended in the Cubs getting shut out, an obvious pattern had developed and it disturbed Joe Maddon as he sat in his office before Game 4.

"If we're going to chase, they're going to kick our ass," he said.

A year earlier, the Cubs reached the National League Championship Series despite failing miserably at situational hitting, the art of advancing runners by putting the ball in play. With so much swing-and-miss in their game, the 2015 Cubs regularly killed rallies with strikeouts. Among all 30 major league teams in 2015, the Cubs had the most strikeouts (a club record 1,518), were last in hitting with two strikes (.154), had the most strikeouts with runners in scoring position (404), were last in hitting with a runner at third and less than two outs (.237), 28th in hitting with runners in scoring position (.237), and—in a flaw that became a fatal one against the hard-throwing staff of the New York Mets in the NLCS—24th in hitting against power pitchers (.213).

Epstein and Hoyer set about fixing the lack of contact in their offense when they went shopping on the free agent market after the season. They signed outfielder Jason Heyward and infielder/

outfielder Ben Zobrist for a combined $240 million. Heyward and Zobrist made the Cubs one of only three teams in the league with two everyday players who did not strike out 100 times. The Giants (Buster Posey and Denard Span) and the Braves (Adonis Garcia and Ender Inciarte) were the only other such teams.

The additions of Heyward and Zobrist, as well as improved two-strike approaches by second-year players Kris Bryant and Addison Russell, made the Cubs a vastly improved situational hitting team. In 2016 they improved across the board in all key contact categories. They improved to 21st in strikeouts (1,339, a 12 percent reduction), 6th in hitting with two strikes (.184, a 30-point improvement), 27th in strikeouts with runners in scoring position (381, a small improvement), 10th in hitting with a runner on third and less than two outs (.332, a whopping 95-point jump), 21st in hitting with runners in scoring position (.252, a 15-point increase), and 16th against power pitchers (.229, a 16-point betterment).

The bottom line was that the 2016 Cubs were better equipped for the postseason than the 2015 Cubs because they made more and better contact, especially in high-leverage spots. The ability to make contact becomes even more valuable in the postseason because managers rely more on their best pitchers. With extra off days built into the postseason schedule, managers never use their fifth starter and rarely use their fourth starter or middle relievers. The Cleveland Indians, for instance, had as many off days to play 15 postseason games (16) as they did to play their final 142 games of the regular season.

Because of that lighter schedule, and because of injuries to starting pitchers Carlos Carrasco and Danny Salazar, Cleveland manager Terry Francona opted to use a three-man rotation in the World Series: Corey Kluber, Trevor Bauer, and Josh Tomlin. That meant that Kluber, who had chewed up the Cubs in Game 1, was back to face them in Game 4.

The improved situational offense of Chicago, however, was nowhere to be found through three games in the World Series. The Cubs were getting exploited by breaking balls, not by velocity.

Francona's best pitchers all had devastating breaking balls: Kluber threw sliders and curves with various-sized breaks, Tomlin threw a big-breaking curveball, reliever Andrew Miller owned a wicked slider, and closer Cody Allen showcased one of the best curveballs in the game.

Against them Cubs batters looked like they were playing a losing game of whack-a-mole: the pitches disappeared just when they thought they had them lined up. Often the pitches they whacked at were not strikes, but broke out of the strike zone. Entering Game 4, Kluber, Tomlin, Miller, and Allen had combined to shut out the Cubs over $16\frac{1}{3}$ innings, during which Chicago batters managed only three walks against 22 strikeouts. Maddon and hitting coaches John Mallee and Eric Hinske preached patience and an opposite-field approach, but batter after batter anxiously chased spinning pitches out of the zone.

Maddon, borrowing on his days as a roving hitting instructor, injected himself into the search for a remedy. He pulled aside both Addison Russell and Javier Baez before Game 4 for one-on-one discussions. The emphasis again was on hitting the ball a little deeper in its course to the plate—a contact point based on hitting the ball to right-centerfield—rather than trying to hit it farther in front, an anxious approach that is exploited by spinning, off-speed pitches.

"The last game Kluber pitched he had a low pitch count," Maddon said, referring to how Kluber needed only 88 pitches to cruise through six innings. "Yesterday I guess [Josh] Tomlin was making good pitches. We wanted to stay middle-oppo. We didn't do it. We knew about the curveball. We were taking the curveball strike and swinging at the curveball in the dirt.

"We knew what we wanted to do, we just didn't do it. We can hit spin. But if we can take the breaking ball that is a ball, we'll be fine. We have to."

The pattern raised a dark possibility about the Cubs: maybe they were just too young to win the World Series. Facing elite breaking-ball pitches in the cauldron of World Series pressure, maybe they just didn't have enough experience to curb their anxiety and show more discipline. Maddon considered the possibility himself. He knew youthfulness was causing them to chase pitches.

"Of course it is. Yeah. I totally believe that," he said. "That's why I keep trying to make a point that the area we're going to get better at over the next couple of years is hitting. I mean, if you're a scout, the area you project upon the most is hitting. The areas you project least with would be running speed, arm strength, defense—those are the things that are more static. So if a guy is here now, whatever you see now, like with Baez, whatever you see with baserunning and defense now is what you expect the next five, six years.

"The thing you can anticipate better is his hitting. All of our guys. So I'm really pleased that the other parts of their game that don't normally progress are pretty damn good already. The part that has the most improvement is the one they have to improve at. In my mind's eye, my God, whew! You just anticipate two years from now those at-bats are going to be different. I know they're going to be different. So that's the part I'm really encouraged about."

Two years. Game 4 was only three hours away.

Maddon made some tweaks to his lineup to try to jump-start the offense. He moved Russell from eighth to sixth ("Addison is the RBI guy," he said) and dropped Baez to eighth. Baez represented the most extreme case of youthfulness showing its downside. With two strikes he was virtually already out, because he was chasing the next pitch no matter how badly it was located.

"He's reverting just a click," Maddon said. "So I moved him back down. In a perfect world he should be hitting eighth. Then you just take what he gives you. You can't anticipate he's going to move the ball all the time because he can be so out of control at times."

Kluber had the kind of deep array of weaponry to exploit anxiety. His ERA over four postseason starts was just 0.74. In Game 1 he relied on a devastating two-seam fastball that he started at the front hip of left-handed batters and ran back over the inside corner of the plate. The best approach against such a pitch would be to back off the plate slightly to be able to hit the pitch as it runs back.

"We could," Maddon conceded. "But the hardest thing to get a hitter to do is move them in the batter's box. Theoretically, yeah it makes perfect sense. To get somebody to do that is really hard.

"We'll have to find out if he has that pitch going on again. What he had the other night was otherworldly. He may. I don't know. The other thing is our guys have seen him recently. That should help a little bit. When a guy is that good and you haven't seen him, he's as good as he can be. That's a problem."

THE CUBS' FIRST batter of the game, Dexter Fowler, dug into the batter's box against Kluber—from a spot a few inches farther off the plate than where he stood in Game 1. Kluber, on a 1-and-2 count, threw him one of those fiendish two-seam fastballs he had featured in Game 1. This time being farther off the plate gave Fowler room to pull his hands in and get the barrel of the bat on the ball. Fowler dumped a double into leftfield.

After Bryant popped out, Rizzo, the next left-handed batter, dug in. He, too, had moved off the plate. "I felt like I was a million miles off the plate," said Rizzo, who typically stands so close to the plate that his toes nearly reach the white chalk line of the batter's box. Rizzo ripped an 0-and-1 pitch to centerfield to drive in Fowler. The Cubs led, 1–0. They had dented the machine-like pitcher known as Klubot and they had done so by adjusting their feet in the batter's box. Even one run was a very good start.

Maddon likes to yell in the dugout, "Score first!" And if the opposing team scores first he will yell, "Score second!" Scoring first in the postseason, with the way teams emphasize hard-throwing specialized bullpens to protect leads, proved to be golden. Entering Game 4, the team that scored first in 2016 was 14–0 in the LCS and World Series, and 23–8 overall.

This time, however, Chicago starting pitcher John Lackey could not make the lead hold up. The Indians would win going away, 7–2. They clipped Lackey for two runs in the second, one facilitated by two throwing errors by Bryant, the second on a slow roller hit by Kluber he threw away in his haste.

"Our biggest deficit is contact on our part at the plate," Maddon said about the loss. "And we made a couple of mistakes. I can't believe K.B. threw the second ball. The chopper? Just eat it. I know Kluber was running, but just eat it."

Cleveland tacked on another run off Lackey in the third, when Jason Kipnis doubled and scored on a single by Francisco Lindor. Cleveland broke open the game in the seventh when Kipnis smashed a three-run homer off Travis Wood into the rightfield bleachers.

In his mind's eye, ever since he was a boy growing up in Northbrook, Illinois, 21 miles from Wrigley Field, Kipnis had hit hundreds of World Series home runs at the Friendly Confines. A Cubs fan, he was always batting the bottom of the ninth, full count, two outs.

The power of a boy's dream is one of life's little miracles, the way it wraps itself around the heart and remains through old age to the last breath. Kipnis's dream formed in his backyard, through Wiffle ball, softball, "an acorn that just fell off the tree—it didn't matter. It was anything and everything." Wood's pitch was just another acorn, and Kipnis knew just what to do with it.

"When I dreamed them," he said of his backyard homers, "they went farther."

The crowd went silent as he floated around the bases.

"Inside," he said, "I was smiling ear to ear."

As he floated on, Kipnis raised a hand in salute in the direction of his family and friends. He provided the first three-run World Series homer at Wrigley by a visitor since one of the sport's most famous homers, the called shot by Babe Ruth in 1932.

It was almost too much for a Cubs fan to bear. Getting beat again was one thing; getting beat by one of your own kind was especially cruel. Kipnis knew all about the "lovable losers" culture of the Cubs.

He was 11 years old when Sammy Sosa chased Mark McGwire, and 14 when the Cubs came within one win of the pennant. Between family trips, Cubs' instructional camps, field trips, and a ticket to Game 2 of the 2003 NLDS, Kipnis visited Wrigley Field a dozen times or so as a boy.

Just down the block from his house lived another Cubs fan who rode the school bus with him when they were small, and who also attended a 2003 Cubs playoff game: Steve Bartman, the fan who gained infamy around Cubs Nation for his attempt to catch a foul ball in 2003 NLCS Game 6.

Goats, black cats, Leon Durham, Steve Bartman, and now cursed by one of their own. What else could possibly go wrong for a Cubs fan?

Perhaps the worst of the news was that Maddon's fears about the youthfulness of his team were being realized. After Fowler and Rizzo adjusted to Kluber's two-seam fastball in the first inning, the Cleveland ace countered. He emphasized his slider as his weapon of choice. Kluber increased his usage of the pitch from 31 percent in Game 1 to 43 percent in Game 4. The young Chicago hitters continued to flail at it. Kluber pitched six strong innings again, shutting out the Cubs after the first inning and needing only 81 pitches in all. He became the first pitcher in a generation to start and win Games 1 and 4 of the World Series. José Rijo of the 1990 Cincinnati Reds had been the last such workhorse.

Were the Cubs too young to win the World Series? Were their offensive games not advanced enough to deal with the elite Cleveland pitching? After four games, those remained legitimate questions. The Cubs had scored just seven runs and were hitting .204. Bryant, Russell, Baez, and Contreras—all of them no older than 24—were batting .102, on just six hits in 59 at-bats.

Down three games to one, and even with their three best starters—Jon Lester, Jake Arrieta, and Kyle Hendricks—lined up and fully rested, the young Cubs hitters were running out of time to get it right. After 206 games stretching from spring training to the

World Series, they had no more room for error. One more defeat and their season was over. One more defeat and the curse remained intact and they would have to move on to a 109th try at winning another World Series.

In the bowels underneath Wrigley Field, in a groundskeeper's storage area used as a press conference room, Maddon grasped for hope.

"More than anything," Maddon said, "when you're not hitting like that, the whole vibe's very difficult to push in that real positive direction. So you'll continually try to be positive in the dugout during the course of the game. But, you know, it's difficult. It's difficult especially this time of year.

"We just need that offensive epiphany somehow to get us pushing in the right direction. And if we do that, I really think, based on what they have left pitching-wise, going back over there and what we have, I kind of like our chances."

Meanwhile, for a second straight night, there was no party in the Cubs' clubhouse celebration room. The franchise had waited 71 years to see another World Series at Wrigley Field, and after two nights this was the summation of the reprise: two runs, two losses, too young. Heads bowed, the Cubs retreated to their clubhouse in silence. The *feng shui* of the room didn't seem so powerful at a time like this. The mournful quiet suddenly broke when a lone *thwack!* rang out, the percussive result of one of the frustrated young Cubs firing his glove into the back of his wood locker.

"No, we're not going to do that!"

Teammates turned toward the voice. The loud admonition came from David Ross, the 39-year-old backup catcher—the eldest of them all. Ross was a .229 hitter for the season and for his career, and the personal catcher for Lester, the team's starting pitcher for Game 5.

"We've got a Game 5 tomorrow at Wrigley Field and Daddy's playing tomorrow!" Ross said, referring to his nickname, a twist on the Grandpa Rossy nickname started by Rizzo. "We're fine! Daddy's in the lineup tomorrow! Don't you worry. I'll take care of it!"

It had the perfect tone to it. Ross didn't want the young players brooding. It smacked of confidence and swagger, but at the same time, as with most things with the self-deprecating catcher, it was laced with the right touch of humor. He knew it was exactly how the Cubs would have to play Game 5: confident and loose. And that is how the comeback began.

CHAPTER 14

FLIPPING THE CULTURE

J oe Maddon didn't sleep so well on the night before he addressed the entire Cubs team for the first time as spring training opened in 2015 in Mesa, Arizona.

"It was a little *nervioso*, absolutely," he said. "I'd done it before, but
this was a little different venue, different scenario, and actually everybody was there—they had scouts there, minor league dudes, everybody. People waiting on your every word. I'm comfortable doing
it, but you have to get into the flow. Part of the tough part about
spring training is you've been off for a while. If I had to do that same
thing July 1, you could fill up Wrigley and I'm fine. You've done it a
hundred times, but you're in this new situation."

He remembered his first day as manager of the 2006 Tampa Bay
Devil Rays as "daunting." It was his first major league managing job,
and the Devil Rays were still a ragtag, noncompetitive expansion
team with no defined culture and players who needed to be weeded
out.

"I had done a lot of things up to that point, but I never had my
own team," he said. "There is nothing quite like holding your own
baby. So that's pretty much what it came down to. For all the parents

out there, you know the difference. So I got a chance to hold my own baby for the very first time."

It took two years for Maddon to turn Tampa Bay into a pennant winner. With the Cubs, he knew he had the makings of a good team immediately, even with the team having finished fifth five years running. To the core group, and with youngsters Kris Bryant, Addison Russell, and Kyle Schwarber knocking on the door, Epstein and Hoyer that off-season added pitchers Jon Lester and Jason Hammel, catchers David Ross and Miguel Montero, and outfielders Dexter Fowler and Chris Denorfia.

"The message is going to be kind of the same," Maddon said before his speech. "I feel very confident about the message regarding how do you flip a culture, what are the processes, what is the first step? I feel good about that. So when I walk into that meeting in the theater in Mesa I will be more confident in that message than I was even the first day I spoke to the Devil Rays."

Anthony Rizzo already had talked boldly about the Cubs winning the National League Central, and instructed reporters to make sure they quoted him on it. Maddon talked about aiming to go to the World Series. There was more optimism around the 2015 Cubs than perhaps any other team in history coming off five straight fifth-place finishes. Maddon knew it would take much more than optimism. He knew the first step toward flipping a culture, and it would be the theme of his first-day speech. It was his golden rule of managing: connect, trust, and lead—in that order.

"What you need to understand," Maddon told the assembled members of the organization, but especially the players, "is that we need to get to know each other. We need to start trusting each other. And then we have to start bouncing ideas off one another without any pushback. In other words, once you've trusted me and I've trusted you, we can exchange ideas openly without this concern about who's right. That's natural. That's human nature. You've got to get beyond the 'who's right' moment."

He added that he would require only one rule, which they could see painted on the grass beside the baselines of the practice field: "Respect 90," a title he liked so much he used it for his charitable foundation, which provides support for inner-city youth programs.

"Just remember this: choose right," he said. "You know the difference between right and wrong. If you choose right, there will be no issues. We'll all be fine and I won't have to make any rules."

Part of choosing right, Maddon told the players, was choosing to work on their mental skills. As Epstein rebuilt the Cubs with an emphasis on developing the whole player, he understood that improving a player's mental skills deserved as much attention as improving a player's batting stroke or pitching delivery.

"It's a huge part of modern baseball," Epstein said.

During the 2014 season, Epstein conducted a search to upgrade the mental skills program and personnel he had inherited. Just before the 2015 spring training, he announced the creation of a new four-person mental skills department. As director he hired Josh Lifrak, who spent 10 years as mental conditioning consultant at IMG Academy in Bradenton, Florida. He hired former major league outfielder Darnell McDonald as mental skills coordinator and assigned Rey Fuentes to Latin mental skills coordinator. He also brought in Ken Ravizza, a psychology professor who worked in the kinesiology department at Cal State–Fullerton. Ravizza joined the Cubs on the recommendation of Maddon. They had been friends since 1985, when Maddon was coaching in the Angels minor league system, and Angels pitching coach Marcel Lachemann brought Ravizza in to work with Angels players. Maddon brought Ravizza to the Rays in 2009, after which Ravizza returned to the Angels in 2011.

Ravizza, 68, was around the team throughout spring training. At one point, Ravizza gathered the team around him on a practice field. On the ground he placed a line of 162 baseballs divided by seven bats. Each ball represented one game of the season. The bats represented the months of the baseball season, including October.

Beyond the seventh bat were 19 more baseballs, representing the number of games the Cubs might have to play in the postseason to win the World Series. It made for a stark visual reminder of the length of the journey, and how this year the Cubs were preparing not just to get to the playoffs, but also to win them.

Though mental skills coaches such as Ravizza had been around baseball for three decades or more, they still ran up against resistance in the macho world of the clubhouse that questioned their place in the game. Improving your performance through methods like visualization, mindfulness, and proper breathing were resisted by some traditionalists as something between quackery and a service for the weak-minded. In his opening speech, Maddon made sure his players did not think that way.

"If you're not talking to a mental skills guy to get better, you're crazy," Maddon told them. "I do it, you do it, the best players in the game do it. There's a stigma to *not* doing it. If you're not doing it, you're not trying to get better."

Said Epstein, "Joe really legitimized it in our big league clubhouse. The vestiges of the stigma that was associated with it 10 to 15 years ago still remained. It's still a little weird for a guy to talk about it openly. Joe couldn't be more onboard with mental skills training."

After Maddon's opening speech as Chicago manager, the Cubs took the field—actually, a wide swath of grass out in back of their training center—looking like a different team. The best way to measure the immediate change in the Cubs under Maddon was in decibels. As the team began its morning stretch, a huge speaker blasted "Voodoo Child" by Jimi Hendrix. What followed were more tunes from among Maddon's rock-and-roll favorites, including "Brown Sugar" by the Rolling Stones, "Gimme Three Steps" by Lynyrd Skynyrd, and "Tom Sawyer" by Rush.

"I'm a product of the '60s and '70s," he told his new team. "You'll have to put up with that."

The idea behind the loud music, Maddon explained later, was to "get the blood flowing" at the start of the day. Yes, sir, these were not your older brother's Cubs, never mind your grandfather's Cubs. Maddon looked like something of an oddity himself, or some kind of interloper, because he patrolled the fields wearing uniform number 70. It was such a strange number that nobody in franchise history ever wore it before he arrived. Maddon's preferred baseball number was always 20, which he wore in the Angels organization as a player and minor league manager. Then one day in September 1985 he saw a jersey with number 70 hanging in his locker. Equipment manager Leonard Garcia randomly gave him the number after the club traded for pitcher Don Sutton, the future Hall of Famer, who was accustomed to wearing 20 and had the seniority to claim it in Anaheim. Maddon, never wanting to have a number seized again, vowed that day he would always wear 70, such an unpopular number that only five players, all of them journeyman relievers since 2009, have worn it for more than one season in the big leagues. The guy with the white hair, thick-rimmed glasses, and number 70 on his back grabbed the Cubs' attention and confidence from day one.

"I went in, as someone playing on the opposite side against him, thinking this guy was about trickery and gimmicks," Ross said about his expectations for Maddon. "One of the things you feel right away is the genuineness when he talks. He's just talking about the fundamentals of baseball. He wants to be fundamentally sound. I remember thinking, *Wait a minute. This guy reminds me of Bobby Cox—how he teaches, how he talks, how he doesn't have a lot of rules, how he builds a foundation on just doing the right thing.* He establishes an atmosphere where you have a choice between right and wrong, and you choose right. You don't need rules for that."

It didn't take long for the Cubs to understand that Maddon, the old minor league roving instructor, would be a stickler for playing the game the right way. Just a few days into camp, the Cubs were practicing relays and cutoffs when Maddon suddenly stopped the drill. He was appalled that the Cubs were going through the motions, flipping balls casually with a halfhearted effort. He called it the "only time I blew up" at his team in his first two years managing the Cubs.

"Because I felt they didn't get it," he said. "They were a bunch of young guys in the major leagues going through the motions. 'Okay, we've got to do this today and move on.' I didn't like it. I didn't like it at all.

"I was yelling a little bit, making sure they understood I didn't like it. That's not how you win. I told them, 'We need to do things like this better. You've got to care about stuff like this. This is a separator: you have the group that cares about something like this and the group that doesn't.' I made them do it over."

To hammer home his point, Maddon integrated a drill over the next few days that normally is used with Little Leaguers. He split players in lines of five, spread across the outfield. The players would throw the ball to the next man in line, who would catch, turn, and throw to the next in line, and so on, with the ball passed back and forth.

"It was like I was going back to instructional league, like what I did in the early '80s," Maddon said. "A lot of them felt in a way slighted or they were being babied, or 'How dare you have us do this?' But then there were some who got it, and a bunch of them were veterans that liked it. Honestly, it paid off. We might have blown one relay in 2015, maybe two at the most. We were nails. And we were nails again last year.

"It's the fundamental itself. I want your best effort when you go through it, when you go through a fundamental. Whether it's cutoffs and relays, rundowns, first and third defense, bunt defense is big—I just want them to give the drill their full attention until we move on."

Maddon never forgot the mantra from the football coaches at Lafayette he heard over and over as a freshman quarterback: "zero defects." Run the drill, and keep running the drill until you get it right. The ratio of practice time to game time in football is far greater than in baseball, so the importance of drilling is a deep part of the football culture.

"Baseball players, man, they don't get it. They didn't play football," Maddon said. "Too many times on a major league level major leaguers are permitted to do it wrong—by bad habits or you don't call their attention to it in drills. Because some coaches are intimidated. What's the most important attribute a major league coach has? He's fearless. He knows his stuff. He's been doing it for a while. He has this opportunity. But a major league coach if he's not afraid to call BS is a really good major league coach. They're my favorite ones."

On the fourth day of camp, long after everybody had gone home for the day, Maddon sat on a bench at the training facility and took inventory of his new team. It was early, sure, but now he had seen for himself the kind of talent Epstein had told him about in the Chicago system.

"The thin slicing of it is the young players are as good as I've heard," he said. "They're that exciting. You know, a lot of times you read stuff, you hear stuff. I have not been in the National League ever. So I don't know that stuff. But when I see these guys on the field, get to talk to them in meetings, watch their work, and see their skill level, I believe it's absolutely true."

After four days he was convinced that his optimism about the Cubs was real—the team actually had a chance to go to the 2015 World Series.

"That's what I'm saying," he said. "Our biggest thing is that our veterans would be able to stay healthy and be there to complement these guys and ride us when it's going wrong a little bit, primarily in the clubhouse, making sure they don't get down on themselves when things aren't going well. But I think there's the right mixture of veteran players here, too, and the right veteran players, too. I mean, David Ross is as good as advertised. Period."

Then he talked about that first-day meeting and the importance of trusting one another. Every early indication was that this group got the message.

"If we just support each other and work like this? We'll be just fine," he said. "They're talented, man. Whoa! I mean, I've been around a lot of good classes. This is way up there."

The recruiting pitch Epstein gave Maddon and Lester that winter could be seen with their own eyes: the Cubs were loaded.

ONCE THE SPRING training games began, Bryant was the talk not only of camp, but also of all the major leagues. After leading the minor leagues with 43 home runs in 2014, Bryant led the majors in spring training home runs with nine while batting .425. On March 30, 2015, the Cubs sent Bryant, Baez, and Russell back to the minor leagues.

"I could be in this game for a long time and not send down three players that talented on the same day ever again," Epstein said.

The Cubs would not admit it, but the truth about Bryant's demotion was that it was the prudent course of action based on service time rules in the collective bargaining agreement. If the Cubs carried Bryant on the Opening Day roster, he would have been eligible to leave the team as a free agent after the 2020 season, having accumulated six full years of service time. But if they stashed him in the minors for as few as 12 days, it would take an extra year for him to reach six full years of service time—through 2021. In other words, the Cubs could be assured of keeping Bryant for an extra year if they just demoted him for 12 days.

The "trick" of delaying the start of a player's service-time "clock" is a common one around baseball. In 2012, for instance, the Cubs brought up Rizzo from the minors with 100 service days left in the season. Added to the 68 days of service he had with the Padres, Rizzo finished the season with 168 days of service time—conveniently for the Cubs, 4 days short of a full service year, thus "buying" an extra year of control.

The Major League Baseball Players Association was so angered about Bryant's demotion that it released a statement that read, "Today is a bad day for baseball. I think we all know that even if Kris Bryant were a combination of the greatest players to play our game, and perhaps he will be before it's all said and done, the Cubs still would have made the decision they made today. This decision, and other similar decisions made by clubs will be addressed in litigation, bargaining or both."

Just before the Cubs announced the demotion, Bryant walked into Maddon's office to plead his case.

"I'm ready to play up here," Bryant told him. "I know I am."

"K.B., I get it," Maddon said. "Just understand you're going to be here very soon. You're a huge part of our future. Everything is going to work out well. Understand, I know you're very young, but this is going to go by really quickly and you're going to be back here and everything is going to be fine. So if you can just process that, you have to trust me on that one."

For all his talent and acclaim, Bryant is a humble, charming sort with an aw-shucks grin and gentlemanly manners. His measured reaction to being demoted without cause when it came to his performance spoke loudly to his modesty. Bryant went to Triple-A Iowa, where, instead of pouting, he hit three homers in seven games. While Bryant was in the minors, the Cubs used Mike Olt, Jonathan Herrera, Arismendy Alcantara, and Chris Coghlan at third base. They hit .148. The team went 5–3 in the first 12 days. As soon as the 12 days passed, the Cubs promoted Bryant to the big leagues. Bryant would hit 26 home runs and be named the National League Rookie of the Year.

"He's a pleasure," Maddon said. "The beauty about him is conversationally you can talk straight up with him and he will talk straight up back at you—in a very polite, humble way. I learned that the first year, when all that stuff was coming down about him being sent back out. He talked to me and came into the office. I'm just getting to know the guy, and I start thinking, *My God, this guy's different.*"

EXPECTATIONS SOARED FOR the Cubs in the spring of 2015, which placed pressure on Lester, the big free agent addition—and that was on top of the pressure he already felt to live up to the $155 million contract. It was clear immediately in Mesa that Lester felt this burden.

The first time a pitcher faces hitters in spring training is a low-key exercise in a controlled environment. It is live batting practice on a back field in which the pitcher throws with a protective screen in front of him and a batting cage surrounds the area of home plate. A pitcher is limited to a certain number of pitches, typically around 25 to 30. Minor league prospects might overthrow in such a setting to try to catch the eye of coaches and club personnel watching the workout, but veterans know it's nothing more than "getting my work in" to prepare for the grind of a long season.

Lester's first time on the mound for the Cubs, however, had the look of a late-season game. He grinded through his outing with obvious effort and with anger that he wasn't putting his pitches exactly where he wanted them. When pitching coach Chris Bosio told him he was done upon reaching his prescribed limit of pitches, Lester insisted on staying because he wasn't happy with his stuff. He grinded through another 10 or so pitches. Lester would throw with so much exertion that spring that he developed a condition known as "dead arm"—when otherwise healthy pitchers lose the snap on their pitches, reminiscent of his senior year in high school—that carried into April.

Lester's competitive streak had helped him earn that $155 million. But that day in Mesa was an indication that such tenacity could also cut the wrong way. When Epstein told Lester during the recruiting process that he could be for the Cubs what Curt Schilling was for the 2004 Red Sox, Lester nodded in agreement even before Epstein finished the sentence. But there was one big difference between the arrival of Schilling in Boston and the arrival of Lester in Chicago. Schilling was joining a veteran-laden team that had just won 95 games and had come within one victory of the World Series. Lester was joining a young, last-place team that had won just 73 games and finished 17 games out of first place.

Trying too hard, Lester ended his first month as a Cub without a win and with a 6.23 ERA. By June 30, Lester was 4–6 with a 4.03 ERA and the Cubs had lost five straight games to fall a season-worst 11½ games out of first place. Chicago would play its next three games at Citi Field against the Mets. Maddon sensed that the entire team, not just Lester, was tight. So he arranged for a magician to entertain his team before the game that night in New York. Simon Winthrop, a Las Vegas magician originally from Chicago, entertained the Cubs with card tricks and illusions.

"Well, we're looking to create some magic," Maddon explained to reporters. "Just trying to lighten things up a little bit, and we're always trying to create some magic around here, so why not bring a magician in?"

It was pure Maddon. Not only was he lightening the mood around his team, he was also creating a diversion for the media. A magician in a major league clubhouse made for a better story than another day of analyzing what was wrong with the Cubs.

Presto! The Cubs won that night, 1–0. Lester started the next night and threw one of his best games of the season: seven shutout innings with one walk and seven strikeouts as Chicago won in 11 innings, 2–0. The Cubs completed a three-game sweep the next night with a 6–1 victory. Their pitchers allowed New York one run in 29 innings in the three games.

The outing in New York, if not the magician, settled Lester. It was the first of seven consecutive starts in which he threw seven innings. From that start through the end of the regular season, Lester went 7–6 with a 2.80 ERA while averaging almost seven innings per start. In those 17 starts Lester became exactly the elite workhorse Epstein expected when he signed him. He finished the season with 207 strikeouts, the most ever by a Cubs left-hander.

"April was tough on me," Lester said, "especially coming here and all the expectations, and you know, not only personally but as a team. And to go out there and do what I did, I wasn't obviously too proud of that.

"So if I knew how to get off to a better start, it would happen more frequently. But with that being said, just over the years I've been around a lot of guys—the Schills, the [Josh] Becketts—that I've heard them say numerous times that they don't really feel good with their mechanics and stuff until they reach about 100 innings. For whatever reason that is, I guess that's kind of how I feel. I don't know if it's just because we're bigger-bodied guys or just a feel or we pitch better when we're a little bit tired. I don't know. Just the way I'm built, I guess."

Lester's turnaround also coincided with one change Maddon made with him: he stopped trying to cure Lester of his curious case of the "yips" throwing to bases.

A young Lester was a difficult study for any baserunner. From 2006 to 2011 with the Red Sox, Lester allowed only a 67 percent success rate on stolen base attempts and picked off 24 runners. From 2009 to 2011 he made 247 pickoff attempts. But late in that 2011 season Lester suddenly and without explanation developed a mental block about throwing to bases.

"It started surfacing when I was there," said Indians manager Terry Francona, whose last year as Boston manager was 2011. "It was nothing like what it is now, but we did some things to cover for it."

Lester virtually stopped throwing to bases altogether. Francona's successor as Boston manager, Bobby Valentine, had Lester work on his awkward pickoff throws in spring training, but with no progress. That year, 2012, after averaging 82 pickoff throws per season over the previous three years, Lester tried only 5 pickoffs all year. The next year, 2013, Lester tried 7 pickoffs through April 10, then completely stopped trying. He didn't make another pickoff attempt the rest of the season, nor in 2014.

His throwing issue gained national attention in the 2014 American League wild card game when the Kansas City Royals easily swiped three bases against him.

Cases of the yips are equally rare and mysterious. The cause and cure of the malady are predominantly unknown. Pitchers Steve Blass, Rick Ankiel, Kevin Saucier, and Mark Wohlers developed the yips when it came to throwing strikes. Catchers Mackey Sasser, Mike Ivie, and Jarrod Saltalamacchia incurred the phobia throwing the baseball back to the pitcher. Second basemen Steve Sax and Chuck Knoblauch had trouble completing a routine throw to first base. The most similar pitchers to Lester, as it relates to throwing strikes on the mound but hitting a mental block throwing to bases, were Matt Young and Matt Garza.

When Lester and Maddon joined the Cubs the following spring, Maddon's first instinct was to "cure" Lester of this phobia. Under the direction of pitching coach Chris Bosio, Lester would retreat to a back field of the complex and try different ways of throwing the ball to Rizzo, the first baseman. They tried having Lester step off the rubber before throwing. They tried having Lester throw the ball to Rizzo on a bounce. They tried having Lester lob the ball to Rizzo.

"He would do well on the back field," Maddon said.

But game situations produced a much different outcome. The mental block that prevented one of the game's best pitchers from completing a routine throw to first base showed up every game. Maddon suddenly experienced a revelation in June.

"What are we doing here?" he asked himself. "Why do we keep putting these thoughts in his head?"

He sat down with Lester in his office. He told him about a new plan for him.

"Let's get our concentration back on the hitter," he told him. "Let's work on what we do well, not on what we don't do well. The more attention you put on what you don't do well, the stuff you do well is getting away from you. And my contention is if you continue to do well in what you do do well, the other stuff is going to become moot."

So Maddon convened with Lester, Ross, and Rizzo and developed a plan to defend against Lester's throwing issue. Lester would not have to worry about throwing to a base at all. With potential base stealers at first, he would work hard to vary the time he held the ball before throwing home—a tactic to prevent the runner from timing his delivery for a fast start—and he would pitch out of a tucked position (80 percent of his weight on his back foot to start) and with a slide step (in which the stride foot stays close to the ground). With those tactics Lester could deliver the ball to the catcher in 1.3 seconds. Ross was the quickest catcher in the league with his transfer, the time it took him to catch and throw. Ross could catch the ball and get it into the infielder's glove at second base in 1.8 seconds. The combined time of 3.1 seconds was faster than most runners needed to get to second base safely.

Moreover, Maddon empowered Ross to call disguised pitchouts to trigger pickoff plays to Rizzo as he saw fit. Maddon would also intervene if he thought a runner was getting too far off the base after a Lester pitch. Ross would go on to pick off 11 runners in two years, by far the most in baseball. Between Lester's quick move home and Ross's dangerous arm, Lester no longer had to worry about throwing to first base.

"I really believe that was part of the bad start in 2015, that his concentration was being split," Maddon said. "So I got everybody together and formulated a much simpler plan in order to prevent this. At the end of the day, he's much more difficult to steal a base against than a lot of our relief pitchers are.

"It was blown up in the media, rightfully so, but how do you fix it? 'Oh, I'm going to give him this great move. I'm going to take him out there and he'll get this epiphany to free his mind.' No. That doesn't happen. That's not what happens when you're 30 years old. It may occur when you're a teenager and maybe later in life with maybe a different outlook on life. But when it comes to a physical concern and doing something different in front of 40,000 people, it's hard.

"So my epiphany was just that. Let's focus on what he does well, not on what he doesn't do well. The other part is these guys are getting so far off first base they don't know what they're doing. And if he quick-steps, David is going to pick them off. It's still not as easy as they think it is. At 3.1 seconds, you're out."

In August, David Ross left the team to return home to Florida because of a family emergency. His pregnant wife, Hyla, was rushed to a hospital for an emergency cesarean section two months ahead of her due date because of a partial abruption, which occurs when the placenta separates from the uterus. Both Hyla, because of risks from bleeding, and their daughter she was carrying, Harper, their third child, were in danger. With Ross in the room, both mother and child made it through the procedure fine, though Harper would spend a month in the neonatal intensive care unit before she could come home.

Ross spent 10 days away from the team. During that time Epstein and Maddon called him almost every day. Epstein assured him that "every guy in the clubhouse" wanted him to be with his family, and to take as much time as he needed. Maddon told him not to hurry back. "We need David Ross back," Maddon told him, "not just a piece of David Ross." The team arranged to send $500 worth of food to Ross's house so that he and his children would be fed without having to worry about arranging for meals.

"That meant a lot to me," Ross said. "They said, 'Come back when you're right—when mentally you are right.' It made me think about that video they sent me, when I was a free agent, about the way they care about you and your family. It really was true."

On August 29, Lester pitched in Los Angeles against the Dodgers without his buddy behind the plate. Miguel Montero took Ross's place at catcher. Lester gave up five runs and lost, 5–2.

After the season the Cubs sent a video crew to Ross's house. They taped a segment in which Ross talked about how the team cared for him during his family leave, and how the Cubs also had sent him home when his grandmother passed away just two weeks before the family emergency.

"Jason Heyward told me they used that video to show him when he was a free agent, and it meant a lot to him," Ross said. "So that was kind of cool."

As the Cubs folded Bryant, Schwarber, Baez, and Russell into the lineup over the course of the 2015 season, the offense became more formidable. The team batting average improved from .239 in the first half to .250 in the second half. Less obvious, though of even greater import, was the improvement the Cubs made with their pitching and defense. That year the Cubs instituted a run-prevention infrastructure that was at the heart of the team's turnaround.

In 2014 the Cubs were among the nine worst teams in baseball at turning batted balls into outs (68 percent, a rate known as defensive efficiency) and among the nine worst teams when it came to batting average on balls in play against their pitchers (excluding home runs and strikeouts, opposing batters hit .308). In 2015 they flipped the script. They were one of the nine *best* teams at defensive efficiency (69.5) and one of the nine *best* teams when it came to batting average on balls in play (.290). Oddly enough, the turnaround began with a hitting coach.

In December 2014, Epstein hired John Mallee as one of the two Cubs hitting coaches. Mallee, who held a similar job with the Houston Astros, grew up in the south side Chicago neighborhood of Hegewisch. His dad was a Chicago police officer. During the interview process, Mallee mentioned to Epstein how in Houston he benefited from a dedicated support assistant, somebody who could coordinate all things hitting, including scouting reports and video. Epstein liked the idea. He quickly decided to dedicate two "coordinators," one to oversee the offensive side of the game and one for the defensive side. He named video coordinator Nate Halm, then 29 and a former college catcher, to the position of coordinator, advance scouting. Unofficially, Halm became the "run-production coordinator."

As a second coordinator, advance scouting—unofficially, the "run-prevention coordinator"—Epstein hired Tommy Hottovy, then

33, a veteran of 10 minor league seasons who pitched in 17 major league games before he blew out his shoulder in Cubs spring training camp in 2014. While rehabbing his shoulder that summer, Hottovy, who majored in finance with a minor in economics at Wichita State, took a Sabermetrics 101 online course offered by Boston University.

Backing up the coaches and coordinators were 11 back-office analytical wonks with no playing experience. Epstein may have broadened his scope of player acquisition and development over the years to emphasize character, but he did so as an adjunct, not a replacement, for quantitative analysis. If anything, the Cubs drilled even more deeply into analytics than the Red Sox had under Epstein.

The 11-member analytics team included Jeremy Greenhouse, who was hired in January 2014, three years after graduating from Tufts University, where he served as president of the Baseball Analysis Club and the Table Tennis Club. The day before his graduation, Greenhouse, then an analyst for Bloomberg Sports, was a co-presenter at a conference at Harvard titled "Sabermetrics, Scouting and the Science of Baseball." The talk focused on "how Win Probability Added divided by Leveraged Index is calculated, and why he thinks it is a superior stat to Linear Weights."

When Epstein hired Maddon, he designated Greenhouse as Maddon's personal analytics assistant. If Maddon wondered about the optimum situations to bat the pitcher eighth in the lineup, for instance, he could call Greenhouse, who would crunch the numbers to give him an answer.

Working with Greenhouse was Sean Ahmed, whose title was analyst, research and development. Ahmed earned a degree in economics from the University of Chicago in 2006. Greenhouse and Ahmed were just two of the hundreds of millenials with degrees from elite schools who instead of chasing high-paying jobs on Wall Street and Silicon Valley were entering Major League Baseball, no doubt inspired by people like Epstein. Baseball had come a long way since the mid-'90s, when Epstein occupied a desk with the San Diego

Padres that sat between the analytics guy and the scouting guy who had such disregard for one another they didn't talk to each other.

What Epstein did in Chicago, starting in 2015, was to blend the two separate silos of information as never before. Ahmed, for instance, is the "defensive specialist" of the research and development department. His job is to crunch the data from advance scouts and game video to draw up models on where best to position the Chicago defenders for each hitter.

Those models are passed to Hottovy, the bridge between the wonks and the on-field staff who speaks both of their languages. He synthesizes the data with his own observations—he is with the club both home and away and typically watches games in a seat high above the field.

When it is time to formulate specific game plans for pitching and defense—really, it's foolish to try to separate the two—Bosio, the pitching coach, is the point person. He oversees Hottovy and catching instructor Mike Borzello in coordinating the overall game plan of how to attack opposing hitters and where to best position the seven players behind the pitcher. Bullpen coach Lester Strode delivers it to the relievers. Third base coach Gary Jones serves as the infield instructor while first base coach Brandon Hyde and bench coach Dave Martinez make in-game positioning adjustments.

The specifics of pitch calling and sequencing—what, where, and when to throw to individual hitters—is driven by Borzello, a former minor league catcher in the St. Louis Cardinals organization who played in just 42 games over four years with a .151 batting average before his release after the 1994 season. Borzello went home to California to take a job driving a delivery truck for his father, Matt, a childhood friend of Joe Torre in Brooklyn. When the Yankees hired Torre to manage in 1996, Torre invited Mike to try out during spring training for a spot on the Yankees' support staff. Mike would have to pay his own way. Borzello earned a job as a batting practice pitcher and bullpen catcher. The Yankees players respected Borzello so much that when they won the World Series that year they voted him three-quarters of a World Series share, about $180,000—a generous amount for someone who was neither a player nor a full-time coach. Borzello won three more World Series championship rings in New York before joining Torre in Los Angeles in 2008.

Borzello's career reached a turning point in 2009, when veteran catcher Brad Ausmus joined the Dodgers at a time when video scouting information was becoming easily accessible by computer. Twenty of the 30 major league teams at the time, including the Dodgers, were using a video software system called B.A.T.S. from Sydex Sports. The scouting reports that used to take three days of acquiring and breaking down video could be done in 15 minutes. Teams were building "video rooms" around clubhouses to facilitate video study. Ausmus loved digging into the B.A.T.S. system for clues about how to break down opposing hitters.

"I was lucky enough to sit down with him and learn this new age stuff, and it was enlightening and fun at the same time," Borzello said. "Brad was all into it. He had a lot of time to study because Russell Martin was playing every day. So Brad was really the one who brought this to the table. I thought, *This is really, really important and can change the game.*

"I feel like up until the last couple of years so many pitchers went out there and pitched blind. They just pitched off their strengths. This system points out the weakness of the hitters. Over time the system I used kept evolving—kind of like the Ausmus system on steroids. It's become really, really, really in depth."

After the 2011 season, Dale Sveum, who had been a Red Sox coach in 2004–2005, called Borzello with a tentative job offer.

"I think I'm going to get the Red Sox managerial job," Sveum told Borzello. "Would you come with me?"

"Yeah. Actually, I'm probably going to need a job," said Borzello, as the Dodgers were in the midst of an ownership change.

Two days later, Sveum called Borzello back.

"Would you come if it's the Cubs?"

"Sure."

"It looks like the Red Sox are going back and forth. It looks like the Cubs are going to offer me the job and I'll take it. I'd like you with me. I want you to help Bosio and put together an infrastructure of scouting reports like you did with the Dodgers."

Epstein and Hoyer did hire Sveum. They gave conditional approval to his hiring of Borzello, but first wanted to meet with Borzello for an interview.

"I had done a little research going in," Borzello said. "Dale had already told me they were pretty good guys. I made a couple of calls. I talked to Gary Tuck, who was one of their bullpen coaches in Boston. He told me, 'You'll love them.' I thought, *If Tuck loves them they must be great guys.* He's a tough nut to crack.

"First, I sat with Jed [Hoyer] for about an hour. It was almost like two fans talking about the team. He was really reflective about the Yankees–Red Sox rivalry in those years and wanted my perspective from the other side. It was a fun, easy conversation. He's got a great personality anyway, but it was especially fun rehashing those wars we both went through.

"Then, after we wrapped up, I went into Theo's office. He was a little more direct, asking me about what I do and what I would bring to the table. And we talked a little more in technical terms about the catching position—essentially what I was being hired to do. It was very in-depth. He said he had heard a lot of good things about me, some things that weren't as good, and he wanted to hear me out.

"That was it. I flew out the next day. Randy Bush called me a couple of days later and offered me the job."

Officially, his title is catching coach, but not only does Borzello help with game-planning, he also works with the catchers in between innings on scouting reports and pitch selections. When the Cubs come off the field, the catcher will sit next to Borzello and they will review how to pitch at least the next three hitters due up for the opponent. When they are in the field, Borzello stands near the dugout rail to assist in the pitch calling. While he does not call pitches, Borzello is ready with a suggestion if the catcher looks over for help.

"He is our secret weapon," Epstein said. "And I mean that sincerely."

"Borzy is the best," Maddon said. "He *is* the secret weapon. He doesn't exist anywhere else. You have hitting coaches, assistants to the hitting coach, pitching coaches, assistants to the pitching coach, but nobody else has a Borzello.

"His ability to break it down is different from anybody else. First of all, it's the time he puts into it. Then it's his ability to disseminate data and what he's seeing and write it down in little boxes to pinpoint what to do and what not to do against certain guys—to the point of certainty. It's not like he says, 'Maybe.' It's, 'Do this. Don't do this.' There are no maybes.

"I'll test him during games. I'll say, 'I like this here,' and he'll go, 'Yes,' or 'Ahh, I'd rather this.' He's very certain. And that's important. I don't care if it doesn't work. He's very convicted, and I like that a lot."

The Cubs reached the 2015 All-Star break with a record of 47–40. But as their run-prevention infrastructure took root in the second half, they became one of the most efficient pitching and defensive teams in baseball. After the All-Star break, they ranked first in strikeouts (677), first in batting average allowed (.234), first in on-base percentage allowed (.291), and third in earned run average (3.42). Most important of all, they ranked first in wins (50, the most for the franchise after the All-Star break since 1945).

From the whip-smart recent college grads in the back office, to Borzello's insanely detailed game plans, to Bosio's physical and mental preparation of his pitchers, to Hottovy's synthesis of information, the Cubs in 2015 built the baseball equivalent of a Central Intelligence Agency for pitching and defense. Nobody personified the efficacy of this system better than Jake Arrieta. A pitcher once given up as a lost talent by the Baltimore Orioles, Arrieta flourished in the system in the second half of the season. In his 15 starts after the All-Star break Arrieta allowed only nine runs. His 0.75 ERA over 107⅓ innings set a record for the lowest second-half ERA since the All-Star Game began in 1933.

Overall, Arrieta was 22–6 with a 1.77 ERA, the lowest ERA by a Cubs pitcher since Grover Cleveland Alexander in 1920. Only two other pitchers had won so many games with such a low ERA since the mound was lowered in 1969: Dwight Gooden in 1985 and Ron Guidry in 1978.

The Cubs won 97 games, the third most wins in baseball. The only teams with more happened to play in their same division—St. Louis and Pittsburgh. That meant Chicago's rewards for 97 victories would be the second wild card and an elimination game on the road—the National League wild card game at Pittsburgh. The good news for the Cubs is that they would put the ball in the hands of Arrieta.

The routine for Arrieta to prepare for this start, like all of them, begins five hours before he actually takes the mound. It starts with a 40-minute stretching session, in which he pays particular attention to his hips, joints, IT bands, and glutes, and uses a lacrosse ball to roll out his back. Next, he moves to a stationary bike, where for 20 minutes he gets his heart rate up, increases blood flow, and lets "the fascia release."

Then it is time for a small plate of food: roasted Brussels sprouts, marinated chicken, and a quinoa chocolate chip cookie, washed down with a cup of carrot juice.

Next, he finds a quiet place to sit in the players' lounge, where he watches some video, listens to music, and then meditates.

"I use that as my time to focus on breathing," he said. "I feel like we don't take enough time to put some thought into that. A lot of stress can be relieved by inhaling and exhaling. I'm focusing on one singular thought: *How do I create a sense of calm?* I want to feel calm and collected with a clarity of mind in what I am doing for the ultimate preparation for how I am about to perform.

"I feel that meditation is so important for me because there are so many things going on outside of our arena—family, things in the community, health problems with friends or family—and it can be hard to put that aside and just completely focus on this. Sometimes that's difficult for me, but more times than not I can completely separate the outside world from what I'm about to accomplish."

Two hours before game time, Arrieta will start to warm up his body. First he spends 20 minutes on a Pilates reformer, running through a progression of movements designed to "lengthen my obliques, my lats, fire up the shoulders a little bit, get some fast-twitch muscles going, stress every area of the body before moving onto competition.

"I think preparing the body is very important, not just to perform but to prevent injuries. I think a lot of injuries could be prevented by having a better routine leading into competition."

After the work on the reformer, he does some work with stretch bands in the weight room. Then it's time to put on his uniform. He puts headphones on and listens to mellow electronic music. As a young pitcher, he used to listen to heavy metal to get "pumped up" for a start. Now he has learned that it is more beneficial to "lower the heart rate and calm the mind and the body. When I get out there, I know the energy is going to be there. So I try to conserve as much energy as I can leading into the performance, so when I really need it I can have it out there."

After 30 minutes or so, he makes the long, slow walk to the outfield and the bullpen to begin his on-field routine. He will look around the ballpark, taking two or three minutes to simply absorb the atmosphere, and visualize being in the middle of it all on the mound. There is a 2-minute warm-up before he begins to throw. He runs a couple of quick sprints, does a couple of yoga poses, and does a few push-ups.

Then he takes off his jacket, takes a sip of water, and begins to play catch, starting with throws of about 40 feet, stretching it to as far as 250 feet and bringing it back to 120 feet and then 90 feet. For the last five or six 90-foot throws, he takes a little crow hop and airs out fastballs, curveballs, and changeups.

Then he is ready to step on the bullpen mound. He always starts out of the stretch position—the abbreviated delivery pitchers use with runners on base—rather than with the full windup, as most pitchers prefer. Arrieta believes in the same philosophy as Hall of Fame pitcher Greg Maddux: the most important pitches a pitcher will have to make will be made out of the stretch. So why not place a premium on practicing out of the stretch?

His throwing always begins with arm-side four-seam fastballs—four or five of those pitches that Bosio emphasized to help turn around his career. Then he moves to glove-side fastballs. He repeats the sequence with two-seam fastballs.

"I like to keep as little movement as possible until I get the timing and rhythm down," he said.

Next: changeups bounced on the middle of the plate.

"I prefer to bounce it on the plate," he said, "because I know in the game things are going to be going fast, my adrenaline is going to be enhanced a little bit, so I want to put the emphasis on being down."

Next: a few slider/cutters, to both sides of the plate.

Then: a few curveballs, because "once I'm really loose that's when I'll really put some spin on it." Like the changeups, he will try to bounce them on the plate.

Last: fastballs, first a few elevated, because coming off the curveball, "that's the combination I like to use quite a bit. Whether I use it in a game or not is one thing, but to me hitters have a very difficult time differentiating when you can throw that high fastball off the same plane as your curveball." The last two fastballs are thrown right down the middle. He typically throws between 25 and 30 pitches in the bullpen.

"Then," he said, "it's game time. It doesn't matter who is in the box. I've gotten to the point where I respect the competition greatly but at the same time I'll do whatever I can to beat them."

When he climbs the mound and the ball is in his hand, his deep-set eyes and the pitch-black veil of his beard create a slate of emotion that is so blank it borders on disturbing. His gaze and his intentions are as fixed as dried concrete.

Ask him what he loves most about pitching and he will answer, "Being in control. It's the only sport where you're on defense and you have the ball in your hand. That means a lot. Nothing happens until we make it happen. We control the pace of the game. We dictate everything, not only to the other team, to the hitter, but to the crowd and to our guys. I have the ability to set the tone for my fielders, the guys around me.

"If I have the ability to get three quick outs and get them in the dugout, we have a great shot at getting runs on the board. It's a big responsibility, but it's something I really cherish and enjoy."

Arrieta completely controlled the Pirates in the 2015 wild card game. He threw the only shutout in postseason history with no walks and as many as 11 strikeouts. It was the pinnacle of one of the great pitching runs of all time. Late in that game, however, Arrieta felt a slight sense of fatigue washing over him.

"I was like, 'Man, that's probably all the emotions and being physically exhausted after a game like that,'" he said.

His next start was Game 3 of the Division Series against St. Louis, with the series tied at one game apiece. By then he knew that the fatigue he felt late in the game in Pittsburgh remained an issue. When he played long toss in between starts he knew the same explosiveness he had throughout the regular season no longer was there. He told himself, *Okay, I'm going to have to grind this one out and find a way to win this game.*

He did grind out a win, lasting only $5\frac{2}{3}$ innings and yielding four runs for the first time since June. The Cubs' hitters bailed him out with six home runs.

The next night Maddon used eight pitchers to win a nine-inning game—only the second time it happened in postseason history (Don Mattingly of the Dodgers did it in 2014), and the first time for a series clincher. The Cubs had been playing baseball at the corner of Clark and Addison for 100 seasons, and this was the first time they won a postseason-clinching game at the Friendly Confines.

Arrieta and the Cubs ran out of gas against the New York Mets in the NLCS. A weary Arrieta gave up four runs again, this time in Game 2, as his innings count for the season hit $248\frac{2}{3}$—72 more innings than the previous year. New York swept Chicago, holding the Cubs to eight runs and a .164 batting average in the four games.

When it was over, Maddon gathered his team in the ratty old shoebox of a clubhouse—for the last time before it would be replaced with the spacious, sparkling new digs.

"Listen," he told them, "go ahead and lose hard for 30 minutes, like we always do, then let's move along and really understand and celebrate what we accomplished this year."

A five-time fifth-place team made it to within four wins of the World Series under a manager working his first season with the club. Three of Epstein's four pillars made their major league debut in 2015: Bryant, Russell, and Schwarber. The first year of an elaborate run-prevention infrastructure showed enormous gains in the second half of the season. The team won its first playoff clincher in the history of ancient Wrigley Field. Before the Cubs scattered to their homes, Maddon made sure they understood not just what they accomplished, but also what still was to come.

"For me personally, I walked in the door not really knowing anybody in Arizona, when we got there in February, and how we built relationships and created a culture within one year is pretty spectacular within the clubhouse," Maddon said. "I mentioned to them how important it is as we move forward and [when] we go to spring training next year we know exactly what we want to do and how we want to do it. On top of that, our young players have learned how to win on a major league level, which matters. And to get within four games of the World Series in your freshman year is not a bad thing."

The 2016 season would be the Cubs' 108th try at winning their next World Series. Every official Major League Baseball has exactly 108 stitches, just as a mala, or a string of Buddhist prayer beads, has exactly 108 beads. Like stitches and beads, the years spent waiting finally would be exactly enough to close the loop.

CHAPTER 15

GAME 5

Elimination game.

The Cubs franchise had played 21 of these win-or-go-home games since its last World Series championship and lost 15 of them. As hard as Tom Ricketts, Theo Epstein, Jed Hoyer, and Joe Maddon worked to change the definition of "That's Cub," only one defeat stood between Chicago and the continuation of "the curse." One more loss would mean the longest wait in sports would carry to a 109th year, and the reputation as "lovable losers" would persist, no matter how great the team's five-year turnaround had been.

The Cubs brought no momentum into the game. In two nights the Indians had won just as many World Series games at Wrigley Field as the Cubs did in their 101 seasons in the little green jewel of a ballpark. After outscoring all but two major league teams in the regular season, the Chicago offense had gone as cold as Lake Michigan in the middle of January, managing only seven runs in four games. Cleveland pitchers, just as they had done to the hard-hitting Toronto Blue Jays in the American League Championship Series, had baffled Chicago hitters with a heavy dose of breaking balls, exposing what had been an overlooked weakness in the 103-win team.

Curveballs in general are hard to hit, especially because they traffic in deception. They often are thrown in the strike zone early in a count as a surprise (your classic get-me-over, first-pitch hook) or out of the strike zone later in the count as a pitch designed to get a hitter to chase it. Major league batters hit .211 against curveballs in 2016—44 points worse than the overall average. The Cubs were far worse than average against the pitch. They hit .201 against curves. Only seven teams fared worse. No team was worse at making contact on curveballs than Chicago (32 percent). Toronto ranked next-to-last (33 percent).

Few teams, however, exploited the Chicago weakness during the season. Only 9 percent of the pitches the Cubs saw in the regular season were curves. The Indians, a team that threw 12 percent curveballs during the regular season, had dialed up the percentage to 19 percent against the Cubs in the World Series. The strategy to spin the Cubs into submission was working splendidly. The Indians could rely on a server full of data to back it up.

"One thing you realize when you study the data," Indians pitching coach Mickey Callaway said before the game, "is that softer is almost always better than harder. Very few hitters like to hit off-speed better than fastballs. The good thing for us is that all three of our starters have really good curveballs. You don't see that any more in baseball."

Chicago figured to see more of the same tricks in Game 5. To win their first World Series title since 1948, the Indians started Trevor Bauer, owner of one of the most ferocious hooks in the game—even though that pitch went AWOL on Bauer in Game 2. Bauer threw 20 curveballs in that game, but only 10 for strikes, only one of which elicited a swing-and-miss.

To Maddon, all this information meant another round of conversations for him with young hitters Javier Baez, Addison Russell, and Kris Bryant about not chasing breaking balls. (The young and equally anxious catcher Willson Contreras was not in the lineup, owing to keeping intact the buddy battery of Jon Lester and David

Ross.) Maddon's conversations with his youngsters, however, were disguised as confidence-boosting pep talks, not serious discussions about mechanics. Maddon even designed his lineup to give a mental jolt to Russell. After batting him eighth in Game 3 and sixth in Game 4, Maddon pushed him to fifth in Game 5.

"I really like normal routine," Maddon said about the conversations. "There's nothing I can say to all of a sudden make them not chase a ball in the dirt or whatever. Part of it is psychology. Today that is hitting Addison fifth. He's a confidence guy. So, by hitting him fifth, I'm showing confidence in him. I'll reemphasize that when I have a conversation with him. I'll tell him, 'Let's go.'"

As for Baez, Maddon said, "We've talked to him. This is a kid we were hitting fifth in the last two series because he was on top of everything, and now it's speeding up on him. We just have to talk to him. If he has one good game, it could flip just like that, one good at-bat. We've just got to keep talking to him and get him to settle down a little bit. They are young, man. These are youngsters playing in this."

Epstein came to Chicago with designs on building the same offensive profile he built in Boston—a relentless attack that wore down pitchers. In Epstein's nine years as general manager of the Red Sox, his team ranked in the top three teams in the league every year for seeing the most pitches per plate appearance—including at the top of the league six times—and ranked in the top three for runs scored every year but one.

The 2012 version of *The Cubs Way*, the player development manual, defined the organization's "Hitting Development Plan" this way:

> The core purpose of our hitting program is to develop *selectively aggressive* hitters who are under control and can drive the ball to any part of the field. Selectiveness and aggressiveness are of equal importance—selective in that they look very specifically for a good pitch to hit, and aggressive in that they swing to do damage when they get their pitch. . . . They will be better clutch

hitters by possessing the confidence to wait for their pitch rather than chasing a pitcher's best pitches early in a count. . . . Selectively aggressive will be more valuable since they drive up pitch counts and get on base more often. By driving up pitch counts, our teams will consistently chase starting pitchers from games and challenge the depth of opposing bullpens. By getting on base more often, our teams will create more opportunities to score runs and win games. For these reasons, it is critical that we remain disciplined in our commitment to develop hitters The Cubs Way.

The 2016 player development manual included the exact same language—that's how firmly established was the original ideal of the "selectively aggressive" hitter. But the Cubs had lost hold of that ideal in the World Series. The steady stream of spinning pitches from Cleveland pitchers and the anxiety of playing in the World Series caused the young Chicago hitters to abandon their selective nature. Aggressiveness they had in overabundance. It hurt Chicago, too, that Schwarber remained on the bench at Wrigley, still not cleared to play defense.

"We missed him all year," Maddon said. "Just imagine all year with him. We're missing that yin and the yang in the lineup with that lefty/righty mix. We don't have it."

The way the Cubs were swinging the bats, they figured to need a well-pitched game to avoid the end of their season. Managers typically talk about "all hands on deck" when it comes to their pitching plans in an elimination game. Handing the ball to Jon Lester, however, Maddon saw his plans as much more simple than that.

"Our bullpen, you saw it last night, I thought Montgomery was off a little bit last night," Maddon said. "Probably a little bit tired. If we use him tonight it must be up and in. I can't let him warm up, sit down, and warm up again. Same thing with the whole group. I think the whole group needs to be up and in tonight if possible. I think Lester permits that.

"We have to ride Jonny. There's nobody I can bring out of the bullpen, unless he's awful, that's better than him tonight. We've got to ride Jonny."

The emphasis on his starting pitcher ran counter to the dominant trend of the 2016 postseason. Buoyed by the extra off days, managers routinely were asking their best bullpen arms to get more than three outs. Cleveland manager Terry Francona, for instance, had wedged left-hander Andrew Miller into postseason games in the fifth, sixth, seventh, and eighth innings, and Miller had rewarded his confidence without exception.

With Game 4 solidly in Cleveland's favor—7–1 in the eighth inning—Miller did allow a home run to Dexter Fowler. It was the first run he allowed in 53 days, covering $28\frac{1}{3}$ innings over 20 appearances. Miller loved to work often and, unlike many relievers, didn't care when his manager used him. At 6-foot-8 with a slingshot delivery, impeccable control, and the willingness to enter a game at any time on short notice, Miller presented hitters with a unique puzzle almost none of them could solve.

"This guy's a freak," Maddon said. "There's nobody like that. The whole group, Cody Allen and Bryan Shaw, are willing to do the same thing. Those three guys together are kind of an anomaly group. Last year we had a mild version with Clayton Richard and Trevor Cahill and Travis Wood. They were all able to do multiple stuff on a moment's notice. It's unusual to get guys like that. Multiple innings, very durable, get ready quickly . . . it's unusual."

Before the Indians traded for Miller from the New York Yankees on July 31, Epstein had talked to the Yankees about him. It was a brief conversation. When Yankees general manager Brian Cashman brought up the name of Kyle Schwarber, Epstein told him he was untouchable. So, too, was Baez. The same roadblock occurred when Epstein called the Royals to ask about Wade Davis.

The Cubs were running away with the National League Central at the time, but Epstein, knowing bullpens play a bigger role in the postseason, was determined to add a premium closer. Hector

Rondon had pitched well in that role, but Epstein wanted better, and saw the benefit of deploying Rondon and his closer's stuff in a setup role.

Once the Miller talks went nowhere, Epstein pivoted to another Yankees reliever, Aroldis Chapman. The price for Chapman would be lower than for Miller because of the differences in their contract status. Chapman, a free agent at the end the season, would be a two-month rental. Miller was signed for two more seasons at the below-market price of $9 million per year.

Trading for Chapman, however, would pose a philosophical, if not an ethical, dilemma for Epstein. For five years he predicated his rebuild of the Cubs on finding players of high character who thrived in an environment with like-minded, upstanding human beings. Chapman tested the resolve of that position.

Around 11 p.m. on October 30, 2015, more than a dozen police officers responded to a call of a domestic disturbance at a house in Davie, Florida. According to the incident report they filed, a woman identified as Chapman's girlfriend said Chapman choked her, though Chapman, then a member of the Cincinnati Reds, said he used two fingers to poke her on the left shoulder. The girlfriend ran outside the house and hid behind bushes, where she called law-enforcement officials. Chapman went alone to his garage, entered his Land Rover through the passenger side door, sat down, punched the window with his left hand, and pulled a loaded gun from the glove compartment. Chapman, according to the report, then fired eight shots in the garage. A Davie police department spokesman said no charges were filed against Chapman because of "insufficient evidence," which included conflicting stories, no cooperating witnesses, and no physical injuries.

Yahoo! broke the news of the disturbance on December 7 during the Major League Baseball winter meetings. At the time the Los Angeles Dodgers, who already boasted Kenley Jansen as a top closer, were close to acquiring Chapman in a trade with the Reds, but those talks immediately ground to a halt. Said one baseball source at the time, "After the [terrorist] shootings in San Bernardino just happened, there was no way the Dodgers were going to deal with Chapman and a gun issue in Los Angeles."

Said another source familiar with the Dodgers' plans, "I was told they never were going to keep him in the first place. They were going to spin him for something else they wanted. But they were worried after the incident that his value was down, so they walked away."

The Yankees, however, walked into what they saw as an opportunity. Chapman, because of the public relations fallout and the possibility of a suspension, was damaged goods. New York obtained Chapman for a modest package of prospects, with far less value than Chapman would have commanded before the incident. The Yankees did so knowing that Chapman might face discipline from a newly negotiated Joint Domestic Violence, Sexual Assault and Child Abuse policy between the owners and the players. Chapman did become the first player disciplined under that policy. On March 1, 2016, commissioner Rob Manfred suspended Chapman for the first 30 games of the season. Manfred wrote that he found Chapman's "acknowledged conduct to be inappropriate under the negotiated policy, particularly his use of a firearm and the impact of that behavior on his partner."

Almost five months later, Epstein needed Chapman. He reached an agreement with New York general manager Brian Cashman to trade pitcher Adam Warren and three prospects for Chapman. The package Epstein negotiated included 19-year-old infielder Gleyber Torres, one of the top prospects in the game. Epstein insisted on one condition before giving his final agreement on the deal: he asked Cashman for permission for him and Ricketts to speak to Chapman. Epstein said they needed to hear contrition about the incident from Chapman, and they wanted to spell out to him the standard of behavior they expected from all Cubs players. Only if they were satisfied, Epstein said, would the deal be completed. Cashman agreed. A conference call was arranged July 24 with Epstein, Ricketts, Chapman, and Barry Praver, Chapman's agent.

Ricketts told Chapman, "Look, Aroldis, I tell all the players this in spring training and it's important you hear it and I need to hear from you on this: we expect our players to behave. We hold our players to a very high standard for their behavior off the field. And we need to know you can meet that standard."

Chapman said he understood. Epstein and Ricketts were satisfied by what they regarded as his contrition and sincerity. Epstein said he found Chapman "really heartfelt." The trade was announced the next day. It was not well received, particularly when Chapman, in words translated by Cubs coach Henry Blanco, said in his initial news conference with Chicago reporters that he could not recall the details of the conference call with Epstein and Ricketts on account of being sleepy then. Maybe something had been lost in translation, but it was far from the "really heartfelt" emotion Epstein had ascribed to Chapman.

The pitcher a bit later clarified his comments in an interview with ESPN, a transcript of which the team's media relations department made available. In that conversation about the incident, the pitcher said, "I've grown tremendously from that time. I'm with my girlfriend still, with the family, and I feel that I have absolutely changed as a person. I'm working to be a better person. And now that I remember because they just asked me in the previous press conference what the owners asked me, one of the things they did ask me was about being a better person and being a better neighbor to people. And that's something that I think that I am now, much more so."

Chicago had fallen in love with this Cubs team. It wasn't just that they were winning, but also that they were winning with a likable collection of players—a core group of position players that largely was homegrown and a pitching staff populated largely by imported pitchers who raised their game once they joined the team. Now Epstein was introducing in midseason a two-month rental who brought the notoriety of a domestic disturbance and gunplay. If you played out the scenario to what the Cubs had in mind, what Ross called "the Holy Grail of championships" would culminate with the disgraced

Chapman getting the final out in what otherwise would be the biggest, most historic feel-good title moment in sports.

Cubs fans were conflicted. Chapman made their team better, but to some people also less likable. Judging by sports talk radio, Epstein had just willingly introduced the first discordant note of the year into what had been a dream season. Epstein himself wrestled with the move. He had spent five years touting the character of the players he brought to the organization, and yet the last piece of his rebuild contradicted that philosophy. Epstein used the conference call with Chapman to settle this internal conflict. The need of the team won out. Epstein did his best to defend the move.

"We gave that serious, thoughtful, careful consideration over an extended period of time," Epstein said. "We take the issue of character very seriously and continue to. Obviously, we take the issue of domestic violence very seriously. So it was our responsibility to look into this thoroughly and to look at all the facts. Again, we understand there will be lots of different perspectives on this, that there will be lots of strong feelings about this, and that people are going to feel differently about that. And we understand, and we respect that.

"In the end, it was our decision, and we decided it was appropriate to trade for a player who has accepted his discipline, who has already been disciplined by Major League Baseball, who expressed his sorrow and his regret for the incident in a statement at the time, in a meaningful statement today, and, even more importantly, to me and Tom directly today over the phone before we were willing to consummate the trade, a player who is active currently in Major League Baseball and pitching for another team.

"We decided that it was appropriate to trade for that player. It doesn't mean we're turning our back on the importance of character at all. I think because we've emphasized character and building this core that we have, we have a tremendously strong clubhouse culture. We have great character down there. We think that it will help Aroldis as he moves forward."

Not everybody was buying it. Over a picture of Epstein, the back page of the *Sun-Times* sneered, "Spin City." Writing in the *Tribune*, columnist David Haugh ended his take on the Chapman trade with this declaration: "I don't have to like it. Not with the Cubs making their games easier to win but harder to watch."

There could be no debate about Chapman's ability. He was one of the best closers in baseball, and one of the hardest-throwing pitchers who ever lived. His pitches regularly exceeded 100 miles per hour. For his career, Chapman struck out 42.6 percent of the batters he faced, the highest strikeout rate in baseball history.

At 6-foot-4 and 215 pounds, Chapman was a physical marvel. His pitching delivery gave off the frightful impression of a freight locomotive screaming down a mountain. Chapman gathered all his long levers and thick musculature into a tuck position, then, as if spring-loaded, exploded in a burst of energy toward the hitter, his arm swinging long and fast behind him and his front leg extending so far forward that his stride measured seven feet, one of the longest recorded strides in baseball. With that stride, which drew him closer to the hitter by the time he released the ball, Chapman shortened the distance his pitches had to travel not by inches but by feet. Distance equals time, and between his outlier measurements in velocity and stride, Chapman gave hitters less time to react to a pitch than any other pitcher who ever lived.

"He's incredible," Maddon said. "The other day I walked up and patted him on the back. Holy shit—it's wrapped steel. It's unbelievable. There's got to be something to throwing a hundred miles an hour, to coordinate all those movements, but he is some kind of strong."

When it came to how often and when he pitched, however, Chapman was no Miller. Chapman pitched 59 times in 2016, but only six of them before the ninth inning (all of those in the eighth). He saved 36 games, but only once did he do so by getting more than three outs. As closers go, he was something of a diva: he worked best when he had plenty of time to warm up and started the ninth inning with a lead with nobody on base.

Maddon was trying to retrain Chapman on the fly in the post-season to be a multiple-inning threat and to drop him into "dirty" innings—situations with runners on. The first time he tried, it was a disaster. Maddon summoned Chapman in Game 3 of the NLDS in San Francisco with a one-run lead, two runners on, and no outs in the eighth inning. He asked Chapman to get six outs for a save, something he had done only once in his career, and that had been three years earlier. The Giants ambushed Chapman for three runs, keyed by a triple by Conor Gillaspie. The next day Chapman was still visibly shaken by his failure. Maddon saw the despair on his face and spoke with him.

"He was upset with himself," Maddon said. "He was upset with himself when Gillaspie got that knock. He wasn't upset about being in the game. He told me he couldn't sleep that night because he was upset about giving up the hit. He and I have discussed all these scenarios. During the season, the objective was not to use him for more than three outs. Postseason, anything goes."

One of the problems in trying to retrain Chapman is that, unlike Miller, Chapman needs to go through a detailed routine in order to get himself ready to pitch. Disruptions to that routine risk failure. In the fifth game of the NLCS in Los Angeles, Maddon warmed Chapman in the top of the eighth inning with a 3–1 lead. He anticipated asking Chapman to get six outs again. The Cubs blew open the game with five runs in the eighth. Chapman sat down. Then Maddon asked him to warm again to pitch the ninth inning of an 8–2 game. A sloppy Chapman allowed two runs and did not strike out any of the six batters he faced.

"That was our fault," Maddon said. "He had to warm up. He was coming in for two innings, and then all of a sudden we score all those runs and it became one inning, then he had to warm up, sit down, warm up, sit down. So that was part of all that. He threw too much in the bullpen and that's my fault."

World Series Game 5 would begin with Bauer and Lester, the starting pitchers, but, given the tenor of the postseason, it might swing on how each manager deployed his best reliever. Francona already had proved he wasn't shy about inserting Miller into the middle of games for multiple innings—Miller threw 27 pitches over two innings in Game 4. Maddon held a rested Chapman—he did not pitch in Game 4—but when Chapman could pitch and for how long were still abiding questions with the left-hander.

"He's just got to be ready-ready," Maddon said. "Just ride it from there. With him it's so different because he has this absolute routine. Oh, my God. First of all, he has to start throwing the heavy ball. Then if you warm him up and sit him down, it's no *bueno*, man. If I have to warm him up and sit him down once, okay, but if it's more than once, he ain't going to pitch well. It's not going to happen."

Maddon made sure to talk to Chapman before the game.

"I may need you as early as the seventh inning," he told him. "Could you be ready that early?"

"I'm ready," Chapman responded. "I'm ready to pitch for as long as you want me."

Even facing elimination, down three games to one, Maddon saw a clear path for the Cubs to win the World Series. In potential Games 6 and 7 in Cleveland, he liked his fully rested starting pitchers, Jake Arrieta and Kyle Hendricks, over Cleveland starters Josh Tomlin and Corey Kluber, both of whom would be working on short rest. But just to get it there, Maddon would have to ride Lester, push Chapman out of his comfort zone, and hope Game 5 didn't get to Miller with an Indians lead.

"This is obviously very important tonight," Maddon said. "If we get it back to Cleveland, I like it a lot. Grabbing a lead and holding on is big. I don't know how aggressive they will be with Miller tonight. I think they will still. But for him to be that effective as often as he has been is unbelievable. We need to get into the underbelly of the bullpen. If we do, we have a good shot. Their guy, Bauer, hopefully he's missing the zone again and we get to him. And Jon being Jon—that's what we've got to rely on tonight."

The Indians were in command of the series, but they had their own demons to conquer. The franchise's last World Series championship occurred in 1948. It was so long ago only one player remained alive from that team, Eddie Robinson, the 95-year-old former first baseman. Robinson made his major league debut September 9, 1942, against the Philadelphia A's. The manager of the opposing team that day was Connie Mack, who was born in 1862. Since their last championship, the Indians had burned through 28 managers in 68 years.

Francona knew that to end that kind of history he had to put the game into the hands of his bullpen. He used only three starters in the series—Bauer was pitching on short rest in Game 5—because of injuries to pitchers Carlos Carrasco and Danny Salazar. "We would have done it differently if we had our guys," Francona said before Game 5. "When I get Miller up is when I get him in. If you do this with your bullpen during the season, it would last about 10 days before guys start breaking down. But there's adrenaline this time of year and there's no series after this one."

The formula had worked perfectly. Nobody had dented the Indians' bullpen yet in October. His relievers were 4–0 in the postseason with a 1.69 ERA while throwing almost half of the team's innings, 45 percent. The Cubs would face an elimination game knowing it was a baseball version of Beat the Clock: they had to have a lead by midgame, when Francona was sure to go to his lockdown bullpen.

They may not have had the edge in the series, but the Cubs did have Anthony Rizzo. Five seasons before, Epstein had made Rizzo the first of his four pillars, trading for the first baseman with the .141 batting average in large part because he believed in his character. Rizzo rewarded that faith, not only with his big bat but also with the leadership Epstein envisioned.

Ross called Rizzo "probably the most important player we have on the team, just as far as his attitude and how he's able to get along with everybody and gets to know everybody.

"Every time you're around him, whether you're on the field or out to dinner or any place, he wants everybody to have a good time. He's more worried about everybody else having a good time and puts himself second. And I see his personality over everything in baseball. Whether it's his at-bats, batting practice, or anything, he's quick to take a back seat to others. That's unusual for a superstar."

Rizzo came through again in the last hour before Game 5. Rizzo stripped down to nothing, jumped on a couch in the clubhouse, and began quoting every great cinematic motivational line he could think of, from *Any Given Sunday* ("Either we heal now as a team, or we will die as individuals!") to *Rocky* ("Adrian, it's not how many times you get knocked down, it's how many times you get back up!"). The theme from *Rocky* blared over the clubhouse speakers. "We're going the distance!" he shouted. The room cracked up, laughing. Here it was, on the nerve-jangling edge of Game 5 of the World Series, and the Cubs looked like they were deep into a karaoke party. The tone was set. If the young Cubs were going to stare the end of their season straight in the eye, they would do it with a smile on their faces.

THE CLOCK TICKED down with every out.

Three innings—nine outs—had passed for the Cubs and the old scoreboard in centerfield showed them with no runs and one inconsequential single off Bauer. The Indians held the lead, 1–0, because of a home run José Ramírez slammed off Lester in the second inning.

Tick, tick, tick went the outs. With just six more ticks, Francona would be able to put the lead and the World Series championship in the hands of his undefeated bullpen. Bryant, held to one hit in his 15 at-bats in the series, was the first hitter of the fourth inning for Chicago. Following the Cleveland blueprint, Bauer had whiffed Bryant in the first inning—starting and finishing him with curveballs.

"I feel like, as a team, guys are throwing us more curveballs,"

Bryant said. "I don't know. I don't look into the stats. I don't know if we hit curveballs well, but if they keep throwing them, obviously we don't."

No one was throwing in the Cleveland bullpen yet, but the hour was nigh.

"Not a crazy sense of urgency," Bryant said about his thought process as he walked to the plate, "but certainly we want to get some runs there so that they're not going to go to Miller and Allen with the lead there. So for me I wasn't going out there trying to hit a homer or anything like that."

This time Bauer started Bryant with a four-seam fastball. It missed for a ball, high. More tellingly, it was clocked at 91.7 miles per hour, well below his average four-seam fastball in the regular season, 94.6 miles per hour. He came back with a cut fastball, well located down and away. Bryant took it for a strike.

No batter in the major leagues in 2016 rated better against both four- and two-seam fastballs than Bryant. He hit .341 against fastballs, including 27 of his 39 home runs. Bauer wouldn't dare throw him a 1-and-1 fastball for a strike, not to the best fastball hitter in the majors, not with the way Cleveland had throttled Chicago with breaking balls. But he did. He threw a belt-high, 91.5-mph, two-seam fastball on the inside half of the plate. Bryant, as if gleeful to be finally liberated from his weeklong curveball quarantine, smashed it into the leftfield bleachers.

The game was tied. Wrigley was rocking. The clock stopped.

Bauer is considered one of the game's eccentric personalities, a reputation galvanized during the 2016 American League Championship Series when the propeller of one of his drones sliced open the pinky of his pitching hand. The wound was stitched and bandaged, but when he returned to the mound in Toronto, and by rule could not pitch with a bandage, the gash opened. Blood oozed and dripped-dripped-dripped out of the wound like a faucet leaking crimson, creating one of the more grotesque visuals in postseason history.

His eccentricity distracted from the quality of his stuff and the depth of his effort to improve. Bauer purchased a TrackMan system and super slow-motion video cameras for his house to learn more about the spin rates and movement of his pitches. The TrackMan system, which runs about $30,000, uses military-grade, 3-D Doppler radar technology to track 20,000 measurements per second of a baseball. With TrackMan's help, Bauer tweaked the spin rate and spin axis of his curveball.

With the help of the slow-motion video, Bauer adjusted the way the curveball leaves his hand. Like most right-handed pitchers, Bauer throws the curveball with his index and pointer fingers coming off the baseball on the side facing third base. But the slow-motion video taught him that he could generate more spin if, as his fingers came off the side of the ball, his wrist turned in the opposite direction, or pronated. It's the same concept as throwing a tight spiral with a football.

By 2016 Bauer had developed such confidence in his curveball that he threw it nearly twice as often as he had in past years. He increased his usage of the pitch from 12 percent in 2015 to 20 percent in 2016. Left-handed hitters, in particular, had little clue about how to hit the pitch. Bauer threw them 300 curves in the regular season, only 7 of which resulted in a hit.

So where was the curveball?

After Bryant smacked a fastball for a home run, Rizzo was up next, a left-handed hitter, not to mention the famed clubhouse singer and thespian. The fans hadn't even settled back into their seats when Rizzo crushed the next pitch from Bauer: it was another fastball—another elevated two-seam fastball. The ball whistled to rightfield until it smacked against the ivy on the wall. Rizzo hustled into second base with a double.

Bauer needed to get back to the script after getting two fastballs whacked. He tried a curveball to Ben Zobrist, but missed, low and in. He missed, too, with his next two pitches, a fastball and a changeup. With the count 3-and-0, Bauer knew he could groove a cookie of a fastball to Zobrist. The Cleveland scouting report made note that Zobrist virtually never swings at a 3-and-0 pitch—he takes the pitch 97.3 percent of the time, to be exact. He had seen 413 pitches in his career at 3-and-0 and swung at only 11 of them, only 5 of which he actually put into play. He had not had a hit on a 3-and-0 count since September 27, 2013, more than three years before.

So Bauer followed along and played the percentages. He grooved a 92.7-mph, four-seam fastball right down the middle. Lo and behold, Zobrist swung at it, and ripped it so hard into centerfield for a single that Rizzo had to stop at third.

If you wanted to affix a brass marker to commemorate the exact spot where the series flipped, you would place it on that three-batter sequence in the fourth inning of the fifth game. The Indians were six outs away from handing a lead to their expert bullpen. The Cubs could do almost nothing against the deluge of Cleveland breaking balls thrown their way the entire series.

And suddenly this happened: home run, double, single on consecutive swings—every one of them against a fastball.

This was the "offensive epiphany" Maddon beseeched.

"He came out really good," Francona said about Bauer. "I mean, really good. And the two pitches—back to back Bryant and Rizzo jumped on fastballs that caught too much of the plate. They were down, but too much of the plate. And Zobrist had a really good at-bat. That was the damage. It's just they got some fastballs they could handle and they whacked them pretty good."

The turning of fortunes was confirmed when the next batter, Addison Russell, mis-hit a curveball and wound up with an RBI infield single to score Rizzo, giving the Cubs a 2–1 lead. After Jason Heyward struck out, Javier Baez, riding a streak of 13 straight at-bats without a hit, swallowed his pride and smartly dropped a bunt for a hit. Ross followed with a deep fly ball to score another run, pushing the lead to 3–1.

Francona lifted Bauer after the inning, and, as if to underscore the importance of the ticking clock, his bullpen allowed Chicago nothing over the rest of the game.

Lester would not squander the lead. He wobbled a bit in the sixth, when his troubles against the running game surfaced again. The Indians needed only two singles to score, because in between the hits by Rajai Davis and Francisco Lindor, Davis swiped second base. But when Lindor tried the same thievery, Lester's battery mate, Ross, covered for him by throwing a strike to second base to nab Lindor.

Maddon yanked Lester in the seventh in favor of Carl Edwards Jr., but Mike Napoli foiled that strategy with a leadoff single. Maddon ordered Chapman to start throwing in the bullpen. There was no way Maddon could allow the lead to be lost with anybody but Chapman on the mound. The tying run, Napoli, moved to second when Edwards bounced a wild pitch. Edwards recovered to get Carlos Santana on a fly ball.

Now Chapman was ready. Maddon walked out to the mound and signaled for him. He was asking Chapman not only to keep the tying run at second base, but also to get eight outs—more than he ever secured in his major league career. Chapman responded with the game of his life: $2\frac{2}{3}$ shutout innings that required a career-high 42 pitches. Half of his eight outs resulted from strikeouts.

The Cubs won a classic nail-biter of a game, 3–2. It was only the third time in franchise history that Chicago came from behind to win an elimination game, matching the season-saving escapes of Game 6 of the 1945 World Series and Game 4 of the 1910 World Series.

"But we're all about writing our own history," Bryant said. "This team is a special one, and we look at so many times throughout the year where we haven't been playing good, but I feel like we turn that around. Someone told me today that 17 times this year we lost a game and went on to win three in a row, so why can't we do that now?"

"K.B. hit the nail on the head," Russell said. "We're writing our own history. We're making history. Why stop? This is entertaining to us. It's fun, and we live for this. We see a lot of challenges ahead of us, and we embrace them. That's what we've been talking about since spring training, I think, since 2015. So that's kind of like the mind-set we've had and we definitely have embraced that."

The elimination game, for all its portent, brought out the best in the Cubs, from Rizzo hitting the right notes before it (at least metaphorically), to the offensive epiphany that came in the nick of time, to Chapman giving more than he ever had before. They played loose and they played clean when under the most duress. As Russell rightly recognized, the makings of the win were easy to trace. This iteration of the Cubs—the four pillars of Rizzo, Bryant, Schwarber, and Russell, joined by Lester and playing under Maddon—first formed in spring training of 2015. Even better days were still to come.

CHAPTER 16

EMBRACE THE TARGET

W hen the Cubs reported to the first full day of spring training workouts in 2016 in Mesa, Arizona, the daily schedule
that hung on a clubhouse wall included a motivational
saying, as would every one of Joe Maddon's daily schedules. Day one's
motto derived from Hall of Fame football coach Vince Lombardi:
"Individual commitment to a group effort—that is what makes a
team work, a company work, a society work, a civilization work."

It sounded slightly more high-minded than another slogan that already was finding its way around T-shirts in Cubs camp and Chicago.
One month earlier, at the annual Cubs Convention in a ballroom at
the Sheraton Grand Chicago, infielder Javier Baez was asked during
a question-and-answer session with fans what sage advice Maddon
gave him when the team called up Baez from the minors the previous September.

Replied Baez, "Try not to suck."

The ballroom erupted in laughter. Another 100 percent cotton
meme was born.

As with all things Maddon, there was meaning behind the humor.
The manager felt a special connection with Baez because of the trip

he made to Puerto Rico to see him just after being named manager. He knew Baez was an immense talent, but he also knew, like most players, he played better when he was relaxed. That's why he told Baez when he first saw him playing winter ball that the result he wanted most to see from him was a smile. And that's why Maddon told him in September 2015 to try not to suck. He wanted Baez to loosen up, to play the game with a light heart, as if he were back in Little League.

Maddon is the Johnny Appleseed of aphorisms. For him, the main seed for the 2016 season occurred to him during a scrum with reporters in December 2015 at the winter meetings. The questions reporters fired at Maddon stemmed from the ominous idea that his young Cubs snuck up on people in 2015, but that in 2016 they would face the "pressure" and "expectations" of being a known quantity.

Fresh in Maddon's head was the Tom Clancy novel *Clear and Present Danger*, and this line of questioning brought to mind a particular scene in which the president's advisors tell him he needs to disavow a friend who had just been killed by a drug cartel. The novel's hero, Jack Ryan, interjects, telling the president, "No. Not only was he your friend, he was your best friend. You have to address it. Sometimes it's better to run toward the fire than away from it."

Maddon loved the imagery of running toward the danger. He retold the scene to the assembled reporters, and that's how an idea was hatched on the spot for the theme of his 2016 Cubs: Embrace the Target.

"My Jack Ryan moment," he said.

For the first day of the 2016 camp, and the first of his three annual team meetings, Maddon was less *nervioso* than he had been in 2015, his first year with the team. He may have been the first major league manager to deliver his opening speech while using an iPad Pro and stylus. Maddon had written the notes to his speech on the tablet in the form of a diagram.

Maddon started with a green circle, and inside the circle in red ink handwrote six key principles for the season:

1. Embrace the target
2. We all have to set aside our personal agendas
3. All do our jobs (9 on 1)
4. Know we are not perfect, but can be present
5. We are our own little planet
6. Rotate around same goal

Atop the circle were two words followed by arrows pointing up, as well as notations that defined those words as having positive connotations:

Expectations. Strong belief something will happen in the future.
Pressure. A motivator. A positive. An indicator you are in the right place.

Below the circle Maddon wrote more notes, which included:

Do simple better
The process is fearless
The process lacks emotion
The process is the moment
The process is the mental anchor
The process simplifies the task

The area below the circle also included a few favorite quotes:

Change before you have to.—Jack Welch
Wisdom is the reward for a lifetime of listening when you would have preferred to talk.—Doug Larson
Communication creates collaboration. Big ears are better than big egos. When you're not listening, ask good questions.—Bill Walsh

The speech was perfect—well, except for a moment when Maddon's stylus quit working, sending him into a brief "state of technological panic." The speech also would wind up, naturally, on the backs of more T-shirts—the whole circle-and-notes design and scribblings from his iPad. Sales of the shirts benefited his Respect 90 foundation. So began one of the loosest, most relaxed, and most confident training camps that had ever been held, at least this side of the most expensive self-help motivational retreats in some five-star desert resort.

Theo Epstein and Jed Hoyer had introduced three key veteran free agents to the group: pitcher John Lackey, second baseman Ben Zobrist, and outfielder Jason Heyward. Otherwise, the holistic culture they had established in the player development system in the minors was now firmly established with the major league club after one year under Maddon. The Chicago Cubs' 2016 spring training camp was the embodiment of the Cubs Way in full flower—either that or it was a new all-inclusive vacation, Cub Med.

Mornings began with a "Sunrise Yoga" class, followed by meditation sessions. Breakfast included fresh, cold-pressed, organic juices from the on-site juice bar and piles of fruits and berries. The morning outdoor stretching class still included classic rock pumped out from five-foot-tall speakers (to start, this time it was the Stones' "Sympathy for the Devil," Hendrix's "Purple Haze," and Bad Company's eponymous hit). Eric Hinske, one of the two hitting coaches, carried around a boom box so that his hitters could hit to music no matter to which of the four practice fields they were assigned. The vast training room facilities included custom-made Pilates reformers. Acupuncturists, massage therapists, dietitians, nutritionists, and mental skills coaches stood at the ready. And at the end of the workout day, players filled out an eight-inch-long order sheet for a custom-made recovery smoothie, choosing from among about three dozen ingredients. The plush training complex—or "Performance Center" as it was known to better reflect its modernity—opened in 2014, a $99 million investment by Ricketts that preceded the $575 million renovation of Wrigley Field.

There were, of course, more than the usual number of absurdities and oddities to break up the monotony of being treated so well. One day Maddon, dressed in a tie-dyed shirt and a stars-and-stripes headband, and blaring "Shining Star" by Earth, Wind & Fire out of the sound system, drove onto the practice field in his 1976 brown Dodge van, the one with a Western landscape painted on the side, an orange shag carpet, and ostrich-leather trim. There were mimes, musicians, comedians, and real-live bear cubs, as well as assorted running gags to celebrate 39-year-old catcher David Ross, who announced that the 2016 season would be his last. Anthony Rizzo and Kris Bryant opened an Instagram account dedicated to "Grandpa Rossy." They posted pictures and videos of what they called his "year-long retirement party," including one video of Ross wearing a "G-Pa Rossy" jersey and hobbling around the clubhouse using a bat as a cane. "Someone had a rough day of catching drills today," the caption said.

Another time they presented Ross with a close-in handicapped parking spot with his name spray-painted in orange, as well as a Rascal motorized scooter with the license plate GDPA. And still another time, after a workout, the whole team gathered in the parking lot for the unveiling of another present for Ross: a self-driving golf bag cart to carry his catching gear and bats from field to field.

"Last year was good," Ross said about the spring training vibe. "Really good. But this year, I don't want to say it's night and day, but it's even better. The young players have a year under their belts, the postseason experience, and everybody thinks in terms of, what can I do to help the team? I'm telling you, it's special. It's genuine."

Said Maddon, "One of the things I stressed [on day one] was be yourself—individuality, authenticity. Spring training is not about batting practice or side sessions or how many repetitions you get in. The most important thing is to get them thinking properly. It's not about how many repetitions of what occur. I want us to think well."

For Epstein, the highlight of the camp occurred on one of the first days of full-squad workouts. Maddon stopped the practice, in which the players were spread among three fields, and called the entire team together on the mound of a back field. Knowing Maddon, pitcher Jason Hammel was sure what was coming next: either a circus animal or a magician. Instead, walking through a gate in the fence at the practice field was Dexter Fowler, the Cubs' centerfielder in 2015 who almost everyone thought was about to sign with Baltimore as a free agent for $35 million over three years. (The media reports had been overblown.) Fowler re-signed with the Cubs that morning for $13 million for one year, with a mutual option for 2017. The beloved teammate was met with cheers and hugs.

Epstein watched with a sly grin. He had just pulled off a coup in today's game: he signed a major free agent without word leaking anywhere.

"Now that's a surprise," Epstein said. "That's Godfather shit. Nothing will top that."

Beyond the theatrics of the signing, it solved the last major concern Epstein had about his team. Without Fowler, the Cubs planned to ask Heyward, a natural rightfielder, to transition to centerfield. An outfield of Kyle Schwarber in leftfield, Heyward in center, and Jorge Soler in rightfield presented as a below-average defensive alignment. Fowler gave Chicago solid defense in centerfield and kept Heyward in rightfield, where he profiled as a defensive weapon.

Maddon knew he had a very good team, but after the first week of camp that's when he was convinced it was something special. That's when Epstein, Hoyer, and Maddon held the Individual Player Development Plan meetings. Every day the clubhouse message board would list the six or so players who were scheduled to meet with them. Each meeting took anywhere from 5 to 15 minutes.

Epstein, when he was in Boston, had stolen the idea from Mark Shapiro of the Cleveland Indians. Epstein was motivated by the two lines from former players that stuck with him: Craig Shipley telling him that all players felt lied to by the front office at some point, and Gary DiSarcina telling him he wished people had shared with him scouting reports on his weaknesses that stayed filed away. Epstein vowed to never let those slights happen on his watch.

Unbeknownst to Epstein at the time he hired him, Maddon was a big proponent of these Individual Player Development Plan meetings. Maddon, on his own, instituted his own version of these meetings with minor leaguers in the Angels system back in the 1980s.

"It was just me and the player, because none of the other coaches thought it was groovy," Maddon said. "So my point is you're developing this rapport with the player, you're communicating with the player like they had never been communicated with before. It's very rudimentary. It sounds really insignificant, but players were never told what administration thought of them. Ever.

"That's the essence of bad coaching. Okay, say me and you are watching DiSarcina play shortstop. This happened all the time. I would explain this to coaches in meetings. We're watching DiSar and I say, 'Damn, DiSar needs to get better at turning the double play.' So many times coaches would say that to each other and never say it to DiSarcina. Never.

"The point I also want to make was, if you want to [badmouth] one of these players, fine. If you keep it to yourself, then you don't have to tell that player. If you think he's a dick, think he's a pussy, and it never comes out of your mouth to somebody else, that's fine. But the moment you say it to somebody else you've got to go tell the player. That's how I explained it to the coaches in the early '80s. That's the difference between good coaching and bad coaching. There are times when you can choose not to say anything. That's okay to keep it to yourself. But the moment it goes to another human's ears, whoever you're talking about needs to hear it."

As Maddon rose to the Angels' major league staff, the meetings disappeared. One day in 2006, after Maddon was hired to manage the Devil Rays, his pitching coach, Mike Butcher, said to him, "Joe, do you remember those meetings you used to do?"

Butcher had been one of those Angels minor leaguers who sat with Maddon in the 1980s. Butcher was a former amateur boxer from East Moline, Illinois, who signed with the Angels after the Royals released him over a fight with his manager. Butcher eventually made it to the big leagues with the Angels.

"Sure, I remember them," Maddon said.

"I loved those," Butcher said. "And all the guys loved those."

"That's all he had to say to me," Maddon said. "We put them back in with the Devil Rays. Then with the Rays. And there were some tough ones there. Delmon Young, back in the day . . . Elijah Dukes . . . Therein lies the difference. Talk to that group and talk to the 2016 Cubs in spring training. You talk about a group you can see has a chance to be special. The other group, it was dysfunctional, although we got it together in three years. I know we made a lot of changes, but those meetings in the beginning were so unbelievable."

When a Cubs player would leave one of the 2016 meetings, Epstein, Hoyer, and Maddon would say to one another, "Wow. That was impressive." And then the next guy would come in, and they would be moved to say the same thing. And the one after that, and the one after that . . .

"You're like, *amazed*," Maddon said. "Really? One after the other you're so impressed with character, makeup, straightforwardness, and then their skill level. It's an incredible exercise to do it with your group every year, but that group last year? You walk out of there going, 'Holy shit, these guys get it! They friggin' get it.' We were amazed. By the time we got done, we were exhausted. It's the first part of spring training. It takes a lot of mental energy to get through it. And when you get through it, it's like, 'That was great!'"

Said Hoyer, "Every single day we would sit there and say, 'Oh, my God, this is the best group of guys I've ever been around.' There were no bad guys. They were all super intelligent and highly motivated. I'm telling you, it never happens like that. There's always at least a couple of players who, when they walk out of the room, you go, 'Oof. We'll see how that goes.' Or, 'That was an awkward meeting.' Or, 'This person is putting himself over the team.' There was none of that. We couldn't get over how great these meetings were."

During the meeting with Jake Arrieta, for instance, Maddon told the 2015 Cy Young Award winner he would not be pitching as many innings in 2016 as he had in 2015. (Maddon actually first broached the subject with Arrieta the first day he saw him in camp, when he bumped into him in the cafeteria.)

"I'm going to be proactive with your situation," Maddon told him. "You will probably not be finishing games with a lead."

Arrieta signed off on the plan.

"Last year my mind-set was I was going to be out there in the eighth or ninth inning every time out," Arrieta said. "In my last two starts I reached a point where I was a little out of gas."

One day in spring training, well after the games were underway, players found an unusual notation on the daily schedule, which typically lists times, places, and instructors for drills. This one called for all hitters to gather for a meeting in the indoor batting cage regarding "Two-Strike Approach," and the instructor who would be running the session would be Maddon. This was highly unusual. Other than the blowup in the 2015 camp when Maddon chafed at the team's lackadaisical approach to relays and cutoffs, staff members could not recall another time when the manager took full control of a drill or a session.

"Our strikeout totals were so high," coach Mike Borzello said, "and he was really getting frustrated watching our at-bats and the two-strike approaches. So he called everybody together to talk about a good two-strike approach. He showed with a fungo bat the way to move the baseball with two strikes and especially the mind-set you have to have with two strikes.

"I'll never forget it. He said, 'We have to start taking our "B" hack.'"

A "B" hack is a swing with reduced length and effort as compared to a hitter's most powerful swing, or "A" hack. With two strikes, for instance, a hitter might choke up on the bat and place a greater priority simply on making contact.

"That became our rallying cry: 'B hack 'em!' It became who we were," Borzello said. "That became a major point. We started approaching our at-bats differently. 'B hack 'em! B hack 'em to death!' You heard it all year long in the dugout whenever anybody got two strikes on them."

In 2015 the Cubs struck out in 24.5 percent of their plate appearances, the worst rate in the major leagues. In 2016, armed with their B hacks, they cut that rate to 21.1 percent, right at league average.

ONE OF THE quieter developments in the entertaining 2016 camp was the frame of mind of Jon Lester. The Cubs immediately saw a better, more relaxed pitcher than the one who had showed up in 2015 trying too hard to prove that he deserved his $155 million contract. Lester was energized by the addition of Lackey, his hunting partner, former teammate in Boston, and alter ego. Lackey is a gruff, no-nonsense extrovert who likes to boast, "In between the lines, I don't care what anybody thinks of me. I'm there to win."

"John Lackey will be great for Jon Lester," pitching coach Chris Bosio said in Arizona. "Jon is quiet and focused, and Lack brings out the beast in him. He'll push him. John Lackey is a great addition because he can pitch, but also because he makes Jon Lester better."

The relationship between the two pitchers was so symbiotic that the Cubs arranged for Lackey and Lester to hold their opening spring training news conferences together. Like a comedy team, they ribbed one another, completed each other's sentences, and challenged one another about which pitcher would wind up with the most hits.

"When you know people as well as we know each other, you can definitely talk to each other a little bit differently than you talk to anybody else," Lester said. "There's no sugarcoating anything around us. You probably don't want to be in a lot of conversations around us.

"It's good having him. It's always good when you have friends on the team. It's nice having guys that don't sugarcoat things and you know exactly what they're going to bring and what exactly they're going to do for you and what you can do for them to make you better."

Maddon came up with his unique way of describing the combination of Lackey and Lester, observing after just a couple of days into spring training that they were "vibrating on the same level right now." The manager reflected on what it would mean to have Lackey joining Ross in the support group around a more relaxed Lester.

"Jon Lester likes to have people around him that he's familiar with," Maddon said. "I think Lackey's the perfect foil, in a sense. Lack's going to tell Jon Lester exactly what he thinks all the time and that's good. I think together, the combination of Lackey and David has the opportunity to bring out the best in Jon Lester."

With Lackey in the same rotation, Ross catching him, and the strain of trying to prove that he deserved his contract behind him, Lester, the notoriously slow starter who complained he needed 100 innings to feel right, opened 2016 with the best April of his career. In five starts he went 2–1 with a 1.83 ERA. It jump-started what was the best year of his career. Lester tied a career high with 19 wins and posted career lows with an ERA of 2.44 and a WHIP of 1.016. The Cubs were 24–8 when he started, including 12–2 in the second half.

Lester reached lofty Triple Crown pitching numbers—19 wins, 2.44 ERA, and 197 strikeouts—that only three pitchers ever had reached before in franchise history: Arrieta in 2015, Greg Maddux in 1992, and Orval Overall in 1909.

IT TOOK ONLY a month or so of the 2016 season before the Cubs began drawing comparisons to the 1984 Tigers, the 1927 Yankees, the 1902 Pirates, and some of the best teams of all time out of the gate. Chicago won its first three games before its first loss, a defeat that left it one game behind 4–0 Pittsburgh in the National League Central. It would be the only day all season the Cubs were not in first place. They finished April 17–5. They didn't lose back-to-back games until the middle of May.

The Cubs weren't just beating teams; they were annihilating them. The 2015 Cubs team that won 97 games needed the entire 162-game season to outscore their opponents by 81 runs; this team did it in just their first 24 games. After only 29 games, the Cubs had outscored opponents by 100 runs, becoming the first team to wipe out the competition by so much so fast since the 1902 Pirates.

The Cubs were 25–6 after 31 games, the fastest-starting team since the 1984 Detroit Tigers. They owned a 9-game lead after only 35 games. The division race was effectively over before school let out.

On and on they rolled. They reached the last day of June with a record of 51–27 and a lead in the division of 11 games. Something really historic happened that day: Joe's mom, Beanie, worked her last day at the Third Base Luncheonette in Hazleton, Pennsylvania, after working there for 46 years. She retired at age 83.

"I just talked to her," Maddon said before a game in New York. "I said, 'How did it go today?' She said, 'Oh, good.' 'Big party?' 'No, just some cake and some balloons. And a lot of the customers were really nice.'

"Talking to her on the phone she sounded really good. Excited. I was always concerned—my dad passed away in 2002—and this absolutely gives her identity, keeps her busy. I always thought it was good for her. But I never heard her as happy as she sounded today. So I do believe she has other things that will fill up her day. So I do believe it's going to work out. That's a big moment."

The Cubs lost that night, 4–3, the first defeat of a four-game sweep by the Mets. After a 47–20 start, Chicago played dull baseball for three weeks. The Cubs would lose 15 of 20 games in their only slump of the year. Maddon knew exactly what was happening: his team simply couldn't maintain the incredible pace and energy it had played with since spring training began.

On Saturday, July 9, before a game that night in Pittsburgh, Maddon gathered his team for the second of his three annual meetings.

He pulled out his iPad Pro and drew from the same speech he gave in spring training—delivering the key points word for word.

"I reemphasized the spring training message, all this stuff on the back of that T-shirt," he said. "I just reminded them about all that stuff. I said, 'I can see we're tired. I get it. Everybody's tired. I see it. We're going to get through this. And while we're getting through this, don't forget about the target, don't forget about pressure, don't forget about expectations, and those are good things, and when we catch our breath and come back on the other side of the [All-Star] break, get back to where we had been.'

"All it was was a rehashing of what we had talked about. They did not forget about it, because I thought it was so on point and worked so well. We just got away from it because we were tired. That's it. There was no other reason. None."

The Cubs sent seven players to the All-Star Game, a game that featured a whopping 11 players who had been acquired by Epstein: Anthony Rizzo, Jon Lester, Mookie Betts, David Ortiz, Jackie Bradley Jr., and Xander Bogaerts from his Boston days, and Ben Zobrist, Kris Bryant, Addison Russell, Dexter Fowler, and Jake Arrieta from his Chicago tenure.

The National League lost the game, 4–2. It turned out to be the best possible outcome for the Cubs.

ON THE OTHER side of the All-Star break, refreshed by the time off and renewed by Maddon's principles, the Cubs returned to the ways of a juggernaut. They would not lose a series for more than a month, reeling off a 24–8 run that was just as impressive as a similar one to start the season.

During that run, and almost two weeks before the trading deadline, Epstein made one of his under-the-radar moves that quietly were becoming a hallmark of his rebuild. He traded for Mike Montgomery, a 26-year-old, left-handed pitcher from Seattle. Epstein gave up Dan Vogelbach, a first base prospect who was blocked by Anthony Rizzo, and Paul Blackburn, a strike-throwing right-handed pitching prospect. On the face of it, the move seemed extremely minor. Montgomery would be joining his fourth team in five years. His career record while bouncing between the starting rotation and the bullpen was 7–10.

What Epstein saw was a pitcher on the cusp of breaking out. He saw not a middle reliever, the way he was used in Seattle, but a potential 15-game winner as a starting pitcher.

"A year from now," he said, "we'd never be able to trade for a guy like that, not without paying a heavy price. We try to get these guys before they are household names, like the way we traded for Andrew Miller in Boston before 2011. Montgomery is not Miller. He actually reminds me some of Jeremy Affeldt when he started to figure it out."

Affeldt, like Montgomery, was a tall left-hander who developed slowly in the Kansas City Royals system. At age 28 his career ERA was 4.55. He then signed with San Francisco, where he posted a 3.07 ERA over the next seven seasons while winning three World Series titles. Epstein's plan was to keep Montgomery in the bullpen for 2016 and convert him to a starting pitcher in 2017. His track record for finding pitchers on the verge of breaking out was remarkable. His haul in Chicago included:

Kyle Hendricks (2012). Instead of getting Hendricks, Epstein nearly traded his best pitcher at the time, Ryan Dempster, to the Atlanta Braves for pitcher Randall Delgado. Dempster, however, used his veto power as a player with 10-and-5 rights (10 years in the majors, at least 5 with his current team) to kill the deal. Epstein needed to pivot with mere days before the trade deadline. He was in a hurry to move veterans he inherited for young players who could help the Cubs in later years. Dempster, pitcher Paul Maholm, outfielder Reed Johnson, catcher Geovany Soto, and infielder Jeff Baker all would be traded within a six-day window.

After the Atlanta deal fell through, the Texas Rangers called on Dempster. The Rangers were motivated to make a deal. They were clinging to a four-game lead in the American League West, and the team chasing them, the Los Angeles Angels, had just acquired ace Zack Greinke.

Hendricks, 22 at the time, and pitching for Texas's Class-A team in Myrtle Beach, was nobody's idea of a hot pitching prospect, if only because he lacked the elite velocity the game craved. What Hendricks lacked in velocity, however, he made up for with pitching smarts. The son of a golf pro, Hendricks was a 4.0 student at Capistrano Valley High School in Mission Viejo, California. He wanted to attend Stanford, but he didn't throw hard enough for the tastes of the coaching staff there. He chose to attend Dartmouth, where as a freshman he threw $7\frac{1}{3}$ shutout innings in the Ivy League Championship Series clincher, advancing Dartmouth to its first NCAA regional in 22 years.

The Rangers selected Hendricks in the eighth round of the 2011 draft, after his junior year. (An economics major, Hendricks completed his degree in 2014 after returning for fall terms after baseball seasons with the Rangers and the Cubs. He wrote his final economics thesis on "Trade Liberalization and Foreign Direct Investment.")

Up against the 2012 trade deadline, the Cubs started to collect information on Texas prospects. Hendricks stood out because of his numbers. He was a premier strike-thrower who put the ball on the ground and did not give up home runs. In 20 starts at Myrtle Beach, Hendricks walked only 15 batters and gave up only eight home runs. Still, as a slightly built (6-foot-3, 190 pounds) right-hander who rarely cracked 90 miles per hour with his fastball, Hendricks appeared to have a limited ceiling. The crafty right-hander was an endangered species in baseball as velocity rose. In 2012, for instance, there were only 12 right-handed qualified pitchers in all of the major leagues who averaged less than 90 miles per hour with their fastball.

The Cubs weren't certain about Hendricks. And then, as the deadline neared, one phone call convinced them to take a chance on him. It came from a rival player personnel director who knew Hendricks.

"We were told his makeup was off the charts," Hoyer said, referring to how scouts describe a player's character. "He said Hendricks had an 80 makeup [on an 80 scale]. Really, that alone sold us. We went with the makeup."

On July 31, just five minutes before the deadline, they traded Dempster for Hendricks and corner infielder Christian Villanueva.

In 2016, Hendricks posted the second-lowest ERA in the history of Wrigley Field, 1.32, a mark bettered only by Grover Cleveland Alexander 96 years earlier. Hendricks won the ERA title (2.13) and finished third in Cy Young Award voting.

Hector Rondon (2012). Rondon was the Cleveland Indians' minor league pitcher of the year in 2009. Two years later he wanted to quit.

After undergoing Tommy John surgery in 2010, Rondon fractured the same elbow the next year while pitching for Caracas in the Venezuelan Winter League. A screw that had been placed in his elbow during the Tommy John surgery dislodged from the bone. He needed another surgery. Doctors told him he had only a 20 percent chance of pitching again. That's when he decided to quit. He told his girlfriend, his father, his mother, and the Indians that he was finished with baseball. He was 23 years old.

Rondon eventually reconsidered. He underwent the surgery. He grinded through his second major rehabilitation program on the elbow. He made it back in time to throw 7 innings at the end of the 2012 minor league season. Rondon added 21 innings in the Venezuelan Winter League. The Indians, believing teams would not want to take the health risk on Rondon, left him off their roster. The decision exposed Rondon to the Rule 5 draft, an annual winter draft in which teams can select certain qualified nonroster players from other organizations, with the catch being that they must keep that player on the major league roster for the entirety of the next season.

One of the Cubs' minor league coaches, Franklin Font, worked on the Leones staff in Venezuela, saw Rondon pitch there, and recommended him.

Rondon pitched so well with the Cubs that in 2014 he became the team's closer, a role he held until Chicago traded for Aroldis Chapman in July 2016.

Jake Arrieta (2013). The worst starting pitcher in Baltimore Orioles history pitched like Bob Gibson in Chicago. Freed from constraints the Orioles had imposed on his delivery and pitch selection, Arrieta became the 2015 Cy Young Award winner with a season for the ages.

Pedro Strop (2013). The Colorado Rockies signed Strop at 16 years old out of the Dominican Republic and released him at 23. The Texas Rangers signed him, but they traded him three years later to Baltimore, where in 2013 he posted a 7.25 ERA while walking six batters per nine innings. Though he threw 97 miles per hour, Strop fought control issues at every stop. The Orioles included Strop in the Arrieta deal that year. With the Cubs, Strop has posted a 2.68 ERA while reducing his walk rate nearly in half, to 3.4 per nine innings.

Carl Edwards Jr. (2013). This is the story of the "String Bean Slinger." As a skinny senior pitcher at Mid-Carolina High School in Prosperity, South Carolina, Carl Edwards Jr., all 6-feet-2, 160 pounds of him, was determined to follow his close friend and high school catcher Will Bedenbaugh to Carolina Southern University. Bedenbaugh, two years older than Edwards, played 10 games at CSU as a freshman before suffering an arm injury. Just after midnight on December 12, 2010, while home in Prosperity, Bedenbaugh was driving his 2009 Dodge Challenger when it left Mount Pleasant Road, hit several trees, and caught fire. Bedenbaugh was killed.

Edwards's plans to attend CSU changed. The following spring he attended a predraft workout held at Capital City Stadium in Columbia, South Carolina. Scouts from the Rangers, Blue Jays, Red Sox, and Padres were on hand for the event. A Rangers scout named Chris Kemp hoped that Edwards didn't bring his best fastball that day. Kemp already believed he might be sitting on a gem. He saw Edwards pitch in an adult league referred to as the "Bush League," a very competitive sandlot league composed mostly of African-American men, some in their 40s, from communities around central

South Carolina. Kemp saw Edwards hit 91 miles an hour and loved the whiplike action of the skinny kid's arm. Edwards remained under the radar for most teams because he did not participate in the elite showcase circuit for top high school prospects. To Kemp's relief, Edwards didn't crack 90 that day.

In all, 1,463 players were selected in the draft before the Rangers—in the 48th round, a round that no longer exists in a draft that has been truncated to 40 rounds—finally called the name of Carl Edwards Jr. The Rangers signed him for $50,000. They also put him on a 6,000-calorie daily diet. Each day Edwards would throw into a blender milk, ice, Nutella, peanut butter, Oreos, and protein powder, and chug the calorie-laden shake. He still had trouble gaining weight, but his fastball gained velocity. He had his first pitching lesson in Texas's 2011 Instructional League.

Hitters couldn't touch him. By 2013 he was ranked as the 14th best prospect in the Texas system. In $170\frac{1}{3}$ innings, Edwards struck out 240 batters and posted a 1.59 ERA. Then, on July 22, 2013, on a night when he was scheduled to pitch, Edwards walked into the clubhouse of the Hickory Crawdads and saw a report on ESPN that the Cubs had traded veteran pitcher Matt Garza to the Rangers for pitcher Justin Grimm, third baseman Mike Olt, Edwards, and a player to be named, who turned out to be pitcher Neil Ramirez.

A short time later his phone rang. It was Epstein. "Welcome to the Chicago Cubs," Epstein told him.

Epstein was impressed with Edwards's athleticism, which allowed his thin frame to generate power, and the natural cutting action on his fastball, which reminded him of the famous cutter of Mariano Rivera. By 2015, convinced that Edwards was not built to withstand the rigors of starting 30 times and pitching 200 innings in the big leagues, the Cubs converted him to a reliever. His average fastball velocity jumped from 91.9 miles per hour in 2014 to 94.1 in 2015, then jumped again in 2016 to 95.8.

In 41 relief appearances for the Cubs in 2015 and 2016, Edwards struck out 56 batters in 40⅔ innings. Among the 122 pitchers who made their first 41 major league appearances with the Cubs, the String Bean Slinger allowed the fewest walks plus hits per inning of all of them (0.86).

Justin Grimm (2013). A struggling rookie in the Texas rotation at the time of the trade that included Edwards, Grimm was throwing 92 miles per hour and working to develop a changeup or slider to complement his fastball-curveball combination. As with Edwards, the Cubs converted him to a reliever and told him to can his changeup and slider. His velocity spiked to 95 miles an hour and his curveball use doubled. Batters hit just .152 and .161 against his curveball in 2015 and 2016, respectively.

THE CUBS USED every available means to find pitchers. It was one of Epstein's strong suits, dating to his early days in Boston when he dispatched a team of interns to photocopy 30 years of batting records filed away at the NCAA offices.

"He gathers information better than anyone I've ever worked for," Borzello said. "He wants as many opinions as he can get from people he trusts before he makes his decision. Ultimately, he weighs everybody's opinions before he signs a player or trades for a player. You're going to be asked and he wants your opinion.

"He hires people that are going to stand up for their own opinions. He doesn't surround himself with yes-men. He likes hearing what you have to say and why. Ultimately he makes the decision, but he's really good at getting the information he wants from everybody.

"When you work other places you learn it's not always like that. It could just be that they decide, 'We're going to do this' or the circle of people being asked is small. With Theo you always feel like he knows he has people working for him who can be a resource, who know people, like if you want a background check on somebody. I may know a clubbie or a bullpen catcher who caught this guy. So it's not just the stat sheet he's looking at. It's, 'What's his personality like? What's it like when things are going good? What's it like when things are going bad?'"

While scouring for pitchers and information before the 2016 draft, for instance, Epstein and his scouts found a 6-foot-7 junior right-hander named Stephen Ridings at tiny Haverford College. Haverford is a prestigious liberal arts school near Philadelphia with just 1,200 students and an excellent Division III baseball program. Haverford had just won its second Centennial Conference championship in three years. It has produced exactly one major league player, Bill Lindsay, who was born in 1881 and played his last game exactly 100 years before.

At the start of 2016, Ridings was a relative unknown in scouting circles. He primarily had been a middle reliever with sketchy command and a mediocre 85-miles-per-hour fastball during his first two years at Haverford. After gaining strength over the winter, however, Ridings suddenly began throwing in the low- to mid-90s, and once hit 98. The Cubs scouted every one of his starts, including his opening start, when he was on no other team's radar.

Several teams invited Ridings to predraft workouts, which usually involved having him throw a bullpen session. Few teams rated Ridings highly, in part because he had pitched in Division III and had inconsistent mechanics. The Cubs, however, invited him to throw on the game mound at Wrigley Field. Why the game mound? They wanted to analyze his form and his pitches with TrackMan, the state-of-the-art pitch-tracking system installed in all major league parks to provide information such as the speed, spin rate, and spin axis of pitches, and the release point and stride of the pitcher.

When the Cubs looked at the information on Ridings from Track-Man, they were giddy with excitement. Two metrics especially stood out. Ridings threw with such a long stride that he ranked among the most extreme outliers in Major League Baseball. Ridings released the ball a full seven feet in front of the pitching rubber, placing him with Cubs reliever Aroldis Chapman and Yankees starter

CC Sabathia among the pitchers who release the ball the closest to home plate.

The other metric that TrackMan revealed about Ridings was his odd release point. Though Ridings is 6-foot-7, because he throws with a long stride and doesn't move his arm far away from his body, he actually throws with a low release point. The ball comes from an area closer to his head than most hitters are accustomed to seeing.

Hitters learn to expect where a pitch will be by a mental process called "chunking," in which the mind synthesizes thousands of pitches into an expected path—based on release, velocity, and spin. Pitchers who throw in a way that is much different than the majority of pitchers—such as submarine pitchers, knuckleball pitchers, split-fingered fastball pitchers—own an advantage because the way they throw doesn't fit in the "chunking process." In 2014, for instance, the Giants won the World Series with key relief work from Yusmeiro Petit, who flummoxed hitters with a fastball that traveled only 89 miles per hour. Despite its lackluster speed, it was hard to hit because he threw from an odd release point—closer to his head than the standard release point.

Perhaps 20 years ago a scout might have written that Ridings had a fastball with "late life." But in 2016 the Cubs could use laser-guided, military-grade technology to compile hard data to measure his fastball. When the Cubs considered his stride length, his unusual release point, his velocity, and his spin rate, they determined that his fastball was the type of fastball that would confound hitters. They used data to see a Division III pitcher with a swing-and-miss fastball. The Cubs surprised other clubs when they took Ridings in the eighth round, much higher than teams expected. (Flush with young position players, Epstein and Hoyer pivoted in that 2016 draft: starting with their first pick, in round 3, they used 13 of their first 14 picks on four-year college pitchers.)

In Mike Montgomery's case, Epstein saw a pitcher still learning how to use the stuff that in 2008 made him a first-round draft pick of the Kansas City Royals. Montgomery labored in Triple-A for four consecutive seasons before getting a chance to stick with the 2016 Mariners in their bullpen.

"I felt like if I could just get my velocity up to the mid-90s, that was the key," Montgomery said. "I gained about 15 pounds over the winter and changed some things in my delivery to use my lower half more. I thought I started to figure out some things right before the trade. I know some people on the Mariners' coaching staff weren't happy they traded me."

In 2016 Montgomery's velocity shot up from 91.2 to 94.3 miles per hour. If, as Epstein projected, Montgomery eventually would transition back to starting, such velocity would be exceedingly rare from a lefty in the rotation. In 2016, only one qualified left-handed starter threw that hard: Danny Duffy of Kansas City, who came up through the Royals system with Montgomery.

The Cubs would make one immediate tweak with Montgomery: they wanted him to throw his curveball more often. Montgomery's curve was a nasty one, but he had been using it in the old-school manner of a complementary pitch. Most pitchers learned the traditional foundation of pitching: pitch off your fastball, sprinkle in your secondary pitches. As teams dove further into data, however, they pushed pitchers with exceptional off-speed pitches to use them more as feature pitches than complementary ones. Clayton Kershaw, Rich Hill, and Drew Pomeranz, for instance, became better pitchers once they threw their best pitch, the curveball, more often.

After Maddon saw Montgomery for a few outings with the Cubs, he was asked September 1 if Montgomery reminded him of Pomeranz, who became a breakout All-Star in 2016 because of his heavier curveball usage.

"No, not Pomeranz—Kershaw," Maddon said. "You're talking about a tall left-hander with mid-90s velocity who can drop that breaking ball at any time on both sides of the plate, plus he has a great changeup. You just don't see left-handers with that kind of stuff very often, other than Kershaw. I'm not saying he's Kershaw right now, but his stuff reminds me of Kershaw. I believe he is a 15-game winner waiting to happen.

"I like Montgomery, I really do. Montgomery, if this guy ever really thinks he's good, he could be really good. I really like him. Physically, this guy is really talented. The moment he really believes it, he can be very, very good. And if that happens this month, so be it. I'll take it."

Montgomery quickly became another in Epstein's long line of pitchers who performed better with the Cubs than elsewhere. Part of the explanation for these breakthroughs was the run-prevention infrastructure the Cubs put in place in 2015. By 2016 it was a mature system humming at optimal efficiency. The 2016 Cubs ranked as one of the greatest defensive teams of all time. Start with this: it wasn't easy to put the ball in play against their pitchers. The staff allowed the fewest balls in play in any full season since the live ball era began in 1920. And when balls were hit into play, the Cubs' defense turned 72.8 percent of those batted balls into outs, the highest conversion rate since the 1990 Athletics.

Heyward in rightfield and Rizzo at first base each won Gold Gloves. Dexter Fowler, playing a deeper centerfield than usual, improved his play on defense. Infielder Javier Baez was a wizard with the glove wherever he roamed, especially when it came to his extraordinary skills at tagging runners. Bryant improved at third base, where coach Gary Jones schooled him in playing lower to the ground and curbing his habitual tapping of the ball in his glove before throwing it.

The Cubs defended the field with athletic players who seemed to be in the right place almost all the time. Judging by batting average by hitters on balls in play, every starter never was better at suppressing hitters in any full season of their careers: Jason Hammel (.271), Lackey (.259), Lester (.258), Hendricks (.252), and Arrieta (.242), all of whom were far below the league average (.301).

"This is a nice example—a pretty extreme example—of what

happens when you marry pitching and defense," Epstein said. "It's a beautiful thing when it works together. It's hard to quantify some of it, like the confidence it breeds in a pitcher. When it works, they aren't afraid of contact. And when you're not afraid of contact, you can be more efficient and more effective. When you're confident that balls in play are going to be outs, it's easier to game-plan."

Said Hoyer, "We ended up being an elite run-prevention team. Years ago if you told me we would win in 2016, I'd probably have guessed we just mashed people. We scored runs, but it wasn't like we were the 2004 Red Sox and destroyed you. We started out with all these bats as our core, but ultimately pitching and defense carried us."

Another key part of the run-prevention infrastructure was tailoring the right game plans for pitchers. Montgomery provided yet another example of making the best use of a pitcher's stuff. The Cubs traded for him knowing his wicked curveball had been underused. In June with Seattle, for instance, Montgomery threw his curveball just 18 percent of the time, even though nobody managed to get a hit off the 45 curveballs he threw that month. By October with Chicago, Montgomery had doubled his curveball usage to 36 percent. Batters hit .111 off the pitch.

With Montgomery, Epstein's batting average continued to be phenomenal on pitching acquisitions. The Cubs won 103 games in 2016, the most for the franchise since the 1910 team won 104 games. Of those 103 wins, 102 were credited to pitchers Epstein acquired from other teams after Tom Ricketts hired him after the 2011 season. The only homegrown win belonged to Rob Zastryzny, a second-round pick under Epstein in 2013.

Chicago would use 11 pitchers in the World Series. Epstein acquired every one of them from other organizations.

TWO DAYS AFTER the season ended, and three days before the Cubs were to begin the National League Division Series against the

Giants, Maddon held his third and final team meeting of the year. He held it before a workout at Wrigley Field.

"Understand this right now," Maddon told his players. "Something bad is going to happen. It will. And when it happens, we have to keep our heads and we've got to fight through it.

"Too many times in the past, in the postseason, I know we've got the other team by the look in the other team's eyes. There's a distant look. They're anticipating bad. It's almost like a concession look. I never want us to be that team. So know that something bad is going to happen. Know it is. Expect it to happen. And when it happens, we have to keep our heads and fight through it."

The speech was inspired by the first major league postseason series in which Maddon participated. It was the 2002 American League Division Series. Maddon was the bench coach for the Anaheim Angels. They were playing the New York Yankees, who had won four World Series titles and five pennants in the previous six years. This Yankees team, however, was a team in transition. Stalwarts Scott Brosius, Paul O'Neill, Chuck Knoblauch, and Tino Martinez all were gone from the 2001 pennant winner.

The series was tied at one game each when the Yankees held a 6–3 lead on the Angels, heading into the sixth inning of Game 3. The Angels rallied to win the game, 9–6, scoring three runs in the bottom of the eighth.

The next day the Yankees held a 2–1 lead in the fifth inning. The Angels stormed back again. They scored eight runs in the fifth inning—smashing line drives all over the yard against pitcher David Wells—and eliminated New York with a 9–5 win. To this day, Maddon can still see the faces on the Yankees players as Anaheim rallied in both games. He saw the look of defeat on them. Yankees captain Derek Jeter would later tell reporters, "This isn't the same team," in response to questions about how the battle-hardened Yankees could crumble in Anaheim.

"I couldn't believe it," Maddon said. "I'm in the dugout and I look out on the field at these Yankees and it's, 'Holy shit. We've got 'em!' which I never knew about because it was my first playoff.

"So I want my teams to never have that look. How do you not have it? You have to be prepared for something shitty to happen and when it does, it doesn't mean it's the end of the world."

It didn't take long in the 2016 postseason for something bad to happen to Maddon's team, and it went by the name of Johnny Cueto. The Game 1 starter for San Francisco was the Cubs' worst nightmare, a pitcher who threw balls that looked like strikes, confusing the young Chicago hitters into a losing guessing game. Cueto's changeup was particularly devious. He threw 23 of them. The Cubs tried to hit 13 of them, and they missed seven times, never managing to get a hit off the pitch.

Through seven innings the Cubs extracted only two hits off Cueto. Only six times did they even hit the ball with enough authority to get it out of the infield. From his perch at the dugout railing, Maddon felt a very bad vibe. He watched as hitter after hitter was retired meekly, and he knew the Cubs' postseason lives came down to one thing: we'd better not see Johnny Cueto again.

Giants manager Bruce Bochy had four starters lined up for the Cubs: Cueto, former Cub Jeff Samardzija, postseason legend Madison Bumgarner, and left-hander Matt Moore. If the series went the distance, Cueto would get the ball again in Game 5 in a winner-take-all game. Maddon decided right then in Game 1 he wanted no part of seeing Cueto again, even if Lester was matching Cueto zero for zero on a windy night at Wrigley.

Then something happened with one out in the eighth inning that could happen nowhere else but Wrigley. On a full count from Cueto, Baez smashed a high fly ball to leftfield. It felt and looked like a home run to Baez, who quickly began to celebrate. But the baseball ran smack into a great wall of wind. Giants leftfielder Angel Pagan drifted underneath it, thinking more and more that he might catch it as it surrendered its fight against the wind. Then, just as Pagan reached up, his back to the ivy, the ball plopped into that wire

"basket" jutting out from near the top of the wall. It was a phenom-
enon unique to Wrigley Field: a home run that neither cleared the
wall nor was a live ball, inside-the-park varietal.

The home run was a gift from the original Bleacher Bums, the
rowdies who populated the Wrigley bleachers in the 1960s as manager Leo Durocher's Cubs began to play well enough to be taken seriously as contenders. Fortified by sunshine and beer, and with their
numbers growing as the Cubs actually began to win, the Bums has-
sled opposing outfielders, threw objects on the field, reached over
the wall to touch balls in play, and, when the urge struck, walked
across the top of the wall just for the heck of it. Not surprisingly,
given the amount of beer consumed in the bleachers, and the rela-
tively narrow width of the wall, it wasn't unusual for Bums to tumble
off the wall and onto the warning track.

In 1970 the Cubs decided to do something about the unruly behavior. They became the first team to install video cameras to monitor the crowd in a baseball park. They also constructed the wire
"basket" as a defense against fans interfering with play and falling
onto the field. Thirty inches below the top of the wall, and angled
at 45 degrees, a 42-inch wire screen was installed. The basket effectively shortened the distance needed for a home run at Wrigley
Field by three feet. Forty-six years after it was installed to quell the
hijinks of the Bleacher Bums, the basket helped win the Cubs a playoff game, 1–0.

Maddon still needed two more wins in the next three games to
avoid seeing Cueto again. The Cubs gave him one of those wins in
Game 2, by a 5–2 score, when Travis Wood, the winning pitcher, became the first reliever to hit a postseason home run since Rosy Ryan
of the 1924 Giants. San Francisco rebounded with the comeback
against Aroldis Chapman in Game 3. Five outs from elimination,
the Giants rallied against the closer before finally winning in the
13th inning against Montgomery, who was working his fifth inning.

Game 4 presented Maddon with urgency: win or face Cueto in
Game 5 with the season on the line. The worst-case scenario seemed

very likely when the Cubs, throttled by Moore, reached the ninth inning down 5–2.

Maddon is not a manager above trying to get into the heads of the opposing team. He admits he likes to be unconventional in part because it can throw off another team. It was part of his extreme defensive shifting with the Rays, for instance, though shifts have become so commonplace that they no longer hold the same powers of confusion and doubt on a hitter they once did. He likes to squeeze-bunt with two strikes, move his second baseman to first base so his first baseman can charge on obvious bunts, and generally make himself a source of annoyance to another manager.

"All the little games within the game you can perform can have a positive effect for you," Maddon said. "That stuff—like when I look in the other dugout, the manager I cannot read his emotion, that's the toughest guy. The guy you can read his emotion all the time, I like working against that guy. I much prefer that. I mean, I learned that in the minor leagues. I used to like to see the guy who got really happy or got really sad."

Those tactics, though, were of little use against the Giants.

"Some guys, like Joe Torre, never gave away anything," Maddon said. "And Bochy? No."

With Cueto looming, Maddon needed something big and he needed it now, in the ninth inning.

"It's just like Game 1," Maddon said. "I'm standing there thinking the whole time, *We cannot play Game 5*."

Bochy removed Moore, who had thrown 120 pitches. It was as if he removed a critical piece from a game of Jenga. Bochy tried five pitchers against the next six batters, all of whom reached base. The Cubs scored four runs by the time the chain reaction of events ended: single, walk, double, single, error, single. Most notably, given Maddon's spring training tutorial about B hacks, Baez knocked in the go-ahead run with a scaled-down swing on an 0-and-2 pitch that sent a grounder tumbling through the middle of the diamond.

"That inning never happens with the way we hit before," Borzello said. "That wasn't the way we were as an offense before 2016."

Chapman closed out the ninth, and the series, with three swinging strikeouts. Something about that inning, however, made Epstein uneasy. David Ross, who had started the game, was behind the plate when Chapman pitched, a rarity during the season. Ross had caught Chapman for just $4\frac{1}{3}$ innings. (Maddon much preferred Contreras behind the plate with Chapman on the mound.) Ross called 13 pitches in that ninth inning. Every one of them was a fastball—not a single slider. Ross seemed to signal an old-school catching mentality: don't get beat by anything other than your best pitch.

Epstein, who likes to sit in the scouts' section behind home plate for road games, looked around him as Chapman threw fastball after fastball. He saw the advance scouts from the Cleveland Indians scribbling notes. If he noticed it, he knew they did, too, so he knew what they were writing down: Ross calls all fastballs with Chapman. Epstein just filed away the observation, hoping—in vain as it would famously happen—it would never come into play.

The inning otherwise was a perfect ending to the series. Maddon could exhale. There would be no more Cueto.

"With all due respect to us," Maddon said, "if we get to Game 5, I don't know if we could have done that, with Johnny Cueto pitching. I don't know if we could have mustered up. We got one point the last time: the 3-and-2 homer by Javy.

"We win the World Series in Game 7. But we might have won it in Game 4 in San Francisco."

Done with Cueto and the Giants, the Cubs would next have to contend with Kershaw and the Dodgers. Eddie Vedder, the lead singer of Pearl Jam, one of the team's leading celebrity fans, buddy of Epstein's, and a texting friend of Maddon's, sent the manager a good-luck text. "The texts from Eddie Vedder," Maddon said, "are almost lyrical. You could make songs out of them."

The postseason on-the-job training of Chapman, from a diva of a closer into a multiple-inning weapon, would hit another bump in the first game of the National League Championship Series. Chicago took a 3–1 lead against the Dodgers into the eighth inning. Before the inning began, Maddon looked at his lineup card, saw that Corey Seager, the Dodgers shortstop and best hitter, was due up fourth, and called over Bosio.

"Tell Chapman he's got Seager," Maddon told his pitching coach.

As it happened, all three hitters in front of Seager reached base against Montgomery and Strop. Maddon summoned Chapman into the fire drill of a jam: bases loaded, nobody out, and Seager at bat, followed by Yasiel Puig. Chapman pitched to the edge of escape, getting two strikeouts. But the crafty veteran hitter Adrian Gonzalez tied the game with a two-run single. Recovering, as well as providing some foreshadowing for Game 7 of the World Series, Chapman at least preserved the tie by getting Yasmani Grandal on a groundout. Chicago won the game in its next at-bat when Miguel Montero slammed a pinch-hit grand slam, with an encore homer by Fowler.

"I really believe Chapman coming in won the game for us," Maddon said. "If anybody else pitches in that particular moment and they get ahead and [Dodgers closer Kenley] Jansen is in the game, then we don't have much of a chance at all. Seriously, who else do you want to pitch to Seager right there?"

As Chapman struggled to master the crash course in the mid-inning appearance, would Maddon be better off just starting the eighth inning with him?

"No, why would I?" the manager answered. "I really don't want to use him for six outs. The matchups were good, and these other guys are here for a reason. Now, if it's an elimination game, I may do something like that."

The Cubs didn't score in their next 21 innings, first getting shut out in a game started by Kershaw, then another one by Rich Hill, and then the first three innings of Game 4 started by 19-year-old rookie Julio Urias.

If Chicago was stuck in a bad dream, Ben Zobrist woke up the team with the smallest of hits. After peeking to see Justin Turner playing a deep third base, Zobrist dropped an exquisite bunt single to start the fourth inning.

"I contemplated bunting as I was walking up to the plate," said Zobrist, who had four bunt hits during the season. "As I got in the box, I took a glance at third base. You do whatever you can to get things going. That's what I was trying to do."

From there, the Cubs B hacked 'em to death. Baez singled to left on an 0-and-2 count, Contreras drove in Zobrist with his own single to left on an 0-and-2 count, and Heyward drove in Baez with a groundout on a 2-and-2 count. It was a clinic of situational hitting crammed into four batters. When Urias fell behind Addison Russell 2-and-0, the shortstop dropped the hammer: a two-run homer to stretch the lead to 4–0.

The five-batter sequence flipped the series. The Cubs would neither lose nor trail again in the NLCS. Starting with the Zobrist bunt, Chicago outscored Los Angeles the rest of the way, 23–6.

Adding to the surreal nature of the turnaround was the storybook awakening of Anthony Rizzo. The first baseman had been 2-for-28 in the postseason when, in the fifth inning of Game 4, he decided to forgo his own Marucci model bat for one that belonged to teammate Matt Szczur. Rizzo told the media that Szczur's bat was the same size and weight, and that he sometimes switched to it when he was in dire need of a hit. Rizzo smacked a home run in that fifth inning at-bat. He would hit .432 the rest of the postseason, all of it with Szczur's bat.

The Cubs clinched their first pennant in 71 years with a 5–0 win in Game 6 at Wrigley Field. Hendricks, with a reprise of the same $7\frac{1}{3}$ shutout innings he threw to clinch the Ivy League championship as a Dartmouth freshman, outpitched Kershaw. With the help of three double plays and one pickoff, Hendricks and Chapman faced the minimum 27 batters, marking only the second time the ultimate in pitching brevity occurred in postseason history. The other occasion was the perfect game thrown by Don Larsen of the New York Yankees in the 1956 World Series.

"We played our best game of the year," Hoyer said, "and I'm happy for that. I think the players played their best because they know what this means to these people."

Never before had "That's Cub!" been so obviously different from the century-old culture that had existed for so long in Chicago. Laughingstocks no more, the Cubs were going to the World Series. Nobody had been able to say that since Gertrude Stein, Al Capone, Henry Ford, and Seabiscuit were alive, and before Jackie Robinson signed a contract with the Montreal Royals, the first affiliated team to break the color barrier. The Cubs, yes, the Cubs—the team of Phil Cavarretta and Phil Brickma, of Fergie Jenkins and Ferris Bueller, of Ernie Banks and Ernie Broglio, of Steve Bartman and Leon Durham, of pet goats and black cats—were a source of juvenile amusement no more.

Shortly after Maddon was hired, and upon attending that midwinter Hajj known as Cubs Convention, the manager met an 80-year-old lifelong Cubs fan named Rhena Knourek. In the gift bag she received as part of her entry to the convention was a ticket for a free autograph from Maddon.

"Do you know what this is?" she said, holding it aloft. "It's a godwink."

A godwink? Knourek went on to explain that a godwink is one of those little events in life that seem random but happen for a reason. The Cubs, the supposedly cursed Cubs, suddenly were surrounded by godwinks. The home run by Baez in the basket . . . The five relief pitchers who failed Bochy and allowed them to avoid Cueto . . . The bunt by Zobrist . . . Rizzo switching to Szczur's bat . . .

There were more godwinks in the clincher. A pop fly by the penultimate batter, Carlos Ruiz, landed near the spot where Bartman had tried to catch a similar foul ball 13 years earlier; this one landed harmlessly. The game began at 7:08 local time—that's 19:08 on 24-hour time. It took two hours, 36 minutes—the exact time of the game the last time the Cubs clinched the pennant, back on September 29, 1945 in Pittsburgh. It was played on the exact date, 46 years later, of the death of Billy Sianis, the tavern owner and original conjurer of the Curse of the Billy Goat.

With one on and one out in the ninth, with the team on the precipice of the pennant, scouting director Jason McLeod, who worked with Epstein and Hoyer dating back to their Boston days, took a moment to reflect on the team on the field. He saw Anthony Rizzo, Albert Almora Jr., Kris Bryant, Willson Contreras, and Javier Baez, all of them either drafted or developed by the trio.

"All from either in Boston or Chicago," McLeod said. "And the next thing I thought about was, *Wow. They're all so young.*"

Chapman threw the next pitch, and that, too, was a godwink: a double play, Russell to Baez to Rizzo, which served as the perfect homage to Tinkers to Evers to Chance of the world champion 1908 Cubs. On the grounds where once stood a Lutheran seminary before there was Wrigley Field, it was time again to sing hallelujah.

Rizzo stuffed the baseball in the back pocket of his uniform pants. After the game that night, most of the Cubs repaired to Lester's house for a victory party. Rizzo took the ball with him as he drove away from Wrigley, and left it in his curbside parked car as he celebrated at Lester's house.

"I was nervous the whole time," he said. "I thought maybe the car was going to get towed or somebody was going to break into it."

When Rizzo left the party to drive home, he was relieved to find the historic baseball still in the vehicle. With the team flying to Cleveland the next day for the World Series, Rizzo decided to store the baseball in a secure, private place while he was gone.

"I put it in my sock drawer," he said. "That's where I keep it."

Even later that night, after the party at Lester's ended, two men slipped into Wrigley Field and onto the diamond. It was five o'clock in the morning, about two hours before sunrise. The pandemonium of the first pennant for the Cubs in 71 years had given way to the stillness of the otherwise empty old ballpark. The two men played catch and took batting practice. In those small hours of an historic night, carefree, Eddie Vedder and Theo Epstein looked not like the rock stars we expect but like children at play.

CHAPTER 17

GAME 6

The Cubs came prepared to Cleveland. They brought with them from Chicago their proprietary organic juices and their nutritionist. Next to a row of bat bags, they filled an entire refrigerated case in a clubhouse hallway with healthful concoctions with handwritten labels such as "Wrigley Firekiller," "Wrigley Peppermint," "Plant Fix," "Immunity," and "Spiritual Matcha." The search for any edge was a boundless pursuit that included shots of turmeric, organic yogurt, grapes, apples, pears, coconut water, and bottled water.

The Cubs had arrived in Cleveland late the previous night, Halloween, making Joe Maddon most likely the first manager in World Series history to delay travel so that his players could enjoy trick-or-treating at home with their kids. Jon Lester and David Ross, naturally, trick-or-treated together with their children. Maddon was thrilled to be back in Cleveland for Game 6. For one, it meant that his team remained alive, having staved off elimination behind Lester in Game 5 in Chicago. For another, it meant a return to American League rules, and the return of Kyle Schwarber in the starting lineup as the designated hitter. This time Maddon moved him from fifth, where he hit in Games 1 and 2, to second. With Kris Bryant behind him, rather than Addison Russell, Schwarber was more likely to see pitches to hit. Maddon knew that the threat of Bryant's home run power behind Schwarber would prompt Cleveland pitchers to be more aggressive against Schwarber—rather than risk a two-run homer by passively walking Schwarber.

"I think, based on what Schwarber did in that last series, the Indians say, 'This is no joke, he's okay.'" Maddon said. "So once they found that out, if I hit him in the five hole they go straight to Addison every time. That was the whole thing: Where do you protect a guy?"

Maddon gave great credence to lineup protection, or how the order of hitters influenced the manner in which they were pitched. He clustered his best hitters together, so that if you thought about "pitching around" one good hitter, the next one could make you pay a price. Maddon prioritized protecting Schwarber, Bryant, and Rizzo, who had the switch-hitting Zobrist behind him. Zobrist was especially valuable in protecting Rizzo because his ability to make contact made him dangerous with runners on, and his skills from either side of the plate gave opposing managers no obvious choice when it came to matching up relief pitchers against him.

"And Zo is the consummate protector," Maddon said. "So it kind of ends there. After that, everybody is on their own life raft. Russell might catch something, Willy might catch something, Heyward, they all might catch something. But that top part, they're all protected by something. That's how I see it."

The guys on their own life raft, without protection, were Russell, Contreras, Heyward, and Baez, the six-seven-eight-nine hitters. Combined, they were batting .169 in the World Series.

"You look at the last four guys in our lineup, that's all defense there," Maddon said. "Hope we get some knocks there. The last two guys—Heyward and Baez—I can't take them off the field right now. I look out there and we're better with them out there."

Baez, Maddon's wild-swinging second baseman, had fallen into a canyon of an offensive funk. Baez had managed one hit, a bunt single, in his previous 16 at-bats, half of which ended with him flailing at third strikes that usually were nowhere near the strike zone. The co–Most Valuable Player of the National League Championship Series was as good as done when the count reached two strikes. Maddon called him into his office for yet another chat.

"You need to create more time for yourself," Maddon told him. "You're subtracting time from everything you do. Your time management at the plate is poor right now. You need to play with the big part of the field. You need to think left-center [and] over. Think singles. Let the ball get deep. Jam yourself. If you crack your bat, I don't care.

"But to move the baseball it has to be the other way, to create more time. Now listen to me . . . Right now everything is like this, like a gate . . ."

With his arm Maddon made the swinging motion of a gate. Baez was casting the barrel of the bat away from him—creating a long path to the ball—which meant the only way he could hit a baseball is if he caught it well out in front of the plate. It was rudimentary stuff, but an indication of how lost Baez had become at the plate.

"I went through it very slowly," said Maddon, who said hitting coach John Mallee would follow up with Baez on the conversation. "He left smiling. Mallee has talked about all the things we're talking about. Johnny is handling that. I wanted it to be more visualization. The first at-bat, if he whistles a rocket to rightfield, heads-up. He's going to have a good night.

"John has all of that data: only 25 percent of pitches are in the zone with two strikes on him, 30 percent overall. We've got it all, and he knows. He's just a young kid in swing mode right now. I just wanted to give him a different game plan. Let it get deep. Jam yourself. Give yourself more time. I explained it to him as a time-management problem.

"I didn't want to put this on him right now, but there's this other thing I used to do. Guys like that, your first at-bat you've got to take a strike, second at-bat take a pitch, third at-bat you can swing at first pitch, and all bets are off if there's a runner in scoring position, even in your first at-bat. I don't want to hamstring you with runners in scoring position. But otherwise, take a strike, take a pitch, you're on your own your third at-bat. And when you take that pitch, just don't take it. Go through your whole process. Get loaded, get on time, put your foot down, and see the ball.

"Now if this was April, May, that's exactly what I would have told him to do. But right now I just tried to present it to him that way."

Baez and the Cubs figured to see more of the steady diet of Cleveland breaking balls, especially with curveball specialist Josh Tomlin starting on short rest. The Indians had thrown Chicago 30 percent breaking balls in the first five games. The Cubs had little success against spin. They were hitting .190 against the Indians' sliders and .163 against their curves—overall, .172 against breaking balls with only one home run.

Tomlin had made a late-season adjustment with his curveball to turn it into a more effective weapon. He used to throw his curveball with a true overhand delivery that caused him to tilt his head to the first-base side to allow his arm and hand to reach that high spot of his release. By moving his head to the side and reaching up, Tomlin gave hitters an early look at how the curve "popped up" out of his hand at release. (The upward motion of the ball out of the hand is a giveaway that a curveball is coming; fastballs come out of the hand straight.)

In mid-August, Tomlin revamped his throwing motion to create a lower release point while keeping his head on a direct line to the plate. The change eliminated the "giveaway" that the pitch was a curveball. He now released his fastball and curveball out of virtually the same release spot and without that "popping up" action on the curve. The change brought another benefit: Tomlin increased the spin rate on his curveball from 2,720 revolutions per minute to 2,855, gaining more bite on the pitch. His curveball usage spiked from 15 percent in the regular season to 35 percent in the postseason, heading into Game 6.

Still, the Cubs held the decided pitching advantage for Game 6. Tomlin, despite the adjustment he made on his curveball, was 32 years old, the longest-tenured player with Cleveland, and still had yet to establish much of a footprint in the majors. A former 19th-round draft pick in 2006, Tomlin had made 109 starts in the majors and 108 starts in the minors, all in the Cleveland organization. His career ERA of 4.58 was the third-worst in franchise history among pitchers with 100 starts, behind only Dave Burba (4.65) and Roberto Hernandez (4.64). Tomlin would be starting on three days' rest for only the second time in his career. The only other time he started on short rest occurred six years earlier.

Maddon gave the ball to Jake Arrieta, the 2015 Cy Young Award winner and owner of the lowest career ERA by a Cubs starter since the live ball era began in 1920 (2.52 in 98 starts). Arrieta had the benefit of extra rest over Tomlin's short rest—five days to three days—a condition that suited him well. Arrieta was 24–6 over the previous two regular seasons with more than the standard four days of rest.

For most of the year—22 of 33 starts entering the World Series—Arrieta threw to catcher Miguel Montero. But in the World Series, fearful of Cleveland's speed on the bases, Maddon started the strong-armed rookie, Contreras, over Montero and David Ross in both of Arrieta's starts.

"With Jake, Jake's not really good at dotting up the ball," Maddon said, referring to how Arrieta relied more on power and movement than precision. "That's Ross's strength, if he's got a pitcher he can orchestrate. I think you just catch Jake. And Jake, when he's good, it's not as if he's grabbing edges all the time. Jake is going to get weak contact from movement or swing-and-miss in the zone because his ball moves so much.

"You don't need that orchestrating catcher dotting up pitches. You just need somebody to receive it, be athletic. To this point, I think Willson has acted as a deterrent to running, and that's a big part of their game—not that Rossy can't.

"Jake's Jake. Jake's set in his ways pretty solidly. He is who he is. To get him to game-plan in a way that's different from what he believes is very difficult. I'm just going to keep a close eye on Jake. He normally doesn't get bludgeoned. It's just the walk that shows up."

Calling balls and strikes was Joe West, an umpire known among players for adjusting his strike zone depending on if the pitcher, catcher, or manager dared question his calls. Arrieta had started two games in his career with West behind the plate, and was 1–0 with a 2.08 ERA in those games. He knew, more than with any other umpire, you show not the least bit of aggressive body language if you felt that West missed a call. "Just get the ball back and move on," Arrieta said.

Maddon's pitching plan was to ride Arrieta as long as he could, use Montgomery as his first option out of the bullpen, and close the game with Chapman, who had one day off after throwing a career-high 42 pitches in Game 5.

"I haven't seen him yet, but he was giggly on the airplane flying here," Maddon said of Chapman. "He was very good walking on the plane. Guys like that you just read their face. If he's happy, he's good."

Then Maddon would utter what would be the most important—and controversial—strategic element of the night:

"Chapman, I think, is capable of one-plus [innings] again tonight."

THE FIRST CURVEBALL Tomlin threw, with his seventh pitch of the game, dropped into the strike zone against Kris Bryant. It ran the count to 0-and-2. The pitch moved Tomlin one strike away from a one-two-three first inning. Why not throw another curveball? Tomlin did, but this curveball was an ugly one. The pitch had no side-to-side break to it and little drop. It just floated, thigh-high, on the inside half of the plate.

"My favorite pitch," Bryant said.

He smashed it into the leftfield seats for a 1–0 Chicago lead.

"Maybe the biggest swing the whole postseason," Hoyer said. "It's certainly one of the biggest. That place was so loud, it's an 0-and-2 count, they're about to go one-two-three, and then Kris hits the home run and we score two more runs. Even at the time it felt like the biggest moment of the game, because early on you felt like the game could start to go their way if they got any momentum."

Rizzo, the next batter, whacked a changeup for a single. Tomlin tried another curveball to Zobrist, but it was another ugly hanger, and Zobrist drilled that one for a single. Tomlin quickly lost confidence in his best pitch. He scrambled to come up with another plan. He threw nine straight cut fastballs, one of which Russell lofted toward rightfield for what should have been the third out. Centerfielder Tyler Naquin, however, inexplicably took his eyes off the ball to look for rightfielder Lonnie Chisenhall. It was an inexcusable violation of the cardinal rule of playing centerfield: the centerfielder has priority on all balls within his range. Naquin turned passive and stopped. The ball fell between them. Two runs scored.

The Cubs handed Arrieta a 3–0 lead before he even threw his first pitch. How important was that, in their second elimination game, this one on the road? Arrieta was 46–5 over the previous three years when Chicago gave him three runs with which to work. He would get more.

Schwarber walked to start the third. After Bryant flied out, Rizzo rapped another sloppy curve to centerfield for a single. By then it was clear: Tomlin was pitching without his best weapon. He threw only seven curveballs in all. Three were balls, one was the called strike to Bryant, and against the rest the Cubs went 3-for-3 when they chose to swing at his hooks. Tomlin tried a fastball to Zobrist, but Zobrist jumped on that for a single that loaded the bases.

Cleveland manager Terry Francona had seen enough. He went to the mound to remove Tomlin and replace him with Dan Otero. Mallee called over Russell, the next batter, for a quick scouting report on the sinkerball pitcher.

"He's going to run a couple of those two-seamers on you to try to get the double play," Mallee told him. "Make sure you get him in the [strike] zone."

A right-handed sinkerball pitcher relies on movement to both sides of the plate to induce contact toward either end of a right-hander's bat: tailing inside toward the handle of the bat, or, starting off the plate and tailing back toward the end of the bat. It's a barrel-averse pitch, designed for weak contact. The first sinker ran inside, off the plate. Russell didn't bite. He took it for a ball. The next sinker was on the inside corner, but down, and a keen-eyed Russell took that one, too.

Tremendous discipline earned Russell a 2-and-0 count with the bases loaded, a nightmare for Otero that forced him into the zone with his next sinker. This one arrived over the heart of the plate, thigh-high. Russell drove it over the wall in centerfield for a grand slam. It was only the third inning, the Cubs led 7–0, and Russell already had tied a World Series record with six runs batted in. On his own "life raft" without protection in the lineup, Russell surely did "catch something," as Maddon hoped. (The three batters behind him, Contreras, Heyward, and Baez, continued to struggle, going 1-for-11.)

A stalwart Arrieta took the ball into the sixth inning, striking out nine batters and putting him in line for his second World Series win. The plan Maddon gave him in the cafeteria on the first day of spring training in Mesa—shave innings from his season workload in order to be strong through the World Series—paid dividends. Here it was November 1 and Arrieta hit 97 miles per hour with his fastball, a velocity he had not reached since August 12, the only other time all year he threw that hard. Adrenaline likely helped the cause, as well. Arrieta, the creature of very specific habits on game days, found himself out of sorts for Game 6.

"The whole day just grinds on you," Arrieta said. "Everywhere you go, everywhere you turn, all you hear about is the game. It's like I can't wait to get to the park to hit the weight room and start my routine and start sweating. And then the game isn't a seven o'clock game. It's an eight o'clock game. So you wait even longer.

"I'm telling you, it wears on you. When I was on the mound, I was jittery. The ball was in my hands and I was jittery, just from the emotions and all the noise around you all day long. I had to calm myself out there. It's not easy."

"Jittery" would be a good word to capture how the endgame turned out for the Cubs and Maddon. Montgomery, as planned, was the first reliever into the game once Arrieta departed. He stumbled a bit in the seventh when he walked Roberto Perez, Cleveland's ninth-place hitter. Maddon looked at his lineup card. If he was going to use Chapman, he wanted him facing the heart of the Cleveland lineup. So he ordered Chapman to start getting loose, even though Chicago held a 7–2 lead and it was only the seventh inning.

Montgomery recovered to get Carlos Santana on a fly ball. But when Jason Kipnis followed with a single, that was enough for Maddon. He called for Chapman. He had said before the game that he thought he could use Chapman for "one-plus" innings, but this was a monumental stretch—with *seven* outs to go and a *five-run* lead.

"I had actually honestly thought about that exact situation to preserve a big enough lead," Maddon said. "There were two guys on when I brought him in.

"First and second when Lindor came up. That was a tough situation right there. Two guys on, here comes Lindor, and I don't want him hitting left-handed. It can't be Stroppy [Pedro Strop] and it can't be Ronnie [Hector Rondon].

"It could have been Montgomery, but again, it's an elimination game so you've got to think a little bit differently right there, and I'm thinking if we can hold them there and add on, I can get him out. That's exactly what I thought.

"The Chapman situation specifically, if we don't hold it right there he's pitching in the eighth plus another inning with a lot more stress on him. Part of the plan for me was hold the lead, and hopefully augment it, and get his ass out of there."

Chapman retired Lindor on a grounder, a play in which the original safe call at first base was overturned by replay. In the eighth, Chapman worked around a single when Baez turned a spectacular double play, catching a poor feed at his ankles and throwing on the run with a low release. Chapman had thrown 15 pitches, two days after getting extended to 42 pitches. Would Maddon preserve him for Game 7 by taking him out and trusting some combination of Strop, Rondon, Travis Wood, and Justin Grimm to get the final three outs before five runs scored? The answer was an emphatic "no."

"I empathize with him," coach Mike Borzello said. "It's an elimination game in the World Series. If anything really strange happens in the ninth inning, and you've taken out your best pitcher because you're starting to manage the next game, and you lose? I can't imagine many things that would be harder to live with as a manager."

With two outs in the top of the ninth, Bryant singled to leftfield, his fifth hit in seven at-bats since that mood-altering homer off Trevor Bauer in Game 5. Rizzo, still smoking-hot since he picked up Szczur's bat, then crushed an 0-and-1 changeup from Mike Clevinger into the rightfield seats. Now the score was 9–2. Now the other relievers could be asked to get three outs before *seven* runs scored. But after the home run, neither Maddon nor Bosio made a move to the dugout phone to call the bullpen to get someone warm. Instead, they stood side by side in the dugout debating what to do. Bosio was in favor of getting Chapman out of the game. Maddon wasn't so sure.

"I'm still not comfortable," Maddon told him.

Bosio told Maddon that Chapman, with 15 pitches, would be in fine shape to pitch in Game 7 if he removed him now. He told Maddon that 92 percent of Chapman's saves were "in the 20-pitch window, so this is nothing for him at this point."

Bosio advocated for a pitching change.

"We've got plenty of guys to match up against them in the ninth," he said.

Maddon finally agreed. The next thing they needed to do was decide who should replace Chapman. Who was due up for the Indians?

The bottom three hitters, all right-handed: Brandon Guyer, Rajai Davis, and Perez. Who could warm up the quickest? Strop, Rondon, or somebody else? Did they want a left-hander to be ready when the lineup reached Kipnis and Lindor? That would mean getting Wood ready, too. The conversation seemed to go on forever.

"It did," Maddon admitted, and then he recalled the ambiguity that took place in their conversation. "It was like, 'Who do you get up? Strop and Rondon?' And somebody else I think.

" 'Can we get him up and get him in?'

" 'Does he have enough time?'

" 'Do we leave Chappy out there longer?'

" 'No, let's get him in there. Just get them ready as quickly as we can.' "

Complicating Maddon's thoughts about rushing a reliever into the game was a scenario he remembered from the Division Series against the Giants.

"There was a time when Chappy didn't have enough time to warm up and we got him in and it was in San Francisco," he said. "And he did not pitch well in that one and he was upset about it. I did not want to do that to the next guy, not have him warmed up enough, then bring him out there and something bad happens.

"So I decided let [Chapman] face one guy, and we'll be ready by then. I thought with that kind of a lead, one guy, get him out, and move on from there. And that's what we did."

As Maddon and Bosio decided what to do, Zobrist drew a two-out walk. Finally, as Russell grounded out, Strop started throwing in the bullpen. Clevinger threw eight more pitches after Rizzo hit the home run, but because Maddon and Bosio debated what to do, Strop didn't have enough time to get ready to start the bottom of the ninth. Maddon had no choice but to send Chapman back to the mound to face at least one more batter. That's how his closer came to throw five more pitches (Chapman walked Guyer) with a seven-run lead.

Strop gave up a run-scoring single before Wood retired Kipnis on a pop fly for the final out of what became one of the more nerve-racking 9–3 wins in memory. Maddon's use of Chapman was the talk of the clubhouse after the game.

Rizzo, for instance, when asked if he tried to think along with Maddon in anticipation of his moves, replied, "No, I gave up a long time ago. But you know, [Reds first baseman] Joey Votto told me a while ago that the more Chappy pitches the stronger he gets. I've seen it."

Said Chapman, who had thrown 62 pitches in the past three days, through a translator, "I do feel stronger the more I pitch. I can't say if that is actually the case, but I do feel stronger."

Chapman did not complain that night about the way Maddon used him, though he would do exactly that one month later on a conference call after signing a five-year, $86-million contract with the New York Yankees.

"Personally, I don't agree with the way he used me, but he is the manager and he has the strategy," Chapman said during the conference call. "My job is to be ready, to be ready to pitch, however that is, however many innings that is. I need to be ready for that. I need to go in and do my job.

"There were a couple of games, but the one I can point to is Game 6. The game was open and I don't think he needed to [leave] me in the ninth. The important game was going to be Game 7 because we had that game almost won. The next day I came in tired."

The next day, with a night to sleep on it, Maddon admitted he erred in not getting a reliever warm on a standby basis even before Rizzo hit the home run. It would have saved Chapman from going back to the mound for the ninth, warming up for a third time on the game mound, and throwing five additional pitches. A few hours before Game 7, sitting in his office, Maddon said, "The mistake I made was not having somebody warming up for the top of the ninth, in case we did score the two points and just get him out. So he was forced to throw a couple of extra pitches to get Stroppy ready.

"But otherwise, I saw no other way. I saw no other way with Lindor and Napoli coming up—just based on who I wanted on those guys. To me there was no other way to do that."

In two games over three days, Chapman had thrown 62 pitches, faced 15 batters and had pitched, sat down for a half inning, and returned for the next inning four times—a rarity for him to do even once in the regular season. Maddon considered the status and strength of Chapman for Game 7, the most anticipated game in baseball history. Surrounded by his totems—the dark chocolate, the pictures of Earl Weaver, Dick Howser, and Chuck Tanner, the lineup card with its personal necrology and marginalia, the hat that belonged to his deceased father—Maddon hoped for the best.

"I believe he's going to be fine tonight," Maddon said. "I do."

CHAPTER 18

SEVEN

J ust before Dexter Fowler left the dugout to take the first at-bat of Game 7, he made sure to stop by Joe Maddon for their usual pregame ritual.

"You go, we go!" Maddon cackled, and then the two of them intertwined the fingers of their right hands, and quickly pulled them back to mimic an explosion. Both of them laughed. Maddon estimated they had done it "90 percent of the time" at the start of games in 2016.

For whatever reason, perhaps even the secret greeting if you wanted to believe the power of such rituals, Fowler in the 2016 regular season was one of the best hitters leading off games in recorded history. In first plate appearances of a game for Chicago, whether at home or on the road, Fowler batted .390, the fourth-best batting average in such spots going back at least 50 years. He also reached base 48.3 percent of the time, also the fourth-best leadoff rate, and posted an on-base-plus-slugging mark of 1.203, bettered only by Brady Anderson in 1996 and Hanley Ramírez in 2007. The man was instant offense.

"Without Dexter it never happens," Maddon said about the Cubs' title.

More than fraternal good-luck hand gestures, good old-fashioned preparation combined with cutting-edge technology explained Fowler's fast starts. Few Cubs players consistently invested more pregame work with the NeuroScouting training software than Fowler. Some players dabbled once in a while with it on laptops and others occasionally tried out the Cubs' latest toy, an 80-inch monitor near the indoor batting cage at Wrigley Field, which allowed a hitter to stand with a bat in his hand and track the speed and spin of the pitches of the opposing pitcher that night. But Fowler often preferred using the NeuroScouting technology on his tablet before games. Before facing Indians starter Corey Kluber, for instance, Fowler could watch the spin, speed, and path of actual two-seam fastballs thrown by Kluber that were captured by PITCHf/x. Over and over, as if cramming years of at-bats into one study session, he "learned" how to hit exact copies of the pitch by timing the tap on the space bar.

"You see the exact pitch just as it would come at you," coach Mike Borzello said. "With a two-seamer, you'll know exactly how fast it goes, what the spin looks like, how much it runs. Does it have some tilt? Is it flat? After a while a hitter can make the slightest adjustment to his swing path based on all that knowledge. Dexter really, really liked to use that stuff. He was on it all the time."

With his big smile and perpetual upbeat nature, Fowler was yet another high-character player acquired by Epstein. Fowler's father, John, a business owner, and his mother, Trudy, an elementary school teacher, stressed the importance of education when Dexter was growing up in Georgia. Recruited by Dartmouth and Harvard before committing to Miami, Fowler instead signed out of high school when the Colorado Rockies offered him $925,000 as a 14th-round pick in 2003. The Rockies traded Fowler to Houston before the 2014 season, after which Epstein traded pitcher Dan Straily and infielder Luis Valbuena to bring Fowler to Chicago. Fowler's "return" to the Cubs in 2016—announced via Epstein's "Godfather" stunt in the middle of practice—made the team whole and happy.

Fowler spread his good cheer off the field as well. One day before a game in late August, and remembering how his mom would put his back-to-school supplies and clothes on layaway, Fowler walked into a Kmart store on the North Side of Chicago and announced he was picking up the store's entire layaway bill. The tab for 43 families amounted to more than $5,000.

Properly prepared for Game 7, including his ritual with Maddon, Fowler brought his good vibes to the plate to lead off the most anticipated game in baseball history. At 8:02 p.m. on November 2, 2016, Kluber wound and delivered a perfect two-seamer that ran down and away from an observant Fowler. It nipped the bottom and outside edge of the strike zone. Home plate umpire Sam Holbrook called it a strike. It was because Kluber could replicate so many of these exquisitely placed pitches, and with so much movement, and do so without the expression on his face changing even the slightest bit, that he earned the "Klubot" nickname.

Klubot entered the game with the sixth-lowest postseason ERA of all time, 0.89, just behind Mariano Rivera, Harry Brecheen, Wade Davis, Jeremy Affeldt, and Babe Ruth. The whole lot of his postseason work, covering $30\frac{1}{3}$ innings, had come in 2016. This was his sixth start, tying a postseason record, including his third in nine days. His extraordinary workload was straight out of a bygone era, before specialized bullpens, pitch counts, and night World Series games. Klubot was trying to become the first pitcher to win five starts in one postseason, and the first since Mickey Lolich of the Detroit Tigers in 1968 to win three starts in a single World Series.

Maddon and the Cubs were on the lookout early for a sign that the machinery of Klubot wasn't humming with quite the same efficiency—a crossed wire, a half a quart low on oil, a blinking warning light, or, better yet, a misplaced pitch. It didn't take long. With the count 2-and-1 to Fowler, after Kluber missed with two fastballs, there it was: a two-seamer, over the fat of the plate, with none of the usual arm-side run on the famed Klubot sinker. Fowler, or "Hugo" as he sometimes was known (the shortened form of "you go, we go"), crushed it over the wall in centerfield. It was the first leadoff home run in World Series Game 7 history. It was as if he had seen the pitch many times before.

The lack of action on that pitch was the blinking light the Cubs wanted to see. It told them that on this night Klubot was simply Kluber—pushed to the fatigue point Arrieta reached the previous year.

"What I thought from the home run was he's not as good as the last time we saw him," Maddon said. "I thought that was validated right there. The fact that Dexter could do that as the first hitter of the game told me that Kluber was not the same, that his stuff could not be as sharp as the last time. So that's kind of an uplifting thought, but I'm not convinced of everything. The leadoff home run sometimes can be your only run of the game. I've seen that way too many times.

"But under those circumstances, yes, number one, scoring first and, number two, if he's going to do that to Kluber in his first at-bat, then Kluber's stuff might not be as good. That had to be the residue at that time of year. That's a lot of work. But listen, he's so good. But once he hit that home run I thought we're in a little better shape."

KYLE HENDRICKS TOOK the ball for the Cubs, with the chance to complete a personal championship hat trick. He had thrown $7\frac{1}{3}$ shutout innings to win the 2009 Ivy League championship and $7\frac{1}{3}$ shutout innings to win the 2016 National League championship. Before the game, Hendricks huddled with Borzello, pitching coach Chris Bosio, and catcher Willson Contreras to take advantage of Chicago's formidable run-prevention infrastructure.

Unlike Arrieta, the Cubs' Game 6 starter, Hendricks liked to use a malleable selection of pitches. The right-hander relies primarily on a darting sinker at the edges and bottom of the strike zone and, most unusually, *two* versions of a changeup: the traditional right-handed changeup that fades to his arm side, and a unique "cut" changeup that slides in the opposite direction, to his glove side. He complements his base pitches with two selections that rely on the element of surprise: an elevated, 90-mile-an-hour, four-seam fastball and a modest curveball, thrown rarely enough to almost always get a called strike.

In a sport in love with power, Hendricks owned little of it. The hardest pitch he threw all year was 91.5 miles per hour. The genius of Hendricks, however, came from two distinctive traits—one physical and one mental.

The physical anomaly is a slight bend in his wrist when he brings the ball up to the loaded position in his delivery. The wrist turns back slightly toward his head and remains "tucked" as he begins to bring the ball down and back. The unhinging of this loose, tucked wrist helps give life and movement to his pitches. On the mound, because of this wrist action, he looks like a man throwing a paper airplane, and often can make the baseball dip and dive just like one.

The mental edge Hendricks owns is his love and understanding of the cat-and-mouse game with hitters. He stays out of patterns with his four pitches, a particularly valuable trait with the Indians seeing him for a second time in five days. Borzello enjoyed working with Hendricks. It reminded him of his days with the Yankees when he would spend hours working with Stanford grad Mike Mussina. They didn't have nearly as much information then, but they would scour video for hours and talk about the best way to attack hitters. Hendricks, like Mussina, thirsted for information about how to keep hitters off balance.

"The more hitters get a look at pitchers, the tougher it is for the pitcher," Borzello said. "A lot of the stuff we put in the plan for Game 7 had to be put together in the right way based on what we did the last time. All the stuff is the same, as far as the information and his pitches, but now it had to be scrambled. You're kind of moving pieces around as far as when you throw pitches.

"So going into Game 7, me and Willson and Kyle met like we always do, going over everything with each other. We talked to each other, go over video . . . the key is you don't want guys sitting on pitches. You don't want to be too predictable. It's tricky.

"I felt pretty good about it because I felt really comfortable in Kyle. The thing about Kyle is he's not going to go off the page. We're going to win with the plan or go down with the plan. Kyle was not going to beat himself. I felt good about that."

In Contreras, the Cubs also were putting the game plan into the hands of a former minor league third baseman who, out of boredom, converted himself to a catcher, and until June 17, 2016, had never caught a major league game. His inexperience was obvious when he first joined the Cubs. Contreras played the game in a hurry, putting down signs almost as soon as he threw the ball back to the pitcher from the previous pitch.

"When you watch a guy go too fast, he's not thinking his way through the game," Borzello said. "He's just trying to get by. That was the hardest part in the beginning.

"Luckily for me, I'm on the bench. I'm talking to him every half inning. That's my job. That's all I'm doing. I'm going over the next three hitters with the catcher throughout the entire game. 'Okay, we've got this guy, and start him with this . . . this is what you want to do here' . . . just going back and forth, going by the reports but also how we're going to sequence it. 'If it's 0-1 do this, if 1-0 do this' . . . It's all count-specific. He got a really good understanding of my language and personality. It's a lot to handle, but I tell him every day, 'I don't care if you go 0-for-4 and strike out four times. It doesn't matter to me. I care about the catching.'"

Before the season started, Borzello had met with Contreras in Arizona to get to know him. He told him, "One thing I can never have you do is take your at-bats to the field with you. Does that happen with you sometimes?"

"Yes, it does," Contreras replied.

"From now on it can *never* happen. And I'm going to stay on you about it."

Contreras's youthfulness and great skill were evident on almost a daily basis in the NLCS. In Game 4, Contreras struck out in the top of the ninth with the Cubs holding an eight-run lead. Borzello noticed that Contreras seemed distracted and distant behind the plate in the bottom of the ninth. The next day Borzello grabbed him and said, "Remember what I told you in Arizona? I felt that happened yesterday. I can't have that happen."

In Game 5, an 8–4 Cubs win, Contreras left the field after the last out arguing with home plate umpire Alfonso Marquez. It was the continuation of his chirping about calls that had been going on for two innings.

"Contreras was up his ass in Game 5," Maddon said.

Marquez later told Maddon, "If it was the regular season, I would have kicked him out," to which Maddon replied, "Thank you for not doing that."

In Game 6, the clincher, Contreras hit a home run off Clayton Kershaw to put the Cubs ahead, 4–0. Contreras ran up and down the dugout, high-fiving everybody in sight, then quickly remembered his priority. He calmed himself and sat down next to Borzello.

"Okay, let's go over the next three," he said.

Said Borzello, "That was pretty cool. You could see him growing up as we're playing. He's so passionate about the whole game—his part of the game and the team's success. He's really into it. You have to let him play with that passion, but also, mentally, you have to keep him in the right frame of mind. He gets frustrated and overall he's very emotional. But it's like I told him, 'Do not change who you are, because that's why you are the player that you are.'"

Borzello knew he would have to prepare three catchers for the game, a highly unusual World Series possibility. Maddon had told David Ross to be ready to enter the game when Jon Lester came out of the bullpen; he trusted nobody else to work with Lester. And Borzello made it a point to tell Montero to keep himself mentally sharp—that he should expect to play if, for instance, Maddon pinch-hit or pinch-ran for Ross.

"Most teams don't even carry a third catcher," Borzello said. "If they do, usually the third catcher doesn't even think he's going to play. You're there just in case of some extreme emergency. But the way we were going to use these line changes, with Rossy coming in with Jon, I knew there was a good chance Montero would get in the game."

"Don't check out on me," Borzello told Montero. "I'm telling you, you're going in this game at some point."

"I'll be ready," said Montero, a proud veteran who was unhappy about his diminished role as Contreras earned more time.

The idea of using three catchers was almost absurd, based on how rarely it had happened in the history of the World Series. Only twice did a team use three catchers in a game, both times in losses: the Phillies did it in Game 2 of the 1950 World Series, and the Dodgers did so in Game 3 of the 1978 World Series.

Before this World Series began, the Cubs' front office held a meeting with the coaching staff to formulate the 25-man roster. There was some talk in the room about adding an extra pitcher—the name of right-hander Trevor Cahill was discussed—and some talk about adding a bench player with speed. Any alteration would likely have cost Montero his roster spot. The consensus was to keep the three catchers: a rookie, a veteran in midcareer, and a veteran playing his final season.

"It doesn't seem like that big of a decision as you're sitting there," Borzello said. "Turns out to be one of the biggest decisions of the series. The decision to carry three catchers was as important as any decision we made."

The catching conga line would start with the rookie, Contreras. That alone, at least on paper, was a huge risk. It would be just his 50th major league start behind the plate. This game marked only the third time a team trusted a catcher to start one of the 38 decisive Game 7s of the World Series in the same year he made his major league debut. The other teams to be so bold were the 1946 Cardinals, with 20-year-old Joe Garagiola, and the 1912 Red Sox, with 26-year-old Hick Cady.

"The hardest part over the last few months was getting Willson to a point where we felt not only me, Joe, and the coaching staff, but also the pitching staff was comfortable having a rookie catcher behind the plate in such meaningful games," Borzello said. "Leading up to the postseason, it was really getting Willson to understand the scouting reports, understanding the words on the page and what picture it paints, and having the recall in real time. He did an amazing job and was really diligent.

"By Game 7 we really trusted Willson with the information. That being said, you have a guy on the mound who doesn't forget one thing. Kyle Hendricks is so prepared, it was going to be exactly the same as it's been all year. The information doesn't grow because of the size of the game. With Kyle, believe it or not, it's in depth whether it's the middle of the season or Game 7."

CONTRERAS WARMED UP Hendricks in the bullpen. Bosio and Borzello watched. Hendricks gives nothing away in terms of body language or emotion. Maddon, in fact, had to learn that when Hendricks drops his chin, as he often does, it is not a sign of a loss of confidence. It is simply the way Hendricks carries himself on the field—that is, as calmly as if he were exploring the stacks of the Feldberg Business and Engineering Library back at Dartmouth. But on this night, Hendricks's pitches in the bullpen were not as crisp as usual. Borzello harbored a concern, which he kept to himself.

"He was a little off," Borzello said. "Generally, he's the same all the time. His command is always there and his stuff is there each start. For this start, he was a little erratic warming up, a little jumpy. I was concerned a little bit. You're afraid of giving up a run early in a game like this. You're facing Corey Kluber, so you know you can't give up many and win this game. I thought the first inning or two he wasn't right, then I thought he got comfortable. But one thing about Kyle: his demeanor never changed."

Hendricks, spotted the one run on Fowler's home run, worked around an error by Baez in the first inning and two singles in the second inning. In the middle of the second inning, as planned, Lester and Arrieta walked from the dugout to the bullpen, accompanied by Ross. Maddon was bound to get Lester in the game, but Arrieta, who threw 102 pitches the night before, wasn't even listed on his lineup card among his available relievers.

More trouble percolated in the third against Hendricks when Coco Crisp led off with a double. Indians manager Terry Francona, however, played the situation more conservatively than he had all year. Francona had never asked one of his position players to bunt before the seventh inning with a runner on second while trailing. But here, in the third, he handed Chicago an out when Perez bunted Crisp to third base. Maddon brought the infield in, but it did not matter as Carlos Santana singled to rightfield, tying the game at one. Francona played for one run early in the game, and, as it turned out, that was all he would get.

Baez extended the Cleveland rally with another error, this time when he dropped a toss from Addison Russell at second base while rushing to complete a double play.

Now Maddon was getting uneasy about Hendricks. He sent Bosio to the mound to kill some time as Carl Edwards Jr. and Mike Montgomery scrambled to get ready in the bullpen. The Indians had runners at first and second, one out, and their best hitter, Francisco Lindor, at the plate. The bullpen was busy and the crowd was roaring at full throttle, especially when Hendricks missed with each of his first three pitches to Lindor. (In truth, Cubs fans accounted for a good chunk of the 38,104 people in the ballpark, as some Cleveland fans opted to stay home and cover college tuition bills with prices they could glean from reselling tickets. Game 7 was the most expensive baseball game in history. Tickets sold for an average price of about $4,000, with a seat behind the Cubs dugout costing $19,500.)

Each missed pitch moved Maddon closer to getting Hendricks out of the game, though the situation, with two baserunners and the haste in which it occurred, was too "dirty" for Lester.

"I had Montgomery up, to get out of the inning," Maddon said. "I think Edwards got up, too, to try to get out of the inning before we turned it over to Jon. That would have been too quick to get Jon ready.

"It just looked like Kyle was a little bit off. I didn't see the movement you normally see from the side. I was concerned, because if it's going to get bad on him real early then it could get real bad and it's hard to recover from a big number. So I was . . . I didn't know what to think. In June it's a different story. But it's the last game of the year. You just can't take any chances that he's going to settle down or not."

The count was 3-and-0 to Lindor. The young Cleveland shortstop had seen 48 pitches in his fledgling big league career on 3-and-0 counts. He didn't swing at any of the first 47. Then, on the last weekend of the season, after Cleveland already had clinched the American League Central, in a meaningless game in Kansas City against a pitcher named Brian Flynn, Lindor decided, for the heck of it, to swing at a 3-and-0 pitch. He slammed a three-run homer. Of such insouciance ideas are born.

Now here he was in the seventh game of the World Series with a 3-and-0 count against a pitcher barely holding on to his place in the game. Hendricks threw a sinker, almost to the exact spot down and in where he missed for ball three. Lindor, for the second time in his big league life, decided to swing at a 3-and-0 pitch. He fouled off the borderline pitch. Hendricks came back with the same pitch—the third straight sinker, all between 87 and 88 miles per hour and all to nearly the same spot. This time Lindor flied out to leftfield.

The next batter was Mike Napoli, one of five Cleveland starters with a Matrix number highlighted in blue on Maddon's funkadelic lineup card—denoting the matchups that most favored Hendricks. (Those blue Matrix hitters would be as cold as Maddon's math predicted, going 1-for-9 against Hendricks in the game.) With the count

0-and-2, Hendricks threw one of his cut changeups, but it cut too far away from Napoli for the hitter to be tempted to swing.

Hendricks came back with his other changeup, the traditional fade changeup. It was one of the worst pitches he would throw all night. The pitch stayed in the strike zone, above the knees and on the inner half of the plate, running right into Napoli's barrel. Napoli hammered it. By the time he could start running, however, it was cradled in the glove of third baseman Kris Bryant, who barely had to move to catch the line drive for the third out.

"That's another thing," Maddon said regarding his worry over Hendricks. "He had pitched well at Napoli, and then all of a sudden when Napoli turns it loose like that I was a little concerned."

The third inning so spooked Maddon that even after Hendricks escaped it he ordered Lester to start throwing. Lester would throw in the bullpen for the next two innings, throwing a virtual game out there.

"He threw a ton," Ross said. "I don't know what that was all about." Ross caught Lester in the bullpen in the fourth inning, then handed the job to bullpen catcher Chad Noble as he left for the dugout, preparing to enter the game at any time.

VIRTUAL SMOKE WAFTED from the main circuitry of Klubot in the fourth inning, such was the obvious toll of the extreme workload. Unable to put away hitters or command his pitches, he labored through 24 pitches, of which he managed to get the Cubs to swing and miss at just one. The resultant damage was another two runs.

Kluber failed to finish off Bryant, leading off the inning, on four two-strike pitches, the last of which Bryant laced for a single. He then hit Rizzo with an 0-and-2 pitch. Bryant advanced to third on a force-out by Zobrist, and scored, daringly so, on a shallow fly ball by Russell. Kluber gained another two-strike count, this one to Contreras, and hung a curveball, which the thankful catcher roped for an RBI double. The Cubs led, 3–1.

It was downright shocking to see Kluber powerless to put away hitters. During the season he held batters to a .121 batting average with two strikes. Among all qualified pitchers, only Arrieta was tougher to hit with two strikes than Kluber.

Francona sent Kluber back out for the fifth inning, virtual pools of leaked oil collecting on the mound. The manager did so with half a heart. Über reliever Andrew Miller already was throwing in the Cleveland bullpen.

As it turned out, Francona allowed Kluber to throw just one more pitch. It was one pitch too many. It was a slider to Baez, the hitter who had been unable to locate breaking balls all series if you gave him a GPS device. This one, though, invited violence. It was a hanger, a ball that spun up in the zone and had no bite. For days on end Maddon had been coaching Baez before games about letting the ball travel deeper on its path to the plate—to conquer his anxiety at the plate by buying himself more time in the hitting process, which meant hitting the ball the other way. Baez finally made good on all his manager's tutorials. He cranked it over the rightfield wall, an opposite-field home run.

Kluber left on the wrong side of a 4–1 game. He had faced 18 batters and struck out none of them. It was the first time in 145 career games he failed to strike out a batter.

As Miller warmed up, Rizzo walked up from behind to Ross, who was standing on the top step of the dugout by the rail. He threw his arm around Ross's shoulder and, smiling, made a confession.

"I can't control myself right now," Rizzo said. "I'm trying my best."

"It's understandable," Ross said.

"I'm an emotional wreck."

"I hear you. It's only gonna get worse. Just continue to breathe. That's all you can do, buddy. That's all you can do. It's only going to get worse."

Rizzo, the clubhouse leader who quoted movies the way English literature scholars quote Shakespeare, pulled from the Ron Burgundy archive.

"I'm a glass case of emotions right now!"

"Yeah. Wait 'til the ninth with this three-run lead."

Recalling the conversation, Rizzo said, "At first, yeah, I meant it. I'm a wreck every pitch. When I said the 'glass case of emotions,' I was just lightening the moment. It's just that so much goes into every pitch. You try not to think about the outside noise as far as what's on the line. But I don't care who you are, there's always some self-doubt and some nervous energy. It's so hard to block it all out when it's the biggest game possible. It was like that every night."

If you wanted to understand the brotherhood of the Cubs, the relationship between Rizzo and Ross was a good place to start. They first met in October 2008, when Ross was playing for the Boston Red Sox in the American League Championship Series against Tampa Bay. Rizzo was recovering from the chemotherapy to treat his cancer. The two of them shared the same agent, Ryan Gleichowski. Rizzo wanted to attend Games 6 and 7 in St. Petersburg.

"My agent said, 'I may need you to leave tickets for one of my minor league guys,'" Ross said. "So I met him there. It was the first time we met. My agent always raved about him, what a great guy he was."

Six years later, Ross was guesting as a postseason studio analyst for ESPN in Bristol, Connecticut, when Rizzo swung by to make a few appearances. They went to lunch and hit it off. A few weeks later, Rizzo called Ross, who lives near Tallahassee, Florida, to ask for a field pass for the Notre Dame–Florida State football game. Rizzo knew that Ross's brother-in-law was the chief of police there.

"Sure, but with one condition," Ross told him. "I have to be there with you."

Said Ross, "We ended up talking shop the whole game. The wife and kids were in the stands. What stood out in our conversation was he's really mature in a lot of ways. He can relate to the old and the new. He's young, but he can relate to everybody.

"I was a free agent at the time. We talked a little bit like, 'Man, it would be awesome to play together.'"

Rizzo turned to Ross and told him, "We need somebody like you."

Ross signed with the Cubs and they became fast friends. Rizzo loved learning about the strategies and intricacies of baseball from Ross, whose experience as a catcher helped Rizzo understand how pitchers wanted to attack him. Ross considered Rizzo to be the most important player on the team, not only because he played every day and was a run producer, but also because he connected with all players, regardless of their age or background. Knowing Rizzo's importance, Ross made it his responsibility to ride Rizzo, making sure he kept grinding at his job, because if Rizzo eased off his work ethic it would send clues to the rest of the team to do the same.

"I ride him hard," Ross said. "Honestly, I don't know why he likes me. I'm on his ass all the time."

The two became so close that Rizzo gave Ross a Father's Day card during 2016. Rizzo signed it, "Thank you for everything you have done for me! Love, your son, Anthony."

Ross and Rizzo were also the two biggest influencers in the clubhouse, a leadership status never more apparent than when Chicago faced elimination in the World Series. It was Ross who began to turn the tide in the immediate wake of the Game 4 loss, when he heard someone throw their glove into the back of a locker and the room filled with dejection and negativity.

Rizzo picked up on Ross's lead in setting the right tone the next day. An hour before Game 5, he broke out his pregame inspirational and comedic presentation, quoting motivational lines from movies with no clothes on. The Cubs won, so Rizzo did it before Game 6, too. They won again, so he did it before Game 7 as well.

After batting practice was over, and only an hour before the seventh game of the World Series, Rizzo stripped off all his clothes, cranked the theme from *Rocky* on the clubhouse stereo one more time, jumped on top of a coffee table, and began quoting lines from the movie and throwing his best shadow-boxing punches. Pitcher Hector Rondon, joining in on the hijinks, picked up an aerosol can of shoe cleaner and sprayed it in the direction of Rizzo's groin.

Startled and angered, Rizzo stopped and yelled, "What the heck, man!"

He cut the music and stormed off toward the bathroom, where he went into the showers to clean off the spray.

"I'm thinking, *Dang, what's he doing?*" Ross said. "*We can't have this negative vibe right before the game.* I go by there. I can tell he's a little irritated. He *is* irritated."

Ten minutes went by. Rizzo finally emerged from the shower. He walked back silently to his locker with a towel around this waist. The room was quiet and uneasy.

Ross walked up to Rizzo and broke the silence.

"Hey! It's not how many times you get knocked down . . . *it's how many times you get up!*"

Rizzo chuckled.

"You know what?" he said. "You're right!"

Said Ross, "He rips the towel off, runs up, turns the music on again, and he jumps back on the coffee table and starts doing the *Rocky* motions again and shadow-boxes."

AFTER RIZZO AND Ross shared their Ron Burgundy moment in the dugout, it was time for the Cubs to try something they hadn't accomplished all series: dent the Cleveland bullpen. Andrew Miller, Bryan Shaw, and Cody Allen combined over six games to go 1–0 with a 0.69 ERA. They had struck out 43 percent of the batters they faced while allowing one run in 13 World Series innings. They were dominant.

Fowler, who had homered off Miller in Game 4, the lefty's last outing, greeted Miller in the fifth inning with a single. Miller restored order by getting Schwarber to hit into a double play.

Bryant, as he did against Kluber in the fourth, pieced together another gallant at-bat. With the count 2-and-2, Miller threw Bryant five consecutive sliders, his signature pitch and his go-to option with two strikes. Batters hit just .133 off Miller's two-strike slider during the regular season. But Bryant refused to yield against all five of them. He took one for a ball, fouled off the next three, and then took the last one, which barely missed the outside corner, for ball four.

Rizzo was next, and with the count 1-and-2, Rizzo knew what was coming next from Miller: the slider. He was 0-for-3 against Miller in the series, including two strikeouts.

"I was looking to not look like an idiot off Miller," Rizzo said. "He had my number the whole series. Really, I was just trying to see a ball that [looked like it] would hit me, because I'm so on top of the plate off him—off lefties."

Rizzo's entire postseason changed in the fifth inning of NLCS Game 4, when he switched from his Marucci model bat to one that belonged to teammate Matt Szczur. To that point, Rizzo was 2-for-26 in the postseason, and his first two at-bats in that game were typical of his struggles: rookie pitcher Julio Urias blew fastballs by him for strikeouts, one at 95 miles per hour and one at 94. Upon borrowing Szczur's bat, Rizzo immediately hit a home run, and then a two-run single, and then another single.

The press ate up the story. The bat, as the story went, was identical to Rizzo's own model in size and weight but was full of amazing karma. Chalk it up to another godwink in this magical year. Szczur, who wasn't even on any of the playoff rosters, became a minor national star simply by lending his equipment.

The story sounded great, but there was one catch to it: it was built on a white lie.

I pulled Rizzo aside on the eve of the World Series, just after he had finished his media day obligations at Progressive Field, in which yet again Rizzo led people to believe that his bat and Szczur's bat were similar, but for the incredible luck Szczur's bat brought him. Rizzo made a confession to me, but only after he made me promise it was off the record while the World Series was being played. I agreed. Szczur's bat was significantly smaller than his own: one inch shorter and two ounces lighter. Rizzo switched bats not for luck, but as a concession to losing strength and bat speed due to the length of the season.

"It allowed me to free up my hands and not have to use my body," he said. "Because at the end of the year I was so beat, I guess. In the beginning of the playoffs I was missing fastballs. I kept asking myself, 'Why am I missing these fastballs?' My swing is good. It could be psychological, but I think not. But I think taking the extra inch off and lightening my bat, I started to get to those pitches again."

Rizzo played along with the crazy "good-luck bat" story because he didn't want opponents to know that he was using a shorter, lighter bat. He knew that because of the way pitchers beat him early in the playoffs that the scouting report on him said his bat was slow and that he could be beaten with fastballs. Meanwhile, with Szczur's smaller and lighter bat, he actually was much quicker to the ball. It was a secret he enjoyed for the final 10 postseason games, during which he hit .432 with Szczur's bat.

Cornered in a 1-and-2 count against Miller, and seeing Miller for a fourth time in 10 days, Rizzo had familiarized himself with the sweeping, aggressive plane of Miller's slider. If the pitch started over the plate, he learned, it was unhittable because it continued sweeping off the outside corner. The only slider that was hittable, especially because Rizzo stood on top of the plate, was the one that started at his body. That one would sweep into the strike zone.

Swing at the ball that looks like it's going to hit me, he told himself.

As Miller unfolded his long frame, Bryant took off running from first base. The pitch was a slider. It was headed right at Rizzo. He started his swing as the ball swept to the outside half of the plate.

"It was a pretty good pitch," Rizzo said. "Maybe he left it up a little bit. I was able to get my arms extended off of him."

Because he was so committed to the pitch, Rizzo pulled it into rightfield for a single. Bryant never stopped running. He scored easily. At 6-foot-5, Bryant pulled off one of the more stunning baserunning feats in World Series history. He became only the third player in World Series history to score from first on a single. The other two were far smaller: 5-foot-11 Frankie Frisch in 1924 and 5-foot-7 Joe Morgan in 1972.

The Cubs led, 5–1. At one point the sound system at Progressive Field played "Seven Nation Army" by the White Stripes. Hoyer and Epstein looked at each other and smiled. They took it as a sign of good fortune—in such heavy rotation, it had been their unofficial theme song of the 2004 spring training at Phi Signa Playa in Cape Coral.

The positive signs were everywhere for the Cubs. They had dented Kluber and Miller as never before in the series. Impressively, they had sent 23 batters to the plate against the two strikeout artists and nobody struck out. Through five innings, Kluber and Miller threw 19 pitches with two strikes and failed 19 times to get the third strike. Schwarber, Bryant, Contreras, Fowler, and Rizzo combined to reach base seven times on two-strike counts.

They were B hacking 'em to death. Maddon watched this unfold like a proud father. He also watched Kyle Hendricks very closely.

HENDRICKS, LIKE A boxer who survived a standing eight count, suddenly found his equilibrium. After the second error by Baez in the third inning, when the Chicago bullpen became a hubbub of haste and hassle, Hendricks retired seven batters in a row. After the 3-and-0 count to Lindor, Hendricks took care of those next seven outs by throwing an amazing 83 percent strikes (19 of his 23 pitches). Paper airplanes never flew with such precision.

First Ross was in the bullpen to catch his buddy Lester there, but as the fifth inning began, Ross relocated to the dugout—with his shin guards on, ready at a moment's notice for the "line change."

"How's he look?" Maddon asked Ross about Lester.

"He's really sharp," Ross replied with obvious enthusiasm. "*Really* sharp."

Maddon looked at his lineup card. Kipnis owned the highest

Matrix number against Hendricks: .270 in a white box. He was due up fourth in the inning. Behind him was Lindor, a switch-hitter Maddon feared more from the left side.

"My only concern was Kipnis and Lindor—Lindor hitting left-handed," Maddon said. "That was my concern. And the fact that Jon already had been warming up. And I talked to Rossy.

"So okay, my concern is shelf life. How much do you warm him up and not use him? Warm him up and sit him back down? He's not used to that. Before the game I was about Kyle to Jon to Aroldis. That was it. I just wanted those three guys."

So Maddon turned back to Ross.

"If the inning gets to Kipnis, Jon is coming in," he told him, "and you're coming in with him."

Hendricks pushed his streak of consecutive outs to seven by getting Crisp and Perez. He worked the next batter, Carlos Santana, to a 2-and-2 count when he threw a beautiful changeup, one that passed over the middle of the plate and above the knees of Santana. It was, to most observers, strike three, a pitch to end the inning and send Hendricks and Chicago into the fifth inning with a 5–1 lead. One observer, the most important one of all, disagreed.

Before the series began, Major League Baseball officials told Maddon that the assignment of the umpires was driven by data accumulated over the course of the season. Sam Holbrook, they told him, rated at the top when it came to balls and strikes. That's how, they told him, Holbrook was assigned home plate for Game 7 of the World Series.

Holbrook made his major league debut in 1996 at the age of 30. Three years later he took part in an ill-fated strategy during a labor dispute in which 22 umpires had their resignations accepted. For three years Holbrook found work as a welder, meter reader, and stockbroker. He was rehired in 2002. Holbrook worked home plate in Game 2 of the 2010 World Series, a 9–0 win for the San Francisco Giants and pitcher Matt Cain. That same year, his wife, Laura "Susie" Glass, was diagnosed with cancer. She lost her fight just before the

2014 season. Holbrook spent the entire year on the bereavement list. He returned in 2015, and in 2016 rose to the top of charts on ball-and-strike calls.

Hendricks had pitched twice before with Holbrook behind the plate, in 2015 and 2016, and both turned out poorly for him: 0–2 with a 6.35 ERA.

Contreras held the 2-and-2 changeup to Santana in his mitt over the plate, but Holbrook wasn't buying it. "Ball," came the call.

Instead of walking back to the dugout, Hendricks would have to throw another pitch. He missed high. Ball four. Maddon walked out of the dugout and signaled for Lester. Why?

"Because of Kipnis," Maddon said. "If it wasn't Kipnis, if it was another righty or a switch-hitter I thought he had a better chance with, I probably would have left him out there. But Kipnis, he's just really good. It could be 5–3 and then it's an entirely different thought.

"So Jon was ready, they told me he was really good, and Lindor I like hitting right-handed more a lot. The guy that bothered me was Napoli. But he already had that good at-bat against Kyle. So once he walked [Santana] with two outs, and Jon was ready and they said he was good, my thought was I'd much prefer him on Kipnis rather than Kyle. And then here comes Lindor and I have to go to Jon anyway if it got through Kipnis."

But Maddon had insisted before the game that he would not bring Lester into a "dirty" inning, not with his yips throwing to the bases, not with his lack of experience coming out of the bullpen. It was the very last thing Maddon and Epstein talked about before the game and it could not have been any clearer: Lester would not enter the game in the middle of an inning.

The same question again: Why?

"So I thought, *Even though there's a runner on first base*—I had talked about the dirty inning—*it was 5–1, Santana was on first, and he wasn't going anywhere*," Maddon said. "I wasn't worried about any of that. I told Jon, 'Don't worry about it. He's not going anywhere.' So it was Kipnis.

"I didn't think it was a dirty inning: two outs with a four-run lead, Santana on first. I didn't think it was dirty. That's where I was at with that. Honestly, I didn't think [it was dirty]. I told Jon, 'Man, there's nobody on. You're just getting this guy out. Don't worry about that guy at all because he's not going anywhere.' But I didn't have any concern over that."

What would Maddon have done if Holbrook had called the third strike on Santana? Who would have started the sixth inning?

"I probably would have sent Kyle back out," Maddon said. "But if Kipnis had gotten on, I probably would have gone right to Jon on Lindor."

Instead, with Santana on first base and the fifth inning still breathing, Maddon not only brought in Lester but also replaced Contreras with Ross, Lester's personal catcher.

"Think about it," Borzello said. "Willson goes in knowing he's catching Kyle Hendricks, and that's it. Of the three catchers, most people would say he's far and away the best player. And we're pulling him out and bringing in David Ross to catch Jon Lester, and that means you may have Miguel Montero to finish it.

"The domino effect of taking Kyle Hendricks out of the game was huge. That was the plan going in. It's just that I don't think that's ever happened where you would knowingly have a line change with your pitcher and catcher. And now Chapman is probably going to have to be caught by Ross, not Contreras, when it's time for him to come in the game."

The spotlight immediately found Ross. Kipnis hit a cutter from Lester off the end of his bat, sending the baseball skittering, as if wounded, into the grass in front of home plate. Ross picked it up, struggled to find a proper grip as he wheeled, and threw it far askance of where Rizzo expected it at first base. The throwing error put Santana on third and Kipnis on second.

Just two pitches later, Lester bounced a curveball while pitching to Lindor. After hitting the dirt, the ball bounced off the convex grill of Ross's goalie-style catcher's mask and ricocheted toward the Cubs' dugout on the first base side. Ross tried to plant his left foot to pivot to his right, but his foot gave way. He stumbled on his 39-year-old legs. By the time he recovered, fetched the ball, and threw to Lester, both Santana and Kipnis scored. It was the first two-run wild pitch in the World Series in 105 years. The Indians had just turned a comfortable 5–1 Chicago lead into a 5–3 game without managing to hit the ball more than 30 feet.

"First I get a terrible grip and I throw it in the crapper," Ross said. "I let the game speed up on me. I'm the one guy that should be calm, and I throw it away. Then the ball hits my mask and I trip over my own feet. I feel like a fool out there.

"I just get in the game and five pitches later two runs are in. I pride myself on keeping runs off the board, and look what happened."

Maddon had no second thoughts about injecting Lester into the dirty inning.

"Kipnis looks bad against Jon," Maddon said. "He swings and misses. Then he hits the ball off the end. And the ball just rolls far enough that David can't throw him out.

"Then it hits him in the mask.

"Those are the things that are so unpredictable. Of course, it's no fun to watch that, but Jon did his job. He gets Kipnis to hit a dribbler and he strikes out Lindor. You get a dribbler guy on first and then you get a wild pitch and two runs score. That's pretty unpredictable right there. . . . Again, I have no concerns about what we did. It worked out exactly like I thought, other than they score two runs on a wild pitch, because Jon gets us to Aroldis."

Hoyer, watching with Epstein from the scouts' seats behind the plate, could not believe the change of events.

"The 2-2 pitch by Hendricks was tremendous," he said. "We were out of the inning with nothing, feeling great about things, but wait . . . Then all of a sudden a walk, and Lester comes in and gives up an infield hit, error, wild pitch . . . Wait a second, we just gave up two runs and nothing happened! That was an unnerving feeling. I felt like the game was in our control, and then we just literally handed them two runs."

When Ross came to the bench, Borzello met him with a worried look. The coach thought Ross, whose concussion history helped drive his retirement decision, may have been concussed by the wild pitch, if only because of the way the baseball staggered him.

"Now I'm thinking, *Uh-oh, we're going to be down to just Montero now with a long way to go,*" Borzello said.

"It's my ankle," Ross told him. "I tried to get up and my ankle gave way."

Ross clearly was agitated. His haste on the dribbler by Kipnis gnawed at him.

"I didn't get a good grip on the ball," he told Borzello. "I should have taken my time. Kipnis has a bad leg and I didn't process it."

"Relax," Borzello said. "It's okay. We're winning. Let's talk about the next three hitters."

They didn't have much time. Ross was due to hit second in the sixth inning. Russell, in another at-bat extended after it reached two strikes, popped out.

Ross had faced Miller once in the past six years: an at-bat in the seventh inning of Game 1 with the bases loaded and two outs. Miller struck him out on a full-count slider in that at-bat.

"I knew Andrew, just from watching," Ross said. "I watched a lot of video on him. I knew how nasty he was. I knew he was more of a stuff guy than a command guy."

Miller started Ross with two nasty sliders, one for a called strike and one that Ross fouled off. The next pitch was a fastball, well wide of the plate.

"I just saw slider, slider, fastball," Ross said. "I saw the fastball real well. In my mind, I had no chance on the slider."

The next pitch figured to be the slider, Miller's go-to two-strike pitch. Miller peered in toward Perez for the sign. Miller shook his head. He didn't want to throw the pitch Perez wanted. An alarm went off in Ross's head. He remembered all the video he watched on Miller. One nugget of information suddenly came to the fore.

"When he shook when he was ahead, I saw on the video, it was a fastball," Ross said. "Maybe not 100 percent of the time, but mostly. I thought, *If he throws me a fastball again I'm going to hit it.*

"When he shook like that I thought, *He's going to his fastball.* Listen, I think like a catcher too much. But I'm thinking, *The catcher must be calling a slider.* That's his money pitch. If he shakes, it's going to be a fastball 90 percent of the time. In my heart and in my gut I felt like it was going to be a fastball. I wouldn't say I completely sold out for fastball, but I was 90 percent sure."

Miller threw a fastball. It split the middle of the plate, low, "where I like it," Ross said. Ready for it, Ross drove it high to centerfield.

"I knew I got it all, but I was choked up on the bat, so I didn't know if I had enough leverage to get it out," he said.

Cleveland centerfielder Rajai Davis turned and ran for it.

"I saw him eyeing it," Ross said, "and I thought, *If he robs this ball, I'm just going to keep running out of the stadium.*"

The ball carried and carried and carried until it dropped on the other side of the wall. Home run. At 39 years old, Ross became the oldest player to hit a homer in the seventh game of a World Series. Ross was wearing a microphone for Fox. As he rounded the bases, the mic picked up . . . nothing. Ross, one of the biggest chatterboxes on the team, was dead quiet sprinting around the bases.

"It felt like relief more than excitement," he said. "I didn't show a whole lot of excitement. My teammates were so much more excited for me. I know how hard he is to catch. I caught him in Boston. To hit him is even tougher. To do that, and to hit a home run in Game 7, I was like, 'Okay, that's one,' because I was more worried about the runs I let in.

"I was just glad I got one back to help the team get closer to the win. I got to third and Jonesie was real serious and I was like, 'Holy crap, I just hit a home run.' And I run home and Dexter is doing the crotch high-five thing they do for me, and J-Hey is super excited. Everybody is going crazy in there, and I'm going, 'Wait a minute. It's only the sixth. We've got a long way to go.' I was so focused on the end result that I really couldn't enjoy what was going on.

"Then I thought, *I've got really good numbers with the lead all year. This is what I'm really good at. We got this World Series. Don't mess it up.*"

The home run was the first allowed by Miller in six years on a 1-and-2 count. It also was another two-strike dagger for Chicago. Kluber and Miller would throw 25 pitches with two strikes until they finally obtained a third one, to Baez for the last out of the sixth.

"The thing that gets lost is people were concerned about Aroldis being tired," Maddon said. "Miller is well rested and we kicked the shit out of Miller. It's about hitters. I was really surprised we did as well against Miller as we did. But David's home run was very large there. It was a very big play."

The home run by Ross pushed the Chicago lead to 6–3, which Lester, who was as sharp as Ross predicted from his bullpen warm-up, protected with ease. Maddon's pitching script remained in play: Hendricks to Lester to Chapman. He began to think that Lester looked so strong that he might pitch all the way through the eighth inning, leaving Chapman for his preferred role: start the ninth inning, clean.

IN THE SEVENTH inning, before Cleveland batted, Maddon left the dugout. He came back in time for the start of the half inning. The same pattern happened in the eighth inning, and again in the ninth inning. Nerves?

"Bathroom," Maddon explained. "I was fine. Honest to God. I planned the game out before it begins. Everything was working. Everything was right on. Outside of the wild pitch everything was right on. So I was good.

"What I do is I go to the bathroom up in my office, so I can run a little bit . . . get away from it, refocus, and come back—almost like offense and defense. So I like to use the bathroom up in the office in Cleveland, so I go up and down the steps a little bit and come on back. It's kind of refreshing."

Baseball is a wonderful game because it is built on simplicity—everyone takes turns at trying to complete a trip around the four bases—but it also invites a complexity of ideas about how best to accomplish or prevent that. For many children it is their initial gateway into sports, and from there fans earn a license to think they can manage a baseball game, sometimes even better than dues-paying baseball lifers like Maddon.

The beauty of baseball is multidimensional, appealing to the eye and the mind. There is beauty, for instance, in its geometry, the space between the bases and the fielders; beauty in the arc of the season, which brings us out of doors to gather, until fall calls us back in; and beauty in its democracy, that each player hits in turn. But one of its greatest beauties is that, more than any other sport, it emboldens an expertise from those who watch it. Everybody can manage. That does not happen as easily in other sports.

In real time, though, in the seventh game of the World Series, with a five-year rebuild on the line, and 108 years of waiting distilled to one game, only one man makes the calls that count. Maddon needed only to look at the spine of his lineup card to find guidance: be present, not perfect, and, to honor Zimmer, be irreverent. His task was to stay in the moment, without regard for everything that hung in the balance with this game.

The first time Maddon saw Wrigley Field as a visiting manager, he fell in love with the daylight pouring through the grandstand and he daydreamed about *Gladiator*. Once he became Cubs manager, he would make a point during every game to look up from the dugout to the most extreme corner seat in the upper deck toward rightfield. He did so to remind himself how lucky he was to work in such an historic venue and for a fan base that loved the Cubs so much that the seat was always filled.

But asked if he took a moment's reflection during Game 7,

Maddon said, "I don't think I did. I'm that guy, but I don't think I did. I was definitely in the moment. I was not all over the place. Please take it the right way: I didn't feel unlike a regular-season game. I ran everything the same way, except maybe the bullpen might be different, pinch-hitting patterns might be different. Jon Lester's not available to come out of the bullpen during the season. So these are the different things you think about.

"You have this weapon you don't normally have, and there's no tomorrow, so your mind-set, your thinking, is obviously different during the regular season. But before the game I told Bosio everything. I told Theo what I was thinking. I told David, 'Be ready.' I said, 'When Jon goes down to warm up, I want you to warm him up,' and then, after they warmed him up, he came back in the dugout the first time, I said, 'How is he?' He said, 'He's really sharp.' That was nice to hear.

"Then my concern with Jonny, not being a relief pitcher, you can't warm him up, sit him down, warm him, sit him down. I know that's what a starter does, but he's not on regular rest. I don't want to leave all of his best pitches in the bullpen. So if you're going to utilize Jon, you have to utilize him. You just can't be yo-yoing Jon Lester in that situation. That was a concern.

"Believe me, man, talking about it now retrospectively, it was a real crazy moment. But in the moment? I was fine."

As THE EIGHTH inning began, Maddon gave word to Bosio to have Chapman begin to warm. Lester kept cruising. He retired Lindor on a groundball and struck out Napoli. The Cubs were four outs away from winning the World Series. One of those outs, the last one Maddon would need out of Lester, appeared to come off the bat of José Ramírez. It was a groundball to the left of Russell, the shortstop. It was a play in the deep catalog of plays made by the rangy Russell. This one, however, remained unmade, the ball ticking teasingly off his glove for an infield hit.

"The big thing there is, Ramírez hits the ball off Addison's glove," Maddon said. "Because I really wanted to see Jonny get through a solid eighth right there. I just wanted to give Aroldis one inning. That was the plan."

Said Ross, "Perfect pitch. Addison makes that play 9 times out of 10. He was shaded in the hole with Jon pitching in."

Hoyer agreed with Ross, saying, "He was shifted over in the hole. If he's playing straight up he makes it easily. It made for a harder play. But, okay, I still felt like the game was in control. It felt stable."

The hit moved Maddon to replace Lester, who had thrown 55 pitches on two days' rest. It was time for Chapman, who now was being asked to pitch in multiple innings for the third time in four days—after doing so only four times in the entire regular season.

At a time like this, the questions about his extended use in Game 6 seemed more pertinent than ever, as did Maddon's blithe appraisal of Chapman before Game 7:

"I believe he's going to be fine tonight. I do."

It quickly became apparent that Chapman was not fine. He threw seven pitches to Brandon Guyer, all of them fastballs. Six of them were below his average velocity of 101.3 miles per hour. Guyer ripped the last one, which was clocked at "just" 99.2 miles per hour. He drove the ball into the right-centerfield gap, sending Ramírez home, and bringing the potential tying run, Rajai Davis, to the plate.

"Guyer worked a good at-bat," Maddon said. "That was the key to that thing. And he hit an elevated fastball, to his credit, to right-center. That was pretty big."

Davis stepped in next. Not much of a power threat, Davis had not hit a home run since August 30. Chapman had faced 158 batters since joining the Cubs and had not allowed a home run. He threw another fastball, one that missed outside. It was clocked at 99.9 miles an hour. Then two more fastballs, both down and in, each one slower than the last: 99.2 and 98.4 miles per hour. Davis fouled off both of them.

Hoyer and Epstein began to grow nervous about what they were seeing from Chapman. Hoyer was alarmed that Chapman had neither the usual zip nor the location on his fastball.

"The thing with Chappy was I always felt when he got that ball up and away to a righty he was pretty much untouchable," Hoyer said. "Those at-bats, if he threw the fastball in the zone early, then once he went up and away I almost felt like it was automatic he got you out."

Hoyer's intuition was exactly correct. In the regular season, Chapman threw 207 up-and-away fastballs to right-handers. Nobody managed a hit off any of those pitches. Against such pitches that ended at-bats, hitters went 0-for-34.

But it was clear this version of Chapman was nothing like that one. Guyer, a right-handed hitter, smashed his ringing double off what used to be an unhittable Chapman pitch, the up-and-away fastball. Now, against Davis, Chapman could not even get the ball there. Worse, with his fastball leaking down and in to right-handed hitters, and especially losing about three miles an hour off the pitch, Chapman was flirting with his most dangerous zone.

Among all pitchers with at least 300 career innings, Chapman is the toughest pitcher to hit all time, yielding just a .155 batting average. But he does have his own kryptonite. He becomes extremely hittable when he throws his fastball down and in to right-handed hitters. They batted .500 against that pitch in the regular season, with 6 hits in 12 at-bats. The two fastballs Davis fouled off tempted fate.

Something else troubled Epstein. He remembered Game 4 of the NLCS, when he noticed the Cleveland scouts scribbling notes as Chapman, in one of his rare games with Ross behind the plate, threw 13 pitches, all of them fastballs. The next time Chapman and Ross worked together, Game 1 of the NLCS, Chapman threw 17 pitches—and all of those pitches were fastballs. This was their third postseason game together, and Chapman so far had thrown 10 pitches—all of them fastballs.

Chapman's next pitch was another fastball, this one well off the plate. At 2-and-2, Chapman threw two more fastballs, and Davis fouled off each one.

The seventh pitch to Davis was yet another fastball, this one matching the least velocity of the inning, 98.4 miles per hour, nearly three full ticks below his average fastball. Worse, it was Chapman's kryptonite pitch: a down-and-in fastball to a right-handed hitter. It was the 44th pitch Chapman threw to Ross in the postseason. All 44 were fastballs, including 14 in this game.

Davis, choking up on the bat, took a short, violent swipe at the baseball. The pitch ran right into his barrel. The ball jumped out of the park so fast—it smashed against the lens of a television camera atop the high wall in leftfield—that there was no time to process what had just happened.

"For an instant I thought, *Okay, we're still up,*" said Bryant.

No. Just like that, the game was tied.

Owner Tom Ricketts, also seated in the stands, but not with Epstein and Hoyer, stood up in disbelief as the ball left the park. An Indians fan, unaware that the man standing near him owned the Cubs, threw his arms around Ricketts in celebration. Ricketts wrested himself from the hug and, shouting in anger and frustration, had to remove himself from the crowd and into a suite to calm himself.

Hoyer, as if hearing the screeching tires that preceded a crash, had anticipated trouble.

"Chappy just couldn't get [his fastball] to that place up and away," Hoyer said. "Nothing was above the zone. Even the ones away were middle, height-wise. The ball he hit was down and in. There were four balls in that sequence in that same area. He had seen four balls in roughly that same spot."

But a home run? By Davis? Off Chapman? Who saw that coming? It ranked, because of its timing and the likelihood of its protagonists, as one of the most stunning home runs in World Series history.

It matched a home run hit by Hal Smith of the Pirates against the Yankees in 1960—also hit four outs from elimination—as the latest home runs in Game 7 history to wipe out a deficit.

"There was absolutely no place in my psyche where I was thinking home run right there," Hoyer said. "I was completely stunned. Chapman hadn't given up a single home run as a Cub. This was a great battle, but I wasn't thinking it was a battle that would be won by a home run. Maybe a single, a double, or a walk. But there was no place in my mind I was thinking about a homer.

"I was in total shock. Off the bat I thought it was a double. I think I was in shock because never was I thinking home run. It wasn't a hitter you expected a homer from.

"We joked after the game, Theo and I, that for a couple of seconds after that ball went out I let myself go to the darkest possible places. Then I convinced myself the game was only tied."

Epstein, too, visited that dark place when Davis's home run went out.

"You blow a three-run lead with four outs to go . . ." Epstein said. "I'm thinking five years of sacrifice and hard work by so many people is about to go by the wayside . . ."

After the ball went out, Maddon turned to his bench coach, Dave Martinez.

"Davey, who do we have coming up?"

Martinez told him the Cubs had their bottom three hitters due to bat: Ross, Heyward, and Baez.

"I started thinking about the next inning," Maddon said. "Who do we have coming up? The other thing was okay, let's get through this inning, going into the next inning, if Chappy was okay I wanted him to go back out there. Had to. He's there for a reason. He's been there for a reason since the beginning of August."

Crisp followed the Davis home run with a single—off another fastball. Chapman would start the next hitter, Yan Gomes, with two more fastballs, running the streak to 48 consecutive fastballs with

Ross behind the plate. Finally, Chapman broke off a slider for a swinging strike and then another, for another swinging strike. He finally ended the inning with a fastball he threw past Gomes.

"I hadn't caught him much," Ross said. "It was kind of a little uncomfortable for me just because I hadn't caught him since [NLCS Game 1]. Willy had caught him most every game. It's one of those things where this guy throws a hundred, so when in doubt I'm just going to throw a fastball.

"I'll tell you Guyer was one of the tougher at-bats in their lineup. He threw a really good at-bat on him. He hit that double in the gap. And obviously Rajai. We threw him a shit-ton of fastballs. I was hesitant to throw him a slider and speed up his bat. If he connects with a slider I'm not going to be able to live with myself.

"With a guy like Chappy, who throws that hard, I'm thinking, *If I give up a homer on a slider to tie this game I'll never be able to forgive myself. And everybody would be asking me why I called a slider when this guy throws 105.* He threw a fastball down and in, and he was choked up so much . . . the wind just went out of our sails. When that thing went over it was a bad feeling."

Ruminating again about the string of 48 consecutive fastballs, Ross explained, "That's kind of where my unfamiliarity and my comfort level was. I wasn't locked in where I wanted to be. I'm not calling a slider. Those guys hit breaking balls good, from the scouting reports—Rajai and Guyer. I could have gone for chase, but . . . you don't know.

"That's the nightmare of being a catcher—the second-guessing. You don't want to get beat with a secondary pitch. Those are the things I grew up with: don't get beat in a big situation with a guy's second- or third-best pitch. So I'm like, 'It's Game 7. The closer's out here. We need one out. Surely someone is going to pop up a fastball or swing and miss at one.' I think he was just out of gas, too."

Maddon had reached the ninth inning using the only three pitchers he wanted to use, Hendricks, Lester, and Chapman—straight off his script. But a cascade of events turned the story into a horror tale.

The trouble began with a missed 2-and-2 call with Hendricks on the mound, which led to a walk, which led to Maddon forcing Lester and Ross into the game in the middle of an inning, which led to two sloppy runs, which led to Chapman, fatigued from his work the night before, making another early appearance, and throwing for a rare time to Ross, which led to a 44th consecutive fastball being slammed over the wall.

Maddon harbored one major concern as his team trudged off the field: Chapman's state of mind.

"He was really distraught when he came off the field," Maddon said. "That was the only concern I had: over how upset he was."

Maddon approached him on the bench.

"Are you okay? Can you go back out there?"

"I'm okay. I can do it."

Maddon heard enough to be convinced that Chapman would stay in the game to pitch the ninth—not that he was eager to make a change regardless of what Chapman had told him.

"But I knew it had to be him for the next inning," Maddon said. "I thought he had the best chance of getting them out. I knew that would be it for him, too."

THE NINTH INNING began, and so did a light rain. Ross drew a walk against a tiring Cody Allen. Maddon sent Chris Coghlan to pinch-run for Ross. Montero began to put his gear on to catch Chapman in the bottom of the ninth.

Coghlan quickly was erased when Heyward reached base on a groundball that forced out Coghlan at second. Francona brought in Shaw to throw his 95-mile-per-hour cutter against Baez. Heyward stole second base and continued to third when Gomes threw wildly trying to catch him. The Cubs had the potential World Series–winning run at third base with one out. Francona removed Crisp, his outfielder with the worst throwing arm. He moved Guyer to Crisp's spot in leftfield and put Michael Martinez in rightfield.

The count on Baez went full, 3-and-2, after Baez swung through a cutter. Maddon decided Baez had no chance against Shaw, not against that cutter, not when throughout the series Baez had been nearly an automatic out chasing and flailing at two-strike pitches. So Maddon relayed to third-base coach Gary Jones the sign for a safety squeeze. Jones gave the sign to Baez, who, out of uncertainty, disbelief, or both, called time to talk to Jones.

"Horrible matchup," Maddon said about why he asked Baez to bunt with two strikes. "He was striking out over 80 percent of the time when he got to a full count. He's going to swing. Okay. So I also thought if he's going to bunt, he might take a ball. Because you don't have to bunt the pitch if [the safety squeeze] is on. So I thought, *He may take it, and he has a much better chance of moving it.*

"The other thing, Jason is the runner at third base. Perfect guy. You don't do that if Rizzo is up. Everything has to happen. To me, he had a higher chance of doing that than moving the baseball. I thought if he's bunting he might take. If he's swinging, he's not taking. Because he's proven that he doesn't.

"Those are the things you think about before the game begins, and I did. When the opportunity presents itself you have to be ready to enact. The only bad part is he didn't get the sign and he had to go talk to Jonesy. I should have just taken it off, I don't know.

"They weren't expecting that at all. If he gets that down at all, Jason walks home. That was the best way I thought to score. The other thing with the two-strike bunt most people don't understand is that most guys—their two-strike batting average is abysmal. It's beyond abysmal against certain pitchers. It's nonexistent. I would like for some of our guys to do that with two strikes once in a while. Lester won a game with a two-strike safety squeeze. Lester's the best bunter on the team."

Shaw threw a 95-mile-per-hour cutter down the heart of the plate, the fattest of the six pitches in the sequence. Baez squared late, stabbed awkwardly at the pitch, and fouled it off. Strikeout. Two outs.

"I still feel really good with Dexter at the plate next," Hoyer said. "I'm thinking we might take the lead. I'm sitting behind the plate. He hits the ball and off the bat it looks like it's going up the middle. My wife screamed and grabbed me."

Lindor, the Cleveland shortstop, ranged far, scooped up the ball and threw to first base.

"Dexter gets thrown out by three feet."

THE GAME MOVED to the bottom of the ninth. Chapman, distraught and weary, returned to the mound. Montero was his catcher. Montero practically creaked with rust on his way behind the plate. He had caught only two games in the past 32 days. The Indians' top of the lineup was due up: Santana, Kipnis, and Lindor. Chapman was poor at holding runners and Montero was poor at throwing. With stolen bases in order, Cleveland seemed one *baserunner* away from winning the World Series.

"They had all that momentum and three really good hitters to start the inning," Hoyer said. "I thought, *This is unbelievable. How is Chapman, on total fumes, going to get through these guys?*

"It is the untold story of the World Series."

Chapman had thrown 83 pitches in the past three games over four days, plus the approximately 60 pitches he threw warming up to pitch in eight different innings. He fell behind Santana 3-and-1.

Oh my goodness, Hoyer thought, *if he walks him here, all of a sudden this place is going to be* so *loud.*

Chapman threw his worst fastball of the night: 97.8 miles per hour and in the upper half of the strike zone. Santana took it for a strike. At 3-and-2, Montero called for a slider and set his target low. The pitch hung in the middle of the plate with no bite to it—a worse pitch than the previous one. Santana popped it up into leftfield. One out.

Kipnis was next in what would be another at-bat that reached a full count. Chapman threw him six consecutive sliders. Montero, going heavy with sliders, was calling a completely different game with Chapman than Ross did the previous inning. What was going on?

"To be honest," Montero said, "I hadn't been out there behind the plate in so long, and catching a guy throwing a hundred is not easy when you haven't played. I didn't feel comfortable about catching his fastball."

Chapman was unable to throw a hundred. His fatigue showed not just in his diminished velocity on his fastball, but also on the lack of tilt on his slider. He hung three of the six sliders to Kipnis: one on the first pitch that Kipnis took for a strike, one on 1-and-1 that he fouled hard and fairly deep down the rightfield line, and one at 3-and-2 that he fouled straight back, causing him to whirl around in anger, knowing he had missed his chance at a fat pitch.

"The truth is, I thought Kipnis had ended the game when Chapman hung a slider to Kipnis," Hoyer said of the 1-and-1 pitch. "He put a really good swing on it and hit it foul. I give Chapman so much credit. He was clearly tired. He was right there in the middle of the plate, and he just kept coming back with another one. Then the 3-2 slider up. Every pitch was 86, 85 upstairs.

"That at-bat was terrifying. That was an amazing at-bat. Kipnis was so good the whole series. And the story line is too easy if he beats us: the kid from Chicago who grew up on the same street as Bartman beats the Cubs."

With the count full, Montero called for a fastball. He set the target down and away. Chapman threw whatever he had left—it was 99 miles per hour—and missed badly above the strike zone. But Kipnis, after seeing six straight sliders, chased it and missed. Strikeout. Two outs.

Next: Lindor. Chapman started him with a fastball. It was his 97th pitch over three games in four days. It was another dangerous fastball in his kryptonite zone: down and in. Lindor popped it up to Heyward in rightfield. Three outs.

Game 7 was one of the most frenetic Game 7s in World Series history. The Cubs and Indians combined to put 34 runners on base.

The only Game 7 with more baserunners was played 104 years earlier, in 1912, when the Red Sox and Giants put 38 runners on. Chicago and Cleveland put at least one runner on in 16 of their 20 turns at bat.

But the most amazing half inning of all might have been one of those four half innings when "nothing happened." It was the bottom of the ninth. Facing Cleveland's three best hitters, when one run would have ended the World Series—and one baserunner might easily have led to that run—Chapman threw 14 pitches: 10 sliders and 4 fastballs. At least 6 of the 14 pitches were full-blown mistakes in the strike zone. Somehow, Chapman got away with all of them.

"People don't give him enough credit for going out there the next inning [after losing the lead] and getting three outs," Maddon said. "That's pretty large. Nobody even talks about that. I know there were a lot of breaking balls. But that's also the thing . . . even if his breaking ball is not a good breaking ball, coming off the fastball it's a good pitch a lot of times.

"No, listen. That was very fortuitous. Nobody talks enough about that, because that kept Montgomery and C.J. out of the game for the next inning. Most of the time I like Contreras in there with Aroldis. That was a concern when I put Jon in and put David in. Because I knew I wouldn't have Contreras to catch Aroldis. Not to say that he can't. I'm just saying Willson and Aroldis had built a nice rapport. That was part of my concern also.

"But again, it's the seventh game. You have no game tomorrow. You have veteran players. You just have to trust them. It goes back to trust."

CHAPTER 19

INTERLUDE

Rain. Not in torrents and sheets did it arrive, but just barely on the side of too hard and too much to play baseball. It was almost midnight. Umpire Joe West, the crew chief, ordered play stopped and the field covered by the tarpaulin. He walked past Joe Maddon as he exited the field through the Cubs dugout.

"They don't think it's going to be that long," West told him.

"Good."

The Cubs quietly filed out of the dugout and began walking back to the clubhouse, their heads dropped and their faces blank. It wasn't quite the lost look Maddon remembered from the 2002 Yankees, and the look he warned them before the postseason he never wanted to see from one of his teams, but it was the look of a team that knew "something bad" had happened to it. The Cubs blew a three-run lead four outs away from their first World Series title in 108 years, and now they would have to try to win an extra-inning World Series Game 7 as the road team—something that had never been done before.

"Guys, weight room! Won't take long!"

A strong voice suddenly pierced the quiet. It belonged to Jason Heyward, the Chicago rightfielder who struggled to hit all year after signing a $184 million contract, who began the World Series on the bench, and who was hitting .106 for the postseason, including four more hitless at-bats in Game 7. Heyward was calling a players-only meeting.

To get from their dugout to their clubhouse at Progressive Field, visiting players walk out the rightfield end of the first-base dugout, down a short, wide hallway, turn left to go up one short flight of stairs, then turn right up another short flight of stairs and through double doors. To the right of the hallway, directly behind the dugout, is a weight room about 50 feet long by 25 feet wide. One by one the Cubs traipsed into the weight room, where they stood shoulder to shoulder or found places to sit on or lean on equipment.

Maddon walked past the weight room on his way to his office, where he was going to check the weather app on his iPad. The door to the weight room was glass. Maddon turned his head in that direction as he walked by.

"I saw the boys run into that weight room," he said. "I liked the idea the guys got together."

The room filled. Then someone asked, "Where's Chappy? Somebody go get Chappy."

One of the Cubs' in-uniform support personnel walked back to the dugout. There, Chapman sat alone atop the bench. He was told, in Spanish, there was a players-only meeting and that he should come right away. The hulking man Maddon said was built "like wrapped steel" stood up slowly, as if wounded or exhausted. At the time, to get out of the rain from my spot in the first-base camera well, where I was stationed for the Fox broadcast, I stood in the Cubs' dugout toward the rightfield end. Chapman turned to me. He was crying. Tears ran down his face. As he walked past me, as if to comfort or steady himself, he reached his right hand toward my left hand and gently held my wrist. The pain he wore was visible.

Chapman slowly made his way to the weight room. He was the last one in. He stood next to Ross, who was standing guard at the door. Chapman was still crying.

"When we got in," Rizzo said, "it was like, 'Ahh, we just blew a three-run lead in the World Series and there's no game tomorrow.' The mood was definitely down. All of us were just kind of pacing, and then Jay starts speaking."

Heyward started in.

"I know some things may have happened tonight you don't like . . ."

Uh-oh, Ross thought to himself, is this going to be about Maddon? In fact, after the meeting and before the 10th inning began, Ross would tell teammate Matt Szczur, "At first I was afraid it was going to be negative, and I thought this is nothing any of these young players needed to be hearing."

"But it wasn't that at all," Ross said. "There was no negativity."

"We're the best team in baseball and we're the best team in baseball for a reason," Heyward said. "Now we're going to show it. We play like the score is nothing-nothing. We've got to stay positive and fight for your brothers. Stick together and we're going to win this game."

Other players began to speak up.

"Keep grinding!"

"Chappy, we've got you! We're going to pick you up."

"This is only going to make it better when we win."

Ross turned to Chapman. The reliever had only been with the team for three months, and tended to be quiet around his teammates. Ross saw Chapman still in tears, and knew the big man cared much more deeply than he let on.

"Hey, man, we wouldn't be here in the World Series without you," he told Chapman. "This ain't over."

As the players gathered in the weight room, Epstein and Hoyer had left their seats to walk to a room behind home plate that MLB established as what it called "the rain room," where officials could update executives from both teams about the latest weather information. One of the MLB executives there was Peter Woodfork, senior vice president of baseball operations, who had worked under

Epstein in Boston, and was with him at the 2003 Pearl Jam concert the night Epstein first met Eddie Vedder, and was with him in the Cape Coral 2004 spring training house, Phi Signa Playa.

Already in the room were Indians president Chris Antonetti and Indians general manager Mike Chernoff.

"It was surreal," Epstein said. "Chris and I looked each other in the eyes and both thought the same thing, without having to say it. At that point everything was tied. The World Series was tied and the game was tied. We both knew somebody was going to win and somebody was going to lose. The moment was surreal."

The room also defined "state of the art" in baseball. Epstein was 42 years old, Hoyer was 42 years old, Antonetti was 41, and Chernoff was 36. None of them played professional baseball. They were graduates of Yale, Wesleyan, Georgetown, and Princeton, respectively. They represented the new generation of great minds in the game, a new way of thinking.

The meeting was short. The news on the weather was good: the rain should not last long. Epstein and Hoyer left the room, by way of the field and the Cubs' dugout, to pass along the weather information to Maddon. Epstein had been anxious and down ever since Davis hit his home run. His thoughts remained dark, worried that the hard work of so many people in the Cubs organization over the previous five years stood to be wasted after blowing the lead. As Epstein and Hoyer left the dugout and entered the hallway, both of them noticed the players gathered in the weight room. They stopped.

"Go tell Joe what's going on with the weather," Epstein said.

Hoyer continued to the stairs that led to Maddon's office. Epstein lingered in the hallway and eavesdropped on what was being said in the meeting. The darkness over him suddenly lifted.

"I saw our guys meeting and it snapped me back," he said. "It reminded me of how much I admired them and how tough they are, how connected they've stayed with each other, and the great things human beings can accomplish when they set out to achieve for other people, not for themselves.

"That's something that made this organization what it is now. From my position, I can see it: the sacrifice the scouts make when they drive the extra miles to get that last look at a player, the minor league coaches putting in extra hours, the big league coaches crushing video, the players working on their weaknesses, picking their teammates up—you get to see that stuff all the time. That's what makes a great organization. That's Cub.

"Right then I thought, *We're winning this fucking game!*"

Hoyer met with Maddon, briefing him on word that the game should be resuming in a matter of minutes.

Just before he left, Hoyer told Maddon, "Let's win one inning. We win one inning, we win the World Series."

Maddon smiled.

"No doubt," he confirmed.

Said Hoyer about Maddon's outlook, "He was good. Everyone got to take a deep breath with the delay, Joe included."

The entire delay took only 17 minutes, not much longer than the time it takes to fully cover the field with the tarp and remove it. As Maddon prepared to return to the dugout, he reached into a backpack next to his desk and pulled out the faded periwinkle blue Angels cap—the outdated one with a wings logo—and stuffed it into the back of his waistband and underneath the hoodie he was wearing. It was time for his father, Joe the Plumber, to watch the end of another World Series Game 7, just as happened in 2002.

Downstairs, a different team came out of the weight room than the one that had entered it.

"No doubt, it reset us," Rizzo said. "It had been just guys hanging their heads a little bit. The rain delay really helped as far as being loud and outgoing and loose as we always are. It was just a different feel."

"What's fitting," Ross said, "is Jason Heyward called it, the guy who struggled the most out of our starters and was dealing with the most. He could have just been wrapped up in himself and not been a vocal leader. But Jason is the kind of guy who never takes a pitch off, never takes an at-bat off. For him to call a meeting, for him to be the one to speak up, was huge.

"He doesn't talk often, so when he does your ears perk up. 'This must be important.' When he said that, he was absolutely right. He reset the focus of who we are. We're playing for one another. That's a huge learning moment for the young guys."

It would not be until after the game that Epstein was told that Heyward called the meeting.

"That's amazing—that he stayed not only connected to this team but in the middle of everything and despite his offensive struggles he stepped up," Epstein said. "It speaks to his character and professionalism."

Heyward is the son of parents who met while attending Dartmouth: Eugene, an engineering consultant for the Air Force, and Laura, a quality analyst for Georgia Power.

"I'm fortunate to come from great parents and a great family," Heyward said. "No matter how tough it was for me at times this year, I think I gave something to this team with my character, and I think this team gave something to me."

The players returned to the dugout. Shaw prepared to go back to the mound for Cleveland. Schwarber, due to lead off the inning, headed to the bat rack. "Borzy, I've got this," he told Borzello. "Don't worry. I'm telling you, I've got this. I'm locked in." Rizzo, due up third, stood next to him and smiled. The same dugout that 17 minutes before was lifeless and tearful suddenly was alive with shouting and joking. Ross, sitting midway down the length of the bench, suddenly remembered what happened in the clubhouse before the game, when he rousted Rizzo from "the bad vibe" after Rondon mistakenly abbreviated Rizzo's pregame jocularity by spraying him in the groin with shoe cleaner.

Ross turned in Rizzo's direction and yelled at him, "Hey, it's not how many times you get knocked down . . ."

On cue Rizzo completed the battle cry, yelling back, "It's how many times you get back up!"

Rizzo then launched into a clothed version of his pregame routine, yelling, "This is like Tyson-Holyfield! . . . This is a heavyweight bout! . . . This is going to make it that much better when we win! . . ."

The dugout laughed at the encore performance.

"He brings that energy, and that kind of goofy, funny energy that everybody gets," Ross said. "It could be cheesy if you want it to be, but he's the same guy. He does that a lot. It's not like he gets anybody pumped up. He loosens the mood. It's not like, 'Yeah, let's go get 'em!' It's more like, 'Yeah, whatever he's doing, he's an idiot.' And he's got this huge, 12-year-old grin on his face. That baby face. The way he smiles, he's just so likable when he smiles.

"And we have a lot of those guys. Dexter, when he smiles, he laughs. And Jason Heyward when he laughs, everybody laughs. He's got one of those contagious laughs. Javy Baez, when he laughs and smiles, he's just one of those guys you can't help but be in a good mood with him."

In 2008, as manager of the Tampa Bay Rays, Maddon was involved in the longest World Series rain delay on record. The Rays and Phillies waited two days to complete Game 5, which ended in Philadelphia winning the World Series. This one took only 17 minutes. He could tell immediately the difference it made in his players.

"They were so jacked up," he said. "Seriously, the rain absolutely permitted us to recalibrate. There's no doubt about it. If you're talking about a fortuitous moment in the history of time and place as it relates to baseball, that rain delay was the most perfectly timed ever. I've been involved in two rain delays in the World Series: the most nonfortuitous one in Philadelphia and the most fortuitous one for us in Cleveland."

The Cubs and the Indians in 2016 had combined to play more than 400 games, including spring training, and just when they were tied after nine innings in the final game of the World Series and after 176 combined years waiting to win another title, the heavens opened up—just hard enough and just long enough for the Cubs to hit the reset button. It was the ultimate dramatic pause in the telling of a story, a final godwink before fortune really turned for the Cubs.

"Even at the time, it felt like an amazing stroke of luck for us," Hoyer said. "I mean, which team needs the rain delay? Not them. It's definitely us."

Said Epstein, "A little divine intervention never hurt."

As the two teams prepared to resume play, West, the crew chief umpire who worked his first major league game 40 years ago, walked past me toward his post on the rightfield line.

"What do you think, Joe?" I asked him.

"I think if you don't love this, there's something wrong with you."

CHAPTER 20

HEAVEN

The Cubs looked like a different team. On the first swing after the cleansing rain, Kyle Schwarber slammed a loud single through the shifted Cleveland defense on the right side, and ran to first base, pumping his fist and screaming into the Cubs' dugout, as if he had sacked the quarterback on a middle linebacker blitz back at Middletown High. He left to a hero's welcome in the dugout as Maddon sent Albert Almora Jr. to pinch-run for him.

"We don't win without Schwarber," Maddon said. "We just don't do this without him. We don't. You can talk about everything else that happens, but we don't win without him. Period. He goes up, does that little rocking thing with his hands, and literally beats the shift. The energy in our dugout, all of that . . . but Schwarbs set the whole thing up."

Kris Bryant continued a remarkable night of hitting persistence when, after getting in a 1-and-2 hole, he took one pitch from Bryan Shaw and drove the next deep to centerfield. Bryant arrived at spring training as the Rookie of the Year but unhappy that he struck out in 31 percent of his plate appearances. He dedicated himself to being more selective at the plate and slightly tweaking his powerful, uppercut swing so that his barrel stayed in the zone just a bit longer. He cut his strikeout rate to 22 percent, an enormous improvement for a sophomore player. The fly ball he hit off Shaw came on the 34th pitch he saw in Game 7, 15 of which came with two strikes, and only 1 of those resulted in a whiff.

Such persistence was all the more remarkable because Bryant fought cramps in his body all night. He received treatment for cramps in his right arm between innings. His legs throbbed.

"Never had cramps on any level playing baseball," Bryant said. "Just a lot of nervous energy in Game 7, I guess."

As Bryant's fly ball soared, Almora broke about halfway to second base, where he was prepared to take off if it landed in the outfield or hit the wall. That's when he noticed that Davis, unhurried, was gliding after the deep fly ball, as if he had a good read on it.

"I'm a centerfielder," Almora said. "I can read when a centerfielder looks like he's got a play and when he doesn't. I saw the way Davis was running and knew he had it lined up."

At the same time, somebody in the Chicago dugout yelled, "Tag up! Tag up!"

It was Heyward, continuing to make smart contributions despite his slump at the plate.

Almora dashed back to first base. Davis caught the ball near the wall. Almora tagged and sprinted to second base. He ran the go-ahead World Series run into scoring position with one out. It was a terrific, smart baserunning play by a rookie, but one that was not all that surprising given the strong will of that teenage player who sat with Epstein and McLeod in his Hialeah, Florida, living room in 2012. Almora back then essentially begged the two Cubs executives to draft him. His words were prophetic:

"I'm telling you, all I want is a chance to go out there and help the Cubs win the World Series. I'll do anything. I'll make a catch. I'll run the bases. I'll get a hit."

Epstein, Hoyer, and McLeod all noticed the synchronicity of what had just happened, though none had to say it aloud. With Game 7 of the World Series tied in the 10th inning, their 2014 first-round pick singled, their 2012 first-round pick ran for him, and their 2013 first-round pick hit a two-strike fly ball to move him into scoring position. The Cubs were in position to win the World Series because of their first three first-round selections.

Almora's smarts put Cleveland manager Terry Francona in a bind. To get the next two outs without a run scoring he could choose to pitch to Anthony Rizzo and Ben Zobrist or, by intentionally walking Rizzo, Zobrist, and Addison Russell. Rizzo wasn't sure what to expect, but both he and Francona knew that he was swinging a sizzling bat—but among the two of them only he knew that bat was a smaller, lighter one than usual.

"I don't know there," Rizzo said about whether he was expecting to be walked. "It was one of those things. Earlier in the series I kind of knew going up to the box, 'Okay, they're going to walk me here.' But this time, there was only one out, I was more locked in, and I wasn't completely sure if they were going to do it or not.

"This is where Rossy comes in again, from what I've learned always talking to him about these kind of situations. It's like, 'I'm not going to let this guy beat me.' And that was it right there. They were not going to let me beat them when there's a base open. So I definitely understood it."

Francona elected to intentionally walk Rizzo. This situation confirmed why Maddon batted Zobrist behind Rizzo. "The consummate protector," he called Zobrist, a switch-hitter. The situation also confirmed why Epstein signed Zobrist as a free agent, after the Cubs in 2015 struck out more times than any team in baseball.

Shaw, throwing nothing but hard cutters, as is his wont, jumped ahead of Zobrist 1-and-2. Zobrist went to his B hack. He choked up on the bat. Shaw tried to come in with a cutter, but missed location up and away. Zobrist, shooing it away like a bee, flicked it foul, past the Cleveland dugout. Shaw came back with another cutter, but not as up and not as far away. It was in the strike zone. Zobrist carved it past Ramírez, the third baseman, and well inside the leftfield line. Almora came steaming home with the tie-breaking run, Rizzo pulled into third base, and Zobrist jumped onto second base with a double, punctuating the big hit with a fist pump.

Standing on third base, Rizzo put both of his hands on his head and said aloud, "Oh, my God."

"It's extra innings," Rizzo explained. "It's Game 7, and, the way that game had gone, not even a four-run lead was safe, so . . . But when we came out and punched them right there in the teeth and scored, it was like, 'Okay, that's it. That's the game. We're going to win.' And I'm over there like, 'Oh my God, we're going to win the World Series.' As a kid, any kid—who's the worst team in baseball this year? Pick a team—you want your team to win the World Series. Just put that wish in Chicago, and it's so much bigger."

With first base open, Francona issued another intentional walk, this time electing not to pitch to Russell, which filled the bases and put a double play in order with Miguel Montero at bat.

Five years and one week ago from this night, Epstein was introduced as the president of baseball operations of the Cubs, and almost immediately began to plot how he could find four high-character, high-impact players to be the pillars of his rebuilding plan. Not only did he find them within three seasons, but also no better showcase for their importance existed than the 10th inning of the seventh game of the World Series. All four pillars contributed to the winning rally: Schwarber with his leadoff single, Bryant with his deep fly ball to advance the go-ahead run, and Rizzo and Russell with intentional walks when Francona opted not to pitch to them.

With the count 1-and-1, Shaw tried to bury a cutter on Montero's hands, but he didn't get it inside enough. Montero pushed it into leftfield for a single, scoring Rizzo to put the Cubs ahead, 8–6.

The hit not only gave Chicago an insurance run, it also capped an extraordinary night for the Cubs' catchers. Maddon started with Willson Contreras, only the third first-year catcher to start a World Series Game 7, then used Ross, who was playing the last game of his career, and then Montero, the proud veteran who had lost playing time in the postseason. Each of them drove in a run. It was the first time in postseason history a team used three catchers and all of them had an RBI. It was only the second such game in the history of baseball, the other being an otherwise meaningless game in April 1964 in which three Minnesota Twins catchers drove in runs against the Washington Senators.

"That's the most amazing thing I took away from the game," said Mike Borzello, the catching coach. "It was this three-headed monster catching-wise, and how everyone made a major contribution.

"You had a baby, a 24-year-old who never had played much in the big leagues, a veteran guy who's the heart and soul as far as a spokesman and emotional leader, and then you had Miguel Montero, a guy who lost playing time and isn't that happy about his situation and yet he continues to work hard. Three guys in three different stages of their careers: one starting, one ending, and one not happy where his career is going. It's amazing. And it had to be all three. It had to be all three contributing for us to win."

Trevor Bauer stopped Chicago from blowing it wide open. Relieving Shaw, he left the bases loaded by striking out Heyward and retiring Baez on a fly ball.

During the rain delay, Maddon had used some of the time to recalculate his pitching plan. He knew that Chapman was spent. If Game 5, when Chapman nailed down the last eight outs facing elimination, was the game of his life as far as effort, the ninth inning of Game 7 was the inning of his life in terms of gallantry.

"I know a big rallying cry during the players' meeting was about picking him up," Hoyer said. "Everybody was aware of how tired he was. I know a big part of it was, 'Hey, we're going to do this for Chappy. We're going to pick him up.' I know that was a big thrust of the meeting."

By blowing the lead, preserving the tie in exhausted fashion, and then breaking down emotionally, Chapman presented Cubs fans with a different narrative than the one from July. Back then he arrived as a flamethrowing mercenary, whose behavior in a domestic dispute compromised the buy-in for some fans of the joy the Cubs gave them. No longer did those fans face the potential conflict of watching Chapman secure the end to the biggest championship in sports. By failing, and doing so to the point of physical and emotional exhaustion, Chapman became more humanized to a fan base just getting to know him.

"When he comes back in 5, 10 years or so for some anniversary party," Hoyer said, "he's viewed in a very different way—in a very positive way."

Without Chapman, Maddon had considered his choices during the rain delay for the bottom of the 10th. Jake Arrieta, who had started Game 6, had been in the bullpen since the third inning and told pitching coach Chris Bosio he was good to go. But Maddon decided, whether the game was tied or he held a lead, that Carl Edwards Jr. would start the inning, backed by Mike Montgomery if a matchup presented itself that called for a left-hander. Edwards and Montgomery, combined, had pitched in 106 major league games. Between them they had two saves, both by Edwards. Neither one was even on the team as recently as the middle of June, when Edwards was in the minors and Montgomery was pitching for Seattle.

"C.J. and Montgomery know how to do this. Jake had not done that," Maddon said about trusting the relievers over a starter. "Honestly, Jake was good, but his command, I had no idea. He's pitching on really short rest, so for me to bet on his command right there would be a bad bet. That's what I thought. Those two kids, if you told me at the beginning of the year—C. J. Edwards and Mike Montgomery—would be closing the seventh game of the World Series . . . seriously?"

Edwards, the "String Bean Slinger," a former draft pick out of a round, 48, that no longer even exists, locked down two quick outs. He struck out Mike Napoli and retired José Ramírez on a grounder.

Now the really hard part: the last out to end a 108-year drought. Suddenly Edwards lost the strike zone. He walked Brandon Guyer on five pitches, four of them well below the bottom of the zone. Bosio visited the mound, both to slow down Edwards and to give Montgomery more time to get warm.

Pitching to Davis, Edwards threw another ball, a pitch on which Guyer advanced to second without a throw. The next pitch was a fastball down. Davis hammered it on a line to centerfield for a single, easily scoring Guyer.

"I thought, *Oh my God. Really?*" Hoyer said. "*Two outs and no one on base and we're going to give these guys some air?* That's when you get nervous. You start thinking, *Okay, if we can't win it here with a two-run lead, nobody on and two outs, maybe we just can't win.* It's like, 'C'mon guys. Let's get this last out.'"

Maddon walked to the mound and signaled for Montgomery to face Michael Martinez with the speedy Davis, the tying run, at first base and the championship-winning run at the plate.

"I assumed we did it to keep Davis at first," Hoyer said, "figuring there's a chance Montgomery picks him off, whereas with Edwards I think he steals on the first pitch."

Said Rizzo, "I'm thinking we've got to get Martinez out early, because Rajai is going to steal the base and a single ties the game up. So you're just focused on each pitch, pitch by pitch. You can't get out of the moment."

Said Ross, "I'm thinking, *Oh, no. Montgomery comes in, which makes it a little tough for a stolen base because Davis has to read the lefty, but Miggy's in the game and he doesn't throw that well.* So you're thinking, *Surely he's running soon.*"

Earlier in the game Maddon enjoyed hearing a scouting report from Ross about how Lester looked throwing in the bullpen. "Really sharp," Ross told him. This time Maddon had no idea that Montgomery didn't throw a single strike while warming up in the bullpen. And Maddon knew Montgomery first had warmed up as early as the third inning, almost three hours before.

"I hate when the guy warms up that early in the game, sits, and comes back that late in the game," Maddon said. "But there are no options."

Montero met Montgomery on the mound.

"What do you want to do here?" Montgomery asked his catcher.

"Don't worry," Montero said as he turned. "I'll figure it out by the time I get back there."

Montgomery threw his eight warm-up pitches. He didn't throw a strike with any of those pitches, either. *Oh, my God*, Montgomery thought. *I have no idea what's going to come out of my hand.*

Behind the backstop, Hoyer was worried, too. Davis stole more bases, 43, than any other player in the American League. If he stole second base, the Indians could tie the game with a single, a possibility that would seem more likely because the Cubs would be forced to play their outfield deep to guard against the potential winning run, Martinez, getting to second base with a double. Hoyer turned to his wife and expressed his fears aloud.

"Oh, God, he's going to steal second and we're a broken bat hit away from a tie game," he said.

Explained Hoyer, "I felt with Martinez at the plate I wasn't worried about the damage. I was more thinking, *Don't get a guy into scoring position and he dunks one in.*"

Bryant moved in at third base, guarding against a possible bunt from Martinez, a fast runner.

Montero, once he arrived back behind the plate, decided to start Martinez with a curveball from Montgomery, the pitch the Cubs encouraged him to throw twice as often as before his trade from Seattle. Davis didn't run. The pitch looped perfectly into the outside third of the strike zone. Martinez took it for strike one. The pitch, after all those poor warm-up pitches, immediately relaxed Montgomery.

Okay, he thought to himself, *I've got this.*

Said Borzello, "He told me after the game, 'I don't know if I was nervous or what, but I was in another place. Whatever sign was put down, my only thought was, Let's make the pitch.'"

Montero called for another curveball. Hoyer never saw the pitch. His eyes were locked on Davis at first base, fearful that he would be stealing. Davis did not run. The curveball was a near duplicate of the first one—thrown to the same spot, but slightly harder. Martinez swung, and topped a slow groundball to the left of the mound. The next four seconds were a study in how many thoughts a human mind can process in such a short period of time.

Hoyer heard the contact of the bat hitting the ball and turned toward the interior of the infield.

"Off the bat I thought it was an infield hit," he said. "I really did. It was hit weakly by a guy who can run. Off the bat, my heart sank for a second."

Said Ross, "Off the bat it's like, 'Oh, please be hit hard enough to get him.' It was one of those in-between ones, a dribbler, that are tough. Montgomery didn't move. He wanted no part of that ball."

"When the ball was hit by Martinez," Maddon said, "I couldn't tell if the ball was hit in front of the plate. I couldn't tell, and I see K.B. breaking on it nicely, and I'm thinking is it hit hard enough? And I can see that it was."

Bryant, charging, fielded the ball after a third bounce between the mound and third base, funneled his glove with the ball cradled into it to his transition, and stepped with his left foot toward first base as he drew back his hand to throw with a right arm that had been cramping all night. Just as his plant foot landed, and just as his arm came around to throw the ball to Rizzo at first base, his spike slipped on the wet grass. His arm dropped as the ball left his hand. A smile creased Bryant's face while this moment of danger was happening.

"I see that his foot slips," Maddon said, "and I went 'Oh, shit.' "

"I didn't notice until I saw the replay on the play," Hoyer said. "Oh, my God, his foot slips two or three feet! I have a really hard time watching the last play. You would think you would relish it and watch it over and over. But Kris's foot slipped so much on the throw, I swear I watch that play and I see the ball going in the stands."

"The ball sailed," Rizzo said. "He threw it low and it just sailed up."

On another day, in another year, in another karmic vortex in which the Cubs seemed to be stuck for more than a century, maybe the throw, triggered by one slip of the foot caused by rain that appeared to have saved them, sails over Rizzo's head, down the right-field line, and Davis comes skittering all the way home with the tying run. Those days and such thoughts officially ended when the throw from Bryant arrived on target—at about the height of the "C" on Rizzo's cap—and safely in the mitt of Rizzo at 12:47 a.m. on what was now the first hour of November 3, 2016. From lovable losers to champions, the five-year rebuild of the Cubs was complete, and it ended with the first player on which it was built: Rizzo.

"I think everyone would agree with this," Hoyer said. "The emotion of that Wednesday night was just relief. We stared into the abyss and actually had not fallen in.

"If we win 6–3, Chapman closes it out, the entire atmosphere, everyone's attitude, is a lot different. Because we had nearly blown the game, and given our history, we were forced to play the ninth inning thinking about it, and it turns out okay in the 10th, for me and everyone else we were just relieved that night. It didn't sink in that we won the World Series and ended the drought until later."

"I felt," Ross said, "like the weight of the world was off our shoulders."

The Cubs, for as much as they played the role of the favorite throughout the year, forged a legacy as a great comeback team. Down three runs in the ninth to the Giants, and three outs away from facing Johnny Cueto in an elimination game, they came back to win the Division Series. Down two games to one to the Dodgers, and shut out for 21 straight innings, they came back to win the pennant. Down three games to one to the Indians, and having scored just two runs in the three defeats, they came back to win the World Series with three straight elimination game victories. In the denouement, they came back after blowing a three-run lead, making good on a vow to pick up the vanquished, tearful Chapman.

"That's why this team is world champion right now," Epstein said. "The chemistry is amazing. We all pick each other up. We have that chemistry. If you don't have that, you have nothing."

Immediately after catching the last out, Rizzo removed the baseball from his mitt and stuffed it in his left back pocket, just as he did the pennant-clinching baseball. Instead of going in his sock drawer, though, this one he would give to Ricketts at the parade. The last out triggered bedlam, and so many thoughts and emotions to process.

"He squeezes the glove and it's . . . it is surreal," Maddon said. "It's a moment I've experienced twice now, but of course holding your own baby, being the manager with the Cubs after 108 years, your mind doesn't even know where to go. Your mind has all these options and it doesn't know what to focus on at that point. There are so many things to focus on. Of course, the victory itself, 108 years, your dad, your mom, your wife, your family, your players, your fans . . . there are so many different places your mind can go and my mind went to just Rizzo purely catching the ball. He caught it. He caught it! The game's over. That's it. Season's over.

"It's a feeling like no other. It's incredible. Gratification. It was gratifying that we did it. It was unbelievable that we did it so quickly. Everybody talks about how wonderful our team is. The reflection there is, does anybody realize how young we are? How actually green and inexperienced we are? Nobody's even talking about that when they say you're the favorite to win, you have the best team in baseball. I'm thinking to myself, *Does anybody understand how young these guys are?*

"To be that young and to wire it—from the first day of spring training to the last day of the season—that was the expectation. That was the part I thought was underemphasized. It was stated, but you have to realize the scrutiny and involvement our players are under on a daily basis. So they have no experience to rely on as far as how do I deal with this? How do I process this? What does it mean? There's no experience to rely on, except for maybe what David might say, Jon might say, John Lackey might say, I say, what Miggy might say.

They're out there on their own little diving board experiencing all of this. First time."

That night, not long after the final out, the heavens opened again, this time with more conviction. Many of the Cubs players, their families, and friends lingered on the field in this hard, cool rain on this unusually warm November night. Joyful and relieved, nobody was in a hurry to get out of the downpour. They let it wash over them. It was a feeling that went far beyond Progressive Field. From the packed streets around Wrigley Field, where people had gathered all night around her sacred grounds, to the sons and daughters who watched with fathers and mothers in the biggest baseball television audience in a quarter of a century, to the many who wanted this night even more for the ones they loved and buried than for themselves, the faithful everywhere did not need the cool rain upon their skin to feel the change.

The Cubs, and all of their attendant culture, are redefined. The Cubs are champions. That's Cub.

ACKNOWLEDGMENTS

I needed only one day at the Cubs' 2016 spring training camp in Mesa, Arizona, to understand that the common media narrative about this young team was bunk. It went something like this: after its 2015 surprise breakthrough, Chicago might not be ready to play under the pressure of being expected to win. What I found was one of the most joyful and collegial cultures I had ever been around. I remained several more days and grew even more convinced: this team was ready and able to win.

Spring training is baseball's backstage pass. You see the inner workings of a group. You see how the parts fit with one another. Last year I saw that the Cubs, after careful planning, struck upon a winning collection of individuals who understood the power of teamwork. I am grateful that this book benefits from a similar kind of power thanks to the contributions and cooperation from so many people.

At some point during 2016 I interviewed every player on the Cubs' roster. To a man they were unfailingly polite and insightful. Particular thanks go to Jake Arrieta, Kris Bryant, Dexter Fowler, Kyle Hendricks, Jason Heyward, Jon Lester, Miguel Montero, Anthony Rizzo,

David Ross, Addison Russell, and Kyle Schwarber for the frequency and depth of their cooperation.

Owner Tom Ricketts can enjoy the best kind of success: well-earned and accomplished with good people. A true fan at heart, he provided such accessibility and honesty to me that I sometimes had to remind myself that he actually owned the team.

I am especially grateful for the insights and cooperation of President of Baseball Operations Theo Epstein and General Manager Jed Hoyer. Our many conversations were, without fail, informative and enjoyable. They are impressive leaders in so many ways, never more so than in their humility.

Likewise, Joe Maddon was incredibly giving with his time and wisdom. He is a fountain of baseball knowledge and goodwill, and I am the better each time I share in his company. His entire coaching staff was gracious in their time and assistance.

Thanks, too, to Senior Vice President of Player Development Jason McLeod for his insights and to Media Relations Director Peter Chase and Assistant Director Jason Carr for their patience and professionalism in answering questions and handling requests.

I must thank Cubs fans as well. Without connection to community, sports are just glorified versions of fifth-grade gym class: play for play's sake. Sports at their best bring people together, and I never will forget the joy that pervaded Chicago in October 2016. The people I encountered were delightful without exception—happy to know we all shared in this special time and place.

Getting this project off the ground would not have been possible without David Black, my agent and the Bernoulli effect behind it. I am indebted to his inspiration, guidance, and friendship. Similarly, Mary Reynics was the Joe Maddon of editors. With just the right touch and the right words at the right time, and above all her belief in me, she gave clarity and polish to the pages.

I am indebted, too, to my teams at *Sports Illustrated,* Fox, and Major League Baseball Network. Special thanks go to Chris Stone,

Stephen Cannella, and Emma Span at SI for their encouragement and consideration, and to Eric Shanks, John Entz, Judy Boyd, Bardia Shah-Rais, and Pete Macheska at Fox for their faith in me during what was the postseason most every baseball journalist has wanted to cover for more than a century. I know how fortunate I was to enjoy a true front-row seat to history, including our pregame meetings with Joe Maddon and Terry Francona, two class acts.

Above all, I give the greatest thanks to my wife, Kirsten, and sons, Adam and Ben, for their love. It is hard enough to be gone from home all of October, but then to come home and devote every day of November and December to the grind of reporting and writing this book was a harsh challenge for all of us. Only with their love and understanding is this book possible. To be loved is the greatest gift man can know, and because of my mother and father, sisters and brothers, and wife and sons, I have been truly blessed.

Montgomery, N.J.
2017

CREDITS FOR PHOTOGRAPH INSERT

INDEX OF NAMES

Note: Page numbers in parentheses indicate noncontiguous/intermittent references.

ABOUT THE AUTHOR

TOM VERDUCCI is *Sports Illustrated*'s senior baseball writer and a two-time National Sportswriter of the Year. He is also a two-time Emmy Award–winning game and studio analyst for Fox Sports and MLB Network. He was cowriter with Joe Torre of *The Yankee Years*.